TOURISM

An Introduction

TOURISM
An Introduction

RAY YOUELL

MSc, MTS, MSA

*Formerly Senior Lecturer
at the Centre for Tourism,
Sheffield Hallam University, UK.*

 LONGMAN

Addison Wesley Longman Limited
Edinburgh Gate
Harlow
Essex CM20 2JE
United Kingdom
and Associated Companies throughout the world

*Published in the United States of America
by Addison Wesley Longman, New York*

© Ray Youell 1998

The right of Ray Youell to be identified
as author of this Work has been asserted by
him in accordance with the Copyright,
Designs and Patents Act 1988.

First published 1998
Second impression 1999

ISBN 0 582 35697 0

Visit Addison Wesley Longman on the world wide web of
http://w.w.w.awl-he.com

British Library Cataloguing in Publication Data

A catalogue record for this book is available from the British Library

Library of Congress Cataloging-in-Publication Data

A catalog record for this book is available from the Library of Congress

Set by 35 in 9.5/12pt Garamond Light
Printed in Singapore (COS)

Contents

List of Figures   *page ix*
List of Tables   *xi*
Preface   *xiii*
Acknowledgements   *xiv*

1. ***Tourism – the World's Biggest Industry***   *1*
    Introduction   *2*
    Historical perspective on the development of tourism   *3*
    The politics of tourism   *8*
    Defining tourism   *9*
    Demand for tourism   *14*
    Chapter summary   *21*
    Discussion questions   *21*
    References and further reading   *21*

2. ***Structure and Organisation of the International Tourism Industry***   *23*
    Introduction   *23*
    Destinations   *25*
    The accommodation and catering sector   *27*
    Transportation   *29*
    Tourist attractions   *33*
    Travel intermediaries   *35*
       Case Study: Thomson Travel Group   *40*
    Globalisation and integration in the international tourism industry   *42*
    The role of the public sector in international tourism   *44*
       Case study: Japan National Tourist Organisation   *46*
    International agencies and trade associations   *50*
       Case Study: World Tourism Organisation   *51*
       Case Study: World Travel and Tourism Council   *53*
    Chapter summary   *55*
    Discussion questions   *56*
    References and further reading   *56*

3. *European Tourism*   *57*
    Introduction   *57*
    The changing face of Europe   *59*
    European tourist flows   *62*
    The structure of the European tourism industry   *66*
        Case Study: Cyprus Tourism Organisation   *75*
        Case Study: European Travel Commission   *78*
    The role of the European Union in tourism   *81*
    Future issues concerning tourism in Europe   *91*
    Chapter summary   *92*
    Discussion questions   *92*
    References and further reading   *92*

4. *Tourism in the United Kingdom*   *94*
    Introduction   *94*
    The historical development of UK tourism   *95*
    The significance of the UK tourism industry   *97*
    The structure of UK tourism   *100*
        Case Study: British Tourist Authority   *103*
        Case Study: Association of British Travel Agents (ABTA)   *121*
        Case Study: Association of Independent Tour Operators (AITO)   *125*
    The future of UK tourism   *135*
    Chapter summary   *136*
    Discussion questions   *137*
    References and further reading   *137*

5. *Impacts of Tourism*   *138*
    Introduction   *138*
    Economic impacts of tourism   *139*
        Case Study: Economic impacts of tourism in Australia   *146*
    Socio-cultural impacts of tourism   *148*
    Environmental impacts of tourism   *150*
    Solving the problems of tourism's harmful impacts   *152*
        Case Study: Tourism Concern   *158*
        Case Study: Green Globe   *160*
    Chapter summary   *162*
    Discussion questions   *162*
    References and further reading   *162*

6. *Planning and Development in Tourism*   *163*
    Introduction   *163*
    Planning and development in tourism   *164*
    Tourism policy formulation   *172*
        Case Study: Policy formulation in Wales – Tourism 2000   *174*
    Planning for sustainable tourism development   *176*
    Partnerships in tourism planning and development   *177*
        Case Study: Partnerships in tourism development – York   *178*
    Tourism in developing countries   *181*
        Case Study: Tourism development in Botswana   *182*
    Chapter summary   *185*
    Discussion questions   *186*
    References and further reading   *186*

7. *Tourism Marketing*   *187*
    Introduction   *187*
    Understanding the concept of marketing   *188*
    Marketing research in tourism   *194*
        Case Study: Australian Bureau of Tourism Research   *203*
    Applying the marketing mix to the tourism industry   *207*
    Destination marketing   *218*
        Case Study: Destination marketing – Australia   *219*
    Strategic marketing planning   *222*
    Chapter summary   *227*
    Discussion questions   *227*
    References and further reading   *227*

8. *The Future of Tourism – Issues for the Millennium*   *229*
    Introduction   *229*
    Future demand for international tourism   *230*
    Factors affecting future tourism demand   *231*
    Future sectoral developments   *232*
    Sustainable tourism – the way ahead?   *235*
    Future government involvement in tourism   *236*
    Chapter summary   *236*
    Discussion questions   *237*
    References and further reading   *237*

    Glossary of Terms   *238*
    Selected Bibliography   *247*
    Index   *249*

List of Figures

1.1	*World exports of tourism versus selected product groups, 1994*	*page 2*
1.2	*A simplified model of tourist activity*	*11*
1.3	*Different categories of tourism*	*11*
1.4	*Classification of tourism according to purpose of travel*	*12*
1.5	*Regional shares of international tourist arrivals, 1975 and 1995*	*16*
1.6	*Maslow's hierarchy of needs*	*19*
2.1	*Structural model of the international tourism industry*	*24*
2.2	*The composition of the tourist destination*	*25*
2.3	*The position of travel intermediaries*	*36*
2.4	*The role of travel agents*	*36*
2.5	*The position of tour operators*	*38*
2.6	*Public sector tourism organisation in Japan*	*44*
2.7	*The functions of a typical national tourism organisation (NTO)*	*45*
2.8	*Organisational structure of the Japan National Tourist Organisation*	*47*
2.9	*Structure of the World Tourism Organisation (WTO)*	*52*
3.1	*The new Europe*	*60*
3.2	*Structure of the European tourism industry*	*67*
3.3	*Main European airlines in terms of passenger volumes in 1993*	*68*
3.4	*Proposed UK rail developments as part of the trans-European transport network*	*69*
3.5	*Annual attendances at selected European theme parks, 1995*	*74*
3.6	*Structure of the Cyprus Tourism Organisation*	*76*
3.7	*Structure of the European Travel Commission*	*79*
3.8	*Growth of the European Union*	*82*
3.9	*How EU legislation is developed*	*84*
4.1	*Milestones in the development of UK tourism*	*95*
4.2	*Growth in package tours taken by UK residents*	*97*
4.3	*Overseas visits to Britain, 1981–95*	*99*
4.4	*BTA networking*	*104*
4.5	*The structure of the UK tourism industry*	*105*
4.6	*The National Express network*	*108*
4.7	*National Parks and Areas of Outstanding Natural Beauty (AONBs) in England and Wales*	*118*
4.8	*Market shares of the top five UK travel agency chains, 1995*	*120*

4.9	Vertical integration in the Thomson Travel Group	128
4.10	The structure of public sector tourism in the UK	129
4.11	The regional tourist boards in England	133
5.1	Tourism's contribution to the balance of payments in Spain and Germany 1990–94	142
5.2	Employment in world tourism, 1988–2006	145
5.3	Relationships in tourism	154
6.1	The relationship between tourism planning, development and management	164
6.2	Interrelationships in tourism planning	166
6.3	The strategic planning process for commercial tourism enterprises	168
6.4	Stages in the tourism planning process	170
7.1	The marketing process in tourism	189
7.2	Various marketing research sources in tourism	196
7.3	An extract from a self-completed questionnaire	198–99
7.4	Stages in effective questionnaire design	200
7.5	The marketing research process in tourism	206
7.6	The marketing mix in tourism	207
7.7	The product life cycle (PLC) concept	209
7.8	Channels of distribution in the tourism industry	211
7.9	Stages in the execution of a direct mail campaign	216
7.10	Origin of overseas visitors to Australia by region, 1994/95	220
7.11	The strategic marketing planning process in tourism	222
7.12	The Boston Consulting Group matrix	225
8.1	International tourism regional growth rates, 1990–2000	230

List of Tables

1.1 *Growth in international tourist arrivals and receipts, 1950–95*   *page 15*
1.2 *World's top ten tourism destinations, 1995*   *17*
1.3 *Tourism receipts of the world's top ten countries, 1995*   *17*
2.1 *Total visitors to Spain, 1985–95*   *27*
2.2 *World stock of hotels*   *28*
2.3 *Main accommodation used by Australian residents on domestic travel, 1985–86 and 1993–94*   *29*
2.4 *Sales revenues of Thomson Travel Group companies, 1995*   *40*
2.5 *Overseas offices of the Japan National Tourist Organisation*   *48*
2.6 *Annual budgets of the Japan National Tourist Organisation, 1994 and 1995*   *50*
3.1 *Tourism in the economy of selected European countries, 1994*   *58*
3.2 *International tourist arrivals and receipts, 1994/95*   *63*
3.3 *Regional percentage shares of international tourist arrivals and receipts, 1960–94*   *63*
3.4 *Tourism balance of payments in EU member countries, 1994*   *65*
3.5 *Europe's principal markets for incoming tourism*   *65*
3.6 *Hotels and similar establishments in the European Union, 1994*   *72*
3.7 *ETC's 1995 budgets for overseas markets (ECU)*   *80*
3.8 *Selected EC Directorates General (DGs) and their associations with tourism*   *83*
3.9 *The 'philoxenia' programme model*   *89*
4.1 *Spending by overseas visitors to Britain, 1981–95*   *99*
4.2 *Top ten UK airports by passenger numbers, 1994*   *109*
4.3 *Top ten hotel groups in the UK, 1994*   *112*
4.4 *Top ten free attractions in the UK, 1995*   *115*
4.5 *Top ten UK attractions charging admission, 1995*   *115*
4.6 *Top five UK tour operators, 1995*   *124*
5.1 *Tourism economic indicators in selected countries, 1994*   *140*
5.2 *Regional growth in employment in travel and tourism, 1996–2006*   *145*
5.3 *International visitor arrivals to Australia, 1988–95*   *147*
5.4 *Origin of overseas visitor arrivals to Australia, 1995*   *147*
5.5 *Australian tourism's long-range forecasts*   *148*
6.1 *Visitor numbers to selected attractions in York 1993–94*   *178*
6.2 *International tourist arrivals in selected country groupings*   *181*
6.3 *Total arrivals in Botswana by country of residence 1980–90*   *184*

6.4 *Expenditure by visitors to Botswana, 1981–90*   *185*
7.1 *Socio-economic classification*   *193*
7.2 *Key features of the International Visitor Survey and Domestic Tourism Monitor*   *204*
7.3 *Advantages and disadvantages of selected advertising media*   *214*
7.4 *Promotional expenditure in Australia's key overseas markets, 1994/95*   *220*

Preface

The cry 'not *another* new book on tourism!' is frequently heard in the corridors of our academic institutions. There are, indeed, growing numbers of textbooks, academic journals and other resource materials devoted to learning about and understanding the phenomenon and industry that is tourism. This book is designed to fill the gap for an industry-relevant book that contains up-to-date tourism data and analyses the burning issues of the moment in international tourism, the 'world's biggest industry'. It is primarily designed as an introductory textbook for staff and students at undergraduate/HND level, but will also be of interest to those working in the industry and can act as a useful 'conversion' text for students on postgraduate programmes who may be unfamiliar with the tourism industry.

The book can be divided loosely into three sections. Chapters 1 to 4 investigate the demand and supply sides of the tourism industry, working from the international level, through European tourism to an analysis of tourism in the United Kingdom. Chapters 5, 6 and 7 focus on the key issues of tourism impacts, planning and development in tourism, and tourism marketing respectively. Chapter 8 considers the future of tourism and the many factors that will influence its development. There is, however, much interplay between all chapters and cross-referencing where appropriate.

Included in the book are international case studies to highlight significant themes, issues and organisations within the tourism industry. To make these as useful as possible, each contains ideas for discussion points and essay questions. The end of each chapter also has a summary, discussion questions on the chapter content, references and suggestions for further reading. A selected bibliography and glossary of common tourism terms can be found at the back of the book immediately before the index.

I hope you agree with me that tourism is a fascinating industry, ever-changing to meet new challenges and improve people's quality of life. I hope, also, that you will agree that this text helps to understand the contemporary nature of the international tourism industry and the issues it faces in the future.

Ray Youell
Aberystwyth, 1997

Acknowledgements

Thanks are due to all the people who have helped this book come to fruition. I am indebted to the many individuals and organisations who have helped with material for case studies and industry examples. Their co-operation is acknowledged in the appropriate sections of the book. Thanks are also due to Ian Little and the team at Longman for their usual very professional approach. But, as always, the biggest thanks go to Sue, Megan and Owen, without whose sacrifices the book would never have materialised.

Chapter One

Tourism – the World's Biggest Industry

Chapter Overview

This chapter explores the development and global significance of tourism as the twentieth century draws to a close and the new millennium dawns. It analyses why tourism is increasingly referred to as 'the world's biggest industry' and investigates landmarks in the past development of tourism, summarising major historical trends and investigating how they can inform the current tourism debate. An analysis of the attempts that have been made to define tourism and explain its different forms is followed by comment on the characteristics of the contemporary international tourism industry. Aspects of the demand for tourism feature strongly in this chapter and include an investigation into the pattern of international tourism flows, determinants of demand and the complex subject of motivation in tourist behaviour. The chapter provides a sound statistical and analytical basis for the more detailed investigation of the supply side of the tourism industry, the subject of Chapter 2.

Key Topics

- The historical development of tourism
- Definitions of tourism
- The politics of tourism
- Characteristics of the tourism industry
- The demand for tourism
- Seasonality in tourism demand
- The pattern of international tourist flows

Introduction

Against the background of unparalleled growth in the latter half of the twentieth century, tourism now finds itself at a crossroads in its development. On the one hand, it is heralded as 'the world's biggest industry' by a number of global organisations including the World Travel and Tourism Council (WTTC) and the World Tourism Organisation (WTO), which highlights the fact that tourism overtook both crude petroleum and motor vehicles to become the world's number one export earner in 1994. Its economic significance is also illustrated by the fact that tourism receipts were greater than the world's exports of other selected product groups, including electronic equipment, clothing, textiles and raw materials (see Figure 1.1).

In addition, receipts from international tourism have achieved growth rates in excess of exports of commercial services and merchandise exports during the period 1984 to 1994. For the period 1985 to 1995 the trend is similar, with the following average annual percentage growth rates:

- Tourism   12 per cent
- Commercial services   12 per cent
- Merchandise exports   10 per cent

WTO data also indicate rapid and sustained growth in international tourist arrivals and receipts from tourism over the last 30 years. Today, tourism is seen as a major contributor

Figure 1.1: World exports of tourism versus selected product groups, 1994

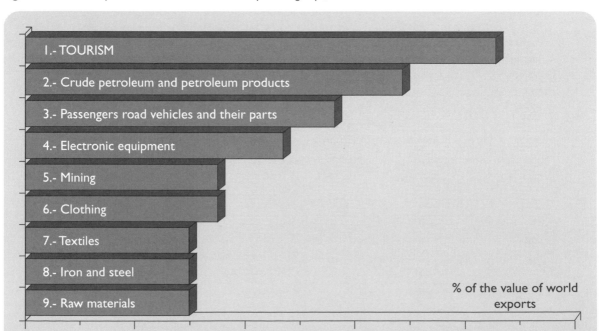

(*Source:* WTO, GATT, WNCTAD)

to global economic development, creating employment and generating wealth on a truly international scale. An increasing number of countries rely heavily on receipts from tourism for their economic and social well-being.

In direct contrast to this very positive outlook for the industry, many national governments are reluctant to invest public funds in tourism development and promotion, with tourism spending often being cut when more pressing social and economic needs arise. The decisions, in 1997, by the governments of Canada, the United States of America and Belgium to transfer responsibility for tourism to private sector enterprises or regional authorities serve to illustrate this point well. In Britain, the funding of the English Tourist Board has been cut drastically since the early 1990s, the decision of a government that considered the industry to be sufficiently mature and able to fund its own expansion with diminishing public financial support. At a time of increasing concern for the environment and the retention of cultural identities, tourism is also viewed by governments and consumers alike as a potentially destructive force, causing harmful environmental and socio-cultural impacts in destination areas and on host communities. Paradoxically, it is not difficult to argue that the withdrawal of public funding and control from tourism development may well accelerate the industry's harmful environmental and socio-cultural effects.

It is against this background of a complex and rapidly expanding industry seeking to maintain its credibility and promote its economic benefits, often in the face of declining governmental and host community support, that this chapter begins its investigation of tourism, the world's biggest industry.

Historical perspective on the development of tourism

The mass tourism that exists in many parts of the world today has its origins in the years immediately following the conclusion of the 1939–45 Second World War. Rising standards of living, increased leisure time and developments in transportation resulted in a sharp increase in demand for international travel, which has grown steadily to the present day. Tourist destinations responded to this demand by developing a wide variety of tourist facilities and amenities. The origins of tourism can, however, be traced back much further than this to pre-Egyptian times, when there was a limited amount of travel associated with festivals and celebrations of a religious or spiritual nature. The early Egyptian civilisation displayed a primitive social structure that rewarded the privileged classes with leisure time to enjoy such activities as dance, music, drama and archery. Travel in Egyptian times tended to be for the purpose of trade or associated with religious activities.

The Greeks, the Romans and the Reformation

The Greek civilisation was the first to espouse the benefits to individuals, and society in general, of a healthy balance between work and leisure, including travel. There is evidence of travel for purely recreational purposes, with the Greeks hosting international visitors during the first Olympic Games, which took place in 776 BC. The Romans propounded the notion of a purposeful approach to the use of leisure time, in contrast to the Greeks' aesthetic approach to the subject. Roman engineers built public leisure facilities for the masses of the urban populations who practised recreation for physical fitness and in preparation for war. The extensive road network developed by the Romans allowed faster and more convenient travel for business and leisure purposes. There was growth in international travel within the Roman Empire for trade, while the wealthier Romans made visits to friends and relations, and began to appreciate the healing powers of near and distant spa waters for the first time.

The austere times between the fall of the Roman Empire around AD 400 and the Middle Ages provided little opportunity for travel and leisure pursuits. The rise of Christianity during these so-called 'dark ages' relegated leisure activities to those associated with worship and religious festivities. The term 'holiday' developed from the holy days designated by the Church in the latter Middle Ages, which gave the mass of the population their main opportunities for leisure. Travel continued to be the preserve of those in power who journeyed for sporting and cultural purposes.

The development of the Reformation movement in Europe in the sixteenth century led to the spread of the Protestant work ethic, which attacked the excesses and corruption of the pleasure-seeking nobility. This led to a sharp decrease in the availability and respectability of leisure, and restrictions on travel for purely pleasurable purposes.

Post-Reformation tourism developments

In the post-Reformation period of the seventeenth century, attitudes towards leisure and travel changed direction once again. From a tourism perspective, two features are of particular note:

1. The development of the 'Grand Tour'
2. The rise of spa resorts

From 1670 onwards, young gentlemen of the aristocracy were sent on the 'Grand Tour' of the great cultural centres of Europe to widen their education and experiences of life prior to seeking positions at court on their return home. Cities such as Paris, Venice, Rome and Florence gave these young tourists the opportunity of sampling different cultures and societies. The popularity of the 'Grand Tour' reached its peak in the mid-eighteenth century, but was halted abruptly by the onset of the French Revolution and the Napoleonic Wars.

Although the medicinal benefits of spa waters had been recognised in Roman times, it was not until the sixteenth century that their full tourist potential began to be exploited and spa resorts grew in popularity. The healing potential of spa waters became widely accepted amongst the aristocracy, leading to the development of spa resorts in Britain and on the Continent. Towns such as Buxton, Leamington Spa, Llandrindod Wells and Bath prospered until well into the eighteenth century. Baden-Baden in Germany was one of the most popular spa resorts in Europe.

The Industrial Revolution

The Industrial Revolution of the eighteenth and nineteenth centuries brought about profound changes to the way of life in Britain, not least in the context of leisure pursuits and developments in tourism. Greater mechanisation and the introduction of mass production techniques in industry led to rapid urbanisation and a flow of population from rural to urban areas, scenarios that were to be found subsequently in many western industrial nations. The stresses and strains of monotonous working methods, coupled with dirty and often dangerous working conditions, encouraged people to escape to the relative peace and tranquillity of the coast and countryside. The Bank Holiday Act of 1871 created four public holidays per year, which, with the increased spending power of the majority of the population, stimulated demand for travel and tourism facilities to satisfy their needs. Two associated developments at this time, namely the rise in popularity of seaside resorts and the introduction of steam power, were to have far-reaching impacts on the future patterns of tourism.

The development of seaside resorts

As was often the case with the historical development of tourism, the initial popularity of seaside resorts was the result of patronage by the nobility and other wealthy minorities in society, although this was to change dramatically after the introduction of the railways in the mid-nineteenth century in Britain. In the early eighteenth century, the medical profession began to realise that the beneficial minerals present in spa waters were also to be found in the sea. It was not, however, until the publication of Dr Richard Russell's noted work *Concerning the Use of Seawater* in 1752, that seaside resorts saw their popularity increase, originally for health-giving reasons. Accommodation, catering and entertainment facilities were developed in many British resorts, including Scarborough, Skegness, Margate and Blackpool, some of which also benefited from the introduction of steamboat services in the early nineteenth century, a factor that led to the construction of the piers still seen at many British seaside resorts today.

The influence of steam power

The introduction of steam power was to have a very important effect on the development of tourism from the nineteenth century onwards. The first steam-powered passenger train service linking Liverpool and Manchester was introduced in 1830, and the network expanded rapidly to service the manufacturing heartlands of the Industrial Revolution. The growth of the rail network also served to bring many British seaside resorts within easy travelling distance of the main centres of population, thereby encouraging visits by a wide cross-section of society, including the emerging working classes; Brighton and Margate were notable successes in this regard. The expansion of the railway network led a number of entrepreneurs to consider how they could capitalise on this new form of travel. One of the most successful was Thomas Cook who was destined to have a far-reaching impact on the early development of tourism and travel. In 1841 he organised an excursion from Leicester to Loughborough for his local Temperance Association. Within 15 years, spurred on by the success of his first trip, Cook was running a fully commercial travel company arranging tours and excursions both at home and overseas, including visits to the Great Exhibition in London in 1851 and 'inclusive tours' to the Paris Exhibition in 1855. The completion of the Suez Canal in 1869 provided Cook with the opportunity of organising his first tours to Egypt.

In the early nineteenth century, just as steam power on land was radically changing the patterns of tourism and travel, the same was true at sea, with the introduction of a new generation of steam-powered ships serving North America, the near Continent and the Far East. The Peninsular and Oriental Steam Navigation Company (P&O) introduced the first regular long-distance services to India and the Far East in 1838. The Cunard Steamship Company started services to North America in 1840. Following his successes in Britain and on the Continent, Thomas Cook organised the first steamship excursion to America in 1866.

Tourism in the twentieth century

The early years of the twentieth century saw a consolidation of domestic tourism activity in the UK, punctuated by the two World Wars of 1914–18 and 1939–45, and the recession of the 1930s. After World War One, the growth in ownership of motor cars heralded the beginning of a steady decline in the use of the railway for holiday trips, a trend that was to continue throughout the twentieth century. British seaside resorts grew in popularity and many became firmly established tourist destinations in their own right during the inter-war years, for example Blackpool, Bournemouth, Southend and Colwyn Bay. The introduction of the first holiday camp by Billy Butlin at Skegness in 1936 provided a boost to overnight stays by offering good value, mass market, all-inclusive holidays for the first time. Above all, the inter-war years saw the emergence of today's consumer society.

Developments in the period immediately after the end of the Second World War were to have far-reaching impacts on the future patterns of travel and laid the foundations for the dramatic growth in domestic and international tourism seen since the 1950s. In addition to general improvements in the social and economic conditions after the war, two factors can be singled out as of particular importance to the growth of tourism, namely developments in aircraft technology and the introduction of overseas package holidays.

The development of jet aircraft

One positive outcome of the Second World War was the rapid advance in aircraft technology, which led to the growth of a viable commercial aviation industry in Britain and the USA. The surplus of aircraft in the immediate post-war years, coupled with the business flair of entrepreneurs including Harold Bamberg of Eagle Airways and Freddie Laker, encouraged the development of holiday travel by air. Comet aircraft were used in the 1950s, but it was not until the introduction of the faster and more reliable Boeing 707 jets in 1958 that we began to see the possibility of air travel becoming a reality for the masses of the population. The 1960s saw a surge in demand for scheduled and charter flights, the latter being combined with accommodation, transfers and courier services to form the overseas 'package tour' that is so familiar today.

The growth of the package tour

Vladimir Raitz of Horizon Holidays is credited with having organised the first modern inclusive tour by air when he carried a party of holidaymakers to Corsica in 1950. The holiday consisted of full-board accommodation in tents and travel in a 32-seater DC3 aircraft. From a modest start with just 300 passengers carried in its first year of operation, Horizon repeated the formula in subsequent years with increasing success. Although it has not been without its casualties, most notably Clarkson in 1974 and Intasun in 1991, the UK package holiday industry has grown rapidly by offering its customers an all-inclusive arrangement at a value-for-money price. Currently, Thomson, Airtours and First Choice Holidays are the biggest ex-UK tour operators in terms of numbers of holidays sold. Elsewhere in Europe, German and Dutch tour operators, including LTU, NUR and Holland International, became key players in the package holiday market. The industry also includes many smaller, independent operators that offer a wide variety of destinations and holiday products. For all operators, the Mediterranean countries are still the most popular with British and the majority of northern European tourists. However, long haul destinations, including the Caribbean, USA, the Far East and Australia, are rapidly gaining favour as overseas destinations for package holidaymakers as travel costs fall.

Tourism today

Notwithstanding the long history of developments in travel and past attitudes towards the work/leisure divide, the mass tourism that exists in the world today is a phenomenon of the post-industrial society of the latter half of the twentieth century. Tourism has become an integral part of the move away from economies based on heavy engineering and manufacturing to a rapidly expanding service sector. The growth in international and domestic tourism since the 1950s has been nothing short of dramatic, with international tourist arrivals climbing from 25 million in 1950 to a record 592 million in 1996 (World Tourism Organisation, 1997). When we add to this the fact that the volume of domestic tourism worldwide is estimated by the World Tourism Organisation to be approximately ten times greater than that of international tourism (World Tourism Organisation, 1983), the scale of the tourism phenomenon can begin to be appreciated. Greater wealth, higher educational standards, increased mobility and more leisure time have all contributed to unparalleled demand for holidays and excursions at home and abroad. Overseas travel is no longer the preserve of the privileged few, but is available to the majority, as developments in transportation, increased competition and global communications technology have reduced the real cost of holidays. Private and public sector organisations have responded to the increased demand by providing a wide range of facilities and products to meet the needs of an increasingly discerning travelling public. It must be remembered, however, that tourism is a very recent phenomenon that has hitherto been allowed to grow in a business environment relatively free of regulation and trade restrictions. Such an unrestricted environment is unlikely to continue in years to come.

The current scale and scope of the international tourism industry is illustrated in recent data from the World Travel and Tourism Council (1996a), which indicate that in 1996 the world travel and tourism industry is estimated to have:

- Employed 255 million people
- Generated an output of US$3.6 trillion
- Contributed 10.7 per cent of global gross domestic product (GDP)
- Invested US$766 billion in capital projects
- Generated US$761 billion in world exports
- Paid US$653 billion in taxes worldwide

Such figures demonstrate the economic significance of the tourism industry on a global scale and confirm that the age of mass tourism has truly arrived in spectacular fashion. Key aspects of the economic importance of tourism are examined in greater detail in Chapter 5, which includes an appraisal of the economic impacts of the industry.

Patterns in the historical development of tourism

In summarising the past and recent history of tourism, it is apparent that there are a number of significant patterns that have emerged, namely:

- *Effects of social mobility.* Since the earliest days of tourism and travel it is clear that small, privileged and wealthy sectors of society have been the first to experience tourist activities and discover new destinations. Once such areas have been discovered by the masses of the lower and working classes, members of this tourism 'élite' have been able to move on to more exclusive surroundings, often further afield. This trend still exists today, with exclusive resorts in such places as the Caribbean being the preserve of the nobility and wealthy personalities.

● *Importance of transportation.* From the construction of the first road networks in Roman times, the introduction of the railways in the early nineteenth century to the development of jet aircraft in the 1950s, much of the growth of tourism has been interdependent with developments in transportation.

● *Increasing pace of development.* Like many other aspects of recent history in western society, the growth of tourism has accelerated dramatically in the latter half of the twentieth century, with resulting positive and negative effects on economies, environments and cultures. The introduction of new technologies has revolutionised the tourism products on offer and the way they are presented and sold to potential customers.

Looking back in history is an important discipline since it can help predict future trends and may influence thinking and practice in the industry. One thing is clear, however: if tourism expands by the same rate over the next 50 years that it has grown since the end of the Second World War, the industry of the future will assume an economic and political significance of truly global proportions.

The politics of tourism

As international tourism involves the movement of people from one country to another, or even from one continent to another, governments may encourage the development of tourism to further their political objectives. It is often suggested that the Spanish government encouraged tourism development to broaden the political acceptance of Franco's regime. In Israel, the development of tourism has done much to stimulate political sympathy for that nation and to boost national morale. In the Philippines, Marcos actively exploited tourism to meet the political needs of his 'New Society'. Other nations, particularly Far Eastern states such as Korea and Taiwan, are also finding that the political benefits of international tourism may be as rewarding as its much vaunted economic advantages.

Outside these examples of overtly political exploitation of tourism development, there are many 'softer' political reasons for countries, regions and even local areas to become involved in tourism. The development of tourism can, for example, help to:

● Change the image or perception of an area: tourism is often regarded as a relatively 'clean' economic activity and, as such, one that can present a favourable image to the outside world. The inclusion of tourism in many urban regeneration projects is a good example of this phenomenon.

● Create a national identity: the promotion of tourism in overseas markets and with domestic tourists can cement a nation's identity, for example Spain, Greece and many of the countries bordering the Mediterranean.

● Promote regional prosperity: tourism can be used as a springboard for further economic and social developments in urban and rural regions. The regional development and promotion of tourism in France is a good example of this.

● Improve quality of life: ultimately, well-planned tourism development can bring a host of benefits to nations and regions, thereby contributing to an enhanced quality of life for their residents.

- Promote cultures: countries and regions with particular cultural and linguistic traditions can use tourism to further their political aims, for example the Basque region of Spain.

- Promote peace and human understanding: the social benefits of tourism, such as meeting people from different cultures, religions and races, can contribute to greater understanding on a global scale and to the promotion of world peace.

As international tourist arrivals continue to grow, there is little doubt that the political aspects of tourism development will increase in significance, in both the developed and developing nations of the world.

Defining tourism

Agreement on a comprehensive, easily understood and universally accepted definition of tourism has proved difficult to accomplish. This is due, in most part, to two principal factors, namely the broad nature of the subject and the fact that the tourism industry comprises a multitude of diverse, yet interrelated, industry sectors. If we consider that the study of tourism impinges on such disciplines as geography, psychology, sociology, economics, anthropology, planning, business studies, politics and economics, to name but a few, it is easy to understand the difficulty in agreeing a workable definition. On the industry side, sectors as diverse as hotels, leisure centres, local government planning departments, airlines, conservation bodies, travel agencies, museums, transport providers and entertainment complexes all lay claim to inclusion in any definition of tourism.

There have, nonetheless, been many attempts at defining exactly what we mean by tourism. The United Nations Statistical Commission has accepted the following definition of tourism on the recommendation of the World Tourism Organisation (WTO). It states that tourism comprises:

> '. . . the activities of persons travelling to and staying in places outside their usual environment for not more than one consecutive year for leisure, business and other purposes'. (World Tourism Organisation, 1993)

A definition that is often quoted in the UK context is the following proposed by the Tourism Society in the early 1980s:

> 'Tourism is the temporary, short-term movement of people to destinations outside the places where they normally live and work, and activities during their stay at these destinations; it includes movement for all purposes, as well as day visits or excursions'. (Tourism Society, 1982)

Both of these definitions offer a clear insight into the scope and context of tourism. They demonstrate that it is an activity embracing all aspects of the movement of people away from their normal surroundings and the activities they undertake and facilities they use in their destination areas. More specifically, these two definitions demonstrate that people we would categorise as tourists are:

- Away from their normal place of residence, although they will be returning home at some point in the future

- On a visit that is temporary and short-term, but is not greater than 12 months in duration

- Engaged in activities that one would normally associate with tourism

- Not necessarily staying away from home overnight, but merely on a day visit (excursion)

- Not always away from home for holiday purposes, but may be away from home on business

In attempting to define tourism it is important to distinguish between those visitors who stay overnight in a destination and those who do not. From a technical point of view, domestic or international visitors who stay at least one night in the place or country visited are known as tourists, whereas those who do not stay overnight are categorised as same-day visitors, day visitors or excursionists.

While both definitions quoted above encapsulate the technical nature of tourist activity, neither makes reference to the considerable impacts that tourism can have on destinations and host communities, nor the complexities of the industry that has evolved to support tourist movements. We investigate tourism's negative and positive effects in Chapter 5, while Chapter 6 concludes that without sensitive planning the growth of tourism in an area can destroy the very characteristics that attracted the visitors in the first place. Given the importance now attached to the development of sustainable policies and practices in world tourism, any definition that fails to include reference to this issue can be only partially complete. With this point in mind, we can begin to identify the major elements necessary for inclusion in a comprehensive definition of tourism, namely:

- There is travel between a tourist's home area and a destination.

- The visit is temporary and short-term.

- The visiting tourist will undertake activities normally associated with tourism, but may be on business or visiting friends and relatives.

- The tourist will make use of a variety of tourist products and facilities in reaching and staying in the destination.

- The tourist's visit will result in negative and positive impacts on the destination area and its people.

These elements can be assembled into the simplified model of tourist activity shown in Figure 1.2. This figure demonstrates that tourism, like much economic activity, is essentially a demand and supply relationship, concerned with satisfying the requirements of domestic and international tourists by providing a range of facilities and amenities, often grouped together in destination areas. A variety of sectors provide transportation to and from destination areas, while tourism intermediaries (for example travel agents, tour operators, wholesalers and brokers) facilitate the matching of destinations to prospective tourists. The nature of the demand, which is considered in more detail later in this chapter, will be influenced by a variety of factors, such as consumer buying behaviour patterns, travel propensities, lifestyle characteristics, technological developments and political factors. On the supply side, destination areas will experience negative and positive impacts, which may be economic, environmental or socio-cultural. The regulatory framework depicted in Figure 1.2 impinges on both demand and supply; the development of tourist amenities and facilities will, to a greater or lesser extent, be regulated in destination areas, as will the means of outward and return travel. Demand-side regulation will include health and safety issues, consumer protection and advertising practices.

Figure 1.2: A simplified model of tourist activity

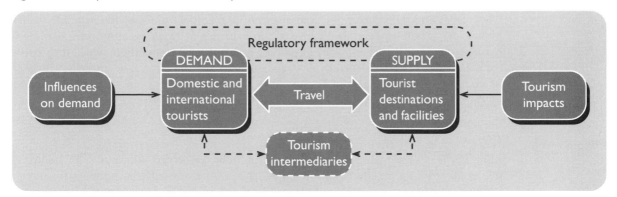

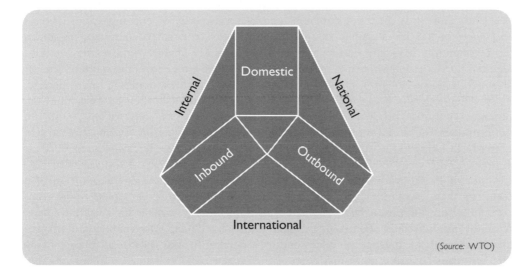

Figure 1.3:
Different
categories
of tourism

(Source: WTO)

Different types of tourism

For any given country, the World Tourism Organisation suggests that there are three basic forms of tourism, namely:

1. *Domestic tourism* – involving residents of the given country travelling only within their own country, e.g. a family from New York visiting the many theme parks and other attractions of Florida.
2. *Inbound tourism* – involving non-residents travelling in the given country, e.g. a student from Denmark visiting relatives who live in Phoenix, Arizona.
3. *Outbound tourism* – involving residents travelling in another country, e.g. the family from New York deciding to have a long vacation in Australia.

These three basic forms of tourism can be combined in a variety of ways to derive the categories of tourism shown in Figure 1.3. With reference to this figure it is possible to identify three principal categories of tourism:

1. *Internal tourism* – comprising domestic and inbound tourism
2. *National tourism* – made up of domestic and outbound tourism
3. *International tourism* – composed of inbound and outbound tourism

Although such categorisations are primarily intended to facilitate the collection and ana-lysis of statistical data concerning tourism, they nonetheless are a useful starting point when analysing the structure of domestic and international tourism. For example, some organisations will concentrate exclusively on a particular category of tourism, e.g. most mass-market tour operators focus on sending residents of the country in which they oper-ate on overseas holidays, thereby working solely in the outbound tourism sector. By way of contrast, a hotel in central London may work across the domestic, outbound and inbound categories by welcoming both British and overseas tourists.

Purpose of travel

Although it is easy to imagine that tourism is only concerned with travel for holidays, this is far from the reality of the situation. There are many different motives for travel, which can usefully be categorised for statistical and analytical purposes into leisure tour-ism, business tourism and visiting friends and relatives (VFR), as shown in Figure 1.4.

Leisure tourism is the most common type of tourist activity, encompassing holidays and short breaks for a variety of motives. Residents of northern European countries most commonly associate leisure tourism with long (4+ nights) holidays to southern Mediterranean destinations, such as Spain, Italy, Portugal, Greece and the south of France, although short breaks are a growing feature of many countries' domestic tourism scene. As travellers become better educated and more sophisticated in their lifestyles, and the providers of tourism products more responsive to their needs, the range of leisure tourism opportunities on offer becomes ever more diverse: anything from cycling holidays in China or trekking in the Himalayas to white-water rafting in the Rocky Mountains or art appreciation tours in Italy, are available to those with the inclination and ability to pay.

Although business tourism generally accounts for a relatively small proportion of a country's share of all tourism activity, its economic importance is often greater than com-parable leisure tourism activity. This is because business tourism is high value tourism, with business travellers often paying premium rates for travel, entertainment and accom-modation, both for prestige purposes and as a penalty for the short lead time of many business trips. Business tourism is also economically beneficial for a number of other reasons, including the fact that it is less seasonal than most leisure tourism and it spreads the benefits of tourism to areas not normally associated with tourist activity. Business tourism often plays an important complementary role to leisure tourism in many destina-tions; accommodation providers, for example, will often sell to business people during weekdays and offer reduced rates for leisure tourists at weekends, thereby making max-imum use of their available resources.

Figure 1.4:
Classification of tourism according to purpose of travel

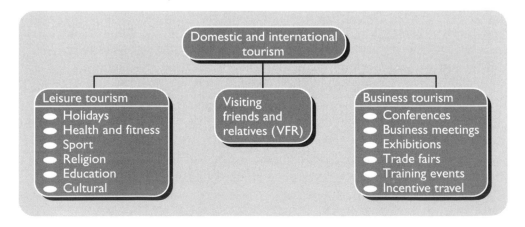

Visiting friends and relatives (VFR) is a significant, if often overlooked, category of tourism in many developed and developing nations. In the UK context, data from the *Tourism Intelligence Quarterly* (British Tourist Authority/English Tourist Board, 1996) demonstrate that visits to friends and relatives accounted for 27 per cent of all tourist trips by UK residents in 1994, with holidays at 57 per cent, trips for business purposes totalling 11 per cent and trips for other purposes at 5 per cent. Thus, out of a total of nearly 110 million trips in 1994, 30 million VFR trips with an expenditure of some £2.4 billion were made by UK residents. On first analysis, it may be difficult to understand how it is that somebody who stays free of charge with a friend or relative in their home, is helping tourism in an area. The answer lies in the fact that the visitor, although enjoying free accommodation, is likely to spend money on other goods and services in the locality, such as food, entertainment and transport, so contributing to the local economy. Indeed, the very fact that he or she is not paying for accommodation may well be an incentive to spend more on such things as eating out and entertainment.

Characteristics of the tourism industry

Having considered the historical development of tourism and examined definitions of the concept, we will now concentrate on key aspects of the industry that has evolved to support leisure and business tourism. Chapter 2 on the structure of international tourism focuses on the interdependence and relative importance of the principal industry sectors, while this section investigates its underlying characteristics. The following is a selection of the most prominent characteristics of the tourism industry that exists in many of the world's developed nations today:

● Dominated by private sector enterprises
● Dynamic and entrepreneurial
● Many small and medium-sized enterprises
● Serves domestic and international markets
● Thrives on face-to-face communication
● Makes extensive use of new technology
● Rudimentary management structures
● Vulnerable to external presssures
● Has positive and negative impacts

Before we expand on these features, it is important to highlight two points. Firstly, it should be emphasised that the tourism industry has evolved over a very short period of time; the earlier part of this chapter on the historical development of tourism indicated that tourism is essentially a phenomenon of the 50-year period since the end of the Second World War. As such, it lacks the maturity, credibility and status of more established economic activities. Secondly, there are good grounds for debating whether tourism is indeed an industry in its own right; as we shall discover in Chapter 2, tourism consists of a very wide range of interrelated sectors, many of which can justifiably claim to be industries themselves, for example hotels, airlines, tourist attractions, tour operators and travel agencies. Grouping such sectors together under one industry banner certainly helps from a political point of view, helping to give tourism a more united voice when negotiating and promoting its economic credentials. This author considers that, since all sectors of tourism are ultimately engaged in providing products and services to meet the needs of leisure and business travellers, it is indeed an industry; this is the term that is used throughout this book.

Turning to the characteristics of the tourism industry as shown in the list above, it is clear that it is dominated by private sector enterprises. Public bodies have an important role to play in tourism planning, regulation and development, but the great majority of tourism providers operate in the commercial world. This dynamic, commercial slant to tourism gives the industry a rather glamorous image, with many small and medium-sized enterprises trading in a highly competitive and entrepreneurial business environment. However, the reality of operating in the tourism industry is generally far from glamorous and its competitive nature often forces companies to operate at levels of profitability that affect their long-term viability. One problem associated with an over-dependence on private sector operators in the tourism industry is the potential to ignore tourism's social, cultural and environmental problems while focusing on maximising profits. This is where a public sector organisation can exert its influence by ensuring that the interests of communities and society in general are not forgotten as the tourism industry expands its operations. The list of characteristics shows that it is important to remember that the tourism industry serves both domestic and international markets. It is all too easy to become immersed in the glamour of international tourism and to forget that, in purely economic terms, domestic tourism is far more important than international travel to an individual country.

Operationally, the tourism industry is first and foremost a 'people business' that thrives on face-to-face communication methods. This is apparent not only in the way that tourists are managed in destination areas, but also in terms of the human resource inputs surrounding transportation and the selling of tourism products and services. To be successful in tourism requires a substantial investment in staff training and development, particularly in customer care, languages, selling skills and the use of new technology equipment and systems. Regrettably, such investment in operational and the associated management training has, save for a small number of excellent examples, been insufficient hitherto in a number of tourism sectors. Consequently, many tourism businesses lack clearly defined management structures, a factor compounded by the large number of small enterprises operating in tourism and the relative immaturity of the industry.

Demand for tourism

The simplified model of tourist activity described in Figure 1.2 demonstrates that tourism operates within a demand and supply exchange environment; tourists travel to destination areas in their own country or overseas, making use of a variety of facilities and services before their trip, *en route* and in the destination area. Earlier in this chapter, the three principal purposes of travel, i.e. for leisure, business or visiting friends and relatives (VFR), were identified. But what actually influences people when they are making their choices on where to travel? What determines, for example, whether an individual takes a holiday in Florida or Florence, prefers a short break in Vermont to Venice, or chooses an activity holiday rather than a world cruise? Indeed why do tourists travel at all? The remainder of this chapter, on the demand for tourism, explores the complexities of individual motivation and the determinants of tourist travel, beginning with an overview of the demand for tourism at the international level.

Patterns of international tourism demand

It has been stressed elsewhere in this chapter that today's mass tourism is a phenomenon of the second half of the twentieth century. The rapid growth in demand for international tourism since 1950 is clearly shown in Table 1.1.

Year	Arrivals (millions)	Receipts (US$ billions)
1950	25.3	—
1960	69.3	—
1970	159.7	17.9
1980	284.3	103.1
1990	455.9	260.0
1995 (provisional)	567.0	371.7

Source: Adapted from WTO sources

Table 1.1:
Growth in international tourist arrivals and receipts, 1950–95

Table 1.1 demonstrates that the number of international tourist arrivals increased more than 20-fold between 1950 and 1995, from 25.3 to 567 million arrivals over the 45-year period. Year-on-year rates of growth in arrivals over the same time period have been equally impressive, averaging approximately 6 per cent and 5 per cent per annum respectively in the 1970s and 1980s. Data relating to the first half of the 1990s indicate a slowing down in the rate of growth of international arrivals to just over 3 per cent per annum. It is clear, and not surprising, that these variations in the demand for international tourism are related to fluctuations in the performance of the global economy; in general terms, the 'boom' periods of world economic activity have seen the fastest growth in international tourism, a reflection of the greater confidence of both leisure and business tourists to spend on travel, and of tourism enterprises to expand their operations; the growth in demand in the latter half of the 1980s illustrates this point well. The opposite has been true when growth in the world economy has been suppressed, for example in the early years of the 1990s when there was a general recession in national economies, compounded by the effects of the 1991–92 Gulf War in the Middle East. There were also significant reductions in demand for international tourism in the mid-1970s and the early 1980s, both related to the decision by the oil producing and exporting countries (OPEC) to limit the world production of oil, thereby raising its price and consequently increasing the costs of international travel.

Regional demand for international tourism

Just as there are fluctuations in tourism demand at an international level, regional demand also changes over time, as shown in Figure 1.5. This clearly demonstrates that Europe dominated international tourism arrivals in 1975 and 1995, but with a significant reduction in its market share of 9.7 percentage points over the 20-year time period. Chapter 3 on European tourism considers in detail the underlying reasons for this fall, which is largely the result of increasing competition from regions such as east Asia and the Pacific Rim countries. Figure 1.5 indicates that the Americas remain a distant second to Europe in overall share of arrivals with 19.7 per cent of the market in 1995, a loss of 2.8 percentage points from the 1975 figures. Among those areas that have been increasing their market share of world arrivals since 1975, the east Asia/Pacific region has made the most significant gains. Since 1975, this region has increased its share of international arrivals by 10.8 per cent to 14.7 per cent in 1995. Africa increased its share by 1.2 percentage points to 3.3 per cent in 1995, while less dramatic gains were achieved by south Asia (from 0.7 per cent in 1975 to 0.8 per cent in 1995) and the Middle East (from 1.6 per cent in 1975 to 1.9 per cent in 1995). If the data from 1994 and 1995 are compared, however, these two regions achieved the highest growth rates of all world regions, with the Middle East showing a growth of 11.8 per cent and south Asia 11 per cent of total world tourist arrivals (World Tourism Organisation, 1996).

Figure 1.5: Regional shares of international tourist arrivals 1975 and 1995

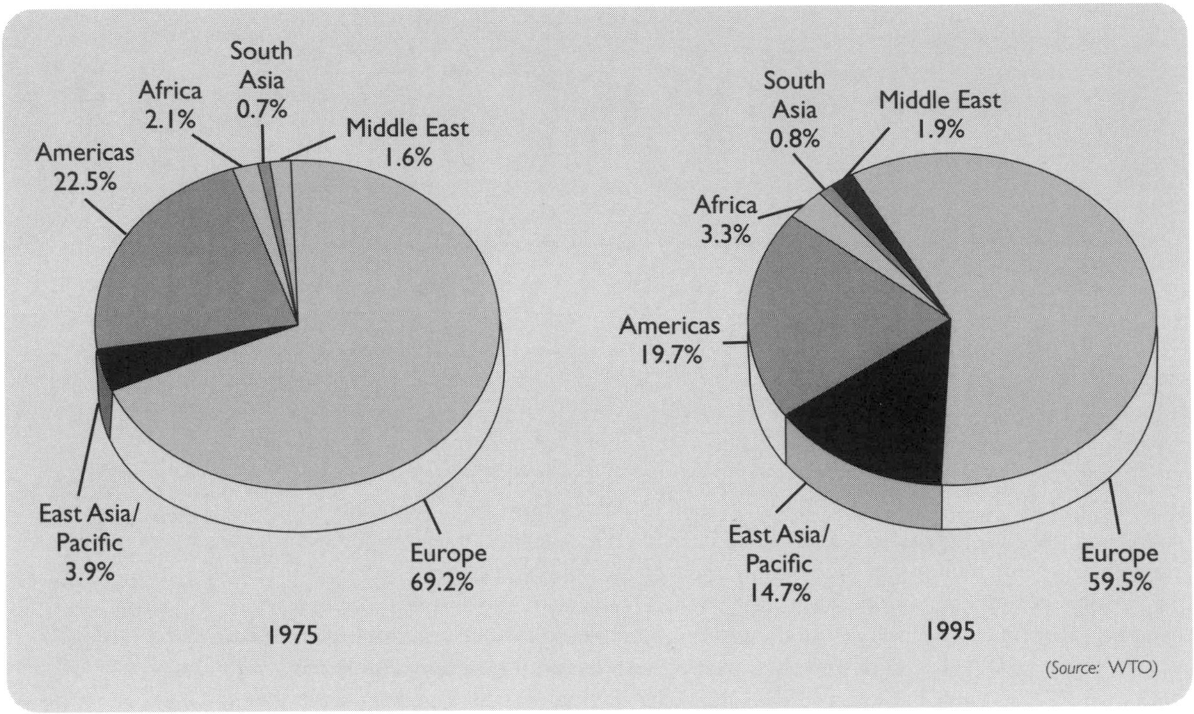

1975

1995

(Source: WTO)

The world's top tourism destinations

The pattern of international tourist flows in the mid-1990s reveals, first and foremost, a heavy concentration of tourist arrivals in a relatively small number of countries. In fact, the world's ten leading tourist destinations account for 54 per cent of the total volume of tourist flows (World Tourism Organisation, 1996). Moreover, since the beginning of the 1990s, there has been a gradual diversification of tourist markets with the emergence of new destinations such as China, Hong Kong and Singapore. The same phenomenon has been apparent in central and eastern Europe where such destinations as Hungary, Poland and the Czech Republic have all achieved significant gains in their share of total international tourist arrivals.

Table 1.2 lists the world's top ten destinations in 1995 in terms of visitor arrivals. This shows that France was once again the world's premier tourism destination with 60.5 million visitors in 1995, equating to a 10.68 per cent share of the world market. For the first time, Spain ousted the United States of America as the world's number two destination. It is interesting to note that seven of the top ten tourism destinations actually lost market share between 1990 and 1995, mainly at the expense of the 'tiger economy' countries of the Far East and certain eastern European destinations; of the top ten, only China, the United Kingdom and Poland increased their share of international tourist arrivals between 1990 and 1995.

If we concentrate on receipts from tourism, there is a similar pattern of dominance among a small number of countries. In 1995, the 20 countries with the highest tourism receipts accounted for 72 per cent of total world revenue. The ten leading countries alone represented 55 per cent of the world total (see Table 1.3).

Table 1.3 indicates that the United States of America leads the world in receipts from tourism, while third-place Italy's figure for receipts moved even closer to that of France

Table 1.2:
World's top
ten tourism
destinations, 1995

Country	International tourist arrivals (000s)	Share of world total (%)
1. France	60 584	10.68
2. Spain	45 125	7.96
3. United States	44 730	7.89
4. Italy	29 184	5.15
5. China	23 368	4.12
6. United Kingdom	22 700	4.00
7. Hungary	22 087	3.90
8. Mexico	19 870	3.50
9. Poland	19 225	3.39
10. Austria	17 750	3.13

Note: All results provisional
Source: Adapted from WTO (1996)

Table 1.3:
Tourism receipts
of the world's
top ten countries,
1995

Country	International tourism receipts (US$ millions)	Share of world total (%)
1. United States	58 370	15.70
2. France	27 322	7.35
3. Italy	27 072	7.28
4. Spain	25 065	6.74
5. United Kingdom	17 469	4.70
6. Austria	12 500	3.36
7. Germany	11 922	3.21
8. Hong Kong	9 075	2.44
9. China	8 250	2.22
10. Singapore	7 550	2.03

Note: All results provisional
Source: Adapted from WTO (1996)

in 1995. Countries in east Asia and the Pacific, in particular China, Australia, Hong Kong, Indonesia, Singapore and Taiwan, all achieved growth rates in excess of 10 per cent in 1995 when compared with the 1994 statistics. Receipts from tourism in many central and eastern European countries, notably Poland, have grown steadily since the beginning of the 1990s.

Seasonality in tourism demand

So far, this section has investigated variations in tourism demand from a geographical or spatial perspective, but temporal fluctuations in demand are also an important aspect of tourist travel. Seasonality in tourism refers to the tendency for tourist demand to be concentrated into relatively short periods of time, the result of favourable climatic conditions, institutional factors such as school holidays and work leave, or the staging of events, for example the annual carnival in Rio de Janeiro or the Winter Olympic Games. During these peak season times, demand for tourist facilities and amenities is at its greatest and prices at their highest. It is common, for example, for tourists from northern European countries to pay more for a holiday in a Mediterranean destination during the summer months of July and August than in the 'off season' months of January, February and March. Conversely, the price of skiing holidays in European resorts is highest in the winter months when demand is at its peak.

Seasonal fluctuations in the demand for tourism can have serious environmental, economic and social repercussions on destination areas and their host communities, as well as causing problems to organisations providing tourism facilities and services. Areas that cannot sustain a year-round tourism industry are unable to provide full-time employment opportunities for workers and can suffer from image problems associated with the closure of facilities at certain times of year. In peak season, conversely, it may be difficult to recruit enough staff of sufficient quality to provide a high standard of customer service. High seasonal demand also places a strain on the residents of tourist areas who are commonly forced to endure extra congestion, pollution and all the problems associated with an influx of visitors. The strain on an area's infrastructure and utilities is also apparent, for example extra demand for water, electricity and sewerage services. Individual tourist enterprises also encounter financial difficulties when faced with seasonal demand, which can have serious effects on cash-flow, day-to-day management and planning future strategies.

There are many ways of attempting to minimise the problems associated with seasonality in tourism demand, such as:

- *Differential pricing*: using the price mechanism to offer reduced rates at periods of low demand, thereby spreading demand to the 'shoulder' times either side of the peak season.
- *Targeted marketing*: identifying customers who could take tourist trips out of season and developing appealing products and services, e.g. couples whose children have left home, the so-called 'empty nesters'.
- *Changing the product mix*: developing all-weather facilities and conference venues that can be used throughout the year.
- *Altering promotional techniques*: distributing brochures and other promotional items to highlight off-season facilities and events, e.g. the British Tourist Authority produces a brochure that features tourist attractions that remain open out of season.

There are circumstances when seasonality can be turned to the advantage of a destination area; resorts in countries such as Switzerland, Austria and the Alpine region of France, which attract both a winter and a summer market, can sustain a viable tourist industry all year round and benefit fully from the positive economic effects of the industry.

Influences on tourism demand

Beginning from the standpoint that all individuals have a unique set of characteristics that determines their physical and psychological make-up, then the variety of influences on each person's demand for tourist travel is immense. Certain factors that influence tourism demand are outside the control of the individual and are the predisposing conditions for travel to take place. These factors are often referred to as determinants, while the influences that shape an individual's choice and over which they have a degree of control are termed motivators. The next two sections of this chapter look at the determinants and motivators of tourism in greater detail.

Determinants of tourism demand

Before an individual can take part in any type of tourist activity, whether for leisure, business or visiting friends and relatives, there are certain 'core' conditions that must be satisfied and which may limit a person's ability to travel. Having sufficient time available to travel is clearly a fundamental determinant of tourism demand. An individual must be able to spare the time to be away from home, work, study or other commitments for the duration of their trip. The introduction of paid holiday entitlements and increases in leisure time in the majority of western industrialised nations have contributed to the increased demand for tourism. It is clear, however, that patterns of tourism demand are changing, with a sharp rise in the popularity of short breaks at the expense of traditional long holidays. In addition to having sufficient time, a person must also be able to afford the cost of travel. Although there has been a gradual rise in income levels in western societies, there are clearly sections of the population whose income level does not permit discretionary spending on tourist travel. The income levels of many people living in the developing nations of the world are generally too low to allow them to travel internationally. Moreover, income levels are inextricably linked to rates of employment and unemployment in national economies and at local/regional levels. As well as having sufficient time and money to travel, an individual must live under a political regime that allows its citizens freedom of movement within their own country and overseas. In the former Eastern Bloc states, prohibitions and restrictions on tourist travel were a common feature of the Communist regimes. In times of austerity, countries may limit the amount of foreign currency its citizens can spend abroad, sometimes to a level that makes international travel impossible to achieve. A fourth determinant of tourism demand is the state of health of a prospective tourist; clearly, an individual who is incapacitated through serious illness or injury will be unable to undertake a tourist trip.

Demand motivators

Even when a person has satisfied the necessary determinants of tourism demand, there are complex psychological influences at work within the individual that will affect their demand for tourism. Major travel and tourism organisations invest large sums in marketing research in order to understand better these motivating factors that influence a tourist's choice and patterns of purchasing behaviour, in the hope of improving the products and service they offer their customers. Probably the most widely quoted work on motivation theory is that of Maslow, who developed the widely referenced 'hierarchy of needs' (see Figure 1.6).

In Maslow's model there are five levels of needs that an individual seeks to satisfy, from physiological needs at the base of the pyramid to self-actualisation at the pinnacle. Maslow argues that individuals must satisfy certain physiological needs, such as shelter, warmth, water and food, and safety needs before moving on to the need for belonging and love, esteem and ultimately self-actualisation. Applying Maslow's hierarchy of needs

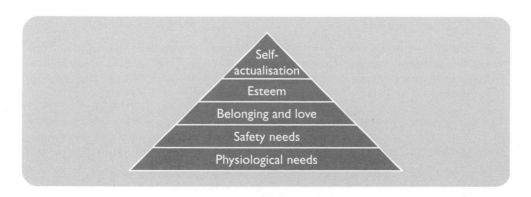

Figure 1.6:
Maslow's hierarchy of needs

to tourists' motivation to travel, it is clear that, depending on the particular circumstances of the individual, tourism can satisfy all levels of needs. A holidaymaker, for example, will choose accommodation, hospitality and travel arrangements that meet his or her physiological and safety needs. Holidays can certainly provide opportunities for developing social relationships, thereby contributing towards the need for belonging and love. Tourists sometimes use their travel experiences as a way of boosting their esteem among peers. Particular types of tourism-related experiences may also contribute to a person's achievement of self-actualisation or self-fulfilment, perhaps becoming spiritually enlightened or learning a new language while on holiday.

One of the earliest attempts at classifying tourist behaviour was developed by Plog (1973). As a result of research into the habits of airline passengers, Plog identified three distinct types of tourists, which he termed:

- *Allocentrics*: those who enjoyed travel and cultural exploration, were in above-average income groups, independent in mind and body, confident and adventurous.
- *Mid-centrics*: the bulk of the population in a destination, who display little desire for exploration and move in after its discovery by allocentrics.
- *Psychocentrics*: individuals who tend to be anxious, self-inhibited and insecure.

Plog found that the travel characteristics of the three groups differed markedly and he suggested that the market for a given destination evolves and appeals to different groups at different times. A destination will be 'discovered' by allocentrics, but as it becomes more popular it will attract increasing numbers of mid-centrics.

In attempting to understand the complexities of tourism motivators, it is clear that tourists' choices are influenced by a wide variety of underlying factors, which, leaving aside the determinants of time, money, freedom to travel and health that have already been considered, include:

- *Education.* This has a profound effect on individuals, not least in relation to their demand for tourism, given the tendency for education to broaden the mind and stimulate the desire to travel.
- *Stage in the life cycle.* Tourism demand fluctuates in relation to a wide variety of life cycle characteristics, such as age, family composition and domestic commitments.
- *Fashions and fads.* Destinations and tourist products go in and out of fashion.
- *Personal mobility.* Access to a private motor vehicle can open up greater tourism opportunities.
- *Rural/urban residence.* Urban dwellers may be motivated to seek the peace and solitude of rural areas for tourist travel, and vice versa.
- *Race and gender.* Cultural surroundings and societal stereotyping can influence the demand for tourism.
- *Destination image.* The techniques used to create a favourable image of a destination and to promote its attributes for tourism, and the methods used to communicate this promotional message to prospective tourists, will influence tourism demand.

It is important to stress that none of these factors works in isolation, but rather each is part of a complex, interrelated mechanism that shapes an individual's motivation for tourism demand. Moreover, the relative importance of each factor to an individual will change over time in response to internal and external influences.

Chapter summary

This chapter has highlighted the significance of the international tourism industry and signalled its potential as a major force in global economic activity. Despite the dramatic growth in international tourist arrivals since the end of World War Two, the industry finds itself at something of a crossroads in its development. Its economic importance is often overshadowed by its associated negative impacts. At governmental level, there are wide variations in perceptions of the economic, political and social benefits that tourism can generate. Nonetheless, the demand for domestic and international tourism continues to grow and this opening chapter has placed the contemporary tourism industry within its historical setting, demonstrating that the mass tourism that is now such a common feature of western, industrialised societies is very much a product of the latter half of the twentieth century. Important aspects of the demand for tourism have been considered along with an analysis of the nature and different types of tourism. We have considered a simplified model of tourist activity and set the scene for the more detailed analysis of the supply side of the tourism industry in Chapter 2.

Discussion questions

1. To what extent is tourism's claim to be 'the world's biggest industry' justified?

2. What factors have contributed to the dramatic rise in international tourist arrivals since the 1950s?

3. International tourism encompasses a wide range of industry sectors; what problems and opportunities does this present for the future development of tourism?

4. What factors have contributed to the recent growth in tourism in the east Asia and Pacific Rim markets, and to what extent is this growth sustainable in the longer term?

5. Which demographic factors do you consider will be of particular importance in determining the future demand for international tourism?

References and further reading

- British Tourist Authority/English Tourist Board (1996) *Tourism Intelligence Quarterly*, Vol. 17, No. 4, BTA/ETB, London
- Burns, P and Holden, A (1995) *Tourism: A New Perspective*, Prentice Hall, Hemel Hempstead, UK
- Holloway, J C (1994) *The Business of Tourism*, 4th edition, Longman, Harlow, UK
- Mill, R and Morrison, A (1992) *The Tourism System*, Prentice-Hall International
- Plog, S (1973) 'Why destination areas rise and fall in popularity', *Cornell Hotel and Restaurant Quarterly*, Vol. 14
- Tourism Society (1982) *British Tourism Yearbook 1982*, Tourism Society, London
- Witt, S, Brooke, M and Buckley, P (1995) *The Management of International Tourism*, Routledge, London

- World Tourism Organisation (1983) *Domestic Tourism Statistics 1981–82*, WTO, Madrid
- World Tourism Organisation (1993) *Recommendations on Tourism Statistics*, WTO, Madrid
- World Tourism Organisation (1996) *International Tourism Overview 1995*, WTO, Madrid
- World Tourism Organisation (1997) *International Tourism Overview 1996*, WTO, Madrid
- World Travel and Tourism Council (1996a) *1996 Research Report*, WTTC, London
- World Travel and Tourism Council (1996b) *Progress and Priorities 1996*, WTTC, London

Chapter Two

Structure and Organisation of the International Tourism Industry

Chapter Overview

This chapter builds on the demand aspects of tourism studied in Chapter 1 by analysing a structural model of the supply side of the industry. We consider the central role played by destinations and investigate accommodation and catering, the most important sector in terms of employment and total revenue. Exploration of the key features of the transportation sector in international tourism is followed by an analysis of tourist attractions and the most important influences on their development and operation. We look at the work of travel agents and tour operators, respectively the retailers and wholesalers of the tourism industry. The role of the public sector in international tourism is followed by an investigation of various international agencies and trade associations involved with the industry.

Key Topics

- Destination organisation
- The accommodation and catering sector
- Transportation in international tourism
- Tourist attractions
- Travel intermediaries – tour operators and travel agents
- Globalisation and integration in international tourism
- The role of the public sector in international tourism
- International tourism agencies and trade associations

Introduction

Chapter 1 highlighted the fact that the demand for tourism has grown rapidly in the 50 years since the end of the Second World War, to a position where it is considered by many commentators and international agencies to be 'the world's biggest industry'. The

Figure 2.1:
Structural
model of the
international
tourism industry

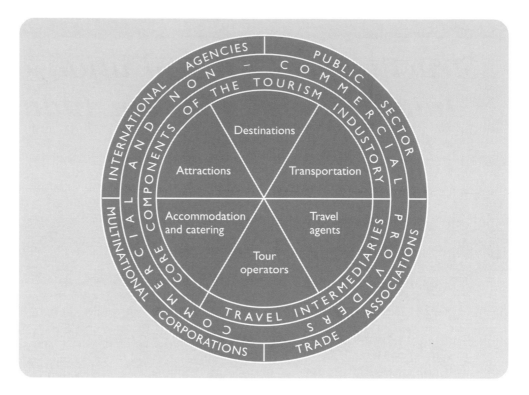

retrospective look at the historical development of tourism indicated that the industry has been very successful in meeting the growth in demand for international tourism. There is a continuing debate as to whether tourism is an 'industry' in the generally accepted sense of the term or merely a collection of related sectors that serve the needs of the travelling public. This chapter affirms the view that international tourism is indeed an industry in its own right and one that, given its status as the world's leading export category, is worthy of the same degree of attention as other sectors of the global economy when planning for economic growth and development.

This chapter's investigation of the structure and organisation of the international tourism industry begins with consideration of the structural model shown in Figure 2.1. This demonstrates that the four core components of the tourism industry are destinations, visitor attractions, transportation and accommodation/catering. Tour operators and travel agents act as intermediaries by packaging tourism products and services and making them available to prospective travellers. These six elements of international tourism are provided by a range of commercial and non-commercial enterprises, although as was shown in Chapter 1, the industry is dominated by private sector providers. The non-commercial arm of the tourism industry consists of public sector enterprises and organisations that operate in the not-for-profit (voluntary) sector, for example conservation societies, civic trusts and wildlife charities. The providers of the core components of the tourism industry are influenced, to a greater or lesser degree, by a variety of organisations, including:

- *International agencies* – such as the World Tourism Organisation (WTO), World Bank, Organisation for Economic Co-operation and Development (OECD) and the European Union.
- *Public sector bodies* – including national tourism organisations (NTOs) and local tourist associations, which seek to organise, co-ordinate, regulate and promote tourism development at local, regional, national and international levels.

- *Trade associations* – for example the Pacific Asia Travel Association (PATA), International Air Transport Association (IATA) and European Travel Commission.
- *Multinational corporations* – such as Hertz, Holiday Inn International and British Airways, which operate across national and international boundaries and have considerable influence on global tourism developments.

In the remainder of this chapter we explore each of the principal sectors and agencies that go to make up the international tourism industry.

Destinations

Although destinations do not represent a sector of the tourism industry in the strictest sense of the word, they are by their very nature the focal point for much tourist activity, concentrating many industry sectors in a single area. In many respects destinations are the external face of the international tourism industry, benefiting from tourism's positive economic and social effects, while at the same time being the location for many of the negative environmental and socio-cultural impacts of the industry. They are also of prime importance in tourism since it is often the destination and its image that attracts a tourist in the first instance, thereby acting as a catalyst to the many sectors of the tourism industry, as shown in Figure 2.2.

Figure 2.2 indicates that a destination can be considered the 'umbrella' under which the diverse sectors of the tourism industry work in partnership to provide facilities and services for leisure and business travellers. A typical destination will have a variety of commercial and non-commercial tourism organisations operating in tandem, with public bodies generally supplying the infrastructure, planning and regulatory frameworks, tourist information services and destination promotion, while private operators provide the bulk of the facilities for visitors, such as accommodation, catering, attractions and entertainments.

Destinations exhibit a number of important features of interest to tourism planners and operators. These are illustrated by the following examples.

- *They exist at varying geographical scales.* A destination may be a continent, a whole country, a region within the country, a capital city, a town, village or countryside/wilderness area. A single visitor attraction may be of a sufficient size to qualify as a destination in its own right, for example Disneyland Paris, Universal Studios and Center Parcs villages in Europe. Equally, a single natural or cultural attraction may have enough drawing power to warrant the term 'destination', for example the Grand Canyon, the Egyptian Pyramids, the Great Wall of China or the Victoria Falls. Clearly, such variations in the scale of destinations can pose problems (and opportunities) for the tourism industry.

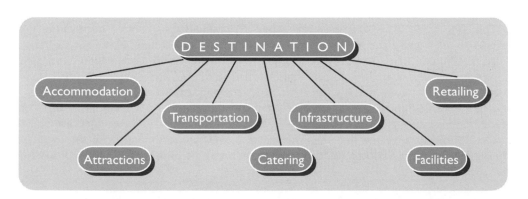

Figure 2.2:
The composition of the tourist destination

● *They encompass multiple products.*   Figure 2.2 demonstrates that tourism destinations support a variety of products, services and facilities that are provided to meet the needs of visitors. These may be part of an area's superstructure, i.e. purpose-built tourist facilities such as accommodation establishments and attractions, or part of its infrastructure, i.e. the 'skeleton' of transport services, utilities and communications channels around which tourist facilities are developed. Such disparate products and facilities, which may vary markedly in terms of scale, quality, availability and financing, must be integrated into an overall development strategy if the destination is to be marketed successfully.

● *They exhibit a multi-ownership pattern.*   The products and facilities on offer in tourism destinations are provided by a wide range of private, public and not-for-profit organisations, each with their own objectives and management styles. Although each organisation undertakes its own marketing activities, the responsibility for the overall marketing of a destination is usually given to a public agency. The fact that the majority of the tourism facilities in a destination are operated by autonomous private sector enterprises means that the public sector destination marketing organisation will have little control over the marketing of individual tourist facilities, a situation that may lead to a rather unco-ordinated approach. To some extent, this situation can be alleviated by the formation of a public/private sector partnership, with the public body providing 'pump priming' funding for destination development and promotion.

● *They serve the needs of a variety of markets.*   Most tourism destinations cater for a wide range of business and leisure tourists, each with their own requirements in terms of product mix and service standards. For example, the island of Majorca provides facilities for mass market, package holidaymakers in its southern resorts, while attracting higher-spending tourists to its northern coastal towns such as Puerto Pollença and Alcudia. In such circumstances, destination marketers have to convey different images and messages to meet the requirements of particular market segments and provide appropriate facilities.

Also, the popularity of destination areas fluctuates in response to a number of demand and supply factors. For example, the development of a wide range of high quality tourist attractions and facilities in Florida, coupled with targeted promotional activities, has stimulated demand for holidays in the state in the 1980s and 1990s. Tourism is Florida's largest industry, generating more than US$30 billion in 1992 and employing some 657 000 people across all sectors of the industry, including accommodation, catering, attractions and transportation. Spain, on the other hand, experienced a slowdown in tourist demand during the latter half of the 1980s from its dramatic annual growth rates of the 1960s and 1970s, culminating in a fall in tourist numbers in 1990 (see Table 2.1).

The statistics in Table 2.1 show that Spain's popularity as a tourist destination has begun to rise again, the result of increased levels of investment in tourist facilities, improved infrastructure and a 'repositioning' of the destination from one offering just sun, sand and sea attractions to one that also has an important cultural and artistic heritage in its coastal areas and interior regions. Visitor numbers rose sharply after the hosting of the World Expo in Seville and the 1992 Olympic Games in Barcelona. In terms of Butler's tourist area life cycle concept (see Chapter 7 for a detailed explanation), Spain could be said to have reached the consolidation and stagnation stages of the cycle in the late 1980s, followed by a period of rejuvenation in the early 1990s that continues to the present day.

Year	Total visitors (millions)	Receipts from tourism (US$ billions)
1985	43.2	8.1
1986	47.4	12.0
1987	50.5	14.8
1988	54.2	16.7
1989	54.0	14.2
1990	52.0	18.0
1991	53.5	19.0
1992	55.3	21.0
1993	57.3	23.5
1994	61.4	26.8
1995	63.3	29.0

Source: Spanish National Tourist Office

The accommodation and catering sector

Sometimes simply referred to as 'hospitality', this sector provides leisure and business tourists with somewhere to stay and sustenance while travelling to or staying in their destinations. It encompasses hotels, self-catering accommodation, restaurants, fast-food outlets, contract catering and a wide range of other enterprises; everything from a luxury five-star hotel in Seattle to a farm guesthouse in Denmark, or a top harbour-side restaurant in Sydney to a kebab bar in Turkey. In purely economic terms, accommodation and catering is the most significant of all the sectors of international tourism, since it is the biggest employer and accounts for the largest proportion of tourists' expenditure. If we examine the UK context, the accommodation and catering sector employs approximately two-thirds of all those working in the tourism industry and represents 60 per cent of total spending on tourism (British Tourist Authority/English Tourist Board, 1996). Similar patterns are to be found in the majority of countries which have highly developed tourism industries.

Classification of accommodation

The divergence of historical, cultural, geographical and political influences throughout the developed and developing nations of the world has given rise to a wide variety of accommodation types available to tourists. Accommodation can be categorised in a number of ways, for example:

- Serviced or self-catering, e.g. staying at an inn or in an apartment in a self-catering villa complex
- Charged or free, e.g. paying for a room in a hotel or staying free of charge with a friend
- Chain or independent, e.g. belonging to a hotel chain such as Inter-Continental Hotels or trading independently
- Static or mobile, e.g. a holiday villa or a rented camper van
- Urban or rural, e.g. a city centre youth hostel or a forest camping ground
- By purpose of visit, e.g. for business or visiting friends and relatives (VFR)

Table 2.2:
World stock
of hotels

	Thousands of rooms			Number of additional rooms (thousands), 1985-1994	per cent change, 1985-1994	per cent share	
	1985	1990	1994			1985	1994
World	9 199	11 060	12 218	3 019	32.8	100.0	100.0
Africa	267	334	384	117	43.8	2.9	3.1
Americas	3 462	4 311	4 493	1 031	29.8	37.6	36.8
East Asia/Pacific	813	1 207	1 557	744	91.5	8.8	12.7
Europe	4 425	4 936	5 462	1 037	23.4	48.1	44.7
Middle East	130	160	179	49	37.7	1.4	1.5
South Asia	102	112	143	41	40.2	1.1	1.2

Source: World Tourism Organisation (WTO)

Accommodation is most commonly classified under one of the following categories:

● Commercial or non-commercial
● Serviced or self-catering

By far the majority of the world's tourist accommodation is provided by commercial companies, although there are examples of non-commercial providers within youth tourism, educational establishments, religious groups and conservation bodies. Classifying accommodation as either serviced or self-catering is dependent on the level of service provided. As its name implies, the term 'serviced accommodation' is used when a service is provided along with an overnight stay, for example meals, valet services and housekeeping. In this category, therefore, we find a variety of establishments, including hotels, guesthouses, inns, bed and breakfast establishments, youth hostels and farm guesthouses. The term 'self-catering', or self-serviced accommodation as it is sometimes referred to, consists of establishments where the tourist is provided with overnight accommodation, but caters for all other needs independently. In this category, therefore, are included villas, apartments, rented houses and cottages, motor homes, camping grounds, caravan sites, holiday complexes, chalets, second homes, boats, home 'swaps', colleges, universities and timeshare accommodation. The distinction between serviced and self-catering accommodation is not always totally clear since increasing numbers of self-catering providers are now supplying a range of services to their guests. For example, it is quite common now for self-catering establishments, particularly if they form part of a complex, to offer visitors the option of buying food and ready-to-eat meals. Some even have on-site restaurants, cafés and snack bars. The Center Parcs holiday villages found in the UK and other European countries are an excellent case in point, offering their holidaymakers a variety of eating places, sports facilities, shopping opportunities and a child-minding service, along with self-catering villa accommodation.

Hotels are the most common type of accommodation used by leisure and business tourists, particularly those travelling internationally. Table 2.2 shows the total worldwide stock of hotels and similar establishments, as well as regional variations.

As the data in Table 2.2 show, the world stock of hotel rooms stood at just over 12.2 million in 1994, a 25 per cent increase on the 1985 figure of 9.2 million rooms. The

Accommodation used (percentage of total nights)	1985–86	1993–94
Friends/relatives house/flat	44	46
Hotel/motel	16	19
Rented house/flat	7	7
Caravan park	13	8
Other	20	20
Total nights (per cent)	100	100

Source: Australian Bureau of Tourism Research

Table 2.3: Main accommodation used by Australian residents on domestic travel, 1985–86 and 1993–94

regional growth rates in hotel supply over the same time period mirror the general trends in international tourism growth that we investigated in Chapter 1. The fastest rates of growth in hotel stock have been in the east Asia/Pacific, Africa and south Asia regions, while Europe experienced the slowest growth rate between 1985 and 1994 of all world regions. Table 2.2 clearly indicates that Europe and the Americas dominate the supply of hotels, with a combined market share of more than 80 per cent of all rooms, although the share of both regions declined between 1985 and 1994.

Although hotels are the dominant form of accommodation used in international tourism, other types of accommodation feature more prominently in a country's *domestic* tourism scene. The types of accommodation used by Australian residents on domestic travel, for example, are given in Table 2.3, which demonstrates that staying in the house/ flat of a friend or relative is by far the most popular category, although the use of hotels and motels has increased since 1985–86.

The pattern of accommodation used on domestic travel in the UK shows that staying in a caravan (21 per cent) was the most popular category of accommodation used on all holidays in 1995, followed by hotel/motel (21 per cent) and staying with friends and relatives (19 per cent) (British Tourist Authority/English Tourist Board, 1996).

Future supply of accommodation

The factors influencing the future supply of accommodation are discussed in detail in Chapter 8 on the future of tourism, but it is important to stress certain points at this juncture. Firstly, future success in the provision of accommodation will depend on a very focused and targeted approach to development and marketing. Companies will need to seek out, or even create, these 'niche' markets and develop appropriate facilities and services to satisfy consumer demand. Also, as tourists become more sophisticated in their purchasing habits, they will increasingly expect higher standards of customer service and product quality, while still demanding value for money. Accommodation providers that are able to respond quickly to changes in the marketplace, in society in general and in the work/leisure divide, through the use of new technology and effective human resource strategies, will be in a position to reap the benefits of the predicted growth in international and domestic tourism.

Transportation

The transportation sector of the tourism industry covers a variety of water, air and land-based services, including travel by coach, train, private car, taxi, hired car, bicycle, aircraft, cruise ship, ferry and canal craft. We saw in Chapter 1 that throughout history the growth of tourism has been synonymous with developments in transportation. This still applies today, with advances in aircraft technology, passenger shipping, road improvements and high-speed rail travel offering faster, more comfortable and more convenient travel. Travel by air dominates the international tourism scene whereas travel by private car is the most popular form of transportation for domestic tourism, offering flexibility, freedom and good value for money. As domestic and international tourists become more experienced and sophisticated in their travel habits, the transport sector is having to respond by offering a wider variety of travel options, using the latest passenger-carrying vehicles and providing the highest standards of customer care. Competition between and within the different forms of tourist transportation is also contributing to the emergence of an international transportation sector that is becoming more customer-centred in its approach. It is important to remember that transportation is often an integral and pleasurable part of a total travel experience and not merely a means of getting from home to a holiday destination. The excitement felt by young children on a charter flight to a summer sun holiday destination or the pleasure given to senior citizens on a coach tour serve to illustrate this point well.

The transportation sector includes not only the services provided for tourists but also the related infrastructure that supports the means of travel, such as roads, motorway service areas, ferry terminals, airports and railway stations. Much of this infrastructure is provided by public agencies, or by public/private sector partnership arrangements. As demand for travel has grown, many transport terminals have developed into large, integrated complexes offering a range of catering, currency exchange, business, retail and entertainment facilities.

Air travel

The rapid growth in international tourism since the end of the Second World War has been closely allied to the expansion of air travel services. Advances in aircraft technology have led to increases in aircraft capacity and the development of aeroplanes with a far greater flying range. These two factors, coupled with increased demand for air travel generally, have enabled airlines to reduce prices and provide the stimulus for the growth of scheduled services and inclusive tours to medium and long-haul destinations. Deregulation of air travel, first accomplished in the USA and planned for completion in Europe during 1997, has increased competition between airlines and helped to keep fares low on an expanding network of routes. Allied to the growth in air services has been the rapid expansion of the associated infrastructure needed to cope with business and leisure tourists as well as freight traffic, including airport terminals and runways. London-Heathrow alone handles more than 50 million passengers per year and is the world's busiest airport.

International airlines have sought to increase their dominance in global markets through acquisitions and strategic alliances with other airlines. British Airways, for example, in attempting to achieve its ambition of becoming the world's biggest airline has established links with Qantas in order to establish a presence in the Asia/Pacific region, TAT (a French domestic carrier) and Deutsche BA, and is currently negotiating an alliance with American Airlines.

Types of air travel services

For statistical purposes, the International Air Transport Association (IATA) classifies air travel services into one of three categories, namely:

1. Domestic
2. International scheduled
3. International chartered

Domestic services refer to air travel within a country, while international represents travel between different countries. Scheduled services are those that operate to a published timetable, on defined routes and under government licence. These services must run regardless of passenger load and are used primarily by business travellers who are prepared to pay a premium for the extra convenience and flexibility offered. Many governments still fund their national airlines, for example Air France, although there is a general move away from state ownership towards private sector operation, or at least private–public sector partnerships.

Chartered air services evolved to serve the expanding package holiday industry and now represent a significant proportion of passenger traffic in many countries with established outbound tourism sectors. Indeed, seat-only sales are one of the fastest growing products in air travel. Although some package holidays do incorporate scheduled air services the majority include a charter flight, known as an inclusive tour by charter (ITC). Charter services are generally cheaper than scheduled flights since their operators aim to fill as many seats as possible, often only offering the flight if they can be guaranteed a minimum number of passengers, known as the break-even load factor. Often this figure will be as high as 85 or 90 per cent, after which the operator begins to make a profit on the flight.

For the 1995 trading year, IATA airlines carried a total of 1107 million passengers on their scheduled services, of which 352 million were on international flights and 755 on domestic services (International Air Transport Association, 1996). Growth of passenger numbers on international scheduled services was 6.6 per cent over the 1994 figures, but on domestic flights only 2.5 per cent. International charter passenger traffic grew by 17.7 per cent between 1994 and 1995, reflecting the increased demand for long-haul package holidays in particular.

Rail transportation

Given that the railway was the dominant form of mass transportation in western industrialised societies until the rise in car ownership of the early twentieth century and the later introduction of air travel services, it is surprising that the demise in the use of rail services has been so swift. It is true that passenger and freight rail transportation still has an important role to play in some developed nations and is the principal form of long-distance travel for people living in the developing countries of the world. In western societies, travel by rail still occupies a small share of most country's domestic tourism transportation statistics. From an international tourism viewpoint, however, rail travel finds itself unable to compete with other travel modes for the mass movement of tourists to their holiday destinations.

The general fall in demand for tourist travel by rail is not just a consequence of the rise in popularity of the private car and the introduction of travel by air. It is also a function of government approaches to rail travel, which vary considerably in different regions of the world. If we compare rail travel in the United Kingdom and France, for example, we see a UK rail transport network that has suffered from insufficient investment in rolling stock, signalling and track upgrading. As such, demand for tourist travel by rail has fallen sharply. The French government, on the other hand, has invested considerable public funds in the rail system, with its 'flagship' TGV (*train de grande vitesse*) network offering a high-speed service across the country. The French rail system is used extensively for tourist travel and the TGV is regarded as a viable alternative to domestic air services for business travel within the country. A similar situation exists in Japan, where the so-called 'bullet' trains link major centres of population. One notable exception to the poorly developed UK rail network is the Eurostar service linking London with Paris, Brussels and other major European cities via the Channel Tunnel, offering a high-speed service to business and leisure travellers. As yet, however, the high-speed line between London and the Channel Tunnel is only at the planning stage and is unlikely to be operational until the early years of the next century. The European Union has recently agreed plans to develop an integrated transport network throughout the continent by the year 2010, including a trans-European rail network (see Chapter 3 on European tourism for more details of the proposed network).

Despite the best efforts of countries such as France, international tourist travel by rail has become a 'niche market' product, serving the needs of two particular categories of travellers, namely young people travelling on cheap discount tickets, often over a long period of time, and older people who can afford the luxury of nostalgic trips on the great railway journeys of the world, for example the Venice–Simplon Orient Express, the trans-Siberian route, and tourist trains operating in the North American Rocky Mountains.

Passenger shipping

In the same way that rail transportation was the dominant mode of surface travel up to the time of the twin developments of the growth in car ownership and the introduction of air travel services, so the ocean-going liners were the most popular form of sea transport for long-distance international travel up to the middle of the twentieth century. Passenger shipping services suffered badly when air travel services were introduced from the 1950s onwards. Companies such as P&O, Union-Castle Line and Cunard withdrew their services to the USA, South Africa and the Far East; such routes were to be serviced by the more accessible and affordable scheduled air travel services.

The demise of the ocean-going liners forced the passenger shipping industry to diversify into cruise shipping. Today, cruising is enjoying something of a revival, with the Caribbean, the Mediterranean, the Baltic, the Far East and Australasia among the principal cruise destinations of the world. Paradoxically, the introduction of the very same air services that signalled the demise of the international passenger shipping industry has boosted cruising, with the development of the fly-cruise holiday, where tourists combine a charter or scheduled flight to and/or from a port with their sea cruise. Whereas in the past cruising tended to be the preserve of rich and famous senior citizens, today's cruising industry has products geared to all ages and budgets. The arrival of mass market tour operators and new-generation vessels onto the cruising scene has heralded a new era of packaged cruises at bargain basement prices.

In many parts of the world, ferries offer inexpensive and reliable services on short sea crossings. Places as diverse as the Greek islands, Hong Kong harbour, the Scottish Highlands and Islands, the Adriatic Sea and the Baltic coastline all rely on ferry services for everyday travel and tourist business. In places where there is strong competition between ferry operators, such as on the short sea crossings in the English Channel, there have been considerable advances in vessel technology, with the introduction of hovercraft, hydrofoils and jet-foils to compete with the fast, new generation of passenger ships. The opening of the Channel Tunnel in 1994 increased competition on cross-Channel services still further. In addition to operating the faster vessels, ferry companies have responded to this challenge by offering price reductions, enhanced levels of customer service and greater on-board shopping and entertainment facilities on their ferry services.

Road transport

The road transport element within the transportation sector of tourism includes travel by private car, bus and coach, taxi and hired car. The private car is the world's dominant form of travel for tourist purposes, especially for domestic tourism and intra-continental travel. It offers a degree of flexibility, comfort and convenience that cannot be matched by other forms of transportation, but it does bring with it considerable environmental impacts. The high levels of car ownership in the densely-populated industrialised regions of the world, particularly in Europe, some Far East countries, South America and the USA, have resulted in sharp increases in the use of cars for long holidays, short breaks and recreational day trips. This has led to problems of pollution, physical erosion, loss of land to car parks and congestion in many popular tourist destinations, especially historic cities, coastal resorts and national parks, where vehicles often spoil the very ambience that attracted the tourists in the first place. Central and local governments are attempting to minimise the impact of vehicles by introducing a variety of techniques, including public transport initiatives, road pricing and pedestrianisation.

Travel by coach is an altogether more environmentally friendly form of tourist travel, transporting large numbers of tourists on scheduled services, on transfer journeys or forming the transport element of an inclusive tour, for example a coach holiday in the Austrian Tyrol. Deregulation of coach travel, which occurred in the USA in 1982 and more recently in Europe, has liberalised the market for travel by coach and offered travellers a wider choice of operators. In the case of Europe, EU legislation allows a coach operator from any member state of the Union to offer coach services in any other EU country.

Tourist attractions

Tourist attractions have an important role to play in world tourism since they often provide the motivating force for travel, thereby energising the many components of the tourism industry. The scope of the attractions sector is immense; logically, anything that has the power to draw visitors to it can be considered an attraction. Moreover, an attraction may not be a readily identifiable place or feature, but a visitor's overall perception of a destination as an attractive place to visit, distilled from a variety of sources and images. London's current popularity as a tourist destination with young visitors from around the world is a good case in point; they are not attracted primarily by the 'traditional' attractions such as the Houses of Parliament, Buckingham Palace and Big Ben, but rather by the image of the capital, real or otherwise, as a 'cool' place to hear good music and have an enjoyable time.

Tourist attractions occur at a variety of scales. Many internationally famous attractions, for example San Francisco's Golden Gate Bridge, Red Square in Moscow and the Pompidou Centre in Paris, are household names on many tourists' 'must see' lists. Domestic tourists travel within their own countries to a variety of attractions, some of which are provided free of charge while others charge admission. These may be day visits or a part of a long holiday or short break. Many larger visitor attractions, such as theme parks and stately homes, will have a regional catchment area. At a local level, attractions meet the need for recreation, education, entertainment and excitement for a wide range of visitor types, from young children to members of organised groups.

Tourist attractions are provided by both commercial and non-commercial organisations. Many historic buildings, areas of landscape or wildlife interest, museums and ancient monuments, for example, are in the care of public bodies and voluntary groups, which aim to preserve or conserve vital parts of a country's heritage while at the same time making facilities available to tourists. In the UK, for example, the Department for Culture, Media and Sport (formerly the Department of National Heritage) helps ensure that the nation's heritage is protected and managed for generations of visitors to come, through statutory controls, grant-aid and other funding mechanisms. The Department also sponsors Heritage Open Days, when the public is allowed free access to buildings that are not normally open or usually charge an entrance fee. Private companies seek to generate profits through the provision of a wide variety of purpose-built attractions, such as amusement parks, entertainment facilities and theme parks. Perhaps the best known of all attraction companies is the Disney Corporation, pioneers of the theme park concept in the USA and now operating attractions in Europe and the Far East as well.

Attractions are not always permanent. Many tourist destinations, at local, regional, national and international levels, host special events as a way of boosting tourism or meeting different event objectives, such as the celebration of an anniversary or the staging of a musical extravaganza. Indeed, areas that lack a critical mass of either built or natural attractions often concentrate on staging a wide variety of events aimed at different market segments, by developing a so called events-led strategy. Many destinations around the world are well known for staging events, for example the carnival in Rio de Janeiro, the Boston Marathon and the Passion Play at Oberammergau, to name but a few.

Types of tourist attractions

Tourist attractions are generally classified into one of two categories, namely:

- Natural attractions
- Man-made (or built) attractions

At an international level, the range and variety of natural attractions is immense, encompassing, among other things, mountains, rivers, deserts, ice flows, forests, lakes, valleys and, perhaps most important of all from a tourism perspective, beaches and the sea. When looking back in history it is apparent that much early tourist activity was stimulated by natural attractions and features. In the eighteenth and nineteenth centuries, destinations with spa waters began to attract visitors in greater numbers and seaside resorts grew in popularity, originally as a result of the health-giving nature of sea water. When considering the drawing power of natural attractions and features, such as the Grand Canyon, the Victoria Falls or Mount Fuji, it is easy to forget the importance of climate as a factor in attracting tourists to destinations. For many people living in the cool temperate climate of the northern European plain, the prime stimulus for their holiday travel is warm weather, hence the strong intra-European tourist flows from countries such as Germany, the Netherlands and the United Kingdom to destinations bordering the Mediterranean Sea.

Man-made tourist attractions come in a variety of types and occur at different scales. Many were not originally built to attract visitors, but are simply the product of history and cultural development, for example churches, castles, cathedrals, monuments and even former industrial sites. Although the range and variety of man-made attractions is very diverse, it is possible to group them under a number of themes for analysis, for example:

- *Heritage attractions*: facilities that depict past events in history through the re-creation and display of artefacts and memorabilia, e.g. Williamsburg in the USA and the Jorvik Viking Centre in the UK.

- *Museums and ancient monuments*: attractions that exist primarily to conserve historic collections and commemorate past events, but which are visited by tourists, e.g. the Louvre in Paris, Stonehenge in Wiltshire, UK, and the British Museum in London.

- *Theme parks*: facilities that offer visitors an exciting experience in a purpose-built, themed setting, consisting of 'rides', other entertainments, catering and retail outlets. Examples include Walt Disney World in Florida and De Efteling in the Netherlands.

- *Entertainments*: nightclubs, discotheques, concert halls, theatres, arenas and opera houses, among others, that provide a variety of entertainment opportunities for visitors, e.g. New York's Free Trade Hall, the Sydney Opera House and the discothèques found in Spanish and other Mediterranean resorts.

- *Sports facilities and events*: can be a powerful stimulus for tourism, e.g. motor racing Grand Prix venues and the summer and winter Olympic Games.

- *Leisure shopping venues*: shopping malls, out-of-town retail complexes and historic city centres often attract visitors to a destination, e.g. Europe's largest retail complex at the Metro Centre in north-east England and the quaint streets of Chester, UK.

- *Wildlife areas*: including zoos, wildlife centres, sea life attractions and botanical gardens, for example Busch Gardens and Sea World in Florida.

In addition to these permanent attractions, events can play an important part in the image of a destination and the mix of attractions it offers to visitors. Most events can be said to be 'man-made', in that they are staged with a particular objective in mind, at a predetermined time in a precise location. We should not forget, however, that many naturally occurring events can be equally powerful as a motivator for tourist activity, e.g. the dramatic sunset over the Grand Canyon and the migration of wildebeest across the African plains.

Issues in the attractions sector

The main factors affecting the future of tourist attractions are discussed in detail in Chapter 8 on the future of tourism, but it is important to stress a number of important issues at this point. The attractions sector will always be a prime motivator in international and domestic tourism; natural and man-made attractions will continue to be the stimulus for much tourist travel. The very dynamic and responsive nature of the sector, however, will mean that the attractions themselves, and how they are planned and managed, will constantly evolve in response to changes in consumer demand. It is important to stress that these changes will affect both man-made and natural attractions. Whatever the type or location of the attraction, its visitors will expect a stimulating experience, well presented, respectful of cultures and the environment, yet with a high standard of customer service. Also, in common with many others areas of tourism, new technologies are likely to play a significant role in how attractions are managed, operated and promoted to visitors in the future.

Travel intermediaries

The term 'travel intermediary' is given to any individual or organisation that makes travel arrangements on behalf of a third party, providing a link between customers and the suppliers of travel products and services, as shown in Figure 2.3.

Figure 2.3: The position of travel intermediaries

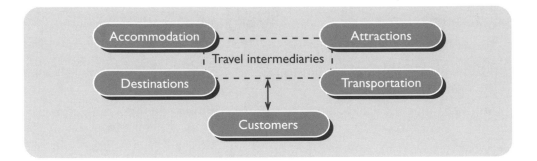

Figure 2.4: The role of travel agents

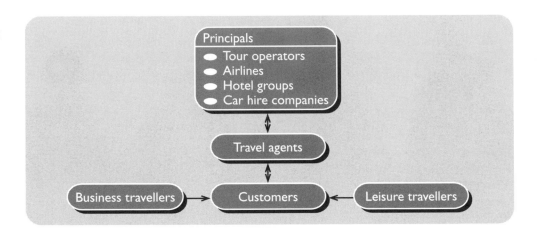

The suppliers of travel products and services referred to in Figure 2.3 include many firms that operate in the core sectors of the tourism industry and include hotels and other accommodation providers, transport companies, tourist attractions and destination marketing organisations. Travel intermediaries liaise directly or indirectly with such suppliers in order to satisfy the needs of their customers. Most travel intermediaries operate in the commercial world, making a profit on the services they offer to their clients by charging a fee or taking an agreed proportion of sales income, known as a commission. The very diverse nature of the international tourism industry means that there is a wide range of organisations that make travel arrangements on behalf of others, including transport companies, conference organisers, business executives, youth group organisers, religious institutions, sports clubs and associations, charities and community group leaders. However, in terms of volume of sales, by far the two most important intermediaries in the international tourism industry are travel agents and tour operators.

To the casual observer there may appear to be little distinction between the work of travel agents and tour operators. This is perhaps not surprising given the degree of collaboration and integration in the travel sector, a subject to which we shall return later in this chapter. In reality, however, each category has its specific roles and functions in international tourism, as the following paragraphs explain.

The role of travel agents

We can consider travel agents to be the retail arm of the tourism industry, acting as intermediaries linking customers with a range of travel providers, known as principals (see Figure 2.4).

In the same way that a clothes shop sells products to shoppers, so travel agencies retail their 'products' to the general public. Indeed, the term 'travel shop' is commonly used to refer to travel agency premises. The one major difference between these two types of retail outlets, however, is that unlike the clothes retailer, travel agencies do not buy in stock in advance, but rather react to the wishes of their customers before contacting the principals.

As Figure 2.4 indicates, travel agencies are generally acting on behalf of two parties when they undertake their work. They provide a service to their clients, on whose behalf they are making the travel arrangements. These may be either leisure or business travellers, travelling individually or as part of a group. They also act as the agent for the companies supplying the travel products. Depending on the particular travel agency in question, these principals may include:

- Tour operators
- Car hire firms
- Airlines
- Ferry companies
- Coach companies
- Cruise lines
- Hotels
- Theatres

The business relationships between travel agents and principals are generally strictly controlled by individual agency agreements. Depending on the nature of its business, a travel agency will negotiate agreements with each tour operator, airline, ferry company, cruise line, hotel group, car hire company, etc., with which it conducts business. These written agreements will include details of a number of points, such as accounting procedures, policies on refunds and cancellations, procedures for issuing tickets and other travel documentation, commission rates, responsibilities on racking brochures, handling complaints, training and promotional support. The commission payments that agents earn from the principals are usually expressed as a percentage of sales and vary according to the product being sold and the commission policy of the principal. In general terms, commission rates range from around 10 per cent for most package holidays to as much as 40 per cent for services such as car hire and the sale of travel insurance.

Although the sale of overseas holidays is the main activity of the bulk of travel agents, many offer a wide range of travel-related products and services, including travel insurance, foreign exchange, theatre bookings, rail tickets, coach excursions, airline tickets, car hire, cruising, visas and passport applications.

Arranging travel for leisure purposes dominates the work of most travel agencies, but some may have a business travel specialist, or even a business travel department, catering exclusively for the needs of corporate clients. There are also some travel agencies, known as business house agencies, that deal solely with business travel services for clients. The requirements of business travel clients are quite different from those of leisure travellers, since they often need to travel at short notice and on scheduled rather than charter services. This does mean, however, that the value of their business is usually higher than that of holidaymakers, making the extra effort needed to secure and maintain their custom worthwhile.

Travel agents that sell airline tickets on behalf of the world's principal airlines must hold a licence issued by the International Air Transport Association (IATA), the international trade body representing the interests of more than 80 per cent (200+ companies) of the world's airlines. Since these airlines, which include major carriers such as British Airways, Korean Air, Indian Airlines, IBERIA, KLM Royal Dutch Airlines and USAir, only pay commission to approved IATA sales agents, an IATA licence is a much sought-after commodity. Travel agents must meet certain approval criteria before a licence can be issued, covering such matters as security of premises, staff qualifications and financial stability.

Tour operators

Unlike travel agents, who sell holidays and a range of other travel products, tour operators actually assemble the component parts of a holiday, i.e. the means of travel, accommodation, facilities, transfers, excursions and other services. If we consider that travel agents are the retail arm of the international tourism industry, then tour operators can be likened to wholesalers, since they buy in bulk from the providers of travel services, such as the hoteliers and airlines, break the bulk into manageable packages and offer the finished product, the inclusive tour (IT), for sale via a travel agent or direct to the consumer. Figure 2.5 shows the role of tour operators and their position as intermediaries between the suppliers of travel products and travel agents. The figure also shows that some tour operators deal direct with their customers rather than selling through travel agents. This practice is often limited to specialist tour operators and a small number of 'direct sell' operators, which profess to sell their products at reduced prices since they pay no commission to travel agents.

There are four principal types of tour operators found in the international tourism industry, namely:

- *Mass market operators*: companies that sell high volumes of 'packaged' products, primarily to overseas destinations, at relatively cheap prices (see the Thomson case study on page 40).
- *Specialist operators*: enterprises that concentrate on a particular segment of the market, for example senior citizens, a particular country or destination, a particular activity or specific type of tourism, e.g. cultural tourism, business tourism or sports holidays.
- *Domestic operators*: companies that provide a range of products geared to the needs of the residents of their own country.
- *Incoming tour operators*: companies that specialise in supplying holidays and other travel services solely for overseas visitors to a country.

Contrary to popular belief, most tour operators found in the international tourism industry are not large, multinational organisations, but rather small and medium-sized

Figure 2.5: The position of tour operators

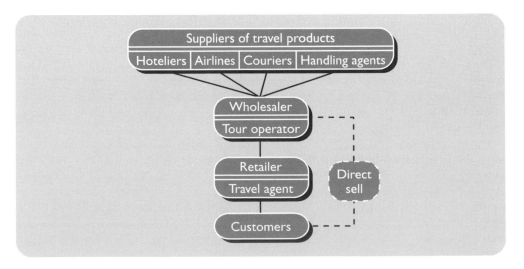

enterprises serving the needs of specialist markets. Regardless of their size of operation, all tour operating businesses will be involved in similar activities to achieve their goal of developing and supplying tour products that satisfy their clients' needs. Depending on the type of tour operator concerned, some of these activities will be carried out by staff in the company's head office while the remainder will be delegated to overseas personnel. Key activities are as follows:

- Market research
- Product development
- Contracting
- Marketing
- Brochure production and distribution
- Reservations
- Sales support
- Administration
- Customer services

These activities relate broadly to the stages that a tour operator goes through when developing its tour products. *Market research* has a key role to play in helping the company to decide on the main elements of its products and to identify market opportunities. Market research information is available from a variety of internal and external sources, including past sales figures, customer satisfaction questionnaires, analysts' reports, industry trends data, official statistics and analyses of competitors' programmes. *Product development* involves using the market research data to determine the overall structure of a tour programme and its precise details, such as the overall capacity of the programme, which destinations and hotels are to be used, and what travel arrangements will apply. Having agreed these details, staff can begin to negotiate *contracts* with the providers of accommodation, transportation, courier and other travel-related services. *Marketing* staff will use a variety of promotional techniques to inform the general public and travel intermediaries of the product's existence and its key features. Large tour operating companies will generally develop a portfolio of products aimed at different segments of the market, for example young people, 'empty nesters', special interest groups and families. The *brochure* has a vital role to play in selling the tour operator's products and is the company's main sales tool. Distribution will be carefully monitored to ensure that the most profitable sales outlets receive the largest supply of brochures. Once the brochures go on sale, *reservations* staff will take bookings from travel agents and/or the general public. *Sales support*, for example point-of-sale materials, staff training and familiarisation visits, will be made available to the travel trade to stimulate sales. The *administration* section of the tour operator will deal with a range of tasks, from finance and legal aspects to staff recruitment and training. The *customer services* function will be concerned with handling queries, dealing with complaints and generally helping the public with any problems they may have.

Issues concerning travel intermediaries

Chapter 8 considers in detail the future for travel intermediaries and the principal factors that are likely to affect their development. What is clear, however, is that, given their role as the 'conduit' linking customers to the suppliers of travel products and facilities, travel intermediaries have a critical role to play in influencing, informing and reacting to future developments in international tourism. The intermediary position of travel agents and tour operaors means that their success will tend to mirror the troughs and peaks in international tourism generally; periods of favourable economic activity will present them with identifiable business opportunities to exploit, and vice versa. The sector will remain highly competitive, with success coming to those enterprises that are the most responsive to fluctuations in the international tourism scene and that are able to predict and capitalise on changes in consumer demand.

The following case study of the Thomson Travel Group is an excellent example of a major business enterprise that must constantly refine its products in line with such fluctuations and changes.

Case Study: Thomson Travel Group

Introduction

The Thomson Travel Group is part of the International Thomson Organisation, which has interests not only in travel, but also in publishing and oil. Thomson Travel is one of the world's leading leisure travel and holiday companies, with 4.8 million holidaymakers and a sales revenue of £1.5 billion (1995 figures). Its overall aim is to develop and retain strong leadership positions in all its markets by providing high quality, competitively priced, leisure air travel and holiday services. Thomson Travel Group companies include:

- *Thomson Tour Operations (TTO)* – one of the world's largest air inclusive tour operators
- *Portland Holidays* – a division of TTO specialising in direct sell inclusive tours
- *Britannia Airways* – Europe's leading leisure airline
- *Lunn Poly* – the UK's largest travel retailer of inclusive tours
- *The Holiday Cottages Group* – the UK's largest letting agency for holiday cottages in Britain

Sales revenues for the component parts of the Group for 1995 are given in Table 2.4.

Table 2.4:
Sales revenues of Thomson Travel Group companies, 1995

Company	1995 sales revenue (£m)
Thomson Tour Operations	1277.3
Britannia Airways	605.5
Lunn Poly	118.4
Holiday Cottages Group	17.6
Corporate and other	5.0
Total	2023.8

History

In 1965, Lord Thomson, a Canadian businessman, took the first step towards the creation of the Thomson Travel Group when he acquired Universal Sky Tours, Britannia Airways and Riviera Holidays. In 1974, when the then number one operator Clarksons failed at the height of the holiday season, Thomson Holidays inherited the enviable number one position which it still retains today. The Lunn Poly travel agency chain with 60 retail outlets was acquired in 1972 and the Thomson Travel Group was made even stronger with the founding of Portland Holidays in 1979, now the UK's leading direct-sell operator. In 1988 the Horizon Travel Group was acquired; this brought Orion Airways and Horizon Holidays into the Thomson Group, plus the Horizon brands of HCI, Wings, OSL and Blue Sky, as well as Horizon Travel Centres. In 1989, Thomson Tour Operations was set up as the new company operating all programmes run by Thomson and Horizon. By summer 1991, all brands and ▷

products had been realigned to operate separately, but under the Thomson banner. Only Portland continues to operate as a separate company.

Thomson Tour Operations (TTO)

This is the most familiar of the Thomson Travel Group's companies, responsible for the largest share of the UK outbound package holiday market. Its mission is: *'To be the leader in terms of quality, profit and volume of the ex-UK tour operating industry'*. TTO's specific aims are:

1. To have the best team of people in the industry working for the company.
2. To provide all its employees with a challenging, rewarding and secure working environment.
3. To ensure that the quality of product and service is better, and is perceived to be better by holidaymakers, suppliers and travel agents, than all major competitors.
4. To operate within a lower cost base, quality for quality, than all major competitors.
5. To be the clear market leader in terms of size of the ex-UK inclusive tour business.
6. To achieve a superior level of profitability compared to all major competitors to ensure the long term viability of the business.
7. To carry out all tasks with due responsibility towards the communities in which they operate and towards the environment.

Thomson Tour Operations' company structure

- *Marketing department.* The job of TTO's marketing department is to identify and plan to meet holidaymakers' needs; in other words to provide the right holiday at the right price to the right person. The department has staff involved in creating products, providing a customer service function, producing brochures, undertaking market research and liaising with the press and media.
- *Overseas department.* This is mainly concerned with operations outside the UK and co-ordinates the overseas operation of all holidays. Its responsibilities include the contracting of all types of accommodation, providing a high standard of service to clients while in the resort and maintaining and improving the standards of accommodation and service on offer. The aviation team draws up the initial flight plans from the capacity requirements, i.e. the number of holidays planned to be sold and the number of aircraft needed.
- *Personnel services.* This section is divided into two departments, one serving UK staff and the other dealing with staff overseas. The main activities of the overseas personnel department include planning staffing levels, recruitment, job evaluation, salary and benefits administration, and staff relations. UK Personnel has the task of assisting managers to recruit the right calibre of staff in the most effective way. This may be by internal progression, transfer or external recruitment. Staff training and development are also handled by the personnel department.
- *Sales department.* One of the main objectives of TTO's sales department is to maintain excellent relationships with travel agents in order to create sales opportunities. This is done through the agency sales force which provides agents with sales and market information and trains agency personnel in products and procedures. Another responsibility of this department is co-ordinating a merchandising team that visits the top agents at regular intervals to check on brochure stocks and visibility on shelves.
- *Systems division.* Staff in this section provide computing services for all areas of the company. The viewdata-based reservation system for travel agents (TOP) is recognised as the ▷

Thomson Travel Group continued

standard for the UK travel industry. There is also an automated funds transfer system for payments from agents. Thomson's computer systems provide the means to hold, change and update all business and holiday related information. They handle all reservations on about 28 000 travel agent terminals around the country.

● *Finance and legal department.* Responsibilities of this department include working with marketing on the pricing of each programme, preparing budgets, reporting actual results against the budgets and analysing any variances. It handles all financial transactions including credit control and payments to accommodation providers and airlines. Company secretarial and legal matters are also dealt with in this department.

The future of Thomson Tour Operations

At the start of 1991, TTO's Managing Director set out the agenda for Thomson Tour Operations for the 1990s. He stressed the following points as the way to ensure that Thomson remained at number one:

● Diversity   ● Efficiency
● Reliability   ● People
● Quality   ● Environment
● Value for money

Whether TTO can hold on to its number one position throughout the 1990s remains to be seen, in the light of the fiercely competitive environment for outbound tour operations.

(*Information courtesy of Thomson Tour Operations*)

Discussion points and essay questions

1. What are the advantages and disadvantages of having a number of different operating companies under the 'umbrella' of the Thomson Travel Group?

2. Who are Thomson Tour Operations' main competitors?

3. Why do you think the company diversified into the UK self-catering market?

4. What are the principal external threats and opportunities facing the Thomson Travel Group in the next five years?

Globalisation and integration in the international tourism industry

Throughout its relatively short history, organisations operating in the international tourism industry have sought informal arrangements with other companies as a way of expanding their businesses and providing better products and services to the travelling public. As competition in the industry has intensified, companies have sought to expand their operations and spheres of influence through mergers, acquisitions and more formal linkages with industry partners. International airlines are an excellent example of this trend; as we saw earlier in this chapter, British Airways has embarked on a globalisation strategy through alliances with a number of the world's airlines, including Qantas and American Airlines, as part of its vision of becoming the leader in the international airline industry.

Globalisation is one of the fastest-growing trends in the development of international tourism. Driven by economic and political motivations, the major commercial operators in tourism are seeking to grow their enterprises, increase market share and, ultimately, achieve world dominance in their particular industry sector. Globalisation is most evident in the airline and hotel sectors of tourism, where multinational corporations reap the benefits of economies of scale and competition suppression by operating at a global level. The world's airlines have been instrumental in establishing computerised reservation systems (CRS) to sell airline tickets and a variety of other travel-related products, such as hotel reservations, car hire and travel insurance. These CRS, for example Sabre, Galileo, Worldspan and Amadeus, have facilitated the moves of the multinational corporations towards the globalisation of their operations.

The most visible sign of the globalisation of the international tourism industry is the growth in size and influence of the multinational corporations (MNCs), sometimes referred to as transnational corporations (TNCs). Multinational corporations in tourism operate commercially across national frontiers and seek to maximise their returns from global partnerships and alliances. MNCs are most apparent in the airline, hotel and tour operations sectors of the international tourism industry, where they benefit from technical, operational and financial economies of scale. Their scale of operation also allows MNCs to take full advantage of computerisation, but it is in the area of political and economic influence that they reap the biggest advantages, especially in the developing nations of the world.

In addition to a general fear that the *modus operandi* of MNCs leads to a standardised or homogenised tourism product, there are a number of specific concerns about the work of multinational corporations in tourism development, particularly in the Third World, for example:

- A high proportion of the economic benefits of tourism are returned to the MNCs' parent countries.

- With their headquarters and power bases in western, democratised countries, the MNCs appear remote and often insensitive to the needs of the indigenous governments and residents.

- Environmental and socio-cultural concerns may have a low priority with the MNCs.

- There are often limited opportunities for local people to reach positions of responsibility within the organisations; the more responsible positions are given to staff from the MNCs' parent countries.

- The strong bargaining power of the MNCs allows them to negotiate rates for accommodation and other tourist services that may not be advantageous to local companies.

The case study on Thomson (see above) demonstrates that there is considerable vertical integration in the UK travel industry, i.e. one company having control over other enterprises that are at different levels in the chain of distribution. The Thomson Travel Group owns Thomson Tour Operations, the Lunn Poly travel agency chain and Britannia Airways, Europe's leading charter airline. Horizontal integration, when companies at the same level in the distribution chain or in the same industry sector merge voluntarily or are the subject of a takeover bid, also occurs in the tourism industry, for example a hotel chain acquiring an independent hotel or a tourist attractions group adding to its product portfolio through a merger with a competing company.

Closer linkages between companies in the tourism industry may result in better products and services for the travellers, but there are fears that monopolies could develop and consumer choice be reduced unless governments monitor such linkages carefully.

The role of the public sector in international tourism

Governments and other public sector bodies become involved with tourism for a variety of motives. Chapter 5 on the impacts of tourism indicates that it is tourism's economic benefits, such as job creation, export earnings, wealth creation, urban regeneration and tax revenues, that are prime motivations for public sector interest in the industry. Some countries realise that tourism can also bring with it a number of political and social benefits, for example improvements in residents' quality of life, a favourable image on the world stage and the fostering of a national identity. As regards tourism's negative impacts, the public sector often takes on the role of guardian of potentially endangered national and local environments, cultures and communities.

National, regional and local public bodies play a significant role in international tourism, both directly and indirectly. Direct involvement includes the provision of infrastructure, information services and some tourist attractions and facilities, such as leisure centres, historic buildings and museums. The public sector's indirect role in tourism, however, is often of greater significance. Public agencies aim to provide a favourable economic climate and establish tourism policies within which the commercial sector of the tourism industry can operate successfully. Public bodies also provide a co-ordinating, promotional and regulatory role in tourism provision, seeking to conserve the physical and socio-cultural resources that attract tourists to destinations. Figure 2.6 shows how these responsibilities are administered within Japan's public sector tourism organisation. The figure shows that Japan's Department of Tourism is the responsibility of the Minister of Transport through the Transport Policy Bureau. Local and regional governments report to the Department of Tourism, which has planning and travel promotion divisions.

Figure 2.6: Public sector tourism organisation in Japan

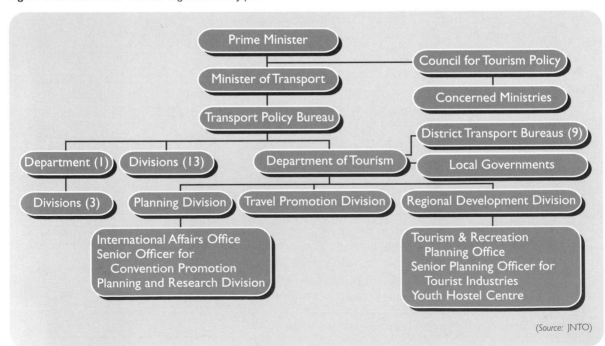

(Source: JNTO)

Functions of public agencies in tourism

Although the functions of public sector tourism bodies vary between nations, any country that has a significant and established tourism industry is likely to have a separate department of government, known as the national tourism organisation (NTO), and/or public agencies that carry out the range of functions shown in Figure 2.7.

The figure indicates that a typical NTO will have four principal areas of responsibility under the direction of a chief executive officer through a number of departments. The functions undertaken by the NTO and other regional and local public authorities include:

- *Establishment of tourism policy.* This is generally the starting point for government involvement in tourism, when its sets out the policies and priorities for tourism development. Chapter 6 on planning and development in tourism considers tourism policy formulation in greater depth.

- *Destination promotion.* This is often the most important function of the NTO, which will be responsible for, among other things, marketing research, marketing planning, travel trade activities and producing promotional materials.

- *Infrastructure provision.* Either independently or in partnership with the private sector, public bodies provide funding for many infrastructure developments that are directly or indirectly associated with tourism, for example road schemes, railway systems, airports and transport terminals.

- *Tourism facilities.* Government departments and public agencies sometimes have the responsibility for maintaining tourist attractions and facilities, such as museums, parks, castles, historic houses, ancient monuments, national parks and forests, coastal areas and galleries.

- *Tourist information services.* National tourism organisations often co-ordinate the provision of tourist information services for visitors, which may be delivered by regional and local authorities.

Figure 2.7: The functions of a typical national tourism organisation (NTO)

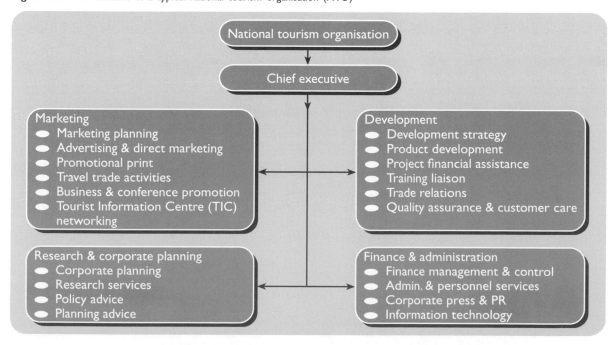

- *Legislation and regulation.* Governments enact a wide variety of legislation and regulation relating directly or indirectly to the tourism industry concerning, for example, health and safety, consumer protection, registration of accommodation and attractions, passport and visa requirements, the licensing of travel agencies, the training of tourist guides and restrictions on transport.
- *Finance for development.* Some governments provide, for example, grants, loans, tax concessions and tariff reductions, as incentives for tourism development.
- *Advisory services and training.* Many public bodies at national, regional and local levels provide, or facilitate the provision of, business advisory services and training as a way of raising standards in the tourism industry.

The precise functions undertaken and degree of public involvement in tourism will depend on the importance attached to the industry by the government concerned. As tourism's contribution to a nation's economy grows and tourist revenues increase, the public funds available for tourism development are likely to increase the range and variety of functions that can be carried out.

The following case study on the Japan National Tourist Organisation gives an indication of the responsibilities and activities of an NTO concerned primarily with the promotion of inbound travel to its country.

Case Study: Japan National Tourist Organisation

Introduction

The Japan National Tourist Organisation (JNTO) was established under Japanese law in April 1959 and subsequently reorganised in 1964, 1979, 1983 and 1985. It is a non-profit making organisation, working under the direction of the Japanese Ministry of Transport, and has two principal aims:

- The promotion of inbound travel to Japan
- The provision of information to Japanese nationals on travelling safely overseas

In order to fulfil its principal aims, the JNTO is charged with undertaking the following activities under Japanese law:

1. Conduct publicity in order to stimulate visits by foreign tourists to Japan
2. Operate tourist information centres for overseas visitors
3. Furnish travel safety information to Japanese overseas tourists
4. Conduct investigations and research on pertinent aspects of international tourism
5. Perform activities incidental to those mentioned above

The original form of the JNTO was the International Tourist Association (ITA), established in 1931 as a promotional body for travel to Japan. The Pacific War saw the dissolution of the ITA and its replacement by the Japan Tourist Association (JTA) in 1955, which was to become the Japan National Tourist Association (JNTA) in 1959. In 1964, the JNTA was split into the two organisations that exist today, namely the Japan National Tourist Organisation (JNTO) and the Japan Tourist Association (JTA), which promotes domestic tourism in Japan.

Structure of the JNTO

The organisational structure of the JNTO is shown in Figure 2.8.

Figure 2.8: Organisational structure of the Japan National Tourist Organisation

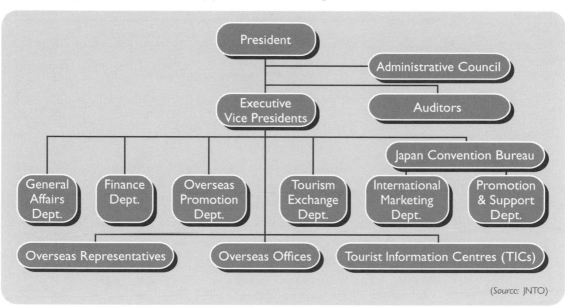

(Source: JNTO)

The Organisation's administrative council investigates and deliberates on matters concerning the operation of JNTO's activities. The council consists of 26 members drawn from experts on international tourism in Japan. They are appointed by the president of the JNTO and are subject to the approval of Japan's Minister of Transport. JNTO maintains six departments in its Tokyo head office and 14 overseas offices in the world's key cities (see Table 2.5).

The responsibilities of the six head office departments are as follows:

● *General affairs*: responsible for JNTO's administrative functions, including legal matters, personnel, staff training, domestic public relations and general co-ordination of the Organisation. It also manages the long-range marketing plans and priority projects, performance and analysis of market surveys, publishing of periodicals and the collection of statistical data on international tourism.

● *Finance*: oversees the formulation of budgets, requests for government subsidies, contracting, procurement activities and reporting financial settlements to the Japanese government.

● *Overseas promotion*: responsible for administering and overseeing the work of JNTO's overseas offices, providing media assistance to travel journalists, participation in travel trade fairs and exhibitions, and carrying out joint marketing activities in conjunction with the Japanese travel industry.

● *Tourism exchange*: responsible for improving reception services for foreign visitors to Japan, administering the tourist information centres and conducting the national examination for guide–interpreters. Since the amendment of JNTO law, this department also provides Japanese travellers with information on how to travel overseas in safety.

● *Japan Convention Bureau*: responsible for convention and incentive travel promotion. The Bureau consists of two departments. The international marketing department administers marketing and promotional activities concerned with the encouragement of convention visitors to Japan, for example the collection and analysis of marketing data, attracting conventions to Japan, advertising and public relations. The promotion and support department manages such activities as training programmes for staff engaged in convention-related duties, providing information and advice for organisers of international meetings in Japan, and supporting tourist programmes for foreign participants attending international conventions in Japan. ▷

Japan National Tourist Organisation continued

Table 2.5:
Overseas offices
of the Japan
National Tourist
Organisation

Office	Countries and territories administered
New York Chicago San Francisco Los Angeles	U.S.A., countries in Central America and in Caribbean area
Toronto	Canada
São Paulo	Countries in South America
London	United Kingdom, Ireland, Denmark, Norway, Sweden and English-speaking countries in Africa
Paris	France, Spain, Portugal, Belgium, Luxembourg and French-speaking countries in Africa
Geneva	Switzerland, Italy. Greece, countries in former Yugoslavia and the Middle East
Frankfurt	European countries excluding those covered by other European Offices
Bangkok	South-east Asian countries excluding those covered by the Hong Kong Office
Hong Kong	Hong Kong, China, Macau and the Philippines
Seoul	Korea
Sydney	Australia and New Zealand

Source: JNTO

The overseas offices implement, under the direction of the Tokyo head office, various tourist promotion activities, including travel information services, media assistance, participation in fairs and exhibitions, and advertising in major consumer and travel trade publications. Areas distant from the JNTO's overseas offices are covered by a network of representatives who provide information on travel to Japan and distribute travel literature. They are stationed in major cities in North America, South America, Europe, Asia and Oceania.

JNTO's activities

The Japan National Tourist Organisation undertakes a wide-ranging programme of promotional and product development activities, which can be summarised under the following headings:

- *General promotion.* JNTO engages in a variety of promotional activities targeted at consumers and the travel trade. These include advertising, public relations work, media assistance, travel trade seminars, familiarisation visits, regional promotion fairs, overseas exhibitions and an information service via its 14 overseas offices and network of representatives. The Organisation has recently established an information service on the Internet.

- *Convention and incentive travel promotion.* The Japan Convention Bureau, a specialist department of the JNTO, is responsible for marketing Japan as an international convention and incentive travel destination. Members of the Bureau undertake market research studies on how to increase Japan's share of international conventions, attend overseas trade exhibitions and organise training programmes for staff working in this sector of Japan's travel industry.

● *International co-operation.* JNTO maintains close working relationships with the following major world tourism bodies: World Tourism Organisation (WTO), East Asia Travel Association (EATA), Pacific Asia Travel Association (PATA), American Society of Travel Agents (ASTA) and Confederacion de Organizaciones Turisticas de la Americana Latina (COTAL). It also works with several individual countries on a bilateral basis to increase inbound tourist traffic.

● *Reception services for foreign visitors.* JNTO continually works to improve, expand and enhance the reception services for visitors from abroad. It aims to improve the quantity and quality of tourist information services, ease any language problems that may arise, promote mutual understanding and friendship between foreign visitors and the Japanese, generate greater international tourism in local areas and reduce the travel costs of overseas visitors.

● *International tourism exchange project.* This JNTO initiative was started in 1995 and is designed to promote inbound tourism to Japan by supporting and developing people-to-people exchange programmes between Japan and other countries. Specific themes include sister city exchanges, school-to-school exchanges and vocational exchanges.

● *Japan tour development project.* This project is designed to explore the possibilities of developing new tour products under the co-sponsorship of the JNTO and local tourism bureaux in Japan. The main objective of the project is to stimulate inbound tourism to local regions in Japan, thereby spreading the economic and social benefits of international tourism to as wide an area of the country as possible.

● *Activities for Japanese overseas tourists.* Since 1979, the JNTO has been given the responsibility of offering services to Japanese people in order to ensure trouble-free overseas travel. This includes providing advice and assistance with such matters as security, etiquette and customs, for both the Japanese travelling public and the travel industry as a whole.

● *Research and statistics.* The JNTO has established a Marketing Council to investigate the further refinement of its targeted marketing activities, particularly partnerships between the public and private sectors of the tourism industry. For this and other promotional work, the Organisation relies heavily on a wide range of statistical data, including surveys of foreign visitors' travel in Japan and the Overseas Visitors Japan Travel Survey, which focuses on impressions and interest before travelling to the country. JNTO also collects and analyses statistical data on worldwide tourism trends and forecasts.

● *Consignment activities.* JNTO is often commissioned by outside organisations to undertake various types of tourism-related activities, including advising on training programmes, promotional work, the development of information networks and the production of PR materials.

Budgets and revenue sources

JNTO's budget for the 1995 financial year was 3.3 billion yen (US$34.7 million), of which 2.4 billion yen (US$25.4 million) was in the form of government subsidies (see Table 2.6).

Contributions of 392 million yen (US$4.1 million) were received from Japanese organisations and enterprises involved with tourism, such as Japan Railways, Japan Airlines, prefectural governments, the Japan Hotel Association and the travel agency sector. JNTO funds for services to Japanese overseas tourists consist of the capital furnished by the government and contributions from the Japanese tourist industry.

▷

Japan National Tourist Organisation continued

Table 2.6:
Annual budgets
of the Japan
National Tourist
Organisation,
1994 and 1995

Item	1994	1995
Revenues (thousand US$)		
Government subsidies	24 500	25 381
Government funds	0	0
Contributions	3 815	4 082
National guide–interpreter examination	364	461
Miscellaneous	4 442	4 698
Total	33 121	34 622
Expenditure (thousand US$)		
Overseas tourism promotion (including overseas personnel expenses)	15 499	16 196
Promotional aids	1 328	1 034
Convention promotion	1 710	1 800
Reception of foreign visitors	2 030	2 359
Services for Japanese overseas tourists	304	325
Statistics and research	120	126
National guide–interpreter examination	371	387
Management (excluding overseas personnel expenses)	11 142	11 683
Reserve	747	749
Total	33 251	34 707

Source: JNTO

(Information courtesy of the Japan National Tourist Organisation)

Discussion points and essay questions

1. Critically analyse the role played by the JNTO in the growth of tourism to Japan since the beginning of the 1960s.

2. What problems do you think the JNTO is likely to encounter when competing for international visitors on a global scale?

3. What influence does the JNTO have on the development of Japan's tourism products?

4. How is the JNTO working towards improving facilities for incoming tourists?

International agencies and trade associations

International agencies and trade associations have an important role to play in influencing tourism policies and practices at a global level. They lobby on behalf of the tourism industry as a whole and its different sectors, aiming to present a positive image of international tourism to politicians, the public and other businesses. Multinational corporations in tourism operate commercially across national frontiers and seek to maximise their returns from global partnerships and alliances. Elsewhere in this book we investigate the roles played by a number of public bodies in the field of tourism, including the European Travel Commission and European Union (in Chapter 3), and the Association of British Travel Agents (ABTA) and Association of Independent Tour Operators (AITO) in Chapter 4. The final part of this chapter investigates the work of two global organisations, the World Tourism Organisation (WTO) and the World Travel and Tourism Council (WTTC).

Case Study: World Tourism Organisation

Introduction

The World Tourism Organisation (WTO) was established in 1975 and is the leading international body in the field of global tourism. With its headquarters in Madrid and a 1997 establishment of 77 staff, WTO is the successor to the International Union of Official Travel Organisations (IUOTO), which was founded in 1947. Membership of WTO comprises 134 of the world's governments plus 328 affiliate members drawn from private operators, regional and local governments. The WTO is unusual in being the only inter-governmental organisation open to the operating sector, which includes airlines, hotel companies and tour operators. This combination of public and private sector involvement encourages a hands-on approach to strategic issues affecting the international tourism industry.

WTO's mission

WTO provides a forum for governments and industry to establish the frameworks and global standards of world tourism and, thereby, the consolidation of one of the world's fastest growing industries. Its stated mission is: '*To develop tourism as a significant means of fostering international peace and understanding, economic development and international trade*'.

WTO activities

In order to achieve its mission, WTO undertakes a wide-ranging programme of work, which can be categorised into the following six major areas:

1. *Technical co-operation for development.* As an executing agency of the United Nations Development Programme (UNDP), WTO provides technical advice and assistance to governments on a wide range of tourism issues, including tourism master plans, the development of environment indicators, hotel classification systems and investment appraisals. Projects range from short-term training seminars on such matters as tourism education, marketing and promotion, to the development of long-term strategies; a recent example of the latter is the tourism master plan for Lebanon with a budget of US$700 000.

2. *Statistics and market research.* WTO is the foremost international centre for the collection, analysis and dissemination of tourism data from over 200 countries and territories worldwide. It continually monitors and analyses tourism trends around the world and has a long-term aim of standardising the collection and reporting of international tourism statistics. WTO produces a series of publications on international tourism including the *Yearbook of Tourism Statistics, Compendium of Tourism Statistics, Travel and Tourism Barometer* and *Monographs and Forecasts of Tourism Trends.*

3. *Education and training.* WTO has a strategic framework for the organisation of tourism education and training, including courses on educating the educators, short-term and distance

World Tourism Organisation continued

learning programmes. It has a network of 14 education and training centres worldwide and aims to contribute to the debate on curriculum standards of tourism courses.

4. *Environment and planning.* WTO is working for sustainable tourism development through the introduction of practical measures, such as the establishment of environmental indicators to measure tourism impacts. WTO participates in forums such as the Earth Summit in Rio and the Globe seminars in Canada, and is a major force in the development of a brand of tourism that is environmentally and culturally responsible.

5. *Quality of tourism development.* Health and safety issues, liberalisation of travel, security concerns and the General Agreements on Tariffs and Trade (GATTs), reflect the wide-ranging and interconnected issues related to improving the quality of tourism services. WTO is working towards the removal of barriers to tourism and is encouraging the liberalisation of trade in tourism services.

6. *Communications.* As well as acting as a publishing unit and press contact for the Organisation, WTO's communications division seeks to improve the image and boost the credibility of international tourism as an important economic sector. It also helps member countries to improve their own communications and undertakes work aimed at helping tourists understand the impacts they can have on tourist regions.

Figure 2.9 shows how these six areas of the WTO's work are reflected in the Organisation's structure, its administrative activities and regional representation.

Figure 2.9: Structure of the World Tourism Organisation (WTO)

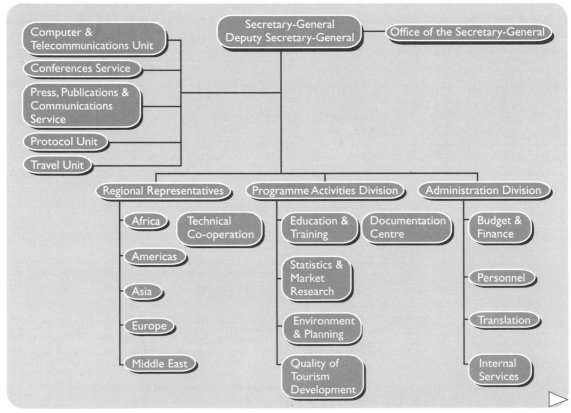

At a time of forecast continued growth in international tourism, the work of the WTO will become increasingly important in helping tourism achieve its full potential as a prime economic and social activity. To prepare for the future, the Secretary General of the WTO issued a white paper on current trends in world tourism at the Organisation's executive council meeting in Manila in May 1997. The paper will be reviewed by a high-level, select working group of tourism experts from the public and private sectors of the industry. These experts will make recommendations on the future of the WTO, to be debated at a World Tourism Summit in Istanbul in September 1997. The Secretary General believes that the WTO must change, modernise and adapt if it is to maintain its prominent role as the champion of international tourism.

(*Information courtesy of the World Tourism Organisation*)

Discussion points and essay questions

1. If you were asked to comment on the future role of the WTO in international tourism, what would you recommend?

2. Can you foresee any conflict between the activities undertaken by the WTO and the tourism initiatives of its member countries?

3. What importance do you attach to the role of the affiliate members of the WTO?

4. How can the WTO help to achieve the goal of sustainable tourism development on a global scale?

Case Study: World Travel and Tourism Council

Introduction

The World Travel and Tourism Council (WTTC) is a global coalition of more than 85 chief executive officers (CEOs) from all sectors of the international travel and tourism industry, including accommodation, catering, transportation, entertainment, recreation and a range of travel-related services. Established in 1990, WTTC's goal is to work with governments to realise the full economic impact of global travel and tourism, by promoting:

● The economic and job creation importance of travel and tourism

● Open and competitive markets for travel and tourism

● Sustainable development

● The elimination of barriers to growth

The Council and its members undertake top-level missions, make proposals and engage in policy discussions with government decision makers. WTTC's work is supported by research undertaken by the WEFA Group, an international forecasting company. The research is designed to determine travel and tourism's total size and contribution to world, regional and national economies based on the United Nations system of national accounting. WTTC has also established a number of research centres to provide information and support to decision makers and the tourism industry on issues concerning the environment, taxation and human resources, for example the World Travel and Tourism Environment Research Centre (WTTERC) established in 1991 and based in Oxford, UK. Other research projects have investigated travel and tourism education and training in Europe, Asia-Pacific and Latin America, air transport liberalisation and the safety of travellers. ▷

World Travel and Tourism Council continued

Organisation of the WTTC

WTTC is led by a 15-member executive committee, which meets twice a year to co-ordinate policy issues and agree strategies for action. Day-to-day operations are carried out by the President of the WTTC and a small team of staff based in London, Brussels and New York. Many members of the Council are household names in the global travel and tourism industry, including:

- Holiday Inn Worldwide
- American Airlines
- The Hertz Corporation
- KLM Royal Dutch Airlines
- Hilton International
- Accor SA
- Cunard Line
- British Airways plc
- Abercrombie and Kent
- The Thomas Cook Group

All WTTC members are invited to an annual general meeting at which members of the executive committee present progress reports and an agenda for future action.

WTTC's Millennium Vision

During the course of 1996, the WTTC reshaped its basic policy agenda to sharpen focus and create a new strategic platform for action. This was published under the title *Travel and Tourism Millennium Vision* (WTTC, 1996b), a document designed to concentrate the attention of the world's governments and relevant agencies on the economic importance of international travel and tourism, while at the same time promoting public and private sector policy initiatives. In the report, WTTC identified four basic policy priorities that would encourage governments, in co-operation with the private sector, to harness the travel and tourism industry's economic dynamism. These Millennium Vision priorities are as follows:

1. Make travel and tourism a strategic economic development and employment priority

2. Move towards open and competitive markets

3. Pursue sustainable development

4. Eliminate barriers to growth

As this list indicates, WTTC believes that the employment and economic development potential of travel and tourism should be given a high priority by international governments, which should be encouraged to include the industry in their mainstream programmes for job creation, export promotion and investment stimulation. WTTC estimates that the industry provided 250 million jobs worldwide in 1996 and has the potential to employ some 385 million people by the year 2006 (WTTC, 1996b). The Council also proposes that national satellite accounts for travel and tourism should be established, so that the industry's full economic significance is recognised. WTTC believes that moves towards open and competitive markets in travel and tourism will be accelerated by implementing the General Agreement on Trade in Services (GATS), further liberalisation of air transport and deregulation of the telecommunications industry. WTTC also accepts the generally held belief that for the world's tourism industry to flourish it must develop in a sustainable manner, respectful of the earth's environment, peoples and cultures. The Council proposes a policy framework for sustainable development based on Agenda 21 and the encouragement of environmental initiatives by the travel and tourism industry, such as the Green Globe programme (see case study in Chapter 5). In 1995, WTTC, the World Tourism Organisation (WTO) and the Earth Council unveiled a joint report (WTTC, 1995), which identified the 10 priority areas for action on sustainability for travel and tourism companies as:

1. Waste minimisation

2. Energy efficiency, conservation and management

3. Management of fresh water resources

4. Waste water management

5. Hazardous substances

6. Transport

7. Land-use planning and management

8. Involving staff, customers and communities in environmental issues

9. Design for sustainability

10. Partnerships for sustainable development

WTTC's Millennium Vision also encourages the elimination of barriers to growth in the international travel and tourism industry by expanding and modernising infrastructure, particularly airports, air traffic control systems and border clearance procedures. The Council also argues for intelligent taxation for an industry that makes significant contributions to national economies and increased investment in human resources, including education and training.

(*Information courtesy of the World Travel and Tourism Council*)

Discussion points and essay questions

1. In what ways does the work of the World Travel and Tourism Council differ from, and complement, that of the World Tourism Organisation (WTO)?

2. Do you consider that the primarily commercial objectives of the membership of the WTTC are compatible with their desire to promote sustainable tourism development?

3. How can the themes of WTTC's Millennium Vision best be achieved?

4. How does a move towards more open and competitive markets help the members of the WTTC?

Chapter summary

This chapter has concentrated on the supply side of the international tourism industry, exploring the interrelationships of its many industry sectors with the help of a simplified, structural model. This model demonstrated that the core components of the tourism industry are destinations, accommodation, transportation and attractions. Tour operators and travel agents, the so-called travel intermediaries, respectively package and retail these core components to the travelling public. We have seen that destinations have a crucial role to play in international tourism, since they are the focus of so much tourist activity and are often the prime motivation for travel; the way in which they are planned, managed and promoted is central to the future success of the tourism industry. The chapter has demonstrated that international tourism is essentially a private sector enterprise, although governments and other public agencies have a very important advisory, regulatory and promotional role to play, especially through National Tourism Organisations (NTOs). We have highlighted the dynamic nature of the different industry sectors and the extent to which integration, in its many forms, is concentrating resources in a growing number of global organisations and multinational corporations. The chapter concluded with an analysis of the role and significance of international agencies and trade associations, and the important part they play in lobbying on behalf of the industry by seeking to maximise their political influence.

Discussion questions

1. Why is the planning and management of destinations so crucial to the future of international tourism?

2. What are the key issues facing the accommodation and catering sector in the next 10 years?

3. What advantages and disadvantages does vertical integration in tourism present to tourism operators and the travelling public?

4. How is the role of governments and public agencies in tourism likely to change over the next 25 years, at both national and international levels?

5. With the rapid development of new technologies, does the retail travel agent have a future in western societies?

References and further reading

- British Tourist Authority/English Tourist Board (1996) *Tourism Intelligence Quarterly*, Vol. 17, No. 4, BTA/ETB, London
- Holloway, J C (1994) *The Business of Tourism*, 4th edition, Longman, Harlow, UK
- International Air Transport Association (1996) *Annual Report 1996*, IATA, Geneva
- Japan National Tourist Organisation (1996) *Tourism in Japan 1996–97*, JNTO, Tokyo
- Lickorish, L (1991) *Developing Tourism Destinations*, Longman, Harlow, UK
- Van Harssel, J (1994) *Tourism: An Exploration*, 3rd edition, Prentice-Hall International
- World Travel and Tourism Council (1995) *Agenda 21 for the Travel and Tourism Industry*, WTTC, London
- World Travel and Tourism Council (1996a) *Progress and Priorities 1996*, WTTC, London
- World Travel and Tourism Council (1996b) *Travel and Tourism Millennium Vision*, WTTC, London

Chapter Three

European Tourism

Chapter Overview

This chapter explores the main issues concerning the development and significance of tourism to Europe, the world's principal destination for international tourism. It investigates the recent political changes in Europe and considers how the tourism industry needs to respond to the new challenges offered. An analysis of the structure of the European tourism industry is followed by an investigation of the particular role of the European Union in tourism, with consideration of the most recent EU measures affecting the industry. The chapter concludes with an appraisal of the factors considered likely to influence the future position of Europe within the global tourism industry.

Key Topics

- The changing political and economic structure of Europe
- European tourist flows
- The structure of the European tourism industry
- The role of the European Union in tourism
- The future of tourism in Europe

Introduction

Its rich architectural, linguistic and cultural diversity, coupled with a wealth of natural attractions, makes the continent of Europe the world's principal destination for international tourism. Preliminary results from the World Tourism Organisation reveal that some 347 million international tourist trips were made to or within Europe in 1996, with international travel receipts for the region totalling more than US$214 billion (WTO, 1997). Tourism plays a significant role in the economies of the majority of European nations, with many countries heavily reliant on incoming tourism for their economic well-being, through employment, wealth creation and economic development (see Table 3.1).

Country	Tourism receipts as percentage of		
	GNP	Merchandise exports	Services exports
Austria	6.70	29.30	44.98
Croatia	11.80	33.50	62.26
Cyprus	23.48	177.08	64.01
France	1.84	10.46	27.04
Germany	0.50	2.55	17.34
Greece	5.04	44.49	42.39
Malta	23.58	41.74	63.90
Spain	4.16	29.82	64.21
United Kingdom	1.42	7.44	25.10

Source: Author's adaptation of WTO data

The table illustrates the marked variation in the economic importance of tourism to a selection of European countries. These statistics from the World Tourism Organisation (WTO, 1996b) show that, at one end of the spectrum, tourism receipts accounted for almost one quarter of the gross national product (GNP) of the Mediterranean island states of Cyprus and Malta in 1994, whereas the northern European countries of Germany and the United Kingdom recorded figures of just 0.5 per cent and 1.42 per cent respectively. When the statistics for tourism's contribution to total service exports are examined, however, even those European countries with less reliance on the economic contribution of tourism display significant proportions, for example for Germany 17.34 per cent and for the United Kingdom 25.10 per cent. Table 3.1 shows that receipts from tourism make up nearly two-thirds of all service exports in Croatia, Cyprus, Malta and Spain, further emphasising the economic importance of tourist activity in these southern European countries.[1]

Despite these encouraging economic indicators at an individual country level, there is clear evidence to indicate that Europe's domination of world tourism markets is in decline, the result of strong global competition coupled with a degree of complacency on the part of certain countries in Europe in their approach to tourism and its potential economic benefits. Data from the World Tourism Organisation (WTO, 1997) show that Europe's share of international tourist arrivals fell by 10.5 per cent between 1975 and 1996, while its share of receipts for the same period fell by 12.7 per cent. These significant reductions, the result of increasing competition on a global scale, particularly from emerging destinations in eastern Asia and the Pacific Rim, are having a serious impact on the future development of tourism in many European destinations.

Nevertheless, Europe can still boast to having six of the top ten world destinations in terms of international tourist arrivals (WTO, 1997). In 1996, France was the number one tourism destination in the world followed by Spain, which overtook the USA for the first time. European countries also hold positions 2–6 in the league table of the world's top ten tourism earners, after the United States of America.

[1] The particular methodology adopted by the WTO in compiling the statistics given in Table 3.1 differs from that used by national governments and other industry bodies, who often quote figures of a higher value than those shown. According to Eurostat data, for example, Spain had a positive tourism balance of payments figure of 14 644 million ECU in 1994, giving tourism an estimated share of gross national product (GNP) of between 8.5 and 9 per cent (Eurostat, 1996).

The changing face of Europe

Before considering the recent political changes in Europe, and their impacts on the tourism industry, it is important to determine exactly what we mean by the term 'Europe'. A definition of Europe from a *geographical* perspective is relatively straightforward: Europe can be considered to be the western extremity of the Eurasian landmass, extending east to the Ural Mountains, west to the Irish Republic and Portugal, north to the Scandinavian countries and south to the Mediterranean Sea. Even within this notion of Europe, however, there are stark geographical differences, for example in climate, land form and accessibility, which offer both opportunities and difficulties for tourism development, leading to the very diverse European tourism scene that exists today.

The *cultural* diversity of Europe is one of its greatest assets in terms of tourism. Europe does not convey a single cultural identity, but rather a multitude of languages, traditions, music, architecture and gastronomy that are magnets for international and domestic tourists alike. Retention of cultural identity within the notion of a union of federal states in Europe is one of the great debates in the final part of twentieth century European history.

Perhaps the most useful approach to defining the word 'Europe' from the perspective of the tourism industry is to investigate the *image* of Europe held by prospective travellers. To those travelling from afar, for example the USA and the Far East, Europe is often perceived as a single entity rather than a number of individual countries. Their perception of Europe is of a collection of internationally renowned capital cities intertwined with a variety of natural attractions spanning national frontiers. To Europeans themselves, their image of the continent will be moulded by many factors, not least the political regime under which they live and their country's economic prosperity. Past restrictions on travel for nationals living in the former Eastern Bloc states, coupled with low levels of disposable income and limited access to the media, have contributed to a restricted and narrow view of 'Europe'. Many look with envy at their neighbours from the more prosperous Western European countries as they continue to travel throughout Europe for business and leisure purposes, helped by recent improvements in transportation, such as the Channel Tunnel and high-speed rail services across Europe. Many Western Europeans consider that the term 'Europe' is synonymous with the 15 member states of the European Union. The entry into the EU of Austria, Sweden and Finland in 1995, and the desire on the part of many former Eastern Bloc countries to join the Union, serves to reinforce this perception.

Recent political and economic developments in Europe

The political history of Europe in the late twentieth century has been one of conflict and division. In the past, the major political divide was between the socialist states of Eastern Europe and the capitalist democracies of the West. The political map of Europe has been redrawn since the collapse of the Berlin Wall in 1989, one of the most significant events in European history (see Figure 3.1).

The map shows the national boundaries of the countries of Europe and reflects four important political changes, namely:

● The breaking down of the barrier between East and West Germany
● Expansion of the European Union
● The dissolution of the Soviet Union and formation of the Russian Federation
● The changes in the former Yugoslavia

Figure 3.1: The new Europe

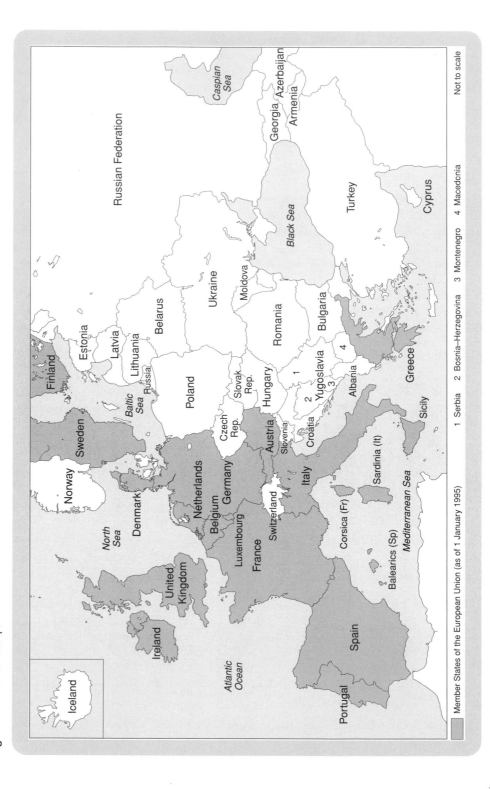

Member States of the European Union (as of 1 January 1995)   1 Serbia   2 Bosnia–Herzegovina   3 Montenegro   4 Macedonia   Not to scale

The war in the former Yugoslavia has all but decimated the area's tourist industry and serves as a stark reminder of the fragility of international tourism when exposed to political threats. The expansion of the European Union is dealt with more fully later in this chapter. The next section considers the consequences of the democratisation of the former 'Iron Curtain' states of Eastern Europe on the European tourism scene.

The rise of the Eastern Bloc states

There is little doubt that the two major political changes that have swept through Europe since the late 1980s, namely the fall of the Berlin Wall in 1989 and the evolution of the former Soviet Union into the Russian Federation (Commonwealth of Independent States), have heralded a new era in the development of European tourism. When considered alongside the gradual easing of state control in countries such as Bulgaria, Hungary, Poland and Romania in recent years, the potential exists for a massive expansion in travel and tourism between the East and West in Europe. Moreover, tourism is seen by many of the former Eastern Bloc countries as an essential part of their economic development and restructuring as they move towards fully democratic, free market economies. There are, however, concerns as to whether the potential for tourism offered by the opening up of the Eastern Bloc states can be fully realised, in terms of both incoming tourism and outbound tourism from East to West. These concerns are considered in depth in the next sections of this chapter.

Prospects for incoming tourism to the East The countries of the former Eastern Bloc have a high curiosity value in the minds of travellers from Western Europe and beyond. Tourists from the free market economies of the West are keen to be among the first to 'peep behind the Iron Curtain'. Countries that have hitherto discouraged incoming tourism on the grounds of its potential corrupting influences are finally realising that the encouragement of a sound tourism industry can play an important part in a move from a manufacturing economy to one based on services. Tourism is seen as an important source of foreign currency, a provider of jobs and, perhaps most importantly, a way of improving the rather poor image of many of the former Eastern Bloc countries. There are, however, a number of obstacles to the development of incoming tourism, which include:

- *Inadequate infrastructure.* Services such as transportation, telecommunications and utilities are poorly developed in certain regions, resulting in difficulties for tourists travelling to, and within, many former Eastern Bloc countries.
- *Poor image.* The economies of many countries have been based on heavy engineering and manufacturing, leading to rather stark images of industrialised landscapes and pollution.
- *Poorly developed government tourism policies.* Many countries have only rudimentary public sector tourism policies and structures, resulting in unco-ordinated approaches to tourism development and marketing.
- *Poor accommodation stock.* Many regions lack accommodation that is of a standard acceptable to tourists from the West.
- *Lack of attractions and entertainment facilities.* Although many countries have areas of great scenic beauty, high-quality built attractions and entertainment facilities are in short supply.
- *Low service standards.* Levels of customer service in hotels, restaurants and other tourist outlets lack consistency. Some city centre hotels and restaurants offer

standards of service that compare favourably with their counterparts in the West, while others found in outlying districts often fall short of expectations.

- *Depressed economic situation.* Countries faced with historic debt burdens and increased costs of moving to a free market economy find it hard to justify investment in tourism development.
- *Little product development.* There has been little innovation in the tourist products offered by many former Eastern Bloc states.
- *Insufficient market research.* Poorly developed government structures for tourism have resulted in a lack of reliable market research data on which to base future planning.
- *Poorly developed capital markets.* The former socialist economies have limited access to capital markets to finance future tourism developments.

In order to fully achieve their undoubted potential for tourism development, the former Eastern Bloc countries will need to develop partnership arrangements between private and public sector organisations to address these limiting factors. Working individually and as part of joint initiatives, the countries will require considerable support and tourism 'know how' from Western nations. The role of the European Union will be crucial in helping the countries to invest in infrastructure, training, travel trade developments, market research, marketing and government structures. The desire on the part of many of the former Eastern states to join the EU is likely to hasten the move towards tourism industries that are fully responsive to the needs of travellers from East and West.

Prospects for outbound tourism to the West In the same way that tourists from the West are curious to visit the hitherto 'closed' Eastern Bloc states, there is considerable interest among Eastern Europeans in travelling to the West. Under the former communist dictatorships, travel to Western countries was severely restricted. These restrictions, coupled with low levels of disposable income, made travelling to neighbouring Eastern Bloc countries for holidays the norm. Very few individuals were allowed the privilege of travel to the Western, democratised nations.

It could be argued that the opening up of the Eastern European states will have little impact on the ability of the majority of their residents to travel to the West. It is certainly true that many of the physical barriers to travel have been eased, but the buying power of most workers has not increased markedly. The prices charged by airlines, hotels and other tourism companies for travel to the West are beyond the reach of those on average and below average incomes. In the short term, travel from East to West is likely to remain the preserve of a relatively small and privileged group of individuals on above average incomes.

European tourist flows

Europe is the world's principal destination region for international tourism, in terms of both tourist arrivals and receipts. Data from the World Tourism Organisation (WTO, 1996a) show that Europe accounted for just under two-thirds of all international tourist arrivals in 1995 (see Table 3.2).

Examination of the figures contained in Table 3.2 demonstrates that Europe's share of total international arrivals in 1995 was 59.5 per cent and it accounted for 51 per cent of total tourism receipts worldwide. While these figures may seem encouraging on first analysis, it should be noted that Europe's growth rate for international arrivals between

Table 3.2: International tourist arrivals and receipts, 1994/95

	Tourist arrivals (thousands)		Percentage change		Tourism receipts (US$ million)		Percentage change	
	1994	*1995*	*95/94*	*94/93*	*1994*	*1995*	*95/94*	*94/93*
World	546 269	567 033	3.8	5.4	346 703	371 682	7.2	10.4
Africa	18 477	18 800	1.7	0.7	6 530	6 915	5.9	8.5
Americas	107 176	111 944	4.4	3.0	95 084	95 239	0.2	4.8
East Asia/Pacific	76 973	83 624	8.6	10.6	61 990	69 349	11.9	18.7
Europe	329 819	337 240	2.3	5.1	174 811	189 820	8.6	11.0
Middle East	9 875	11 041	11.8	10.0	5 129	6 653	29.7	6.8
South Asia	3 949	4 384	11.0	11.0	3 159	3 706	17.3	13.1

Source: WTO

Table 3.3: Regional percentage shares of international tourist arrivals and receipts, 1960–94

	1960	*1970*	*1980*	*1990*	*1994*
Africa					
Arrivals	1.1	1.5	2.6	3.3	3.4
Receipts	2.6	2.2	2.6	2.0	1.9
Americas					
Arrivals	24.1	23.0	21.6	20.6	20.3
Receipts	35.7	26.8	24.6	26.6	18.8
East Asia/Pacific					
Arrivals	1.0	3.0	7.4	11.6	14.0
Receipts	2.9	6.1	8.4	14.9	17.5
South Asia					
Arrivals	0.3	0.6	0.8	0.7	0.7
Receipts	0.5	0.6	1.5	0.8	0.7
Europe					
Arrivals	72.5	70.5	65.6	62.1	60.1
Receipts	56.8	62.0	59.5	53.8	50.0
Middle East					
Arrivals	1.0	1.4	2.1	1.7	1.5
Receipts	1.5	2.3	3.4	2.0	1.1

Source: WTO

1994 and 1995 was only 2.3 per cent, 1.5 percentage points below the world average of 3.8 per cent. Furthermore, Europe's share of both international arrivals and receipts has been declining steadily since the 1960s, as the figures in Table 3.3 demonstrate.

Table 3.3 shows that Europe's share of international tourist arrivals declined from a high of 72.5 per cent in 1960 to 60.1 per cent in 1994. Similarly, the continent's share of receipts from international tourism fell from 62 per cent in 1970 to 50 per cent in 1994, predominantly at the expense of the rapid growth in tourism in east Asia and the Pacific. Looking to the future, the World Tourism Organisation forecasts that Europe, although continuing to retain its position as the world's principal destination for international tourism, will experience the slowest growth rate of all the regions of the world. WTO's estimates for average annual growth rates in tourist arrivals between 1990 and 2000 are as follows (WTO, 1995):

- Europe   2.7 per cent
- World average   3.8 per cent
- Middle East   4 per cent
- Americas   4.6 per cent
- Africa   5 per cent
- South Asia   6.1 per cent
- East Asia/Pacific 6.8 per cent

It is difficult to pinpoint a single reason to explain the significant and steady decline in Europe's share of international tourism since the 1960s. It is possible to highlight a number of negative, supply-side factors that have contributed to the situation, such as environmental problems (for example algal blooms in the Adriatic and the devastation caused by the Chernobyl nuclear incident), the perception that certain countries in Europe are expensive destinations, lack of industry cohesion in tourism promotion, overcrowding in cities, inadequate staff training, poor transport infrastructure and political upheavals. Of greater significance, however, are changes in the nature of the demand for tourism products; increases in the levels of disposable incomes and standards of living of the majority of Europeans have allowed more travel to long-haul destinations outside Europe for main holidays, with a subsequent rise in demand for shorter, more frequent trips closer to home. Another important factor is the comparative attitudes of national governments to tourism development and promotion. With a few notable exceptions, the governments of many long-haul destinations that are keen to enjoy the economic benefits of tourism are investing heavily in promotion and product development, while many European countries are scaling down their public investment in tourism promotion or delegating responsibilities to the private sector. The work of the Australian Tourist Commission, highlighted in the second case study in Chapter 7, serves to illustrate how effective a publicly-funded tourism promotion organisation can be.

Domestic and incoming tourism

The bulk of tourist activity within Europe consists of nationals taking trips in their own country or visiting other European destinations. For visits to other countries within Europe, there is a distinct pattern of travel from the highly urbanised, densely populated and colder northern European countries to the warmer destinations found in southern Europe, particularly around the Mediterranean basin. Germany, France and the United Kingdom, for example, are prime source markets for the tourist-receiving countries of Spain, Greece and Portugal, each of which relies heavily on revenue from tourism for its economic prosperity (see Table 3.4).

With reference to Table 3.4, it is interesting to note that, with the exception of Ireland, the only EU member states that exhibit a positive tourism balance are found in southern Europe, whereas those exhibiting the greatest deficit are located in northern Europe. This further reinforces the notion of a north–south migration of tourists within Europe, taking revenue away from the colder, northern countries to be spent in the warmer Mediterranean destinations.

Although the great majority of tourism activity within Europe is the result of travel by Europeans themselves, incoming tourism from countries outside Europe also makes a

Table 3.4:
Tourism balance
of payments in
EU member
countries, 1994

Country	Credits (million ECU)	Debits (million ECU)	Balance (million ECU)
Belgium*	4 333	6 509	−2 176
Denmark	2 677	3 021	−344
Germany	8 927	34 930	−26 003
Greece	3 272	942	+2 330
Spain	18 116	3 472	+14 644
France	20 801	11 623	+9 178
Ireland	1 515	1 351	+164
Italy	20 004	10 176	+9 828
Luxembourg*	4 333	6 509	−2 176
Netherlands	4 027	7 867	−3 840
Austria	9 963	7 035	+2 928
Portugal	3 430	1 430	+2 000
Finland	1 100	1 323	−223
Sweden	2 379	4 106	−1 727
United Kingdom	13 052	18 689	−5 637

* Belgo-Luxembourg Economic Union
Source: Author's adaptation of Eurostat figures

Table 3.5:
Europe's principal
markets for
incoming tourism

Market	1990 visits	1995 visits
USA	7 530 000	8 700 000
Japan	1 219 000	1 880 000
Canada	1 513 000	1 600 000
Australia	505 000	543 500
Brazil	284 000	500 000
Other Latin America	195 000	320 000
Argentina	128 000	290 000
Hong Kong	84 000	215 000
South Africa	152 000	170 000
Israel	145 000	150 000
Mexico	155 000	150 000
Korea	45 000	130 000
India	110 000	128 000
New Zealand	88 000	82 000
Singapore	49 000	56 000
Thailand	32 000	56 000
Taiwan	40 000	44 000

Source: European Travel Commission, 1996

significant contribution to economic activity. This is due, in part, to the spending per head of overseas visitors, which tends to be greater than that of domestic tourists. Table 3.5 provides statistics on the main markets for incoming tourism to Europe, showing total visitor numbers for 1990 and 1995. The table shows that the USA is clearly Europe's dominant overseas market, with 8.7 million visits in 1995. This dominance by the USA is reinforced when the figures for expenditure are examined; of the total spending of 22.16

billion ECU (US$44.32 billion) for all overseas markets covered by the European Travel Commission, 14.1 billion ECU (US$28.2 billion) was spent by visitors from the USA (European Travel Commission, 1996). The figures in Table 3.5 also indicate the principal growth markets for incoming tourism to Europe. These include Japan, Korea, Hong Kong, Thailand, Brazil, Argentina and other Latin American countries.

Regional variations in European tourism

The countries of the western and southern sub-regions of Europe, for example Spain, Greece, France, Italy and Portugal, are the most popular destinations for tourism. Statistics from the World Tourism Organisation (WTO, 1996a) indicate that these two regions accounted for almost two-thirds of the total of 337 million tourist arrivals in Europe in 1995, although there is evidence of a slow-down in growth due to saturation of the market in certain areas and currency overvaluation in selected countries. Eastern and central parts of Europe are the next most popular tourist destinations, benefiting from both western European tourist flows and long-haul incoming tourism. Northern European countries attracted approximately 10 per cent of Europe's total tourist arrivals in 1995, while the eastern Mediterranean was the fastest growing sub-region in respect of international tourist arrivals and receipts.

The structure of the European tourism industry

Tourism in Europe is a highly fragmented industry with a very high proportion of small and medium-sized enterprises (SMEs). The European Commission estimates that a little under half of those employed in tourism in Europe work in hotels and catering (4 million), and that 95 per cent of the employers in this sector are very small companies with nine employees or less (European Commission, 1994). The European tourist industry is dominated by private sector companies, which operate within a business environment that is, to a greater or lesser extent, regulated by public bodies at local, regional, national, European and international levels. The European Commission refers to the 'horizontal' nature of European tourism, consisting of a broad range of interlinked industry sectors operating across national frontiers. This complexity in the structure of the European tourism industry is demonstrated in Figure 3.2, which highlights a number of key features of the European tourism industry, including the following:

1. Europe competes directly with other world regions for its share of international tourist arrivals.
2. Multinational corporations, for example airlines, car rental companies and hotel groups, operate across continental boundaries and may have interests in a number of regions in the world.
3. Private and public sector bodies work in partnership, and in isolation, to deliver the core components of the European tourism industry.
4. Commercial enterprises, including travel agents and tour operators, offer the distribution channels for European tourism products, both within their own countries and on an international scale. German companies, including TUI, NUR and LTU, currently dominate the European mass market tour operating industry.
5. A range of public sector agencies, including the European Commission, the European Travel Commission (see case study later in this chapter) and National Tourism Organisations (NTOs), seek to influence the planning, development, regulation and promotion of European tourism nationally and internationally.

Figure 3.2: Structure of the European tourism industry

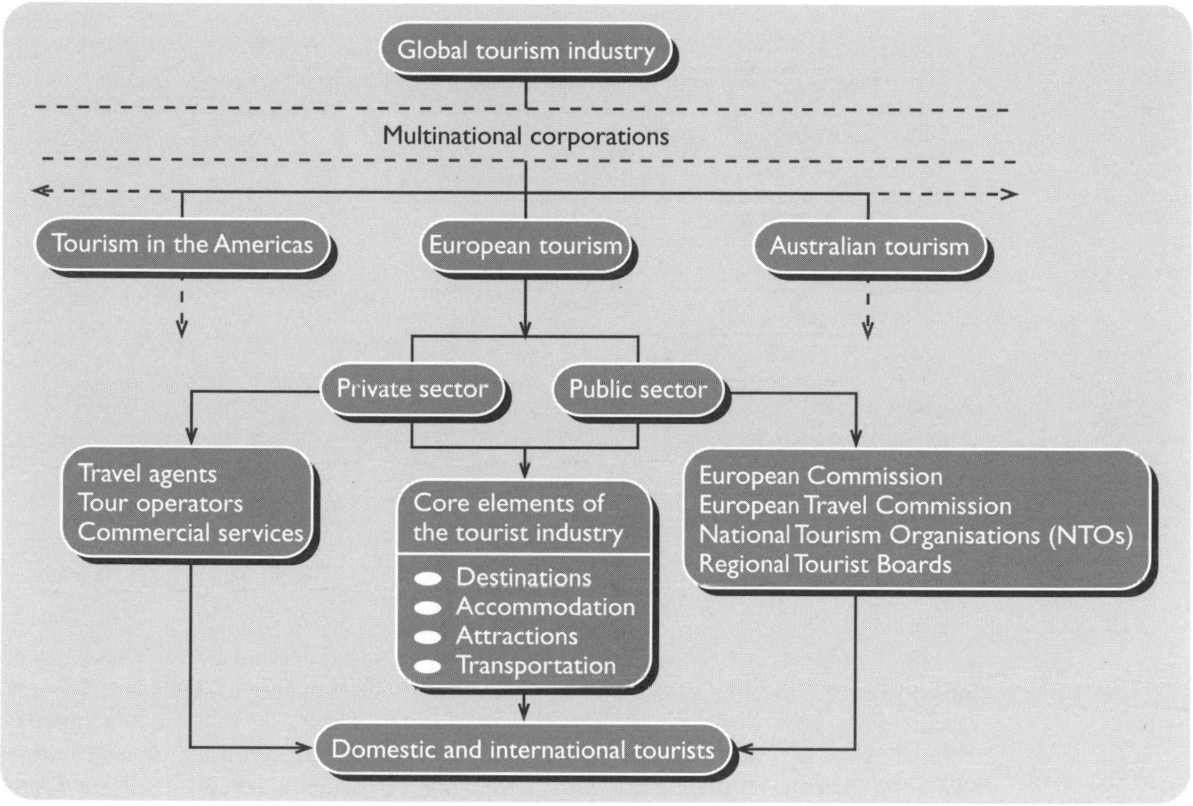

6. The various components of the European tourism industry work to satisfy the needs of both domestic and international tourists.

The following sections of this chapter investigate important issues in the various sectors of the European tourism industry, beginning with transportation.

Transportation

Transportation in Europe is delivered by a wide range of public and private sector enterprises, with marked differences in the levels of public investment in transport in different European countries. Historically, both the transport infrastructure (roads, railway lines, canals and airports) and transport services in the majority of European countries have been financed from public funds. The provision of an integrated public transport network was considered an important part of a country's social policy. Although this situation does still apply in certain European states, recent political and ideological changes have led to the increased deregulation of transport services, with responsibilities being moved from public bodies to private sector operators. In the majority of cases, however, transport infrastructure projects are financed from public funds or are private/public sector partnership initiatives, perhaps augmented with grant-aid from European Union structural funds.

Advances in transport technology are continually offering leisure and business travellers in Europe new or updated services and faster travel to their destinations. There is

Figure 3.3: Main European airlines in terms of passenger volumes in 1993

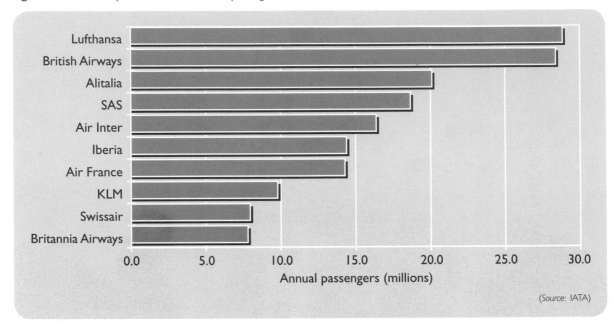

(Source: IATA)

growing competition between the various sectors of the transport industry – road, rail, air and water – to offer leisure and business tourists high quality facilities and services. Competition occurs both within and between transport sectors; different coach companies competing for business to offer sightseeing trips around the major capital cities of Europe is a good example of the former, while competition between Eurostar train services and the airlines on the London–Paris route exemplifies competition between different sectors of the transport industry. Air travel has expanded rapidly in Europe, with seven European airlines carrying over 10 million passengers in 1993 (see Figure 3.3).

Although many improvements in European transport services are not planned primarily to meet a tourism need, the improved situation that arises invariably produces an indirect benefit for tourists. For example, the use of EU funds to upgrade road systems in the less developed member states as part of regional economic development strategies, makes these areas more accessible to tourists, whose spending provides welcome extra revenue for the regions; parts of the Irish Republic, Greece and Spain are good cases in point.

Trans-European transport networks

The European Union's common transport policy of 1992 is aimed at reducing the disparities that continue to exist between different modes of transport in Europe, notably through a more equitable sharing of the costs and through other measures to promote healthy competition, better respect for the environment and greater integration between different transport modes. The emphasis is on developing sustainable transport services, with the reduction of noise, water and air pollution being seen as a priority. In a decision taken in September 1996, the European Parliament and the Council of the European Union formally established the guidelines for the establishment of a trans-European transport network, to be implemented on a gradual basis by the year 2010. The proposal seeks to integrate land, sea and air transport networks throughout all member states of the European Union, in accordance with published maps. Figure 3.4 shows the outline plan for developments in UK rail services as part of the trans-European network. Similar

Figure 3.4: Proposed UK rail developments as part of the trans-European transport network

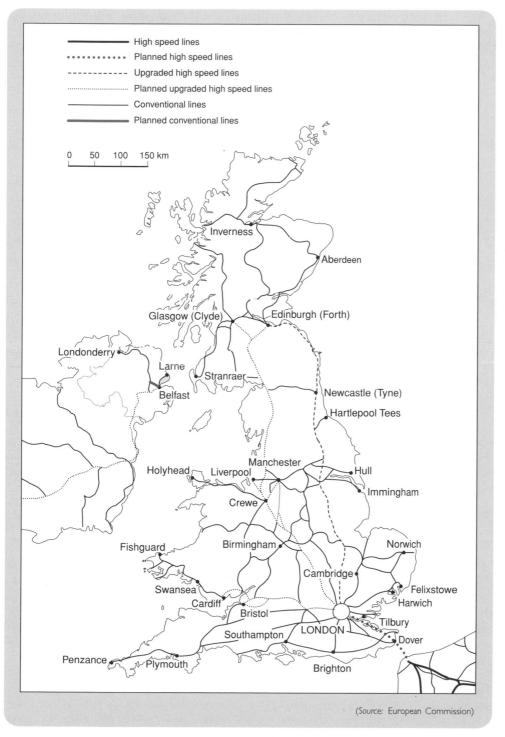

(*Source:* European Commission)

maps have been produced for each of the 15 member states of the EU, detailing rail, road and airport proposals.

The map in Figure 3.4 shows that the UK's part of the completed trans-European rail network will consist of three types of lines: a high-speed line between London and the Channel Tunnel for speeds of 250 km/h and above, a series of upgraded high-speed lines equipped for speeds of the order of 200 km/h, and a number of conventional lines throughout England, Wales, Scotland and Northern Ireland.

The trans-European network is to act as a general reference framework designed to encourage member states, in collaboration with the European Union, to carry out projects of common interest, the purpose of which is to ensure the cohesion, interconnection and integration of the network, including access to adjoining countries. The network has the following specific objectives:

● Ensuring the sustainable mobility of people and goods within the EU under the best possible social and safety conditions

● Contributing to the strengthening of economic and social cohesion in the Union

● Offering users high quality infrastructure on acceptable economic terms

● The inclusion of all modes of transport, taking account of their comparative advantages

● Encouragement of integration between different forms of transport

● Linking the major conurbations and regions of the EU

● Ability to connect to the networks of the European Free Trade Association (EFTA) states, the countries of central and eastern Europe, and the Mediterranean countries

The trans-European network comprises transport infrastructure, to include road, rail and inland waterway networks, seaports and inland waterway ports, traffic management systems and navigation systems.

The upgrading and improvement of transport facilities and services in the years running up to the network's completion in 2010 will have undoubted benefits as far as tourist activity is concerned. Of particular interest will be improvements to the trans-European road network, given the dominance in the use of the private motor car for tourist trips in Europe. The trans-European road network will consist of motorways and other high quality roads, whether existing, new or to be adapted, which:

● play an important role in long distance traffic, or

● by-pass the main urban centres on the routes identified by the network, or

● provide interconnection with other modes of transport, or

● link landlocked and peripheral regions to the central parts of the EU.

The stated priorities for the development of the trans-European transport network include the completion of missing sections of existing major routes, providing infrastructure to enable effective links between peripheral and central regions of the Union, and the optimum combination and integration of the various modes of transport.

Transport liberalisation in Europe

The European Union policy in the field of transport services is to encourage the provision of services by deregulation. Although measures to deregulate coach travel, inland water transport and maritime transportation in Europe have been in place for some time, it is the deregulation of Europe's air services that has proved to be the most controversial measure of all. The aim has been to dismantle the restrictive practices impeding free competition in member states, which have resulted in substantially higher air fares than in other parts of the world where full deregulation exists, most notably the USA. The final stage of air transport liberalisation was underway in 1997 and included:

- the introduction of a single air transport licence covering all EU member states
- establishing Union-wide conditions for access to air routes for air carriers
- passenger fares (including the power of the European Commission to intervene to halt unfair practices).

A number of other initiatives have been taken to ensure that the core liberalisation is not impeded by marginal factors. These cover reservation systems, allocation of landing and take-off slots at airports, denied boarding compensation schemes, standards for aircraft airworthiness and mutual recognition between the member states of licences for cockpit personnel.

Since 1993, all bilateral capacity sharing rules or agreements have disappeared completely. Pricing rules have been progressively relaxed and cheaper air fares have become more widely available. New services have been, and continue to be, introduced as greater access has been provided. The so-called 'fifth freedom' rights were first granted in a limited way in 1990. These rights allow a carrier to transport passengers between member states other than the one which issued the licence. For example, flights from country A could stop off in country B, deposit and collect passengers, and continue on to country C. Since 1993, however, fifth freedom rights have been applied fully, enabling free access to all intra-Union routes. Restrictions on full cabotage, i.e. the right for a carrier licensed in one member state to operate services in another state or between two other member states, are due to be lifted in 1997. The end result of this process should be greater choice, increased flexibility and lower fares, to the benefit of all leisure and business tourists.

Deregulation of air travel in Europe will contribute to a forecast increase in demand for both domestic and international air services up to 2010. The International Air Transport Association (IATA) estimates that total passenger numbers to, from and within Europe will more than double, from 366 million in 1993 to 773 million in 2010 (IATA, 1996). Scheduled international services are predicted to show the greatest annual average growth rate of 5.1 per cent over the same period, followed by domestic traffic at 3.9 per cent and international charter services with 3.6 per cent growth.

Accommodation

The diversity of cultures, history and architecture within the countries of Europe is reflected in the wide variety of accommodation on offer to business and leisure tourists. In general, hotels are the most common type of accommodation used for holiday and business trips, but there are many other forms of accommodation available, including self-catering apartments, youth hostels, bed and breakfast establishments, caravan sites, camping grounds, inns and holiday villages, to name but a few. Even within the hotel sector itself there are wide variations in the type of product on offer; whether it is a secluded country house hotel in the Welsh countryside, a city centre hotel in Brussels that is part of a multinational chain or a high-rise hotel in a bustling Spanish seaside resort, it is clear that the requirements of different sectors of the market are reflected in a wide product variety.

The rich diversity within Europe results in a highly fragmented accommodation sector with no single pan-European market and a high degree of internationalisation. Hotel

Table 3.6:
Hotels and similar establishments in the European Union, 1994

	Number of hotels etc.	Beds (thousands)	Overnight stays (millions)	Percentage taken up by non-residents
Total	177 835	8 363	1 770	11
Belgium	1 980	105	28	48
Denmark	565	99	25	43
Germany	37 307	1 387	314	11
Greece	7 604	508	54	76
Spain	10 063	1 053	175	60
France	20 057	1 193	252	38
Ireland	977	60	—	—
Italy	34 547	1 723	275	37
Luxembourg	373	14	3	88
Netherlands	1 726	138	56	32
Austria	18 402	650	92	75
Portugal	1 728	202	34	60
Finland	951	106	14	25
Sweden	1 855	174	35	19
United Kingdom	39 700	949	414	44

Source: Eurostat

chains are a common feature of the accommodation scene in many northern European destinations, with companies such as Accor, Granada/Forte, Holiday Inn/Bass, Inter-Continental Hotels, Queens Moat Houses, Sol Hotels and Hilton International featuring prominently. Multinational corporations with headquarters in the USA and the Far East, as well as European companies themselves, see Europe as an important region for further hotel developments based on a number of factors, including:

● Expansion in business travel as a result of the introduction of the post-1992 Single European Market
● The emergence of new tourism markets in the former Eastern Bloc countries
● Positive future growth forecasts in international tourism
● Ending of the recession in many European countries

Data on the stock of hotels and similar establishments in the 15 member states of the European Union are shown in Table 3.6, which indicates that there were in excess of 177 000 establishments in 1994 offering a combined total of more than 8.3 million bedspaces.

Table 3.6 also demonstrates the variations in the proportion of non-residents using the establishments in different European countries, an indicator of the importance of incoming tourism to the particular countries concerned. The figures of 76 per cent and 75 per cent for Greece and Austria respectively, for example, indicate high numbers of overseas tourists and, hence, tourism's importance in the overall economies of these countries. In contrast, the low proportion of non-residents using the accommodation establishments in Germany, Sweden and Finland illustrates tourism's limited relative economic significance in these countries, which is reflected in a low value for tourism's contribution to GNP.

Market segmentation and branding in European accommodation

Hotel companies in Europe have sought to expand their operations through targeted product development and promotion, identifying leisure and business travellers as distinct markets with quite different requirements. Growing competition and the need to maximise accommodation stock have led hotels to develop products and services for 'niche' markets and to enter into alliances with other providers of tourist facilities and products, for example tourist attractions, tour operators and transport providers. One of the best examples of the concept of market segmentation and subsequent branding is demonstrated by the rise of the French hotel group Accor, which has a wide product portfolio geared to the needs of a variety of market segments, for example:

- *Sofitel*: luxury, 4-star hotels geared to the needs of international business travellers
- *Novotel*: 3-star, mid-range hotels primarily designed for use by business travellers during the week and families at weekends
- *Mercure*: 3-star hotels of individual character offering a high standard of personal service
- *Ibis*: 2-star budget hotels offering simple accommodation and basic catering at a reasonable price
- *Formule 1*: budget hotels with basic accommodation and 'no frills'
- *Hotelia*: semi-residential hotels aimed at the senior citizens' market

Accor's success in turning a national hotel chain into a multinational travel company through acquisitions, targeted expansion and brand development has led other companies to follow their example. Market segmentation and product branding is seen as the most effective way for European hotel groups to maintain or expand their market share and even in some cases to create new markets.

Tourist attractions

Europe's attractions as a tourist destination are both man-made and naturally occurring. Man-made attractions consist of purpose-built facilities for tourists, for example theme parks, and those facilities which, although not originally developed as visitor attractions, are now of interest to tourists, including cathedrals, castles and historic buildings, for example Westminster Abbey, the Palace of Versailles and the Kremlin in Moscow. Visitors from all over the world are attracted by Europe's scenic beauty and natural features, such as the Alps, the Mediterranean Sea, the Norwegian fjords, the Pyrenees and the Highlands of Scotland, to name but a few. The management of the majority of the cultural and artistic attractions in European countries, as well as their ancient monuments and historic buildings, is entrusted to public sector organisations, which aim to conserve the country's heritage while at the same time making facilities available to domestic and international tourists. Commercial operators provide a variety of purpose-built attractions, including theme parks, entertainment facilities, amusement parks and leisure facilities. Many European destinations host special events as a way of attracting visitors at the same time as achieving other objectives, for example staging a musical or sporting event, or celebrating a national anniversary.

Theme parks in Europe

Although the concept of theme parks originated in the USA through the work of the Disney Corporation in its resorts in California and Florida, Europe can boast a variety of

Figure 3.5: Annual attendances at selected European theme parks, 1995 (millions)

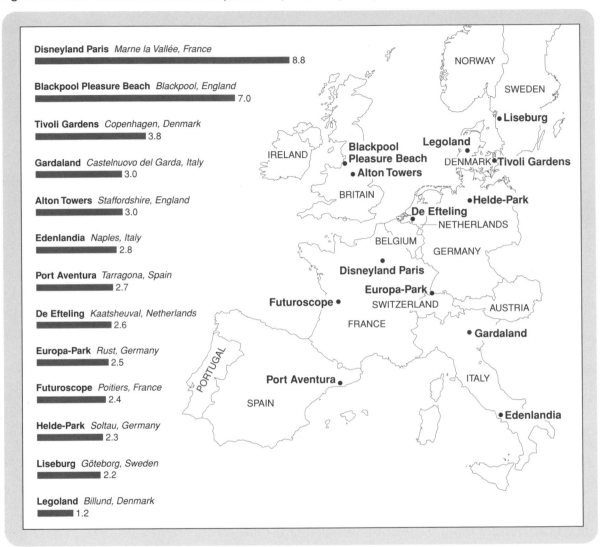

theme park attractions, predominantly located close to the major centres of population in the industrialised northern regions of the continent (see Figure 3.5). The figure indicates that the Disney phenomenon has now spread from the USA to Europe with the opening of Disneyland Paris, originally called EuroDisney, in 1993.

As with all theme parks, those located in Europe must constantly update their facilities and services in order to remain competitive. 'White knuckle' rides remain popular with visitors, while sophisticated animatronics and computer-generated 'virtual reality' experiences keep many attractions at the forefront of developments.

Role of the public sector in European tourism

Figure 3.2 showed us that public sector organisations play two key roles in European tourism, namely:

- Working in isolation or in partnership with commercial operators, they provide a range of facilities, products and services for tourists, for example visitor attractions, tourist information services, historic buildings, leisure facilities and transport services.
- They seek to influence and regulate the planning, development and promotion of tourism through bodies such as the European Union, European Travel Commission and National Tourism Organisations (NTOs).

The role of the European Union in the field of tourism is considered in detail later in this chapter. The following two case studies, featuring the Cyprus Tourism Organisation and the European Travel Commission, investigate the work of one specific NTO operating in Europe and a publicly funded organisation responsible for the worldwide promotion of the whole continent of Europe as a tourist destination.

Case Study: Cyprus Tourism Organisation

Introduction

The stated aim of the Cyprus Tourism Organisation (CTO) is '. . . *the organisation and promotion of tourism in the Republic of Cyprus, through the utilisation of all available possibilities*' (CTO Annual Report, 1994). In order to achieve these aims, the Organisation is engaged in a wide-ranging programme of planning, regulation, inspection and marketing of the Cyprus tourism product. It was established and operates according to the provisions of the Cyprus Tourism Organisation Law 1969–1985, the CTO (Structure and Conditions of Service) Regulations of 1970 and the CTO (Administrative and Financial) Regulations of 1970–1994.

Structure of the CTO

Day-to-day management of the CTO is the responsibility of the Director General who reports to a nine-member Board of Directors, drawn from commercial enterprises and public sector interests in Cyprus tourism. The CTO employs 125 members of staff and has four principal departments, in addition to the Director General's office, covering administration, promotion, tourist organisation (planning) and tourist services (see Figure 3.6).

The CTO's head office is based in Nicosia and there are regional offices located in various parts of the island, offering tourist information and inspection services. In 1994, the CTO operated overseas offices in London, Frankfurt, Paris, Stockholm, Athens, Milan, Zurich, Brussels, Amsterdam, Vienna, New York and Tokyo. In Tokyo, the CTO is represented by the Commercial Counsellor of the Ministry of Commerce, Industry and Tourism.

Administrative functions of the CTO

The CTO's administrative department is involved in a wide range of activities, including providing the secretariat to the Board of Directors and the Organisation's main committees. Staff are also concerned with personnel and legal matters, and the accounting and financial functions of the CTO.

Planning and development of tourism in Cyprus

The CTO's planning function includes the preparation of plans for infrastructure projects, the approval of architectural plans for hotels, surveys, the preparation of studies and the overall ▷

Cyprus Tourism Organisation continued

Figure 3.6: Structure of the Cyprus Tourism Organisation

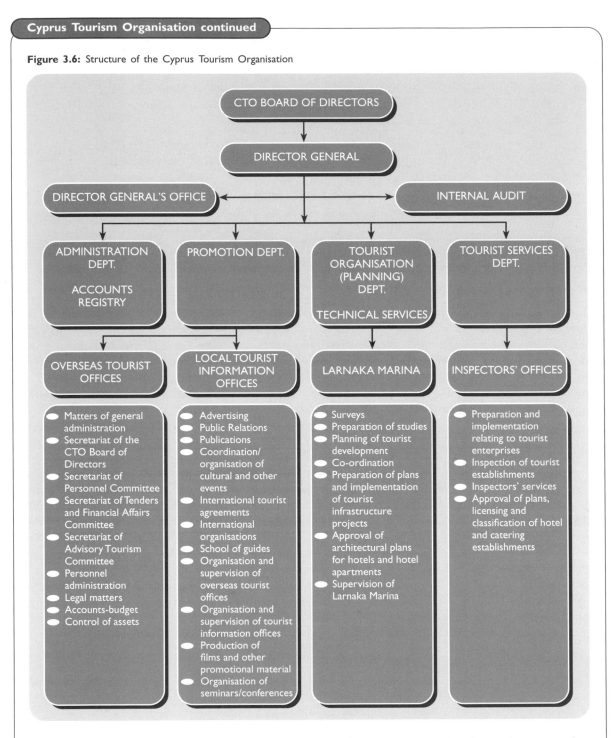

co-ordination of tourism development on the island. Work in recent years has focused on a number of development priorities, including a golf development strategy, a master plan for nautical tourism, a study on the landscaping and presentation of archaeological sites and a pilot project on the European Blue Flag Campaign. Much attention has been paid to the encouragement of agrotourism ▷

in Cyprus, including the provision of an incentive scheme for the conversion and refurbishment of village houses for use by tourists. The planning department have also undertaken research on operational aspects of the agrotourism product, such as the establishment of a central reservations system and the formulation of a marketing strategy.

Marketing the Cyprus tourism product

The CTO initiates and co-ordinates an aggressive policy in marketing Cyprus around the world. The main focus of the current marketing policy is the attraction of tourists with high per capita expenditure. The Organisation also aims to achieve other important objectives, such as the promotion of a positive image for Cyprus, the development of winter tourism and special interest tourism, as well as the growth of conference and incentive travel. The CTO's marketing effort is also geared towards diversification in order to counter the over-reliance on a single market sector.

In order to achieve its marketing objectives, the CTO undertakes a wide range of promotional activities, aimed not only at consumers but also at the international travel trade. The following is a list of the most important of these activities:

- *Advertising*. This includes television advertising in the major markets of Germany, Switzerland, the UK and France.
- *Travel trade events*. All the overseas offices of the CTO organise and take part in a wide variety of events, including trade exhibitions, seminars, receptions and press conferences, plus training events for travel agents and conference organisers.
- *Co-operation with tour operators*. The CTO undertakes joint advertising and other promotional work with tour operators and airlines serving its major markets.
- *Hospitality and familiarisation trips*. The CTO hosts visits to the island by a wide variety of tourist professionals, including journalists, travel writers, tour operators, travel agents, conference organisers, TV and radio crews, and well-known personalities.
- *Participation in fairs in Cyprus*. The CTO participates in a number of events on the island, as a way of promoting domestic tourism.
- *Publications*. In order to service its market diversification strategy the CTO is continually adding to its list of publications for overseas distribution, for example new brochures in Russian, Hebrew, Czech, Hungarian and Polish.

Regulation and supervision of tourist enterprises

The Cyprus Tourism Organisation seeks to regulate tourism development through the implementation of relevant laws and regulations governing the operation of tourist enterprises, covering:

- Hotels and other accommodation establishments
- Travel agencies
- Catering and entertainment establishments
- Tourist guides

Under existing legislation, plans for the building of new accommodation establishments, or the extension of existing premises, as well as their classification, must be approved in the first instance by the Hotels Committee of the CTO and ultimately by the Board of Directors. The CTO publishes the Cyprus Hotel Guide, which lists all registered establishments and their prices. In 1994 there were ▷

Cyprus Tourism Organisation continued

390 licensed travel agencies operating in Cyprus and, during the same year, some 206 licenses were issued to professional tourist guides as provided by the relevant legislation. In relation to catering and entertainment establishments, the CTO examines such matters as the approval of plans, the classification and re-classification of establishments, the prices they charge and other operational matters. Training for tourism professions in Cyprus is provided by both public and private sector organisations. The Ministry of Education operates hotel training departments in the technical schools of Limassol, Pafos, Polis, Larnaka, Paralimni and Nicosia, while the Cyprus Higher Hotel Institute offers hotel management courses.

(*Information courtesy of the Cyprus Tourism Organisation*)

Discussion points and essay questions

1. How does the work of the Cyprus Tourism Organisation help provide high quality facilities and services for overseas visitors?
2. What problems does the CTO face when competing for its share of the international tourist market?
3. How does the CTO seek to influence and regulate tourism developments on the island?
4. What promotional activities does the Organisation undertake to increase visitor numbers?

Case Study: European Travel Commission

Introduction

The European Travel Commission (ETC) is the organisation responsible for the worldwide overseas promotion of Europe as a tourist destination. Established in 1948, first as part of the OEEC (now OECD) and then as a voluntary, autonomous organisation, the ETC operates in all major overseas markets, including the USA, Canada, Latin America (Mexico, Brazil, Argentina), Japan/Asia and Australia/New Zealand. ETC never operates in Europe where its member countries are in competition with each other. The Commission undertakes three principal activities:

- Public relations
- Consumer advertising
- Trade promotion

Prior market research determines the precise choice of activities carried out in each of the ETC's prime overseas markets and assists with the allocation of budgets.

Members of the ETC

To date, 26 European countries belong to the European Travel Commission. They include all EU member states (with the exception of the Netherlands), plus Norway, Iceland, Switzerland, Monaco, Malta, Cyprus, Turkey, Bulgaria, Croatia, Czech Republic, Hungary, Poland and Slovenia. The members of the ETC are the directors of each National Tourist Organisation (NTO) responsible for tourism promotion. They elect a chairman, two vice-chairmen, a steering committee and a planning committee, all for revolving two-year terms of office. A research working group regularly exchanges information and identifies market segments to be investigated and new products to be tested. A small, ▷

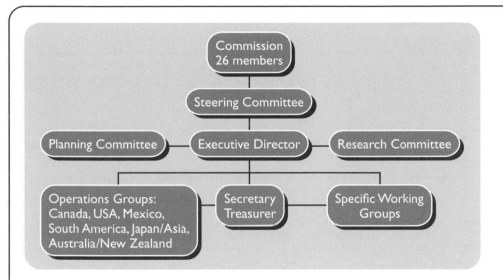

permanently staffed executive unit ensures overall co-ordination of the work of the Commission. Figure 3.7 shows the structure of the ETC and how its work functions interrelate.

Overseas operations

The representatives of the European National Tourist Organisations (NTOs) operating in the various long-haul markets join together to form an ETC chapter and elect a chairman. They decide on a programme of joint activities for the promotion of Europe in the year ahead, propose a budget and seek local tourism industry support. Promotion covers all of Europe, even though there are few markets where every member NTO has representation. The agreed programme of promotional activities is submitted to ETC's members in Europe, who meet twice a year in a General Assembly. After voting the organisation's overall budget, they allocate a budget for each of the five ETC's overseas markets (listed in the preceding paragraph). They then approve or modify the proposed programmes and review past activities.

Each overseas operations' group may hire the services of a promotions or public relations agency, which is also responsible for raising local tourism industry support, both financial and 'in kind'. One of ETC's strengths is that it has very low running costs and can, therefore, allocate the major proportion of its funds to its overseas activities.

Funding of the ETC

The Commission is entirely funded by its members' contributions, calculated according to a set of agreed criteria. Additional financial support for specific campaigns is raised overseas. Long-standing local industry support is testimony to its credibility in the field. Local tourism industry sponsorship means that ETC's seed money is annually enhanced two, three or even four fold, for example from 1 million ECU to nearly 4 million ECU in 1995.

ETC's global budget for promotion and research amounted to 3 519 604 ECU (US$4 223 524) in 1995, distributed as shown in Table 3.7. As the table indicates, the USA received the largest amount of seed money from ETC funds and generated the most from NTO representatives and the local tourism industry in the States. This reflects the fact that the USA is, by far, Europe's principal market for overseas tourists, with Europe welcoming some 8 700 000 visitors from the States in 1995 (European Travel Commission, 1996).

Europe Travel commission continued

Table 3.7: ETC's 1995 budgets for overseas markets (ECU)

Market	Seed money	NTO reps.	Local industry	Other sources	Total
USA	485 000	504 166	1 516 666	—	2 505 832
Canada	97 200	340 000	41 000	30 000	508 200
Latin America	43 750	51 000	6 500	30 000	131 250
Japan	9 972	—	—	—	9 972
Australia	68 050	41 000	51 800	157 400	318 250
Research	41 500	4 600	—	—	46 100

Source: European Travel Commission, 1996

ETC's related activities

In addition to its primary function as a catalyst for the worldwide promotion of Europe as an international tourism destination, the ETC also provides a forum for the directors of European tourism to meet regularly and exchange ideas. Since its establishment, this close consultation has enabled the ETC to take a position on many measures perceived as being potentially damaging to the tourism industry. The Commission is in constant touch with all international and multinational bodies working in tourism, including the following:

● *European Union (EU).* The ETC has recently taken part in the consultations on the Green Paper on the future of tourism in the EU (European Commission, 1995b) and has made representations to Eurostat on the proposed statistics directive to ensure that provision covered both the demand and supply aspects.

● *World Tourism Organisation (WTO).* The ETC regularly attends meetings of the WTO Europe Commission to address the issue of defending Europe's leadership in world tourism. As vice-president of the affiliate members of WTO, the ETC was instrumental in initiating the WTO study on the budgets and promotional activities of National Tourism Administrations published in 1994.

● *Organisation for Economic Co-operation and Development (OECD).* Working through ETAG (the European Tourism Action Group), the ETC supports the work undertaken by the OECD's Tourism Committee on the collection and publication of tourism statistics. OECD officers regularly participate as observers at the annual meeting of the ETC research directors.

The Commission also liaises closely with a number of other important tourism organisations, including the World Travel and Tourism Council (WTTC), Pacific Asia Travel Association (PATA) and the Canadian Tourism Commission.

(Information courtesy of the European Travel Commission)

Discussion points and essay questions

1. In what ways can the ETC help stem the loss of Europe's market share as an international tourism destination?

2. How can the Commission minimise conflict with the promotional work undertaken by its member countries?

3. Why are market research and intelligence gathering so important to the ETC's activities?

4. How is the work of the ETC likely to change in the next 25 years?

The role of the European Union in tourism

The tourism industry has been, and will continue to be, of great importance to the attainment of the broader objectives of the European Union (European Commission, 1996b). Its main contributions to these wider goals are that tourism:

- Creates jobs and wealth and will become increasingly important in this respect;
- Generates jobs rapidly and at low relative cost;
- Gives employment opportunities for varied groups, such as women and young people, which may in some way be at a disadvantage;
- Helps to achieve economic and social cohesion, and often gives less developed and peripheral regions a real opportunity to progress in economic terms;
- Can contribute to the protection and enhancement of the natural and cultural environment;
- Brings Europeans together, breaks down barriers and consolidates European identity and vision.

Tourism is of growing interest to the European Union (EU) as a prime economic sector, with the ability to generate wealth and create jobs in all member states. The exact economic importance of tourism is difficult to assess, but it has been estimated to represent an average of 5.5 per cent of GNP in the EU, with Spain and France reaching almost double this level, and an above-average level in Greece, Ireland and Portugal (European Commission, 1994). According to WTO estimates quoted in Eurostat (1996), tourism in the European Union represented 40.6 per cent of the international tourism market in terms of arrivals and 40.7 per cent in terms of receipts in 1995. Many of the EU member states rank highly in the league table of top international destinations. In 1995, France remained the world's most popular destination in terms of international arrivals and second in terms of tourism receipts, followed by Spain. Italy and the United Kingdom rank respectively fourth and sixth in terms of international arrivals. Of the top seven revenue earners in world tourism in 1995, after the USA, France, Italy, the UK, Austria and Germany maintained their leading positions in terms of revenue, representing a third of all world tourism receipts (Eurostat, 1996). Total employment in tourism in the EU member states is estimated at 9 million, accounting for approximately 6 per cent of total EU employment, in terms of jobs directly linked to tourism products and activities (European Commission, 1995b).

It is important to remember that tourism's contribution to the development of EU member states is considered to generate more than just economic benefits. The EU also recognises the important social role that tourism plays, particularly in the context of a 'People's Europe' and in relation to the social development of young people. Moreover, tourism can help to achieve cultural convergence, as tourism helps to spread awareness about the different European cultures, thus contributing to the development of respect for the different ways of life of Europeans. The Union also believes that tourism can be a useful vehicle for the application of sustainable development techniques, aiming at preserving and respecting the environment in which the tourism industry operates. As the Commission stated in a report on Community measures affecting tourism (European Commission, 1996a), '. . . . *tourism activity, and the benefits derived from it, cannot take place in a downgraded and/or polluted natural, rural, built or cultural environment. It is also evident that tourism development, if it is implemented in a sustainable way, provides long-term benefits to local communities'*.

The following sections of this chapter examine the structure of the European Union and the specific measures adopted or proposed to encourage the development of tourism.

Structure of the European Union

The European Union is a unique grouping of 15 member states, which have joined together to safeguard peace, promote economic development and foster social progress in Europe. The Treaty of Rome, signed in 1957 by the six founding countries of the European Economic Community, sets out the Union's legal framework. This was amended by the Single European Act in 1986, while the Treaty of Maastricht incorporated further changes. The six original member countries were France, Italy, West Germany, Belgium, the Netherlands and Luxembourg. Membership increased to nine in 1973 when Ireland, the United Kingdom and Denmark joined. In 1981, Greece became the tenth member state, followed by Spain and Portugal in 1986. The most recent countries to join are Austria, Finland and Sweden, which became full members of the EU in 1995. This growth of the Union is shown in diagrammatic form in Figure 3.8. Other countries, primarily from the former Eastern Bloc, are seeking membership of the EU, in the hope of regenerating their economies and improving the quality of life for their citizens.

The EU incorporates a number of interlinked institutions, the most important of which in terms of legislative provision are the European Commission, the Council of Ministers and the European Parliament:

Figure 3.8:
Growth of the
European Union

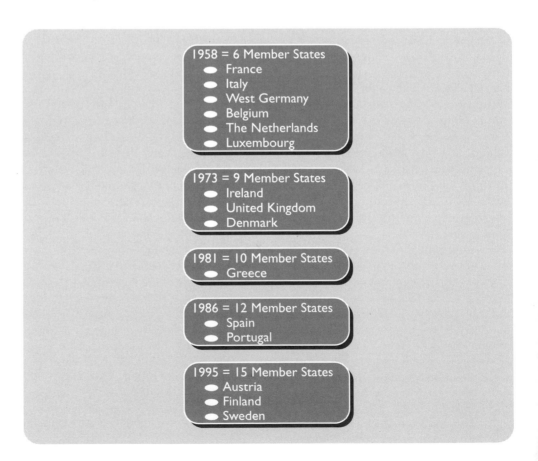

Directorate General	Examples of tourism responsibilities
DG I (External Relations)	Assistance to former Eastern Bloc countries with tourism development initiatives
DG III (Internal Market)	Freedom of movement for travellers
DG IV (Competition)	Competition policy related to transport and tourism matters
DG V (Employment, Social Affairs and Education)	Training programmes for the tourism industry; free movement of labour
DG VI (Agriculture)	Rural tourism projects under the LEADER programme
DG VII (Transport)	Maritime, land and air transport policies
DG VIII (International Development)	Assistance with tourism development projects in developing countries
DG XIII (Telecommunications etc.)	IT projects focusing on tourism in EU member states, e.g. global information systems (GIS)
DG XVI (Regional Policy)	Tourism projects to encourage regional development and social cohesion
DG XXIII (Enterprise etc.)	Tourism Unit

Table 3.8: Selected EC Directorates General (DGs) and their associations with tourism

- *European Commission.* The Commission makes proposals for European laws and ensures that EU policies and practices are followed by member states. The Commission fulfils a similar role to that of the civil service in the UK, except that the Commission actually proposes legislation. Any proposals for new EU laws or regulations pass from the Commission to the European Parliament for debate and then on to the Council of Ministers for approval or rejection. The Commission is made up of a number of separate departments, known as Directorates General (DGs). The department concerned most with tourism issues is DGXXIII, although the work of many other DGs has a bearing on the industry; for example DGVII handles transportation matters, DGXVI oversees regional development and DGIV co-ordinates the work on competition policy (see Table 3.8).

- *European Parliament.* The Parliament debates and amends legislation put forward by the European Commission. The Parliament is currently made up of 626 Members of the European Parliament (MEPs), directly elected every five years from within the member states. Seats are shared out between member states broadly according to the size of the country. The Parliament sits in both Brussels and Strasbourg.

- *Council of Ministers.* The Council decides on all the laws that establish EU policies. The Council consists of Government Ministers from the 15 member states, accountable to their own parliaments, representing national interests on the subjects under discussion, for example trade, agriculture and social policy. Each member state takes a six-month turn to hold the Presidency of the Council, setting the agenda and chairing meetings.

Figure 3.9:
How EU
legislation is
developed

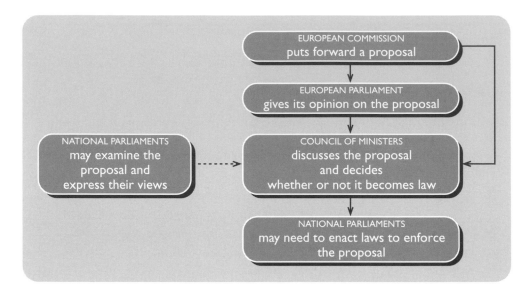

Figure 3.9 shows how these three EU institutions interact in the process of framing EU legislation. As the figure shows, the European Commission puts forward an initial proposal for legislation. The members of the European Parliament are then given the opportunity of commenting on the proposal and suggesting amendments, before the Council of Ministers discusses the proposal and determines what form it might take. At this point, the Ministers will also take note of the views of national parliaments. To become EU law, the proposal may finally require laws or regulations to be passed by the national parliaments of member states.

Tourism measures in the European Union

The title of this section deliberately avoids using the word 'policy' in relation to European Union tourism matters. Although many commentators refer to a tourism policy within the EU, it is debatable whether, in reality, such a policy exists. It is true that since the late 1980s, the importance of tourism has increasingly been espoused by member states, the Council of Ministers and the European Commission, but their actions have fallen short of granting tourism the status of a 'competence', or specific policy powers, within the EU strategic framework, unlike more established areas such as environment and transport. In the early years of its development, the then European Community considered that tourism was primarily a matter for individual member states. As such, the Treaty of Rome did not confer any specific powers upon the Council of Ministers in the field of tourism.

Nonetheless, a 'tourism policy', *per se*, has come a step closer to reality with the inclusion in the 1992 Maastricht Treaty of an acknowledgement that, for the first time, measures in the field of tourism should be included in EU action. The intention is that action in the fields mentioned in Article 3(t), including tourism, should be pursued on the basis of the existing provisions of the Treaty. This major departure reflects the growing awareness of three principal factors, namely:

1. The economic importance of tourism for growth and employment in the Union

2. The compatibility of adherence to the principle of subsidiarity with the need for Community-level action in this area not within the Community's exclusive competence

3. The need to introduce a degree of coherence and linkage in the three associated domains of tourism, consumer affairs and natural/cultural heritage

Declaration 1 of the Maastricht Treaty also states that, since tourism is a sphere referred to in Article 3(t), the question of introducing a Title relating to it in the Treaty should be examined as part of the inter-governmental conference to be convened in 1996. On the basis of the outcome of this conference, the Commission will submit a report on the role of tourism in the EU to the Council of Ministers for consideration.

We will now consider the development of EU measures and action concerning tourism, beginning with the three most important initiatives that have direct relevance to tourism, namely the European Year of Tourism, the Community action plan to assist tourism and the recent 'philoxenia' programme. This will be followed by consideration of a number of EU measures that impact indirectly on tourism and travel, to a greater or lesser degree.

European Year of Tourism

One of the first initiatives undertaken by the EU in the field of tourism was the establishment and promotion of the European Year of Tourism (EYT) in 1990. This was a Community-wide programme of events aimed at raising the profile of tourism within the member states, particularly among young people. The programme, which was adopted by the Council in 1988, had the following principal objectives:

1. To prepare for the establishment of the frontier-free European Community

2. To develop the integrating role of tourism in order to create a 'People's Europe'

3. To stress the economic and social importance of tourism, in regional development and job creation

The specific themes of EYT, set by the Council of Ministers, were as follows:

● To promote greater knowledge among Community citizens of the cultures and lifestyles of other member states

● To encourage the staggering of holidays

● To develop new tourist destinations

● To create new forms of tourism and alternatives to mass tourism

● To promote intra-Community tourism, and to attract tourists to Europe from non-EC countries

Davidson (1992) reports that the EYT initiative suffered from a number of difficulties, not least a limited budget (of just over 8 million ECU) and insufficient time for planning and staff deployment. Despite these drawbacks, EYT achieved some notable successes, including the encouragement of closer links between those working in the highly fragmented tourism industry, the exchange of experience between member states, greater trans-national co-operation in the field of tourism, and highlighting the richness and diversity of the European tourism 'product'.

Community action plan to assist tourism

The Council of the European Communities decided in July 1992 that there should be Community-level action to strengthen tourism and to encourage co-operation between all the public and private sector operators in the industry. The Community action plan to assist tourism was to run for three years from 1 January 1993 with a budget of 18 million ECU. The Commission was required to report annually on the measures adopted.

The decision to develop the action plan emphasised the economic, environmental and cultural importance of tourism and the need to achieve more co-operation between public and private sectors in tourism affairs, at national, regional and local levels. The action plan included measures to strengthen the horizontal approach to tourism in EU and national policies, and to improve the quality and competitiveness of the tourism services on offer within EU member states.

The specific priority areas and associated measures included in the action plan were as follows.

1. Improving knowledge of the tourist industry and ensuring greater consistency of EU measures
   - Development of EU statistics on tourism
   - Detailed studies aimed at improving knowledge of tourism as an activity, assessment of the impact of Union policies to assist tourism, forward analysis of new types of tourism, and the preparation of strategies adapted to keep pace with demand
   - Consultation of tourism professionals with the EU

2. Staggering of holidays
   - Support for the establishment of an international framework whose purpose would be to exchange information and monitor the activities of governments and the tourist industry
   - Support for measures aimed at co-ordinating actions and strategies to encourage the use of tourism infrastructure and facilities outside the peak season

3. Transnational measures
   - Support for co-operation between border regions
   - Support for transnational initiatives contributing to the improvement of tourist information, in particular those using new technology
   - Development of tourist co-operation with Central and Eastern Europe and the Maghreb (countries of North Africa) through the transfer of know-how on training and the implementation of strategies for promotion, as well as on marketing and the creation of small and medium-sized tourist enterprises
   - Support for tourist and technical co-operation in the context of partnerships between towns
   - Support for pilot projects aimed at co-operation between the public and private sectors for the development of traditional tourist regions in decline as well as less developed rural regions

4. Tourists as consumers
   - Support for initiatives which improve the information of tourists and their protection, in areas such as existing classification systems, signposting symbols, timeshare arrangements, overbooking and procedures for redress

5. Cultural tourism
   - Support for initiatives to develop new European cultural tourism routes, in co-operation with the member states, regions and local authorities concerned, and to disseminate information on these routes by means of brochures and publications

- Support for the exchange of experience in the field of visitor management techniques
- Promotion and assistance in the use of European networks enabling tourist operators and cultural institutions to exchange experience, especially as regards highlighting the value of cultural heritage

6. Tourism and the environment

- Support for initiatives aimed at informing and increasing the awareness of tourists and suppliers of services about the interaction between tourism and the environment and in particular through the creation of a European environmental prize
- Support for innovative pilot projects to reconcile tourism and nature protection at local or regional level, in particular coastal and mountain areas, nature parks and reserves, for example by measures for the guidance of visitors
- Support for the development of networks involving transnational exchanges of experience, including experience of environmental problems and their possible solution through visitor management at sites
- Support for initiatives encouraging forms of environment-friendly tourism

7. Rural tourism

- Support for partnership initiatives between operators at local, regional, national or European level, to facilitate exchanges of experience and the transfer of good practice through the organisation of visits, seminars, exchanges of experts and the development of transnational pilot schemes, in particular in the field of vocational training
- Improved information for rural operators and better access for them to the various EU aid schemes available for rural tourism, in particular through the publication of documents for mass circulation and the publication of an operators' manual
- Encouragement for improving the quality of rural tourism supply and support for measures to facilitate access to tourism in a rural environment

8. Social tourism

- Shared information at EU level between public and private sector partners concerning the various methods used in the member states to encourage holiday-taking by certain categories of tourists
- Support for the co-ordination between member states of measures aimed at eliminating barriers to the development of tourism for the disabled, and for the exchange of information in this field

9. Youth tourism

- A feasibility study into establishing links between 'youth cards'
- Support for research into the need to create a network of exchanges with regard to 'European classes' (school travel for pupils from several member states)

10. Training

- Dissemination of information among young people on tourist resources and the profession

● Support for on-going measures to draw up professional profiles for the industry and improvement of mutual information on the qualifications attained in the various member states

● Encouragement of the participation of tourist businesses and their employees in existing EU training programmes and measures

● Support for transnational co-operation projects between universities, tourism schools, tourism professionals, or the authorities concerned, especially for training in the fields of rural, cultural and environmental tourism

● Support for networks aimed at improving the quality of vocational training so as to raise the quality of tourism services

11. Promotion in third countries

● Encouragement of measures confined to pilot projects to promote Europe as a destination in the markets of distant countries, particularly North America and Japan, whose growth is likely to have an impact on tourism with the European Union

The priorities set out in the 1993–96 action plan for tourism made it possible for DG XXIII, the Commission department responsible for tourism, to commission a series of pilot projects, particularly in the fields of rural, cultural and social tourism, vocational training and the environment. The outcomes of a selection of these projects are reviewed in a Commission report (European Commission, 1995a). The projects took place in a number of member states and encompassed a wide variety of tourism themes, for example cultural cruises in the Baltic Sea, Mozart itineraries in Europe, the potential of new technology in cultural tourism, European education and training in sustainable tourism management, the creation of a European tourism campus network and the familiarisation of young people in Greece with careers in tourism. The projects, although limited in their applicability to all sectors of the very diverse European tourism industry, nonetheless laid the foundation for further research and development concerning tourism in EU member states, which has begun with the creation of the philoxenia programme to assist European tourism.

Philoxenia programme to assist European tourism

In April 1996, the European Commission presented a proposal on a first multi-annual programme to assist European tourism to run for a period of four years from 1 January 1997. The proposal builds directly on the work of the 1993–96 Community action plan to assist tourism and acknowledges the growing interest in the economic, social and cultural importance of tourism shown by, among others, the European Parliament, the Economic and Social Committee and, more recently, the Committee of the Regions. The proposal has been given the unusual title of 'philoxenia', meaning the opposite of xenophobia, and considered by those working in the Commission to translate loosely as 'hospitality'. It integrates the results of the consultation on the Commission Green Paper on the role of the EU in the field of tourism (European Commission, 1995b), presented and discussed at the Forum on European Tourism on 8 December 1995.

The ultimate objective of the philoxenia programme is to stimulate the quality and competitiveness of European tourism, in order to contribute to growth and employment (European Commission, 1996b). To ensure a focused approach and coherent set of actions, this objective is sub-divided into four intermediate objectives and seven immediate objectives, as shown in Table 3.9.

Table 3.9: The 'philoxenia' programme model

Ultimate objective	Intermediate objectives	Immediate objectives	Actions
Stimulating quality and competitiveness of European tourism, in order to contribute to growth and employment	A. Improving knowledge in the field of tourism	1. Developing tourism related information	● European statistical system for tourism ● Surveys, studies and desk/field analysis
		2. Pooling tourism information from other sources	● European research and documentation network on tourism
		3. Facilitating the assessment of Community measures affecting tourism	● Establishment of a legal and financial watch
	B. Improving the legislative and financial environment for tourism	1. Reinforcing cooperation with Member States, the industry and other stakeholders	● Organisation and follow up of regular meetings (technical/thematic meetings, round tables, European fora)
	C. Raising quality in European tourism	1. Promoting sustainable tourism	● Local initiatives network ● Environmentally friendly management systems ● European Prize
		2. Removing obstacles to tourism development	● Identification of obstacles and development of appropriate responses
	D. Increasing the number of tourists from third countries	1. Promoting Europe as a tourist destination	● Support for multi-annual promotion campaigns

As the table indicates, the philoxenia programme has, within its overall aim, four intermediate objectives, namely:

● Improving knowledge in the field of tourism

● Improving the legislative and financial environment for tourism

● Raising quality in European tourism

● Increasing the number of tourists from third countries

Each of these has associated immediate objectives and related actions, as described in Table 3.9. If we look at intermediate objective C, 'raising quality in European tourism', for example, its first immediate objective is the promotion of sustainable tourism. The actions necessary to achieve this objective are:

1. Support for a network of local initiatives geared towards sound tourism management

2. Support for the implementation of environmentally friendly management systems in tourist accommodation

3. Organisation of a European prize for tourism and the environment (every two years)

Other corresponding actions within the programme are shown in Table 3.9.

To date, the philoxenia programme has yet to be approved. Consideration of the proposal formed part of the inter-governmental conference in 1996, at which, along with other EU matters, the Council of Ministers considered the future role of the Union in the field of tourism.

EU measures with indirect effects on tourism

In addition to direct measures affecting tourism in member states, there are many EU measures, actions and directives that have an indirect effect on tourism and travel, to a greater or lesser extent. The most important of these include the following:

- *The single market.* The creation of the single market in Europe from 1 January 1993 was designed to provide an area without internal frontiers in which the free movement of goods, persons and services was ensured. As such, the single market established a favourable environment for the growth of trade likely to promote intra-Union tourism and encourage the emergence of a single tourist destination for tourists from outside the EU.

- *Border controls between EU member states.* Article 7a of the EC Treaty on the establishment of the internal market provides for the abolition of controls at the frontiers of member states on the movement of goods, services, capital and persons, thereby facilitating travel.

- *Consumer protection.* EU directives on such matters as package travel regulations, distance selling, fire safety in hotels, timeshare, bathing water quality and accommodation grading, all seek to provide the travelling public with physical and financial protection when things go wrong.

- *Duty-free and duty-paid goods.* Initial Commission proposals to abolish customs limits for goods bought in EU countries have proved contentious. Instead, duty-free allowances have been steadily increased. Since duty-free sales are an important source of revenue for carriers, their abolition is being resisted.

- *Liberalisation of air travel.* The adoption of the EU measures on airline deregulation, scheduled for completion in 1997, is designed to create a 'level playing field' for competition throughout the Union. This is likely to lead to a more flexible system of tariff zones, increases in the use of regional airports and, potentially, lower air fares.

- *Structural funds.* These funds make a significant contribution to the development of tourism in the EU and seek to achieve the objectives of economic and social cohesion. Aid is concentrated on the under-developed regions of the Union (Objective 1), those affected by the decline of industry (Objective 2) and those concerned with rural development (Objective 5b). These regions are defined as priority areas for the application of the structural funds (EAGGF – European Agricultural Guarantee and Guidance Fund; ESF – European Social Fund; ERDF – European Regional Development Fund).

As well as these measures that impact indirectly on tourism, there are many other EU initiatives relating to regeneration that may include tourism within their scope, e.g.

LEADER, REGIS, RECHAR, RESIDER, KONVER and PESCA. There are also a number of education and training programmes where tourism-related projects may be eligible, principally LEONARDO and SOCRATES.

Future issues concerning tourism in Europe

There is little doubt that Europe's share of the international tourism market is likely to continue to decrease in the short term. Europe's response to the growth of high quality tourism products in other world regions is often characterised by a lower quality product offered at a higher price in an indifferent manner. A number of problems relating to product quality and service standards require both immediate and longer-term action, if market share is to be regained. Europe's problems with regard to tourism development and promotion have been caused by a variety of factors, including:

● Insufficient investment in infrastructure
● Ineffective co-ordination of the highly fragmented tourism industry
● Complacency on the part of private and public sector tourism organisations
● Lack of recognition within governments of the importance of the tourism industry
● Insufficient investment in training
● Limited use of strategic planning in tourism development
● Lax development controls leading to negative environmental and socio-cultural impacts

The question that must be addressed by all organisations and individuals with an interest in the future of European tourism is 'how can the industry stem the reduction in its share of the international tourism market?'. There is little doubt that the conditions for the growth of tourism on a global scale are increasingly favourable; higher levels of education, longer holiday entitlements, an ageing population, greater access to new technology, advances in transportation and deregulation within global markets, to name but a few, all point to growth in world tourist arrivals and receipts in the short and medium term. In order to compete effectively with the emerging tourism regions of the world, the European tourism industry must:

● Adopt a public/private sector partnership approach to development and marketing
● Develop high quality products targeted at identifiable market segments
● Place greater emphasis on strategic planning issues in order to reduce the harmful environmental and socio-cultural aspects of tourism
● Increase public sector investment so as to ensure a co-ordinated approach to destination development and promotion
● Provide greater opportunities for training
● Support the large number of small and medium-sized enterprises (SMEs) operating in the European tourism industry
● Raise the profile of the industry locally, regionally, nationally and internationally

The future enlargement of the European Union will focus more attention on *its* role in the development and encouragement of tourism. However, the highly fragmented nature of the industry and its domination by private sector enterprises are likely to mean that the EU's influence on tourism will remain at the strategic level, concentrating on issues such as consumer protection, sustainable development and reinforcing co-operation between EU member states and industry sectors.

Chapter summary

This chapter has highlighted the increasingly competitive business environment that the European tourism industry finds itself in at the end of the twentieth century and the dawning of the new millennium. We have seen that Europe's share of world tourist arrivals has declined steadily since the 1960s and World Tourism Organisation forecasts suggest that this declining trend is set to continue into the near future. Many tourism destination countries, such as those in south Asia, the Pacific Rim and the Americas, are gaining market share of international tourist arrivals by offering top quality infrastructure, products and facilities for tourists. We have investigated the recent political and economic developments in Europe and their impact on tourism development, considering both east–west and west–east tourist movements. With the help of case studies, the chapter has highlighted the complex structure of the European tourism industry and the diversity of its component sectors. Finally, the chapter has addressed the issue of the future of European tourism, suggesting that there are many short- and long-term improvements to both product and service quality that need urgent attention.

Discussion questions

1. What do you consider to be the three most important steps that the European tourism industry must take to help stem the decline in its share of international tourism?

2. Is the geographical diversity of Europe a help or a hindrance in terms of developing a successful tourism sector?

3. Critically assess the role of the European Union in the field of tourism.

4. How should the European Union best advance the cause of tourism as a force for economic and social cohesion?

References and further reading

● Davidson, R (1992) *Tourism in Europe*, Pitman, London
● European Commission (1993) *Tourism Customers in Central and Eastern Europe: Perspectives of Development*, EC, Brussels
● European Commission (1994) *Background Report – Tourism Policy in the EU*, EC, Brussels
● European Commission (1995a) *Community Action Plan to Assist Tourism – Sample Studies and Pilot Projects*, DG XXIII, EC, Brussels
● European Commission (1995b) *The Role of the European Union in the Field of Tourism – Commission Green Paper*, EC, Brussels
● European Commission (1996a) *COM (96) 29 Final*, EC, Brussels
● European Commission (1996b) *COM (96) 168 Final*, EC, Brussels
● European Travel Commission (1996) *Annual Report 1995*, ETC, Brussels
● Eurostat (1996) *Tourism in the European Union: Key Figures 1994–1995*, Eurostat, Brussels/ Luxembourg

- Hall, D (ed.) (1991) *Tourism and Economic Development in Eastern Europe and the Soviet Union*, John Wiley & Sons
- International Air Transport Association (1996) *European Traffic Forecasts 1980–2010*, IATA, Geneva
- OECD (1994) *Tourism Policy and International Tourism in OECD Member Countries*, OECD, Paris
- Pompl, W and Lavery, P (1993) *Tourism in Europe: Structures and Developments*, CAB International, Wallingford, UK
- Williams, A and Shaw, G (1991) *Tourism and Economic Development – Western European Experiences*, Belhaven Press, London
- World Tourism Organisation (1995) *Tourism in 1994 – Highlights*, WTO, Madrid
- World Tourism Organisation (1996a) *International Tourism Overview 1995*, WTO, Madrid
- World Tourism Organisation (1996b) *Tourism Market Trends*, WTO, Madrid
- World Tourism Organisation (1997) *International Tourism Overview 1996*, WTO, Madrid

Chapter Four

Tourism in the United Kingdom

Chapter Overview

This chapter investigates the historical development and significance of the tourism industry in the UK economy, drawing on national statistics and industry data to explore current issues of concern. We consider the principal components of the UK tourism industry and how they interact, within the public, private and not-for-profit sectors. The particular role of public sector organisations involved in UK tourism is considered in detail, highlighting the function of the tourist boards and local authorities in tourism development. The chapter concludes with an appraisal of the key issues facing the future of the UK tourism industry in the short- and long-term.

Key Topics

- Historical development of UK tourism
- Significance of the UK tourism industry
- Structure of the industry
- Analysis of industry sectors
- Public sector tourism
- Future issues for the UK tourism industry

Introduction

British people often demonstrate an ambivalent attitude towards tourism. On the one hand the British have always been great world travellers; indeed many of the milestones in global tourism development are the result of the sterling efforts of UK pioneers (see Figure 4.1). On the other hand, British people have always been slow to recognise that tourism is an important, mainstream industry in its own right, contributing significantly to the UK economy and helping to portray a positive image of the country around the world. To many, it is still regarded as a 'candy floss' industry, even though the total value of tourism to the UK economy was nearly £38 billion in 1995 (British Tourist Authority, 1996a).

Figure 4.1: Milestones in the development of UK tourism

1752 Dr Richard Russell published *Concerning the Use of Sea Water*, leading to a rise in the popularity of UK seaside resorts
1830 Introduction of the railways
1841 Thomas Cook organised his first excursion from Leicester to Loughborough
1851 Tours were organised to the Great Exhibition in London
1866 Cook organised his first excursion to America
1871 The Bank Holiday Act created four public holidays per year
1901 The Factory Act gave women and young people six days' holiday per year
1903 'Trust Houses' opened a chain of hotels in Britain
1936 The first UK holiday camp was opened by Billy Butlin at Skegness
1938 Introduction of the Holidays with Pay Act
1949 First overseas 'package holiday' by air offered by Vladimir Raitz of Horizon
1965 Lord Thomson took the first step towards the creation of the Thomson Travel Group
1969 Development of Tourism Act established the English, Wales and Scottish Tourist Boards, plus the British Tourist Authority (BTA)
1970 Introduction of the Boeing 747 'jumbo jet'
1974 The UK's number one tour operator Clarksons went into liquidation
1986 The number of UK package holidaymakers topped 10 million for the first time
1991 The Intasun holiday company ceased trading
1992 Department of National Heritage created
1994 Channel Tunnel opened
1995 A record 24 million overseas visitors came to Britain, spending more than £12 billion

This chapter gives an overview of the significance and structure of the UK tourism industry, starting with an appreciation of its historical development and concluding with an analysis of future issues and trends. It includes a number of case studies that demonstrate the importance of the various sectors of the tourism industry.

The historical development of UK tourism

Throughout history, people have travelled across Britain for purposes of trade, education and religion and to fight in battles. It was not until the eighteenth century, however, that the foundations of what we now regard as the British tourist industry began to be laid. Spa towns such as Cheltenham, Leamington Spa and Buxton were frequented by the wealthy classes who came to sample the health-giving properties of the saline waters. Seaside resorts, including Brighton, Margate and Blackpool, grew in popularity, helped by the introduction of the railways from the mid-nineteenth century onwards; the first passenger train service was opened in 1830 between Manchester and Liverpool. There followed a massive expansion of the rail network, principally to service industrial centres, but with the capacity to bring many of Britain's seaside resorts within easy reach of the centres of population; Brighton was a notable success with some 132 000 visitors recorded on Easter Monday in 1862.

The Industrial Revolution, which had been the catalyst for the development of the railways, also led to improvements in the road and canal networks in the UK. What the Industrial Revolution also began was the desire for workers to escape from their normal harsh routines and often dirty environments, in favour of relaxation and entertainment in the relative purity of the countryside and coast.

The 1938 Holidays with Pay Act gave a stimulus to mass tourism in the UK, with 80 per cent of workers being entitled to paid holidays by 1945. Holiday camps flourished immediately before the outbreak of the Second World War, the first having been opened by Billy Butlin in 1936 at Skegness. Two years later, there were around 200 camps offering self-contained 'package' holidays to 30 000 people per week. In the early 1950s, two-thirds of all domestic holidays were taken at the seaside and the majority of holidaymakers travelled to their destinations by coach or train. The late 1950s saw the establishment of the British Travel Association, forerunner to the British Tourist Authority (BTA), which was given the role of encouraging the development of hotels and resorts.

The 1960s can be chronicled as the time when UK tourism came of age. The government passed the Development of Tourism Act in 1969, establishing the English, Wales and Scottish Tourist Boards, plus the British Tourist Authority, which was charged with promoting the whole of Britain to overseas visitors. Three important elements of post-Second World War society in the UK, namely the development of jet aircraft, the growth of the overseas 'package tour' and increasing car ownership, were to have far-reaching implications on the UK domestic tourism scene.

Jet aircraft and the overseas package tour

We saw in Chapter 1 that advances in aircraft technology during the Second World War provided the stimulus for the development of overseas package holidays from the 1950s onwards. The pioneering work of Vladimir Raitz of Horizon Holidays in the early 1950s was to have far-reaching implications on the international and domestic tourism scene for many years to come. From these humble beginnings, the package holiday industry attracted more travel entrepreneurs who helped it grow steadily in the 1960s, 1970s and 1980s, to the position in 1994 of a total of 15.1 million overseas holidays sold to British tourists (see Figure 4.2).

In the face of this strong competition from ex-UK tour operators and overseas holiday destinations, the domestic tourism industry in Britain has seen a fall in its share of long holidays taken by British people, although the growth of short breaks in the UK is a continuing success story.

Increasing car ownership

The increase in car ownership after the Second World War provided individuals with greater freedom and flexibility in the use of their leisure time. People travelled further afield, exploring new areas of the British coast and countryside. The number of private cars on the roads of Britain rose steeply from 2.3 million in 1950 to 11 million in 1970. In 1997, the figure exceeded 21 million vehicles. Although this rise in car ownership has brought undoubted benefits to individuals and their families, it has highlighted a number of issues of concern. Firstly, the upward trend in the ownership of cars has resulted in a drop in demand for traditional types of public transport. According to figures published in *Insights* (English Tourist Board, 1993), the use of trains for holiday travel fell from 48 per cent of all journeys in 1951 to just 8 per cent in 1990. Statistics for coach travel for the same time period show a similar trend, with a drop from 28 per cent in 1951 to 9 per cent in 1990. This fall in demand for train and coach travel has led to cuts in services and, in the case of the railways, the closure of unprofitable lines. Those living in the remoter rural areas of Britain have been particularly affected by these service reductions and the loss of choice in their travel arrangements.

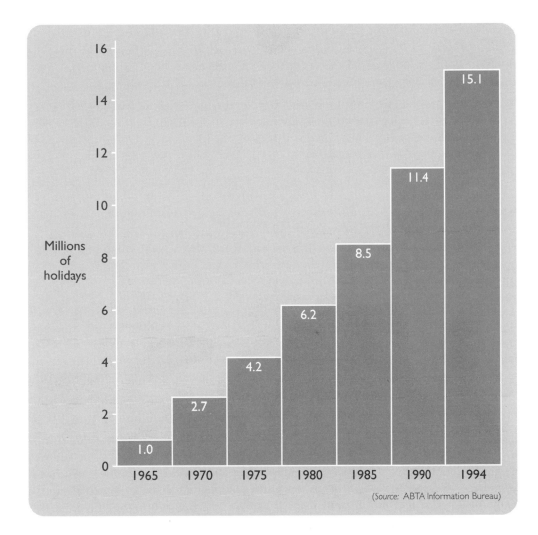

Figure 4.2: Growth in package tours taken by UK residents

Millions of holidays

1965 — 1.0
1970 — 2.7
1975 — 4.2
1980 — 6.2
1985 — 8.5
1990 — 11.4
1994 — 15.1

(Source: ABTA Information Bureau)

A second consequence of the growth in car ownership in the UK has been the rise in associated environmental problems, including pollution, congestion and the loss of land to further road building. These problems are particularly acute in many of Britain's historic cities and most scenic countryside areas. In many National Parks and Areas of Outstanding Natural Beauty, for example, the volume of cars is having a detrimental effect on the landscapes and wildlife habitats, often spoiling what the visitors have come to see and enjoy. These problems have led to calls for cars to be banned from some areas or for their use to be strictly controlled. Popular historic cities, including Canterbury, Cambridge and York, have introduced measures such as 'park and ride' schemes, cycle hire and pricing mechanisms to help alleviate the problems. Managers in the Peak District National Park encourage the use of public transport by working in partnership with local bus and train operators.

The significance of the UK tourism industry

Tourism is one of Britain's leading industries, worth nearly £38 billion to the UK economy (British Tourist Authority, 1996a), categorised as follows:

- £12 775 million (34 per cent) – UK residents staying overnight
- £12 092 million (32 per cent) – overseas visitors in the UK
- £10 056 million (26 per cent) – UK residents on day trips
- £3025 million (8 per cent) – overseas visitors' fares to UK carriers

UK tourism provides jobs for 1.5 million people, 6 per cent of all jobs in the country, and accounts for 5 per cent of gross domestic product (GDP). Quite apart from these economic benefits that tourism brings, it has an important social role to play in rural communities, plays a vital part in urban regeneration and contributes to regional prosperity. As such, tourism plays a major part in enhancing the image of towns, cities and villages throughout Britain, thereby helping to sustain its prominent role in world affairs.

Tourism's contribution to wealth creation

The UK tourism industry generates income and wealth for a wide range of individuals and institutions, including local authorities, companies, private shareholders, voluntary bodies and national governments. At the international level, tourism makes an important contribution to the UK balance of payments, where it is regarded as an 'invisible' item, together with such items as banking, shipping and insurance. In 1994, tourism accounted for just under one-third of all UK service industry exports (British Tourist Authority/ English Tourist Board, 1996). An analysis of the value of UK tourism compared with other leading exports shows that it generates more revenue than, for example, textiles and petroleum products, and has an export value of approximately half that of the UK chemicals industry.

At the local level, the revenue generated by tourism is boosted by an important concept known as the multiplier effect. Research has shown that the amount spent by visitors to an area is recirculated in the local economy and is actually worth more than its face value. For example, £100 spent by visitors staying at a hotel in a small, market town could be worth £100 × 1.3 (the hotel multiplier for that area), i.e. a total of £130. In this example, 1.3 is merely an illustration, since the multiplier effect varies between different parts of the country and different industry sectors (see Chapter 5 for a more detailed explanation of the multiplier concept).

The importance of overseas visitors to Britain

In spite of increased competition from other global destinations and recent periods of world recession, Britain has been very successful in attracting growing numbers of overseas visitors. As Figure 4.3 shows, a record number of 24 million tourists visited Britain in 1995.

Total earnings from overseas tourists to Britain have also risen steadily over the same period (see Table 4.1).

As well as contributing vital income to Britain's balance of payments, overseas visitors also bring a variety of other benefits, for example:

- An influx of tourists to an area helps create or sustain jobs, thus increasing the wage-earners' spending in the locality and leading to an improved local economy.
- The money spent on accommodation, food, transport, entertainment, attractions and leisure facilities creates profits that are used to generate more business for companies.
- The government benefits from incoming tourism since overseas visitors pay VAT and other taxes on a range of products and services including liquor, tobacco, petrol, accommodation and souvenirs.

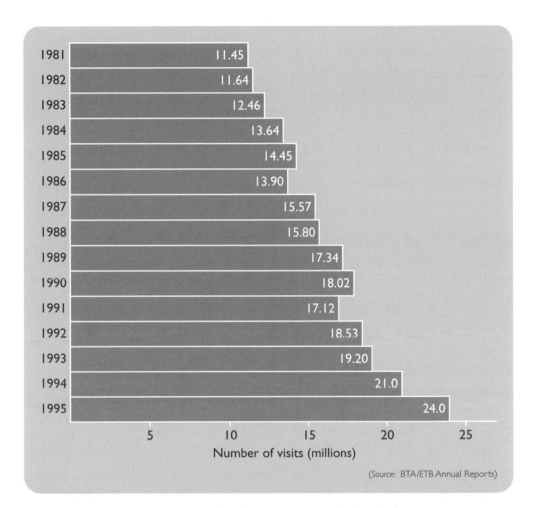

Number of visits (millions)

(*Source:* BTA/ETB Annual Reports)

Table 4.1:
Spending by
overseas visitors
to Britain,
1981–95

Year	Total spending (£m)
1981	2 970
1982	3 188
1983	4 003
1984	4 614
1985	5 442
1986	5 553
1987	6 260
1988	6 184
1989	6 945
1990	7 748
1991	7 386
1992	7 891
1993	9 354
1994	9 919
1995	12 092

Sources: BTA/ETB Annual Reports; BTA National Facts of Tourism

- Overseas visitors' spending on facilities such as public transport and leisure facilities can help to keep costs down for local people, who may also benefit from a greater range of facilities provided for both tourists and residents alike.

- Income from overseas visitors can be channelled into improvements to the local environment, thus improving the quality of life for everyone.

- British theatres and the arts in general benefit from spending by tourists from overseas.

- Income from overseas visitors may help to preserve historic buildings and conserve areas of special environmental significance.

- An international reputation for cultural and sporting events can be maintained if large numbers of visitors are attracted from overseas.

Employment in UK tourism

Tourism's ability to create jobs is one of its main economic benefits and often the principal reason why public sector bodies invest in UK tourism. Data from the *Tourism Intelligence Quarterly* (British Tourist Authority/English Tourist Board, 1996) shows that employment in tourism-related industries in Britain in September 1995 stood at a total of 1 545 300, classified as follows:

- Pubs, bars, night clubs and licensed clubs   389 300
- Hotels and other tourist accommodation   340 900
- Restaurants, cafés and snack bars   338 200
- Sports and other recreational activities   318 300
- Libraries, museums and other cultural activities   83 900
- Travel agencies and tour operators   74 900

Employment in these categories, plus those self-employed in tourism, accounted for some 6 per cent of all the employed labour force in the UK. The World Travel and Tourism Council, using a broader definition of the tourism industry, estimates that employment resulting from UK travel and tourism is expected to total 3.03 million or 11.7 per cent of the UK workforce in 1996, rising to 3.34 million workers (12.2 per cent of the workforce) by 2006 (World Travel and Tourism Council, 1996). It is estimated that for every one direct job in the UK tourism industry, half of an indirect job is created elsewhere in the economy (British Tourist Authority/English Tourist Board, 1996). This can be illustrated if we consider a holiday taken by a family in a caravan at a UK seaside resort. Apart from the direct beneficiaries of the holiday, for example the caravan site owner, other firms not directly associated with tourism will benefit, for example petrol stations, shops, trades people and banks.

The structure of UK tourism

The tourism industry in the UK has a complex structure with many fragmented sectors, providing products, services and facilities for both leisure and business travellers. Everything from high street travel agencies, coach operators and tourist attractions to hoteliers, tourist boards and car hire companies strive to serve the needs of both domestic and overseas tourists. Tourism in Britain is sustained by many thousands of small businesses, a smaller number of large, well-known companies and a host of central and local government bodies that assist the industry at European, national, regional and local levels.

The most common approach to considering the structure of the UK tourism industry is to identify its constituent industry sectors, such as tourist boards, tour operators, airlines and accommodation providers, and to comment on the functions of each and the role it plays in the industry as a whole. Such an approach, however, fails to understand the underlying motivations and objectives of the various organisations within the industry sectors. Is a tourist attraction, for example, merely in business to make a profit for its owners or does it have a wider social or community aim? The next part of this chapter explores the differing objectives of private, public and voluntary sector tourism providers, before going on to analyse in detail the major industry sectors found in UK tourism.

Classification of UK tourism by organisational objectives

The setting of objectives or goals is an essential discipline for the success of all organisations working in the UK tourism industry. Objectives provide a framework within which all the organisation's human, physical and financial resources can be used to best effect. Objectives for individual organisations will be very diverse and will reflect the philosophy of the owners or managers, the size of the organisation, its stage of development and whether it is in the commercial or non-commercial sector of the tourism industry. The objectives will be developed and refined by all those who have an interest in the organisation. Sometimes known as 'stakeholders', they may include:

- Customers
- Owners
- Managers
- Staff
- Shareholders
- Local councillors
- Members (of a club or association)
- Local people
- Society in general

Customers will naturally be concerned about the quality of the experience they receive from the tourism provider and whether they think the organisation gives value for money. Owners and managers will be keen to ensure that the objectives are realistic and achievable and provide a reward for their effort, skill and management expertise. Staff will expect good conditions of employment and future prospects in terms of promotion and the growth, or otherwise, of the organisation. Shareholders will be looking to the owners and/or managers to provide them with a growing return on the capital they have invested in the organisation. Local councillors, representing the local community, will be keen to see that public facilities are being used to the maximum, objectives are being achieved and public funds are being wisely deployed. The members of a club or association will want to be actively involved in setting objectives and helping to achieve them. Society in general has, to a greater or lesser extent, a stake in the aims and objectives of tourism organisations. The benefits of faster travel, instant entertainment and access to a wealth of activities and facilities, for example, need to be balanced against society's wider concerns, including social and environmental exploitation, problems of congestion and cultural changes to areas exposed to tourist development.

Commercial objectives

The UK tourism industry is dominated by private sector organisations whose aims are primarily commercial. Some of the best-known names in the industry are private companies, for example British Airways, Center Parcs, Thomas Cook, Swallow Hotels, Thomson Holidays and Alton Towers, to name but a few. The private sector of the UK tourism industry consists of large and small organisations owned by individuals or groups of people whose primary aim is to make a profit. Many members of the general public invest in these organisations, relying on the profits generated by commercial tourism companies for a part of their income. Profit maximisation is an important objective for any commercial tourism provider, since it helps provide the capital for future business expansion, thereby enabling staff and management to respond better to the needs of customers by providing the products and services they will buy.

Although profit maximisation is the primary objective of the majority of private sector companies, it is by no means the only objective of all commercial tourism organisations. A lot of small businesses in the UK tourism industry are run by people who used to work for larger companies, but became frustrated with the high level of bureaucracy they encountered. Such people value the greater degree of control over their business affairs that self-employment can offer and thrive on making their own decisions. The operators of some tourism companies may not seek to maximise profits to the full, but may be content with a level of profit that gives them the type of lifestyle they are happy with; after all, why work in an industry concerned with holidays and travel and have no time to enjoy yourself and have fun!

In addition to their revenue maximisation objectives, even the biggest UK tourism companies have a variety of related aims. British Airways, for example, is committed to being '. . . *the best and most successful company in the airline industry*' (British Airways, 1993). To help achieve this mission, the company has identified seven detailed objectives, which BA calls goals, that it hopes to fulfil in order to achieve its mission. These are:

1. *Safe and secure* – to be a safe and secure airline.
2. *Financially strong* – to deliver a strong and consistent financial performance.
3. *Global leader* – to secure a leading share of the air travel business worldwide with a significant presence in all major geographical markets.
4. *Service and value* – to provide overall superior service and good value for money in every market segment in which it competes.
5. *Customer driven* – to excel in anticipating and quickly responding to customer needs and competitor activity.
6. *Good employer* – to sustain a working environment that attracts, retains and develops committed employees who share in the success of the company.
7. *Good neighbour* – to be a good neighbour, concerned for the community and the environment.

Clearly, financial strength is of prime importance to British Airways, but these stated objectives make it clear that attention to company finances alone will not achieve its global mission.

Non-commercial objectives

Non-commercial tourism organisations, falling within the public or voluntary sectors of the UK economy, do not usually have profit maximisation as their primary objective. It may be that they have been developed with wider social or community objectives in mind; the principal aim of a tourist attraction developed at the site of an archaeological dig, for example, may well be to provide an educational and recreational experience for the benefit of local people. There are many examples of organisations working in the UK tourism industry that have non-commercial objectives. Local authorities play a major role in the provision of infrastructure and facilities for tourists, as well as marketing their particular areas both home and abroad (see the sub-section towards the and of this chapter for more on the role of local authorities in UK tourism). National, regional and local tourist boards exist to encourage tourists and help their members provide high quality products and services to visitors (see British Tourist Authority case study below).

Charitable trusts working in tourism range from small, localised groups who may be protecting an endangered natural resource, to large organisations such as the National Trust, which protects more than 600 000 acres of coastline, hills and woodland in England, Wales and Northern Ireland and welcomes more than 11 million visitors every year to its 400 buildings and gardens open to the public.

Although profit maximisation is not the primary objective of non-commercial organisations operating in the UK tourism industry, those which are part of local government or are agencies of central government are expected to offer value for money and meet targets and agreed performance criteria. Many local authorities have recruited staff from the private sector and have implemented private sector management practices in order to help achieve their objectives. Similarly, all charitable trusts and voluntary groups will aim to keep their costs to a minimum while striving for their wider social or community objectives. The following case study on the work of the British Tourist Authority is a good example of a publicly funded organisation that has a range of commercial and non-commercial objectives.

Case Study: British Tourist Authority

The British Tourist Authority (BTA) works in the non-commercial sector of UK tourism and is responsible for promoting Britain as a tourist destination overseas. Its central role is to help maximise the contribution that incoming tourism can make to the British economy. It was established under the 1969 Development of Tourism Act, together with the Wales, English and Scottish Tourist Boards; the Northern Ireland Tourist Board was set up in 1948. Unlike the national tourist boards, which are charged with encouraging tourism to their own particular country, the BTA is responsible for promoting the whole of Britain to overseas visitors.

The work of the BTA

BTA's objectives are:

- To maximise the benefit to the economy of tourism to Britain from abroad while working worldwide in partnership with the private and public sector organisations involved in the industry and the English Tourist Board, Scottish Tourist Board and Wales Tourist Board.
- To identify the requirements of visitors to Britain, whatever their origin, and to stimulate the improvement of the quality of the product and the use of technology to meet them.
- To spread the economic benefit of tourism to Britain more widely and particularly to areas with tourism potential and higher than average levels of unemployment.
- To encourage tourism to Britain in off-peak periods.
- To ensure that the Authority makes the most cost-effective use of resources in pursuing its objectives.

In order to meet these objectives, BTA undertakes a wide-ranging programme of market research and product promotion in the major countries of the world. In many respects it acts as the overseas arm of the national tourist boards, gathering market intelligence via its network of overseas offices and representatives. This market intelligence is fed back to the home tourist boards which help generate new products and services to meet the needs of overseas visitors, through liaison with commercial operators and local authorities. Recent BTA initiatives have included the 1995 Festival of Arts and Culture, which helped cement the relationship between tourism and the arts, campaigns to exploit the potential of the Channel Tunnel for incoming tourism, promotion of UK golfing holidays to the Spanish, and joint marketing activities with Belgian travel companies. The BTA has piloted a number of innovative ▷

British Tourist Authority continued

approaches to information dissemination, including a CD-ROM guide to London, Internet services and a fax-back initiative launched in Japan, Australia and the USA. This system enables consumers and the travel trade to request information about Britain 24 hours a day by automatic fax transmission.

BTA's structure and operation

As well as co-operating closely with the British national and regional tourist boards, the BTA also has extensive networks with the overseas travel trade, media and overseas residents interested in visiting Britain, as shown in Figure 4.4.

In addition to running the British Travel Centre in London, BTA operates a network of 40 overseas outlets worldwide, which act as information points for potential visitors to Britain and pass on information about the market from that particular country to the BTA's headquarters in London.

BTA plays an important role in highlighting areas of concern to the tourism industry, such as Britain's comparatively high VAT rate, which has to be passed on to the consumer, and likely effects of the European Package Travel and Distance Selling Directives on UK tourism. It also acts as a catalyst and co-ordinator for the fragmented private sector in UK tourism, helping to develop new partnership arrangements between the commercial and public sectors of the industry.

BTA's principal source of funding is via grant-in-aid from the government. For the year ended 31 March 1995, this amounted to £33.2 million, with a further £15 million generated from other commercial activities, such as selling advertising and space at overseas exhibitions. A record 21 million overseas tourists visited Britain in 1994, injecting over £9.9 billion of additional revenue into the economy, a 6 per cent increase on the previous year (British Tourist Authority, 1996b). According to independent research commissioned by the BTA, £757 million of this was directly attributable to BTA's activities, which when compared to the £33 million grant-in-aid figure, equates to a return of £23 generated for every £1 of public funds spent (British Tourist Authority, 1996b).

(*Information courtesy of the BTA*)

Figure 4.4: BTA networking

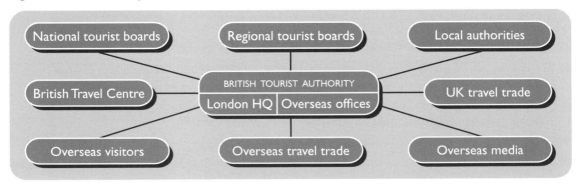

Discussion points and essay questions

1. Consider the value of the role played by the BTA in competing for international tourists.
2. Discuss the influence that the BTA has on the range of tourism products on offer in Britain.
3. What impact is new technology likely to have on the future work of the BTA?
4. What is the justification for spending government money on funding the BTA?

Classification of UK tourism by industry sectors

Having considered the underlying aims and objectives of commercial and non-commercial organisations in UK tourism, we will now investigate the importance of the various sectors of the industry. The way that the major components of the UK tourist industry interact is shown in Figure 4.5.

As Figure 4.5 shows, the UK tourism industry has four core elements, namely destinations, transportation, accommodation and attractions, provided by a variety of commercial and non-commercial organisations. Tourist destinations, whether town, coast or countryside, are the end point of a traveller's journey. Having travelled to the destination by any one of a number of transportation modes, the tourist will need somewhere to stay and something to do. A wide range of accommodation providers will aim to satisfy the first of these requirements, while natural and man-made attractions will offer the tourist entertainment during his or her stay. It is important to remember that these core components are not necessarily mutually exclusive, for example the many attractions offered by a seaside resort such as Blackpool serve to promote the town as a destination in its own right, and vice versa. Similarly, the Alton Towers attraction offers its visitors the chance to stay overnight in its own themed hotel.

Figure 4.5 also demonstrates that these core elements are made available to tourists through three principal distribution channels, i.e. direct to the public and through intermediaries such as travel agents and tour operators. The bulk of UK tourism products are sold direct to the public, for example holidays in hotels, day visits to attractions and coach tours. Large hotel chains, however, do sell through travel agents and negotiate special rates with coach companies and other tour operators. Short breaks to British cities are also sold through travel agents by companies such as Superbreak and Rainbow Holidays. The majority of UK-based tour operators and travel agents, however, specialise in selling overseas holidays to British residents rather than UK holidays.

The non-commercial providers shown in Figure 4.5 include a range of local and national public sector agencies that promote facilities for tourists, while at the same time providing the infrastructure and regulatory framework within which commercial tourist companies operate. The role of public sector tourism is discussed further later in this chapter.

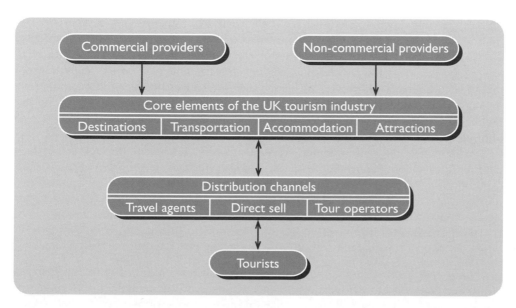

Figure 4.5: The structure of the UK tourism industry

Destinations

Destinations often provide the motivating force for travel and act as a focus for the many components of the UK tourism industry. If we consider the example of a retired couple who read an article in a Sunday newspaper about short breaks in the Scottish islands, it is likely to be the image of the destination itself which initially captures their imagination, but they will depend on a wide range of tourism providers to meet their needs and provide them with a memorable experience, for example a means of travel, somewhere to stay, places to eat, attractions and entertainment while in Scotland. Attracting visitors to destinations is a very competitive business; a browse through the travel pages of any newspaper or magazine will provide evidence of this. Places as far apart as Buxton and Bournemouth, Cardiff and Canterbury, and the Lake District and Dartmoor, are all competing to win a slice of total spending by UK and overseas visitors. The economic benefits of tourism are clearly of interest to a wide range of national, regional and local destinations.

Destinations sometimes pose a dilemma to those studying UK tourism, since there is no clear definition of what actually constitutes a 'destination'. It is possible to argue that the whole of the UK is a destination, particularly to those travelling from overseas. Individual countries in the UK, and identifiable regions within them, are also destinations, as are towns, cities, seaside resorts, areas of great landscape beauty and major tourist attractions. A further difficulty concerning destinations and their role in UK tourism revolves around ownership and control. The great majority of accommodation, attractions and entertainments found in resort areas are provided by private sector operators, whereas the agencies responsible for promoting destinations are invariably public sector bodies, for example local authority tourism departments and national tourist boards. Historically, this has meant that those given the task of marketing an area have had little control over the quality of the tourism products and standards of service on offer to visitors. This situation is gradually changing, with some tourist boards and local councils only agreeing to work with private sector enterprises that have been inspected and approved.

Transportation

Any discussion concerning the development of UK tourism will invariably necessitate a detailed analysis of transportation, since the tourism industry is fundamentally concerned with the movement of people, whether for leisure or business purposes. The provision of safe, reliable, comfortable, fast, convenient and accessible modes of transportation, plus an adequate transport infrastructure, are prerequisites for successful tourism development. The bulk of transport services in UK tourism are provided by private sector operators, including ferry companies, airlines and car hire companies. Many transport infrastructure projects, however, are public sector initiatives, for example road improvements, bridge building and airport developments. Increasingly, we are seeing private/public partnership arrangements in transport infrastructure projects in the UK, for example the high speed rail link to the Channel Tunnel.

Transportation plays an important economic role in UK tourism, through employment and wealth creation. Figures quoted in the *Tourism Intelligence Quarterly* (British Tourist Authority/English Tourist Board, 1996) show that travel within the UK accounted for 8 per cent and 17 per cent of total tourist expenditure by overseas and domestic visitors respectively in 1994, totalling more than £3 billion for both categories of tourist.

Transportation for UK tourists and overseas visitors to Britain can be divided into surface, sea and air travel, each with its own distinctive characteristics and structure.

Surface transport   Surface transport, or land transport, includes travel by road and rail. Road transport in UK tourism is dominated by the private motor car, with more than three-quarters of all long holidays in Britain using this mode of transport in 1995 (British

Tourist Authority/English Tourist Board, 1996). Other less widely used types of surface transport for tourism were bus and coach services (13 per cent) and train (7 per cent). Increasing car ownership and access to private transport have meant that the use of cars for tourist trips has grown dramatically since the early 1950s, at the expense of rail and coach/bus travel, both of which have experienced dramatic losses in market share.

Although the growth in the use of the private car for tourism has given people the freedom to explore the lesser-known parts of Britain which are not well served by public transport, there is increasing concern about the environmental problems that they cause. Congestion and pollution in historic cities, coupled with erosion and congestion in popular countryside areas, have increasingly led to calls for cars to be banned from some areas, or for their use to be strictly controlled (see earlier in this chapter for more on the growth in car ownership in the UK).

Rail travel is an altogether more environmentally friendly mode of transport, but one that has lost popularity with UK tourists in recent years. Tourist trips by train are now at only 15 per cent of their 1951 level. There are, however, one or two growth areas in tourist travel by rail, notably short breaks and the popularity of narrow-gauge scenic railways, particularly in Wales. The number of short breaks by rail increased from 28 000 in 1980 to 135 000 in 1985 (English Tourist Board, 1993). Some operators have successfully exploited the market for 'nostalgia' travel by introducing rail holidays using steam locomotives, for example the Venice–Simplon Orient Express, which is sometimes chartered for special excursions in the UK.

Travel by coach consists of holidays, offered by companies such as Shearings and Frames Rickards, and networked, timetabled services between major cities and towns operated by National Express, a former state-run enterprise which was bought by its management in 1988 (see Figure 4.6).

Many smaller coach companies also run extensive programmes of tours and excursions for their local markets and visitors on holiday in their area. Flexibility and good value for money make coach travel particularly popular with the youth market and senior citizens. The ageing of the UK population will be an opportunity for coach operators to increase their business to the 'senior' market.

Sea transport   Sea transportation in UK tourism is dominated by the ferry companies which operate services between the UK and Ireland, Scandinavia and the near Continent, principally France, Belgium and the Netherlands. Approximately 9 per cent of all overseas visitors to the UK arrive by car using the many seaports around the coast. If, however, we concentrate on European visitors to Britain, the figure rises to 19 per cent (English Tourist Board, 1993). The opening of the Channel Tunnel, plus faster, more frequent and more comfortable cross-Channel services using new generation 'super ferries', hovercraft and hydrofoils, have given the incoming tourist a wide range of opportunities for travel to the UK. Since the beginning of the 1990s, ferry companies have been gearing themselves up for the fierce competition they now face from the Channel Tunnel, which operated its first full summer passenger schedule in 1995. They have sought to compete on price and quality of service, using discounted, duty-free shopping and improved catering as major selling points.

Air transport   There are three principal components of air travel within the UK tourism industry, namely:

● Inbound air travel
● Outbound air travel
● Domestic air travel

Figure 4.6: The National Express network (courtesy of National Express)

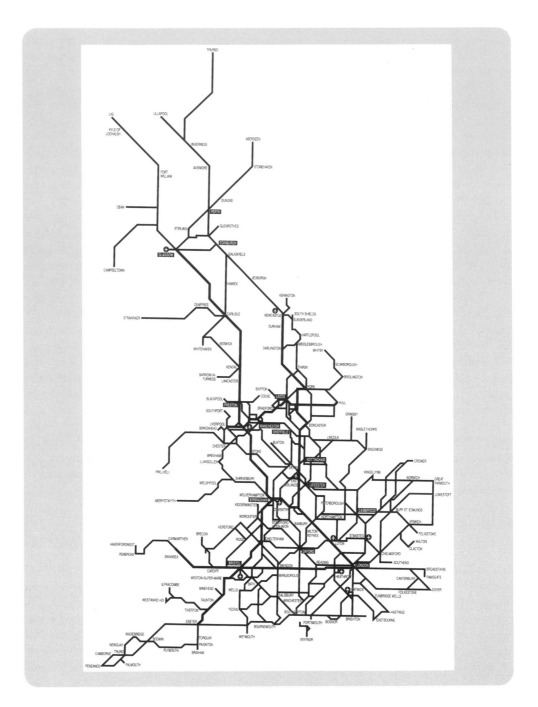

Inbound travel by air is concerned with the growing number of overseas tourists who choose to fly to Britain for their holidays and business trips. Approximately two-thirds of overseas visitors travel to Britain by air, particularly those from long-haul destinations such as Australia, the Far East and the USA. Outbound air travel involves scheduled and charter services that take UK residents away from Britain for leisure and business purposes. Three-quarters of all package holidays sold in the UK use air travel to transport passengers to their chosen destinations. With the introduction of off-peak and stand-by

Airport	Terminal passengers	Percentage of passengers at all UK airports
London Heathrow	51 368 000	42.0
London Gatwick	21 045 000	17.2
Manchester	14 334 000	11.7
Glasgow	5 456 000	4.5
Birmingham	4 784 000	3.9
Stansted	3 256 000	2.7
Edinburgh	2 997 000	2.4
Newcastle	2 417 000	2.0
Aberdeen	2 163 000	1.8
Belfast International	2 039 000	1.7

Source: CAA

fare arrangements and new types of aircraft, such as short take-off and landing (STOL), domestic air travel for holidays and business trips is being given serious consideration by growing numbers of British travellers. Heathrow and Gatwick Airport alone handled 100 000 domestic flights in 1993.

London is the hub of UK air travel and is currently served by five airports:

- Heathrow
- Stansted
- Gatwick
- London City
- Luton

Outside London, there are many important regional airports in the UK serving both domestic and international markets, as shown in Table 4.2.

The number of passengers flying by air is predicted to double in the next 20 years, making airport expansion versus conservation of the environment a very important issue. At present, some of the expansion plans being considered in the UK include:

- A new runway for Manchester Airport to cope with an expected throughput of 30 million passengers per year by 2005
- A fifth terminal for Heathrow
- Expansion of the runway at East Midlands Airport
- A new terminal for Liverpool Airport
- A multi-million pound development at Southampton Airport
- A new terminal for Bristol Airport
- Expansion at Gatwick

There are likely to be heated debates concerning the economic benefits that airport expansion can bring to an area when compared with the environmental and social damage such expansion can cause.

Issues in the UK transportation sector The rapid rise in transport networks and demand for new services and facilities has led to severe pressures on many aspects of the UK transportation scene since the rise in 'mass tourism' more than 30 years ago. The following issues and trends are some of the most important that are likely to influence transport developments in the future:

- *Impact of the Channel Tunnel.* Although still in its early stages of operation, it is becoming clear that services through the Channel Tunnel will have a considerable impact on the UK transportation scene in two principal areas, namely competition between Eurostar services and the airlines on travel to near European cities, and competition between Le Shuttle and the ferry companies for the short sea crossings market.

- *Traffic congestion.* The growth in car ownership and the expansion of air services will continue to have serious impacts on the movement of UK and overseas tourists within Britain. Unrestricted use of the private car is causing traffic congestion and pollution in both town and countryside. London is considered by overseas tourists to have a very poor transportation system when compared with other European cities.

- *Privatisation of the railways.* This may well reduce even further some train services in the UK, particularly in rural areas, many of which rely on income from tourism to help their local economies.

- *Airline deregulation.* Planned for completion in 1997, the deregulation of the European airline industry will further increase competition between carriers, resulting in changes to routes and reductions in fares.

- *New technology.* Improved IT systems will lead to new methods of payment, route selection and booking, as well as more efficient and faster modes of transport.

- *Airport and road expansion.* This will continue to bring conservationists and developers into conflict over the loss of land and buildings. The well-publicised problems concerning the development of Manchester Airport and the extension of the M3 motorway at Twyford Down come readily to mind.

Accommodation

The accommodation sector is an important revenue earner in UK tourism. Data from the British Tourist Authority (1996a) show that spending on accommodation by domestic and overseas visitors to Britain in 1995 exceeded £8.8 billion, representing 36 per cent of total visitor spending. This made accommodation the single largest sector of tourist spending in 1995, ahead of payments for eating out (24 per cent), shopping (19 per cent), travel within the UK (14 per cent), entertainment (4 per cent) and services (4 per cent). The accommodation sector is also a significant employer. Recent figures (British Tourist Authority/English Tourist Board, 1996) indicate that employment in hotels and other tourist accommodation in Britain stood at 340 000 in September 1995, representing 22 per cent of all tourism-related employment. If self-employed numbers are added, total employment in the accommodation sector is estimated to be nearer to 400 000.

The accommodation sector in the UK is dominated by commercial enterprises, providing a wide range of hotels, guesthouses and self-catering accommodation. The only significant non-commercial suppliers of accommodation are the Youth Hostels Association (YHA) for England and Wales, plus the associations for Scotland (SYHA) and Northern Ireland (YHANI), universities and colleges, and premises operated by religious groups. An analysis of the accommodation used by British people on main, long (4+ nights) holidays in the UK in 1995 shows that, in general, self-catering was more popular than serviced accommodation, although the single most popular type of accommodation was hotels, accounting for 23 per cent of all accommodation used (British Tourist Authority/English Tourist Board, 1996). Staying in a friend's or relative's home is a significant category of tourist accommodation, used for 19 per cent of all holidays in Britain in 1995. This category, often referred to as VFR (visiting friends and relatives), is sometimes overlooked as a contributor to tourism revenue; how can it be that somebody who stays free of charge with a friend or relative in their home is helping tourism in an area? The answer to this question is that the visitor, although enjoying free accommodation, is likely to spend money on other goods and services in the locality, such as food, entertainment and transport, so contributing to the local economy. Indeed, the very fact that he or she is not paying for accommodation may well be an incentive to spend more on such things as eating out and entertainment.

Visitors to Britain and UK residents can choose to stay in a wide range of establishments, all of which can be classified as 'accommodation'. There are city centre hotels, motels, farm guesthouses, country house hotels and self-catering cottages, to name but a few. For those looking for something a little different, the Landmark Trust specialises in self-catering accommodation in unusual settings, including a lighthouse and a former railway station!

UK accommodation can be classified in a number of ways, for example commercial or non-commercial, static or mobile, urban or rural. However, it is most commonly classified as either serviced or self-catering, depending on the level of service offered. As its name implies, the term 'serviced accommodation' is used when a service is provided along with an overnight stay, for example meals and housekeeping. In this category, therefore, we find:

- Hotels
- Motels
- Guesthouses
- Bed and breakfast establishments
- Youth Hostels
- Farm guesthouses

Self-catering or self-serviced accommodation includes:

- Cottages
- Villas and apartments
- Chalets and log cabins
- Camping and caravan sites
- Hired motor homes
- Second homes
- Timeshare
- Canal boats
- Educational institutions
- Camping barns
- Home 'swaps'

The distinction between serviced and self-catering accommodation is not quite as clear as these lists suggest; for example, it is quite common now for self-catering establishments, particularly if they form part of a complex, to offer visitors the option of buying food and ready-to-eat meals. Some even have on-site restaurants, cafés and snack bars.

Serviced accommodation Hotels are the most common type of serviced accommodation found in Britain. The annual English Hotel Occupancy Survey (EHOS), commissioned by the regional tourist boards, defines a hotel as:

An establishment having 5 or more bedrooms, not calling itself a guesthouse or a boarding house, and not being listed as providing bed & breakfast accommodation only.

Using this definition, BTA/ETB statistics show that there are in the region of 52 000 hotels in England, Wales, Scotland and Northern Ireland (Confederation of British Industry, 1994). Although gathering data on accommodation stock is always difficult, since different regions use different classification criteria, it can be estimated that, in addition to this figure of 52 000, there are around 20 000 guesthouses, farm guesthouses, boarding houses,

Table 4.3: Top
ten hotel groups
in the UK, 1994

Group	Hotels in UK	Rooms in UK
Forte (acquired by Granada, 1996)	344	30 362
Mount Charlotte Thistle Hotels	112	14 288
Queens Moat Houses	100	10 332
Hilton UK	40	8 440
Swallow Hotels	35	4 379
Accor UK	29	4 338
Holiday Inn Worldwide	24	4 210
Stakis Hotels	33	4 056
Country Club Hotel Group	78	4 000
Jarvis Hotels	46	3 680

Source: Caterer and Hotelkeeper, 1994

and bed and breakfast establishments. Most of this combined total of 72 000 establishments are operated by owner–proprietors who usually live on the premises. Many large hotels in the UK are run by hotel groups, such as Swallow Hotels and Queens Moat Houses, which benefit from 'economies of scale' in terms of purchasing, recruitment and marketing. The top ten hotel groups in the UK in 1994, ranked by number of rooms, are shown in Table 4.3.

Self-catering accommodation Self-catering accommodation in the UK includes all rented premises used for holiday purposes, self-catering holiday camps and centres, all types of caravan accommodation, self-catering youth hostels, second homes and boats (excluding cruises). Using this definition, figures from the BTA/ETB show that self-catering accommodation was used on 52 per cent of all long British holidays in 1992, compared with 31 per cent for serviced accommodation (British Tourist Authority/English Tourist Board, 1996). Many holiday-makers like the freedom and value for money that all forms of self-catering can offer, while families with young children and/or older relatives find it particularly convenient and flexible.

Self-catering accommodation in the UK can take many forms. The former holiday camps, now renamed holiday centres and villages, converted much of their accommodation to self-catering in the 1970s and 1980s in response to customer demand. The market leaders in the UK are Warner's, Butlin's, Haven and Pontin's, which together account for approximately 20 per cent of all UK domestic holidays. Since the mid-1980s, Butlin's has invested £100 million in upgrading its five holiday centres, which between them welcome over 1.5 million visitors every year. The company is currently embarking on a complete refurbishment of its stock of budget accommodation. Center Parcs aims at a more 'up-market' clientele at its UK holiday villages in Sherwood Forest, Elveden and Longleat.

Self-catering cottages throughout the UK are popular with the more affluent AB social groups, who appreciate the rural locations of many of the properties and the convenience of booking through one of the many agencies specialising in self-catering accommodation, for example Blakes, English Country Cottages, Hoseasons, Wales Holidays and Country Cottages in Scotland. The National Trust and the Forestry Commission offer self-catering accommodation throughout Britain in houses, cabins, lodges and cottages.

Self-catering is an increasingly popular form of tourism on farms in the UK. Encouraged by advice and grant-aid from the Ministry of Agriculture and other government departments, many farmers and landowners have converted farm buildings into accommodation units. Such accommodation is popular with families and, from the owners' point of view, is less labour intensive than farmhouse bed and breakfast enterprises.

Timeshare is a particular type of self-catering accommodation involving the purchase of time, usually in blocks of weeks, in a holiday property. The purchaser is then able to use that property at the specified time period each year, or may be able to swap it for accommodation at timeshare properties elsewhere in the world. Although most commonly associated with overseas resorts, there are many timeshare properties in the UK. One of the first was developed on the banks of Loch Rannoch in Scotland in 1974. Most UK timeshare developments are found in the rural areas of Britain, including the Lake District, North Yorkshire, Scottish Highlands and Cornwall. As well as self-catering villas, cottages and log cabins, apartments in seaside resorts and city centres are also available on a timeshare basis.

Camping and caravanning are excellent choices for those looking for good value self-catering accommodation. Caravans were used on 23 per cent of all long holidays in Britain in 1995, with camping accounting for 4 per cent (British Tourist Authority/English Tourist Board, 1996). The owners of many camping and caravanning sites have invested heavily in recent years, to provide their customers with an enhanced range of facilities, including swimming pools, fitness suites, entertainment and eating facilities, aimed principally at the family and youth market. Touring caravans are particularly popular with older age groups, many of whom are members of the Caravan Club or the Caravan and Camping Club of Great Britain.

Accommodation grading schemes The 1969 Development of Tourism Act allowed for the compulsory classification and grading of British hotels, but it was not until 1987 that the English, Scottish and Wales Tourist Boards introduced a workable scheme which had the support of the majority of accommodation providers. This classification system based on 'crowns' was, however, entirely voluntary, unlike many European countries which had implemented compulsory schemes to maintain and improve standards. The scheme categorised accommodation of an acceptable standard within one of six bands:

- Listed   ● Three Crown
- One Crown   ● Four Crown
- Two Crown   ● Five Crown

Establishments were classified solely according to the range of facilities and services they provided. During 1990, by which time the Crown Classification Scheme had more than 16 000 participating establishments throughout England, Scotland and Wales, it was refined to include a subjective assessment of quality, for which establishments could be categorised as:

- Approved
- Commended
- Highly Commended

A fourth category, 'de luxe', has since been introduced to identify accommodation of a particularly high standard. The introduction of the quality gradings was based on the premise that a luxury five-crown city centre hotel may have excellent facilities for guests but poor levels of customer service. A small guesthouse, on the other hand, may have minimal facilities but a welcome which would put any top-flight hotel to shame. The quality gradings, which were introduced first by the Scottish Tourist Board, could be applied to accommodation with any number of crowns or a property that was 'listed'.

The English Tourist Board adopted a similar scheme for self-catering accommodation based on 'keys' rather than 'crowns'. By 1990, over 10 000 self-catering holiday homes had applied for a key rating.

At the time of writing, the UK tourist boards are in discussions with industry representatives and the motoring organisations about introducing a new accommodation classification system based on stars rather than crowns, in the hope of simplifying a somewhat complex scheme that many domestic and overseas tourists have difficulty in understanding. It is likely that the English Tourist Board will adopt the classification based on stars, but the Scottish and Wales Tourist Boards consider that the distinctive nature of their accommodation does not fit easily within such a scheme.

Issues in the UK accommodation sector Accommodation in the UK, as one of the key sectors of tourism, has operated under difficult trading conditions in recent years, not least because of increased competition from overseas destinations and tour operators selling ex-UK package holidays and flights. Some of the most important future issues and trends facing the UK accommodation sector include:

- *Changes in demand.* The growth of self-catering accommodation at the expense of the serviced sector in the UK will provide both opportunities and threats for accommodation providers.

- *Changes in the market.* Some parts of the UK have been slow to respond to the changing demands of an increasingly discerning travelling public. In general, people are looking for accommodation that is of a high standard and is delivered in a professional manner.

- *Product development.* Accommodation providers will need to constantly update their products and introduce new facilities, for example the addition of health and leisure suites and themed restaurants.

- *Short breaks.* The decline in demand for the traditional two-week holiday in Britain provides accommodation providers with scope for the introduction of innovative short-break products based on a wide variety of themes, including activity and special interest, sports, industrial heritage and crafts.

- *Joint marketing.* Linkages between accommodation providers in a region and initiatives with local attractions will continue to generate extra business for mutual benefit. Examples include farm holiday groups, the Best Western marketing consortium and the Virgin hotel group.

- *Growth of 'chain' hotels.* Hotel groups with many properties will continue to expand their operations, bringing greater sophistication in management practices to the UK accommodation sector.

- *New technology.* Businesses will need to keep abreast of developments in new technology, particularly relating to reservations, marketing and financial control.

- *Training.* Many accommodation providers will need to invest more heavily in training, particularly in the areas of customer care and foreign languages, if they are to maximise their business potential.

Visitor attractions

Many of Britain's visitor attractions are the products of geography, history and culture, such as its coastline, mountains, museums, monuments and historic buildings. Others are more recent entrants to the tourism scene, offering visitors entertainment and education, for example theme parks, indoor arenas and cinema complexes. Both types of attraction

Attraction	Number of visits
Blackpool Pleasure Beach	7 300 000
British Museum	5 745 866
National Gallery, London	4 469 019
Strathclyde Country Park, Motherwell	4 150 000
Palace Pier, Brighton	3 800 000
Funland and Laserbowl, London	2 500 000
Eastbourne Pier	2 300 000
Westminster Abbey	2 245 000
Pleasure Beach, Great Yarmouth	2 000 000
York Minster	2 000 000

Source: ETB

Table 4.4:
Top ten free attractions in the UK, 1995

Attraction	Number of visits
Alton Towers, Staffordshire	2 707 000
Madame Tussaud's, London	2 703 283
Tower of London	2 536 680
Chessington World of Adventures, Survey	1 770 000
Science Museum, London	1 556 368
St Paul's Cathedral, London	1 500 000
Natural History Museum, London	1 442 591
Windsor Castle	1 212 305
Blackpool Tower	1 205 000
Thorpe Park, Surrey	1 166 000

Source: ETB

Table 4.5:
Top ten UK attractions charging admission, 1995

feature significantly in the relative popularity of the top ten free attractions in the UK and those charging admission, as shown in Tables 4.4 and 4.5 respectively.

As the tables show, Blackpool Pleasure Beach was once again the UK's most popular tourist attraction with 7.3 million visitors. For the fourth year running, Alton Towers was the most popular attraction charging admission, the result of investment in new rides and targeted publicity.

Attractions have a vital role to play in the UK tourism industry. They are often the single most important reason why tourists visit a destination and are, thus, the stimulus for other sectors of the tourism industry, including accommodation, catering, transportation and entertainment. Different people have different ideas about what constitutes an 'attraction'; a person living in the West Midlands may think of Drayton Manor Park as an example of a tourist attraction. People living in the south of England might mention Thorpe Park or Chessington World of Adventures. Those living in Wales may include St Fagans or Powys Castle on their list of attractions, while residents of Scotland are likely to mention Aviemore or the Burrell Collection in Glasgow. The people of Northern Ireland would surely put the Giant's Causeway towards the top of their list of tourist attractions.

While all these well-known examples clearly fall within anybody's definition of a tourist attraction, it is important to remember that the majority of attractions throughout Britain are not household names. Small museums, craft galleries, shops, leisure facilities and farm attractions, to name but a few, are crucial to the economic well-being of many areas of the country. Together, they form the 'critical mass' of attractions in a locality that forms the basis for encouraging tourists to explore and perhaps stay overnight. As the following English Tourist Board definition of a 'visitor attraction' shows, such places should be promoted to local people as well as to tourists:

A permanently established excursion destination, a primary purpose of which is to allow public access for entertainment, interest or education; rather than being a primary retail outlet or a venue for sporting, theatrical, or film performances. It must be open to the public, without prior booking, for published periods each year, and should be capable of attracting day visitors or tourists, as well as local residents.

The examples of attractions given at the beginning of this section clearly show that attractions can either be man-made or occur naturally. We will now look in greater detail at the role that each of these categories plays in the UK tourism scene.

Man-made attractions Attractions created specifically for the enjoyment and education of visitors occur in a variety of different forms throughout Britain, for example:

- Historic monuments
- Theme parks
- Heritage attractions
- Entertainment facilities
- Sport and recreation centres
- Cultural attractions

Britain is renowned for its wide range of *historic monuments*, which have great appeal to UK residents and overseas visitors. The majority of historic monuments are in public ownership, with many London properties under the management of the Historic Royal Palaces Agency, a division of the Department for Culture, Media and Sport (formerly the Department of National Heritage). Many castles and stately homes in England and Wales are cared for by the National Trust, CADW and English Heritage, who manage the sites and provide facilities for visitors.

Theme parks have been a success story in the UK since the first was opened at Thorpe Park in 1979. Based on a concept that was first developed in the USA, theme parks offer visitors a wide range of permanent rides and entertainments in a themed setting or range of settings, with a single entry charge giving access to all facilities. Most large UK theme parks have experienced growth in their attendances since the late 1980s, through constant updating of their facilities and visitor services. There is evidence, however, that the theme park market is becoming saturated in some parts of Britain, leading to price discounting by parks and the introduction of other incentives to maintain their market shares.

The term '*heritage*' has been adopted by many visitor attractions that depict life at a particular point in time in the past. Many existing attractions have attached the word 'heritage' to their facility, in the hope of attracting greater numbers of visitors and widening their visitor base. They are part of a general trend towards themed attractions in the UK, for example the Jorvik Viking Centre in York and the Tales of Robin Hood in Nottingham. Some parts of Britain have developed attractions that celebrate their industrial heritage, for example Ironbridge Gorge in Shropshire and the Big Pit museum in South Wales.

Entertainment facilities such as nightclubs, casinos, discos, theatres, concert halls, arenas and opera houses, all provide entertainment opportunities for visitors to an area and local residents. Indoor arenas, such as NYNEX in Manchester, Birmingham NEC and Sheffield

Arena, are major venues for concerts, attracting people from a wide catchment area. Much of the appeal of UK tourist destinations is the wide range of entertainment facilities they offer visitors. Seaside resorts such as Rhyl, Blackpool and Brighton, for example, will attract tourists with a variety of live shows, concert events and 'night life' opportunities. Smaller towns and cities will also attract day visitors from their immediate area to enjoy the entertainment at nearby cinemas, theatres, night clubs and arts centres.

As well as being popular with local residents, *sport and recreation centres* also add to the appeal of towns and cities in the UK, helping to attract overnight and day visitors. Swimming baths and leisure centres offer visitors indoor facilities when the weather outside is inclement. There has been considerable investment in sport and leisure facilities in the UK in recent years, with the introduction of wave machines, jacuzzis, health suites, flumes and saunas into centres run by public and private sector operators. On a national scale, sport and recreation facilities are being used to help change the image of certain parts of Britain and attract further inward investment, for example the Don Valley Stadium in Sheffield and the National Cycling Centre in Manchester are both part of urban regeneration projects.

Some parts of Britain have a variety of *cultural attractions* that attract both UK and international visitors. Links with famous people, cultural diversity, associations with the arts and music, are all used to build an image of a destination and attract tourists. Shakespeare's birthplace in Stratford-upon-Avon, for example, is a magnet for UK and overseas visitors alike, while the Cardiff Singer of the World competition attracts tourists from all over the world to Wales. Museums and galleries have long been popular places to visit for entertainment and educational purposes. Britain has an abundance of high quality museums of national and international significance, including the British Museum, Tate Gallery at St Ives in Cornwall, the Burrell Collection in Glasgow, the National Museum of Wales in Cardiff and the National Museum of Photography, Film and Television in Bradford, to name but a few.

Natural attractions   For centuries, people have been attracted to the natural beauty of the British countryside, with its rugged coastline, majestic mountains and picturesque dales. Many of our natural attractions are of international significance and play a major role in attracting overseas tourists, for example the Lake District, Snowdonia, the Highlands of Scotland and the Giant's Causeway in Northern Ireland. The UK's abundance of natural attractions is also a major motivating force for domestic leisure travellers, whose presence helps to sustain the wide variety of tourist amenities and facilities found throughout Britain. A tourist visiting Cornwall, for example, may initially be attracted by the county's scenic beauty, but will also make use of other tourist support services, such as accommodation, transportation, catering, man-made attractions and entertainment. The British countryside is a major resource for leisure and tourism. ETB figures estimate that there are in the region of 550 million day visits to the countryside each year, a quarter of which take place in July and August. The Countryside Commission suggests that some 18 million people visit the countryside on a fine summer Sunday. In certain parts of Britain, the pressure on the countryside is such that the visitors are in danger of damaging the environment permanently and are certainly guilty of spoiling the very beauty that attracted them in the first place.

It is for this reason that many of Britain's most scenic and fragile areas have been granted special status to help protect their environment and provide facilities for their enjoyment by the public. These include the National Parks and Areas of Outstanding Natural Beauty (AONBs) shown in Figure 4.7.

Figure 4.7:
National Parks
and Areas of
Outstanding
Natural Beauty
(AONBs) in
England and
Wales

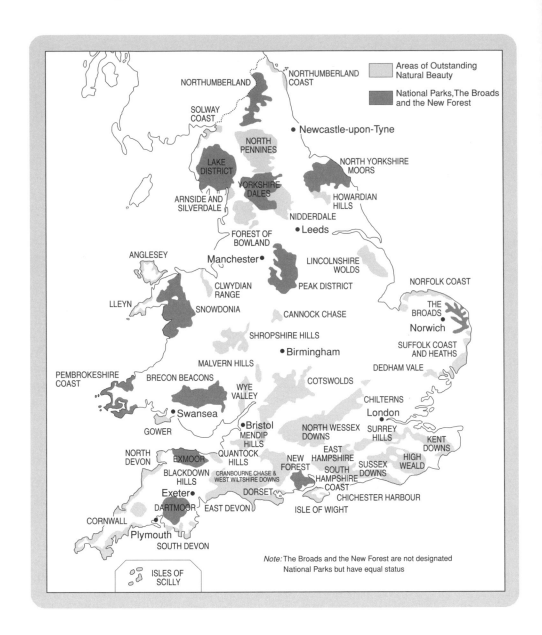

The task of overseeing these protected areas in England lies with the Countryside Commission, whose aim is to conserve and enhance the natural beauty of England's countryside and help give people better opportunities to enjoy and appreciate it. The Countryside Council for Wales does a similar job in the Principality.

National Parks The ten National Parks cover approximately one-tenth of the land area of England and Wales (see Figure 4.7). They were established under the 1949 National Parks and Access to the Countryside Act (the Broads and the New Forest are more recent designations and are not National Parks as such, although they do have similar status). The word 'national' does not mean that the Parks are owned by the government; most of the land within National Park boundaries is privately owned and often under severe pressure from visitors and their vehicles. The Peak District National Park is a good case in point, being located between the large conurbations of Sheffield and Manchester. The total number of visitors to the National Parks in England is more than 70 million in a typical year.

Areas of Outstanding Natural Beauty (AONBs)   Thirty-five of England's most cherished landscapes are protected as AONBs. They range from the wild open moorlands of the North Pennines to the green belt countryside of the Surrey Hills and the intimate valley of the Wye, which straddles the border with Wales (there are another four AONBs wholly within Wales itself). AONBs can be popular destinations for tourists, although, unlike National Parks, they are not designated for their recreational value. The Countryside Commission has proposed stronger measures for their management and more funding for their upkeep. In total, AONBs in England cover around 15 per cent of the landscape.

Issues in the UK attractions sector   The attractions sector in UK tourism is a dynamic and highly competitive industry, having to constantly adapt to changing customer demands, trends and fashions. There are many issues and concerns that commercial and non-commercial enterprises within the sector will need to consider in order to remain competitive. These include:

- *The nature of the visitor experience.*   Rapidly changing lifestyles and changes in tastes and fashions mean that attractions must constantly adapt to the demands of an increasingly sophisticated market that is looking for innovative, high quality products and enhanced levels of customer service.

- *Funding.*   Capital funding will continue to be a problem that will restrict further expansion in the attractions sector, particularly for public sector providers. Local councils faced with static or even reduced budgets for leisure services will look hard at the viability of their local facilities.

- *Health and safety.*   Increased regulation from government and the European Union will force operators to invest more resources in the management of health and safety in their facilities.

- *Technological developments.*   Advances in technology mean that attractions can use a wide range of sophisticated electronic and computer-generated systems to produce exciting and lifelike exhibits, rides and 'hands-on' features. Good examples can be found at Techniquest in Cardiff, the Jorvik Viking Centre in York and Eureka! The Museum for Children in Halifax.

- *'All weather' facilities.*   Building on the success of examples such as Rhyl Suncentre, Butlin's Holiday Worlds and Center Parcs, the operators of attractions will look to develop more facilities that are protected from the vagaries of the UK weather.

- *Media influences.*   The power of the media, particularly television, in the attractions sector has been evident since the mid-1980s with the growth in attractions based on TV programmes or personalities, such as *Last of the Summer Wine* Tours, *Emmerdale* country, and the development of Granada Studios Tour with its re-creation of the set of *Coronation Street.*

- *Increased environmental awareness.*   Attractions based on 'green' themes, or those that subscribe to sustainable principles in their management and operation, are likely to appeal to the growing sector of the UK public that is concerned about environmental issues.

Travel agents

The UK has one of the most sophisticated travel agency sectors operating in world tourism. Approximately 7000 travel agencies are members of the Association of British Travel Agents (ABTA), the trade body representing over 90 per cent of UK travel agents and tour operators (see case study below). The most familiar travel agency names, including Lunn Poly, Going Places and Thomas Cook, are part of large retail networks with many hundreds of branches throughout the UK. Lunn Poly, for example, increased its number of branches to 795 in 1995, making it the number one UK retail travel agency company in terms of number of outlets and turnover. The relative market shares of the top five UK travel agency chains in 1995 are shown in Figure 4.8. This figure illustrates that Lunn Poly, part of the Thomson Travel Group, is the dominant UK travel agency chain with 23.5 per cent of the AIT (air inclusive tour) market, followed by Going Places and Thomas Cook. These top three companies between them account for nearly one-half of all sales of package holidays by air taken by the British.

Travel agency functions

We saw in Chapter 2, on the structure and organisation of the international tourism industry, that travel agents act as the retail arm of the industry, generating revenue from the commission they earn on sales. Although most people associate UK travel agencies with the sale of one particular product, namely overseas package holidays (also known as inclusive tours), an analysis of the work of a typical agency shows that it actually offers a much wider range of products and services, including:

Figure 4.8:
Market shares of the top five UK travel agency chains, 1995

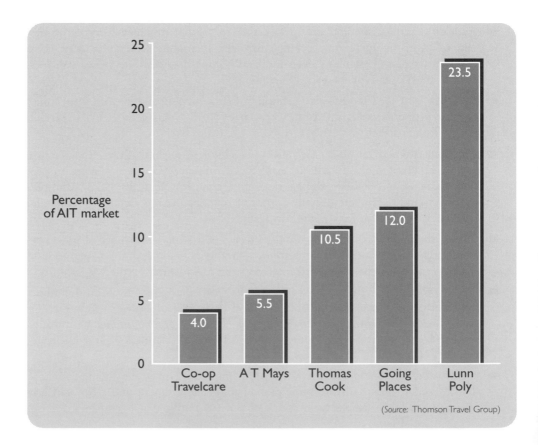

(*Source:* Thomson Travel Group)

- Overseas package tours
- Rail tickets
- UK short breaks
- Coach holidays and tickets
- 'Flight-only' sales
- Travel insurance
- Theatre bookings
- Foreign exchange
- Car hire
- Visa and passport applications
- Cruising holidays

As the market for overseas travel becomes even more competitive, travel agencies will be looking for ways of increasing their income from the sale of products other than the traditional inclusive tours, perhaps offering their clients a more individualised approach to holidays and journey planning.

Most UK travel agencies are members of ABTA, which, as the following case study demonstrates, is committed to furthering its members' interests while at the same time offering high standards of service to UK travellers.

Case Study: Association of British Travel Agents (ABTA)

Introduction

ABTA is the trade body representing over 90 per cent of travel agents and tour operators in the UK. It was formed in 1950 with just 100 members, at a time which coincided with the dawn of a new era for British travellers, when new aircraft technology and greater personal freedom were giving people the means to travel further afield. Foreign travel came to be seen as a temporary escape from the drabness of post-war Britain and the mass market holiday boom was beginning to take shape. Today, holidays are the high point in the year for many millions of UK travellers, with travel for business purposes remaining an important element of the UK travel scene. In our fast-moving society, we have come to take ease of travel for granted, to the extent that some 11 million Britons book an overseas package holiday every year. Many millions will also take short breaks, holidays in the UK, trips by rail or ferry, or travel on business.

ABTA's aims

ABTA's main aims are to maintain the high standards of service among its members, as well as creating as favourable a business climate as possible for the industry. Specific objectives of the Association are:

1. To establish an organisation which is fully representative of travel agents and tour operators in the UK.
2. To promote and develop the general interests of all members of ABTA.
3. To establish and maintain Codes of Conduct between members and the general public, with the object that membership of the Association will be recognised as a guarantee of integrity, competence and high standards of service.
4. To discourage unfair competition without in any way interfering with initiative and enterprise based on fair trading.
5. To promote friendly relations with others in the travel industry.
6. To provide means for negotiations and liaison with other bodies concerned with the development of travel both in the UK and abroad.

Association of British Travel Agents (ABTA) continued

How ABTA works

The Association is a self-regulatory body run by its membership. A network of Councils and Committees, appointed by member travel agents and tour operators, make up the policy-making and enforcing machinery of the Association and help to ensure that ABTA remains in close contact with the whole of its membership. The Association has an education and training function which is carried out by the Travel Training Company (formerly ABTA National Training Board), which liaises with validating bodies such as BTEC and City & Guilds to ensure that the industry has programmes of education and training that are appropriate to its needs.

Up until the end of 1993, ABTA legally operated a type of 'closed shop' arrangement known as the 'stabiliser', which stated that ABTA travel agents could only sell package holidays from tour operators who were themselves members of ABTA, and vice versa. The stabiliser was introduced 20 years ago to safeguard the public against unscrupulous agents and operators. The arrangement was dismantled in 1993, since it was considered to be a restrictive practice and also because, in theory at least, the introduction of the EC Package Travel Directive rendered the stabiliser obsolete.

Membership of ABTA

Those granted membership of ABTA are required to adhere to strict rules governing their business practice. These are contained in ABTA's Codes of Conduct, which regulate all aspects of tour operators' and travel agents' relationships with their customers and which have been drawn up in conjunction with the Office of Fair Trading (OFT).

The Tour Operators' Code of Conduct lays down the minimum standards for brochures, requiring that they contain clear, comprehensive and accurate descriptions of facilities and services offered. It details rules that govern booking conditions in brochures as they relate, for example, to the cancellation or alteration of tours, holidays or other travel arrangements by the tour operator. The Code also contains strict rules concerning the prompt handling of complaints and regulations relating to the business relationships between tour operators and travel agents.

Similar, stringent rules apply also to travel agents who are bound by their own Code of Conduct. The Travel Agents' Code of Conduct regulates all aspects of travel agents' relationships with their customers, covering their responsibility with regard to the standard of service they provide and the information they give to clients. It also lays down rules concerning travel agents' trading relationships with tour operators.

In addition, members of ABTA are required to adhere to precise financial specifications, overseen by ABTA's Financial Services Department, which checks all members' accounts at least once a year.

Protection and redress for the travelling public

In addition to its Codes of Conduct, ABTA seeks to protect the interests of travellers through its Consumer Affairs Department and its own Arbitration Scheme.

Staff in the Consumer Affairs Department offer a service for clients who have booked with an ABTA-registered travel agent or tour operator and who have reason to complain about some aspect of the service they have received. ABTA will look into the complaint and seek to redress the situation without recourse to law. If the dispute cannot be resolved through conciliation, the client may pursue the claim through ABTA's Arbitration Scheme, for which a fee is charged depending on the amount of the claim. The ABTA Arbitration Scheme, administered by the Chartered Institute of Arbitrators, gives the client the opportunity for redress without incurring high legal costs.

▷

Tour operators and travel agent members of ABTA are required to provide bonds to protect their customers in the event of financial failure. The bond can take a number of forms, but is often an insurance policy for the amount required by ABTA, or a bank guarantee. The financial protection offered by the bonding system enables ABTA, in the event of a member's financial failure, to:

● Arrange for clients whose holidays are in progress at the time of the failure to continue their holidays, as far as possible as originally planned, and in any event to make certain that customers abroad are returned to the UK; and

● Reimburse customers whose holidays have not started, the money they paid for their holidays, or make alternative arrangements for the holidays to proceed.

(*Information courtesy of ABTA*)

Discussion points and essay questions

1. What role do trade organisations such as ABTA play in the regulation of the tourism industry?

2. How does ABTA reconcile its potentially conflicting aims of working for the benefit of its members and the interests of the general public?

3. How can ABTA members influence future developments in the ex-UK outbound tourism market?

4. Do you consider that, in general, codes of conduct are sufficiently effective in influencing the activities of members of trade associations?

Tour operators

Chapter 2 on the structure and organisation of the international tourism industry showed us that tour operators can be likened to 'wholesalers', since they buy in bulk from the suppliers of travel products and services, break the bulk into manageable packages and offer these for sale to prospective travellers. Most mass market tour operators choose to sell through travel agents, with a small number dealing direct with their customers. In the case of foreign package holidays booked by British people, 75 per cent of customers use the services of a travel agent rather than booking direct with the operator. There are, however, a number of high volume 'direct sell' operators, such as Portland Holidays, and many smaller, specialist tour operators who prefer to deal directly with their clients, advertising their holidays through newspapers and other media. Direct sell operators stress that, since they do not have to pay a commission to a travel agent, they are able to pass this saving on to the client who should benefit with a cheaper holiday. The more specialist the product on offer, the more likely it is that the customer will deal direct with the operator, for example skiing holidays and mountain exploration tours.

Types of tour operators in the UK The majority of the UK's 600 tour operating companies fall into one of the following four categories:

- ● Mass market operators   ● Domestic operators
- ● Specialist operators   ● Incoming tour operators

Contrary to popular belief, most UK tour operators are small companies specialising in a particular destination of type of product. Although the large, mass market operators dominate the market for overseas package holidays, smaller companies play a vital role in offering customers a wide variety of holiday and travel products, not always featured by the larger tour operators.

Table 4.6: Top five UK tour operators, 1995

Tour operator	Share of total market (%)	Share of through agents market (%)
Thomson Tour Operations	24	29.5
Airtours	15.5	18
First Choice	11.5	12.5
Cosmos/Avro	6.5	5.5
Iberotravel	4.0	4.5

Source: Thomson Travel Group, 1996

Mass market operators Mass market tour operators include some of the best-known names in the industry, such as Thomson, Airtours and First Choice Holidays. Figures from Thomson (Thomson Travel Group, 1996) estimate that these three companies alone accounted for more than 60 per cent of the ex-UK inclusive tour market in 1995. They organised air inclusive tours (AITs), often referred to as package holidays, for approximately 8.8 million British travellers in the 12 months to September 1995 (Civil Aviation Authority, 1996), thereby dominating the UK outbound tourism market. Table 4.6 gives a broader picture of the top five UK tour operators and their relative market shares.

As the table shows, Thomson is the market leader in the UK outbound tour operating market, followed by Airtours and First Choice Holidays, which operates such companies as Sovereign and Free Spirit. Cosmos/Avro and Iberotravel together account for 10 per cent of the through-agents market. There has been a great deal of uncertainty in the outbound tour operating industry in recent years, following Airtours' abortive takeover bid for Owner's Abroad (now First Choice Holidays) in January 1993. Had the bid not failed, due mainly to an injection of capital by Thomas Cook, the industry would have been left with two major companies controlling nearly two-thirds of all package holiday sales. The collapse in 1991 of Intasun (together with the rest of the International Leisure Group, ILG), had already strengthened Airtours' position in the market, since it had gained the majority of Intasun's previous clients.

The top three tour operators all have their own airlines:

- Thomson owns Britannia Airways
- Airtours operates its own airline under the Airtours International name
- First Choice Holidays owns Air 2000

This is an example of vertical integration in the UK travel industry, which we shall explore in greater detail later in this chapter.

Specialist operators There are literally hundreds of small, specialist tour operators working in the UK travel industry. Although less well known than the mass market companies, they meet the needs of the growing number of customers who are looking for specialist travel advice and flexibility in their travel arrangements. Some specialist operators concentrate on offering holidays to particular destinations, for example Paris Travel Service and French Country Camping. Others cater for particular segments of the market, including PGL Adventure Holidays for young children and Saga Holidays for the 'senior' market. The growing interest in activity holidays and breaks has led some specialist operators to focus on specific activities, for example walking holidays offered by the Ramblers' Association and Susie Madron's 'Cycling for Softies', which organises all-inclusive cycling holidays on the Continent. Some operators specialise in cultural tourism, offering art history tours to Italy, musical breaks in Vienna and poetry week-ends in the Cotswolds. These are just a few examples of the types of travel products offered by specialist tour operators, many of whom are members of AITO, the Association of Independent Tour Operators, the subject of the following case study.

Case Study: Association of Independent Tour Operators (AITO)

Introduction

AITO is an alliance of smaller, specialist UK travel companies dedicated to providing a quality product, personal service and choice to the consumer. The Association was established in 1976, mainly in response to the problems posed for smaller travel companies by a sudden, sharp increase in bonding requirements following the collapse of a number of major tour operators. In recent years, AITO has come to be recognised increasingly as the official voice of the smaller or specialist tour operator, whose views had seldom been represented or given due consideration by those who regulate the travel industry. The majority of AITO members are small, owner-managed companies, giving high standards of personal service and attention to detail.

Membership of the Association has grown significantly since 1990, when it introduced its own bonding scheme, administered by AITO Trust Ltd. Currently, AITO has over 150 member companies, whose individual passenger carryings range from several hundred to just under 200 000, with the majority of members responsible for between 10 000 and 20 000 passengers per year. AITO members as a whole carried 1.9 million passengers in 1995, which gives the Association a certain degree of credibility in the travel industry. Member companies include Eurocamp, Explore Worldwide, Allez France Holidays and Cox & Kings Travel.

Aims of the Association

AITO's stated aims are:

- To ensure that the public can book AITO members' holidays with every confidence
- To inform members of the issues of the day and to encourage higher standards and greater professionalism amongst members
- To encourage members and their clients to be aware of environmental issues and to promote environmentally sustainable tourism
- To help members market their wares more effectively to customers
- To ensure that the views and problems of the smaller, specialist tour operators are understood and that the interests of their clients are protected

The work of AITO

The Association's work spans a wide variety of travel concerns, including:

- *A social forum.* AITO acts as a forum for the exchange of ideas and views between its members and the industry in general. It holds regular meetings in the UK and an annual overseas meeting for members, their guests and the travel press.
- *Lobbying.* AITO has become increasingly important as a political lobbying group over recent years, as a respected body of opinion representing a significant section of the UK tour operating

Association of Independent Tour Operators (AITO) continued

market. Its views have been sought by a number of government organisations, including the Mono-polies and Mergers Commission, the Office of Fair Trading and the Department for Trade and Industry.

● *Promotion and public relations.* AITO has worked hard to raise the profile of its member companies with the press and the public in general. It organises press functions for member companies, two main brochure launches each year and a series of smaller press lunches throughout the year. The Association's *Directory of Real Holidays*, produced annually with a 1996 print run of 75 000 copies, is a major part of its marketing activity. It lists all member companies and is distributed to the public, the press, retail agencies, Trading Standards Officers, MPs, Members of the European Parliament and a wide cross-section of representatives of the travel and tourism industry. There is also a *Ski Directory* and a *Guide to Real Holidays*, racked in over 400 independent travel agencies.

● *A regulatory body.* All AITO members agree to comply with the Association's quality charter and code of business practice, laying down basic standards relating to the quality of service to customers, accuracy of brochures, financial security and related matters.

● *Member services.* AITO ensures that its members are kept up to date on all issues that may affect them by providing information, advice and background notes, where appropriate. This includes material on such matters as health and safety, contracting and insurance.

● *Green tourism.* AITO was involved, in 1990, in the establishment of Green Flag International, a non-profit-making company set up to encourage tour operators to understand the importance of environmentally sustainable tourism. The principles of 'green tourism' are promoted in AITO's publications and AITO intends to continue backing initiatives relating to tourism and the environment.

The Campaign for Real Travel Agents (CARTA)

In June 1994, AITO launched a new initiative to link independent tour operators with independent travel agents, with the aim of generating new business for both parties. Originally called the AITO 100 Club, the initiative was expanded in June 1995 and renamed the Campaign for Real Travel Agents (CARTA). To date there are 120 tour operator brands (85 companies) and 442 travel agents in the scheme. Each of the holidays in the Association's *Guide to Real Holidays* can be booked through an independent agent, who can offer advice on product and destination selection and availability. The Guide is designed for racking in travel agencies and the Association has developed a range of point-of-sale materials to accompany the CARTA initiative. Training is an important aspect of the CARTA scheme, as a way of improving links between operators and agents. Public relations activity and local advertising are used to increase awareness among customers, and the campaign has been reported extensively in the consumer and travel trade press.

(*Information courtesy of AITO*)

Discussion points and essay questions

1. Critically analyse the role that AITO plays in the outbound tour operating sector of the UK tourism industry.

2. What benefits does AITO offer to its members?

3. How effective can trade organisations such as AITO be in lobbying for change?

4. Examine how the relationship between tour operators and travel agents can work for their mutual benefit under the CARTA initiative.

Domestic operators   Domestic tour operators working in UK tourism organise holidays, tours and other travel arrangements for the home market. Probably the best known are coach operators, such as Shearings and National Holidays, which offer value-for-money products geared mainly to the older age groups. Although, in general, the British tourism product has not been extensively 'packaged', the development of short breaks to UK destinations has been something of a success story in recent years. Companies such as Superbreak and Rainbow Holidays have led the development of city and country breaks offered for sale through travel agencies. Many tourist boards and local authorities, keen to boost their visitor numbers, have worked with tour operators to feature their particular destinations in brochures and tour programmes.

Special interest groups are well catered for by domestic operators. Activity holidays are growing in popularity and operators, large and small, are emerging to cater for the demand, for example YHA Holidays and HF Holidays. Companies offering specialist services and facilities, ranging from pottery holidays to ballooning breaks, are being increasingly sought by a public looking for something unusual to do in its leisure time.

Hotel groups and marketing consortia (for example, Best Western Hotels) have created and marketed domestic tours for some time, often in conjunction with coach companies. The competitive situation that has arisen in the hotels sector in recent years, however, has forced many more hotels to widen their customer base, by developing themed breaks, activity holidays and special interest tours.

Incoming tour operators   Incoming tour operators meet the needs of the growing numbers of overseas tourists who choose to visit Britain for a holiday or business trip. Just as we would normally visit a travel agency to book our annual overseas holiday or business trip abroad, so overseas visitors do the same in their own country when they want to come to Britain. A travel agent in Japan, for example, who has a client wanting to spend a week in Scotland, has to contact a tour operator to make all the arrangements; this operator, who may be based in Japan or in Scotland, is known as an incoming tour operator, since it is providing a service for overseas visitors to Britain.

There are around 300 UK tour operators in this country that specialise in dealing with the incoming market. Some are little more than handling agents offering a transfer or 'meet and greet' service on behalf of an agent or operator. Others, such as British Heritage Tours, Frames Rickards and Evan Evans Tours, offer complete package tours of the UK, which are sold through overseas agents. The packages are often themed, including tours based on British heritage, gardens or castles. Approximately 100 incoming tour operators in the UK are members of BITOA (the British Incoming Tour Operators' Association). Founded in 1977, BITOA is an independent organisation that aims to provide a forum for the exchange of information and ideas, to follow an accepted code of conduct and to act as a pressure group in dealing with other bodies in the UK with a common interest in tourism matters.

Integration in the UK travel industry

As competition between companies has intensified in the ex-UK travel market, the major UK travel agency companies have developed alliances and mergers with other businesses as a way of maintaining or increasing market share and maximising their profitability. This is most commonly seen in their working relationships with tour operators, for example:

- Thomson Holidays owns the Lunn Poly travel agency chain
- Airtours owns Going Places
- First Choice Holidays has a strategic alliance with Thomas Cook travel agencies
- Inspirations owns the A T Mays travel agency chain

Figure 4.9:
Vertical integration
in the Thomson
Travel Group

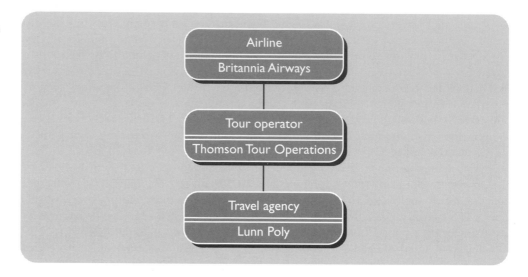

Figure 4.9: Vertical integration in the Thomson Travel Group

These are all examples of vertical integration in the travel industry, when a business has control over other companies that are at different levels in the chain of distribution. Some of the largest tour operators also own their own airlines, giving even greater control over the component parts of package holidays, for example Thomson owns Britannia Airways (see Figure 4.9).

Horizontal integration occurs when companies at the same level in the distribution chain, or in the same industry sector, merge voluntarily or are the subject of a takeover bid. In the airline sector, for example, British Airways is seeking to achieve its ambition of becoming the world's largest airline by acquisitions and mergers with other operators, including American Airlines, Qantas and TAT, a French domestic airline. It has also taken over the former British charter airline Dan Air and has interests in Germany with Deutsche BA. Horizontal integration is also common in the hotels sector, where hotel chains such as Inter-Continental and Queens Moat Houses achieve economies of scale by controlling the operation and marketing of large numbers of individual hotels. Thomson Travel's acquisition of Country Holidays in 1994, and their takeover of Blakes Country Cottages and English Country Cottages in 1995, is evidence that the major tour operators are actively engaged in both horizontal and vertical integration within the tourism industry, as a way of securing competitive advantage.

There is growing concern among consumer groups and the public generally that the concentration of ownership through vertical and horizontal integration is against the public interest, since it may limit choice and reduce competition in the industry. It is for this reason that any large-scale merger between travel and tourism companies is often referred to the Monopolies and Mergers Commission (MMC). The MMC is currently investigating the relationship between tour operators and travel agents in the UK to discover if it is anti-competitive.

Public sector tourism

The preceding sections of this chapter have highlighted the fact that the UK tourism industry is predominantly a private sector enterprise. Companies, large and small, aim to provide a range of tourism products and services to a diverse customer base, at a profit. It would be wrong, however, to conclude that the UK tourism industry is devoid of any

Figure 4.10: The structure of public sector tourism in the UK

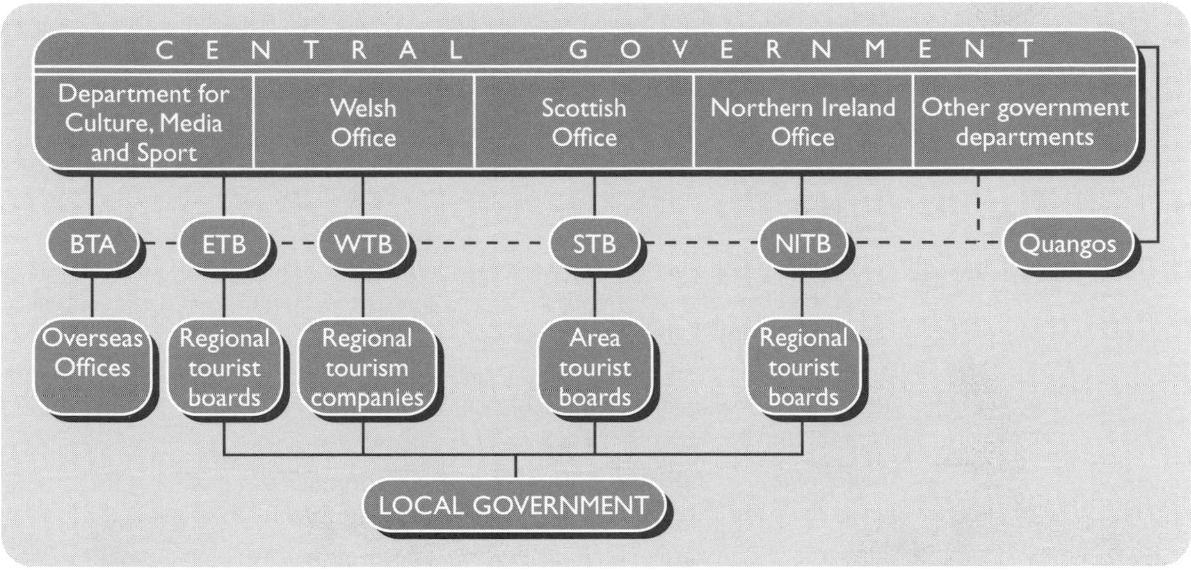

public involvement. Both central and local government, plus a host of 'arms length' publicly funded agencies, play an important role in developing and promoting UK tourism (see Figure 4.10).

As the figure indicates, central government oversees the operation of the four national tourist boards, plus the British Tourist Authority (BTA), via the Department for Culture, Media and Sport (formerly the Department of National Heritage), Welsh Office, Scottish Office and Northern Ireland Office. The national boards, in turn, co-ordinate their particular regional structures and liaise with local authority departments on tourism matters. The BTA maintains a network of 40 overseas outlets worldwide (see case study earlier in this chapter). The quangos (quasi-autonomous non-governmental organisations) include bodies such as Highlands and Islands Enterprise, the Welsh Development Agency, the Countryside Commission and the many development corporations found throughout the UK, all of which have interests in tourism to a greater or lesser extent. While the Department for Culture, Media and Sport can be regarded as the 'lead' government department on matters relating to tourism, other departments, including the Department of the Environment, the Department for Trade and Industry and the Ministry of Agriculture, are all engaged in activities that impinge on UK tourism. Indeed, there are many examples of how government policies seek to provide the foundations on which tourism can continue to build, as follows:

1. *Macro-economic policy.* The industry benefits above all from economic stability, low inflation and low interest rates.

2. *Deregulation.* The Government's deregulation initiative has paid special attention to eliminating unnecessary regulations in the tourism field.

3. *Planning.* The planning system can make a contribution to Britain's ability to attract inward investment in tourism and to the industry's ability to adapt to changes in demand. Local planning authorities must have regard to national and regional planning policies when preparing their plans. Thus their tourism policies must take account of the Government's updated planning policy guidance on tourism.

4. *Transport.* The opening of the Channel Tunnel offers a massive opportunity to expand the number of visitors from Western Europe which already provides 60 per cent of our overseas visitors; and last year all UK regional airports were opened up to US and UK airlines for trans-Atlantic flights, providing a great opportunity for the UK tourism industry in the regions.

5. *Food and drink.* Reforms of the liquor licensing laws – longer opening hours, Sunday opening, the introduction of children's certificates – have greatly strengthened the appeal of the British pub, one of our most distinctive attractions for overseas visitors.

6. *Shopping.* With almost a quarter of spending by foreign tourists going on shopping, the liberalisation of Sunday trading and the removal of restrictions on shop closing hours will add to the attraction.

7. *London buses.* The purchasers of London bus companies will have to retain the red livery on routes in Central London, ensuring that a world-renowned symbol of Britain will remain.

8. *Immigration.* Under the Citizen's Charter, performance standards exist to minimise the time a foreign visitor has to wait before seeing an immigration officer.

9. *Training.* Tourism is all about service, which means that staff training is vital. There are now more than 500 National Vocational Qualifications covering over 80 per cent of jobs, including all areas related to tourism and leisure. The Government provides over £1.8 billion of public funding for training, vocational education and enterprise through the 82 employer-led TECs. TECs are working with the ETB and the regional tourist boards to develop tourism training, including the Welcome Host customer care programme, which is targeting 60 000 participants this year.

10. *Small firms.* The tourism industry is mainly composed of small firms – for example, over 70 per cent of hotels and guest houses have 10 or fewer bedrooms. Small firms will be able to benefit from the Business Links that are being set up – 'one-stop shops' for business support and advice, which will target in particular enterprises with growth potential. Other small firm programmes offer consultancy, loan guarantees, and advice on best management practice.

11. *Sustainability.* The Government recognises that tourism growth can only be sustainable if a balance is maintained between the needs of visitors and the needs of the environment. Special care must be given to those vulnerable locations whose popularity may damage the location itself or the visitor experience. Public bodies such as the ETB and the Rural Development Commission provide guidance to the industry and support for pilot projects to put these principles into practice.

12. *DNH.* The creation of the new Department of National Heritage, with a Minister for Tourism gives tourism a higher profile and links it explicitly with the key elements of Britain's tourism appeal, culture and heritage, an appeal which will be boosted by the substantial funding provided by the National Lottery.

13. *BTA.* The BTA helps the industry market the British tourism product abroad. Next year the BTA will receive £34.5 million from the Government, to which the industry is expected to add £15.5 million. It expects to spend £41 million on marketing and information provision overseas.

14. *ETB.* The ETB centrally and through the regional tourist boards helps the industry to identify market trends and plan accordingly; it seeks to raise standards

through the accommodation classification and grading schemes, the provision of business advice and training; and it helps the industry to market its product at home. Next year the ETB will receive £10 million from the Government, to which the industry is expected to add £2.8 million.

Although these examples (from Department of National Heritage, 1995) demonstrate that government sponsorship for UK tourism occurs in a number of different policy areas, the 1969 Development of Tourism Act remains the only piece of government legislation specific to the UK tourism industry. Now in place for more than 25 years, during a period of rapid developments in UK and world tourism, the Act had four principal outcomes:

1. The establishment of the British Tourist Authority (BTA), English Tourist Board (ETB), Wales Tourist Board (WTB) and Scottish Tourist Board (STB)
2. The introduction of 'section 4' grants for tourist developments
3. The establishment of a hotel development grants scheme
4. Legislation to introduce a compulsory registration scheme for accommodation

The Northern Ireland Tourist Board was not included in the Act since it had already been set up in 1948 under separate legislation. Although many industry representatives are of the opinion that the time for new tourism legislation is well overdue, the present government displays a more 'hands off' role. As a recent government paper on tourism indicates (Department of National Heritage, 1995):

The government sponsors the tourism industry in three ways; it seeks to ensure that the impact of its own policies on the industry is, as far as possible, positive; it helps address weaknesses in the functioning of the market; and it seeks to set a strategic framework, to act as a catalyst for action, and to be a clearing house for information and good practice.

National tourist boards in the UK The UK national tourist boards (ETB, WTB, STB, NITB) seek to maximise the economic benefits of tourism to their particular country by stimulating the development and marketing of high quality tourism products. They do not themselves get involved in the day-to-day management of tourist facilities, but set the framework and policy within which private and public sector organisations can operate. Taking the example of the English Tourist Board, it has the following specific objectives:

- To stimulate the development of English tourism by encouraging the British to take holidays in England and by the provision and improvement of facilities for tourists in England.
- To develop and market tourism in close co-operation with regional and national tourist boards, the BTA, local authorities and public sector organisations, and the private sector.
- To advise government and public bodies on all matters concerning tourism in England.
- To maximise tourism's contribution to the economy through the creation of wealth and jobs.
- To enhance the image of England as a tourism destination by all appropriate means, including undertaking and encouraging innovative marketing.
- To encourage and stimulate the successful development of tourism products of a high standard, which offer good value for money.

- To bring greater recognition of tourism as an industry for investment, employment and economic development, by providing information and, where appropriate, advice and financial support.
- To produce and disseminate information on tourism to the trade and the consumer.
- To research trends in tourism and consumer requirements to show marketing and development needs and opportunities and evaluate past performance, future prospects and the impact of tourism.
- To improve the industry's status and performance by encouraging and stimulating the adoption of up-to-date business methods and appropriate technology and the provision of education and training programmes.
- To ensure that England's unique character and heritage is recognised and protected through the sensitive management of tourism.

In order to achieve these objectives, the ETB is engaged in a wide-ranging programme of work with public bodies and commercial companies, including:

- *Marketing*: direct to the consumer and via the travel trade, through the production of publicity materials and development of new products.
- *Information services*: the co-ordination of the network of Tourist Information Centres and a research function.
- *Development*: co-ordinating national and regional development policies on tourism and advising on local tourism initiatives.

Unlike the Wales and Scottish Tourist Boards, the ETB no longer has powers to fund tourism projects under 'section 4' of the 1969 Development of Tourism Act, meaning that its ability to stimulate new investment and development is severely limited. The ETB suffered a further funding blow in 1992, when the 1993/94 allocation of funds to the Tourist Boards was announced by the government; the ETB's grant-in-aid was cut from £15.6 million in 1992/93 to £14.2 million in 1993/94, with further reductions to £13.9 million in 1994/95 and £11.3 million in 1995/96. For 1996/97, the ETB's government grant has been reduced still further to £10 million. These cuts have resulted in the loss of staff and a reduction in the scope of the Board's operations at national level.

UK regional tourist boards

Although partly funded from public funds, the UK regional tourist boards are essentially commercial, membership organisations that provide a range of services for their private and public sector members. A typical English regional tourist board, for example, will have a wide range of members, from hoteliers, restaurateurs and tourist attractions, to local councils, farm guesthouses and education establishments. There are currently 10 regional tourist boards in England, following the demise of the Thames and Chilterns Tourist Board in the early 1990s and the East Midlands Tourist Board in 1996 (see Figure 4.11).

Many of the UK regional tourist boards now operate as private limited companies, indicating the commercial nature of their work. In order to manage its three designated regions, the Wales Tourist Board, for example, has established associated companies, namely 'North Wales Tourism', 'Mid Wales Tourism' and 'Tourism South Wales'. In England, the Yorkshire and Humberside Tourist Board was incorporated in February 1994 as a company limited by guarantee.

In order to discover the role that regional tourist boards play in the UK tourism industry, we will now consider in detail the main responsibilities of the English regional tourist boards, which are to:

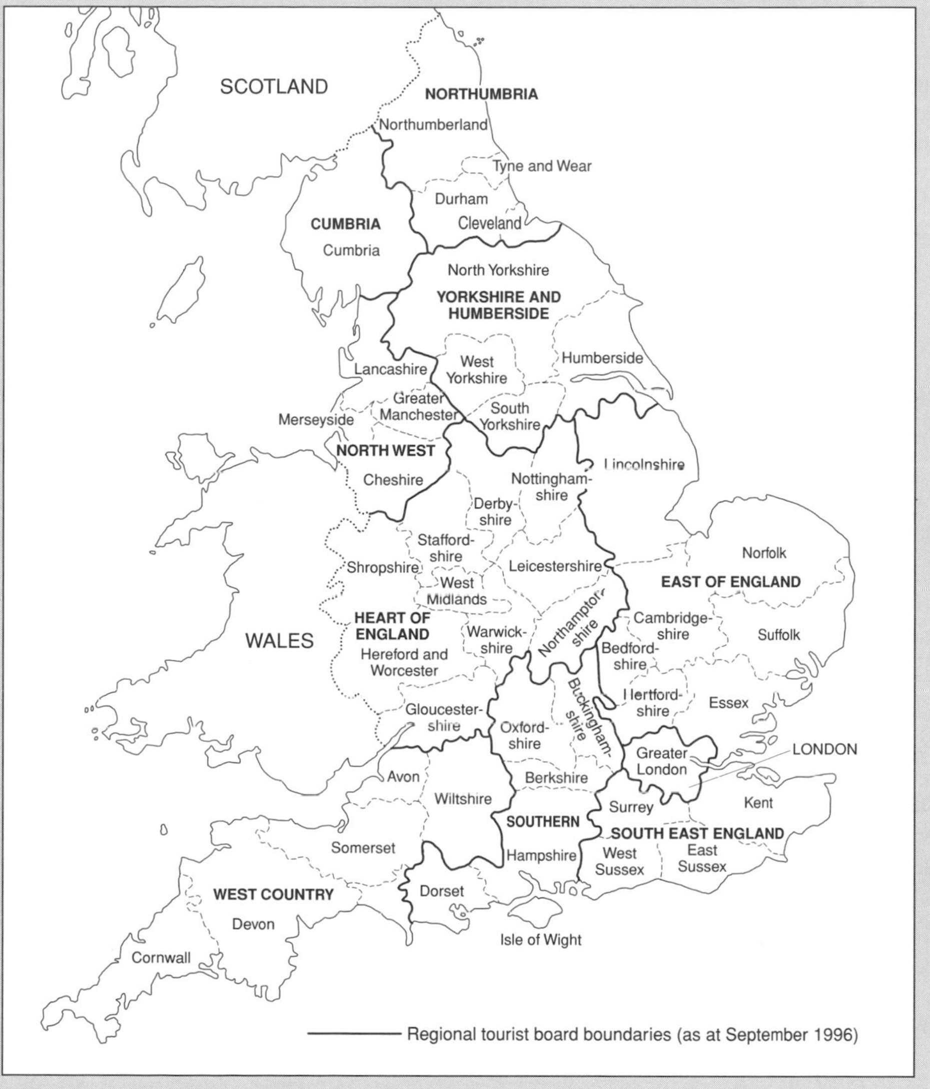

Figure 4.11:
The regional
tourist boards
in England

Regional tourist board boundaries (as at September 1996)

1. Have a thorough knowledge of tourism within the region, the facilities and organisations involved in the tourism industry.

2. Advise the national board on the regional aspects of major policy issues and to supply management information.

3. Service enquiries attributable to nationally developed promotions and to provide literature.

4. Co-ordinate regional tourist information services as part of the national TIC network.

5. Maintain close liaison with planning authorities on policies affecting tourism.

6. Carry out a continuing domestic public relations campaign with the local authorities, the travel trade and the public within the region, with a view to ensuring that issues are understood and the regional and national objectives are known; to

create awareness of the need for tourism to be managed for the benefits of residents as well as tourists.

7. Promote tourism to the region both from other parts of the country and from overseas.

The commercial nature of regional tourist organisations is further demonstrated by the ways in which they have to generate revenue, which include:

- Seeking grants from central government sources via the Department for Culture, Media and Sport, Welsh Office, Scottish Office or Northern Ireland Office
- Collecting subscriptions from local authorities
- Collecting subscriptions from commercial members
- Generating revenue from sales, for example selling advertising space in regional publications and letting space on exhibition stands

Taking the example of the Yorkshire and Humberside Tourist Board, its income for the year ending 31 March 1995 exceeded £2.2 million, made up as follows:

- Marketing activities   £992 161
- English Tourist Board grant   £489 125
- Development services   £225 455
- County Councils/Metropolitan Districts   £198 090
- Accommodation services   £187 744
- Private sector members' subscriptions   £185 171
- District Council   £ 8 551
- Miscellaneous   £ 1 585

These figures clearly indicate that regional tourist boards have to engage in a wide variety of commercial activities in order to generate revenue to sustain their marketing and development functions.

Local authorities and tourism

Local authorities play a key role in the operation and development of UK tourism. Driven by the economic and social benefits that tourism can bring to an area, local councils throughout the UK are investing in tourism facilities and services, while at the same time spearheading the marketing of their destinations to British and overseas tourists. They provide, or contribute to, many of the 'base' infrastructure and facilities for tourists, such as:

- Parks and gardens
- Theatres and arts centres
- Museums
- Sports and leisure centres
- Outdoor activity centres
- Transport services
- Golf courses
- Swimming pools
- Car parking facilities
- Caravan sites

Indeed, it could be argued that there are few local authority services that do not, in some way, contribute to an area's tourism industry, even refuse collection, buildings maintenance and development control. Many councils support the establishment of local tourism groups and associations which will bring together the private and public sector. The Local Government Act of 1948 gave local authorities the powers to set up information and publicity services for tourists. This was reinforced by the Local Government Act 1972 which empowered them to publicise their areas for tourism and provide facilities for visitors.

Today, there are few local authorities in the UK that are not actively involved in some way with promoting their areas to tourists; places as diverse as Barnsley and Bolton, Newark and Nottingham, Sheffield and Scunthorpe, are all competing for a slice of the 'tourism pound'. The scale of involvement is very variable, ranging from authorities with a single person given the responsibility for tourism promotion, to councils with separate tourism departments under a Director of Tourism. Some local authorities see tourism as a natural extension of their planning function and house their tourism officer and staff in this department. The more proactive authorities consider that tourism is an integral part of economic development and so assign individuals into this section. Still others view tourism, and particularly the marketing and promotion of tourism, as a PR activity which lends itself very well to their press and PR department. Irrespective of how tourism is organised within a particular local authority, it is clear that it will remain a vital and increasing part of the work of local councils in the future.

The future of UK tourism

Earlier sections of this chapter have illustrated that the UK tourism industry has been very successful in attracting increasing numbers of overseas visitors to these shores, spending a record £12 billion in 1995 (British Tourist Authority, 1996a). The recent history of tourism in the UK by British residents, however, is less than encouraging. Data from *Tourism Intelligence Quarterly* (British Tourist Authority/English Tourist Board, 1996) show that the number of long (4+ nights) holidays taken by the British in the UK reached a peak in the mid-1970s, when these holidays represented 79 per cent of all holidays taken by UK residents. Since this time, there has been a steady decline in market share to just 56 per cent in 1995, an average annual decline of 1 per cent. This decline in UK holidays taken by the British is in stark contrast to the continued growth in holidays taken abroad, which have increased from 27 per cent to 44 per cent of all long holidays between 1981 and 1995. In 1995, some 26 million of the total of 59 million long holidays taken by the British were spent abroad.

It is against this background that we must consider the future of the UK tourism industry. The present situation facing the industry is the result of a variety of interrelated factors, including:

- Competition from overseas destinations and ex-UK tour operators
- Reduced funding from central government
- Changing nature of the market for holidays
- Lack of investment in 'the UK holiday product'
- Limited investment in infrastructure
- Inadequate management and staff training

The Confederation of British Industry has suggested an action plan for the UK tourism industry with six principal themes (Confederation of British Industry, 1994):

1. *Quality and service*: improve Britain's international and domestic reputation for value for money, particularly by developing the product and raising quality and service standards; encourage active mutual support networks and projects, particularly through the regional and local tourist boards and companies.
2. *Training and careers*: improve training and career development for the industry, by in-house programmes and by encouraging and supporting public education, training and careers programmes.

3. *Marketing*: be active partners with the BTA and the tourist boards in developing and marketing product strengths at national and local level.

4. *The environment*: be active partners with local communities in upgrading the broader environment for visitors, ensuring sustainability.

5. *Product investment*: promote partnership between public and private sectors for major investment projects, for example exploiting the opportunities of the National Lottery and in particular the Millennium Fund.

6. *Public profile of tourism*: spread the message that tourism is good for Britain and for local communities, and that we must promote, not knock, our national heritage and culture.

By championing the cause of UK tourism in this way, the CBI hopes that the industry will begin to invest more heavily in its products and infrastructure, thereby producing a vibrant enterprise culture that will help reduce the impact of overseas holidays on UK tourism.

In a recent parliamentary debate on tourism (Hansard, 1996), the Secretary of State for National Heritage highlighted six key areas of government work in relation to tourism, namely:

- Championing and raising the profile of the industry
- Improving the quality of the product
- Developing a world-class human resource
- Increasing competitiveness
- Making marketing more effective
- Managing the impact of tourism

She noted that the government has worked in close partnership with the industry and tourist boards on measures to improve the competitiveness of British tourism and that government support for the tourism industry involves much more than the provision of funds alone. There is little doubt, however, that the continued reductions in grant-aid for tourism will make it increasingly difficult for the UK tourism industry to compete on a global scale.

Chapter summary

This chapter has surveyed the structure of the tourism industry in the UK and analysed the major issues concerning its operation and development. We have seen that tourism contributes significantly to the British economy, in terms of both wealth creation and employment. The growth in overseas visitors to the UK has been a particular success story in recent years, although fierce competition from ex-UK tour operators is impacting on the number of long holidays taken by the British in their own country. The investigation of the public sector's role in UK tourism has highlighted the concern of reduced government funding for the industry, which is adversely affecting the influential work of the national tourist boards. The chapter concludes with an analysis of the future of UK tourism, suggesting that industry partners, in both the public and private sectors, need to work together to stimulate domestic tourism, through a more professional approach, improved training, greater investment in facilities and more imaginative marketing.

Discussion questions

1. Which key objectives and action points do you think should be included in a revised Development of Tourism Act?

2. What reasons could be advanced for increased public funding for tourism development in the UK?

3. How might the role of local authorities in tourism development and marketing change in the next ten years?

4. Many key commentators on the UK tourism scene consider that the omission of the word 'tourism' from the title of the new Department for Culture, Heritage and Sport is significant. Do you agree?

5. Critically assess the role that technology will play in the future development of tourism in the UK.

References and further reading

- British Airways (1993) *Annual Report and Accounts 1992–93*, BA, London
- British Tourist Authority (1996a) *National Facts of Tourism*, BTA, London
- British Tourist Authority (1996b) *Annual Report and Accounts 1995*, BTA, London
- British Tourist Authority/English Tourist Board (1996) *Tourism Intelligence Quarterly*, Vol. 17, No. 4, BTA/ETB, London
- Civil Aviation Authority (1996) *ATOL Business*, Issue 7, CAA, London
- Confederation of British Industry (1994) *A Wealth of Attraction*, CBI, London
- Department of National Heritage (1995) *Tourism: Competing with the Best*, DNH, London
- Department of National Heritage (1997) *Success through Partnership: A Strategy for Tourism*, DNH, London
- English Tourist Board (1993) *Insights*, ETB, London
- Hansard (1996) *House of Commons Parliamentary Debates 25 November to 29 November 1996*, Stationery Office, London
- Thomson Travel Group (1996) *Annual Report and Accounts 1995*
- World Travel and Tourism Council (1996) *United Kingdom Travel & Tourism Millennium Vision*, WTTC, London
- Youell, R (1995) *Leisure and Tourism*, 2nd edition, Longman, Harlow, UK
- Youell, R (1996) *Travel and Tourism*, Longman, Harlow, UK

Chapter Five

Impacts of Tourism

Chapter Overview

This chapter investigates the contentious issues concerning tourism's impacts at international, national and local level. While it is often the negative effects of tourism that catch the headlines, we discover that tourism also has its beneficial effects, not least in the areas of wealth generation and employment creation. We look in detail at the socio-cultural and environmental impacts of tourism development, and, with the help of industry case studies and examples, investigate ways of reducing tourism's adverse effects. These practical measures are set within the context of the principles for sustainable tourism development, particularly the importance of respecting the needs of host communities and their involvement in the tourism decision-making process.

Key Topics

- Tourism's economic impacts
- Employment in tourism
- The socio-cultural impacts of tourism
- Environmental impacts of tourism
- Minimising the negative aspects of tourism
- Principles for sustainable tourism
- Community involvement in tourism
- Carrying capacity
- Visitor and traffic management

Introduction

The study of tourism's impacts, particularly its detrimental environmental and socio-cultural effects, has come to be viewed as one of the most contentious issues surrounding the industry in the late twentieth century. More attention is now being given to developing and promoting tourism in a way that is sustainable in the long term and that involves local communities in decision making. It is invariably the economic benefits of tourism, however, that persuade governments, local areas and commercial operators to invest in the industry in the first place and develop its full potential. It is all too easy to generalise about the impacts of domestic and international tourism; superficial analysis would indicate that all economic impacts are positive and all environmental and socio-cultural effects are negative. However, these statements oversimplify the complexity of the environment within which tourism operates. Tourism brings with it a range of benefits and problems, which affect economies, environments, cultures and the social interaction of communities. Tourism must strive to maximise the economic benefits of the industry while minimising its detrimental environmental and socio-cultural impacts, if it is to prosper as a major influence on the world economy.

In this chapter we investigate the effects that tourism can have at international, national, regional and local levels, beginning with an analysis of its economic impacts.

Economic impacts of tourism

We saw in Chapter 1 that tourism is now the world's largest export earner and is considered by many to be the world's biggest industry. This justifiable claim is based primarily on tourism's economic performance and potential, creating jobs and generating revenue at international, national, regional and local levels. At the global level, data from the World Travel and Tourism Council indicate that in 1996 tourism generated a total output of US$3.6 trillion and contributed 10.7 per cent of global gross domestic product (World Travel and Tourism Council, 1996). At national level, tourism's revenue-earning potential and contribution to national economies is equally impressive; in 1995, the USA earned more than US$58 billion in international tourism receipts, while tourism dominates economic activity in many Caribbean islands, accounting for over 90 per cent of gross national product (GNP) in Anguilla, 47 per cent in St Lucia and 87 per cent in Antigua and Barbuda. Tourism can also benefit economies at regional and local levels, injecting revenue into urban and rural areas, creating employment opportunities, stimulating the creation of new business enterprises and contributing towards extra inward investment through the promotion of a positive image of an area.

The decision by any government to pursue a strategy of developing its tourism potential is invariably based on the industry's positive economic impacts. The same motivations for tourism development are shown by public agencies at regional and local levels, while commercial operators in the tourism industry also seek to maximise their economic returns. Tourism's economic impacts fall into two broad categories, namely:

● Wealth generation
● Employment creation

Increasingly, developed and developing nations look to the tourism industry to have a positive impact on their economic activity, by contributing to the gross national product (GNP), supporting the country's balance of payments and creating employment opportunities. Central, regional and local governments gain directly from tourism through the collection of direct and indirect revenue. Direct contributions include travel taxes and taxation on incomes generated by tourism enterprises. Indirect sources of revenue include the many indirect taxes levied on goods and services purchased by tourists.

Table 5.1:
Tourism
economic
indicators in
selected
countries, 1994

Country	Tourism receipts as percentage of		
	GNP	Merchandise exports	Commercial services exports
Brazil	0.36	4.42	39.20
Cuba	4.47	42.50	—
Gambia	6.51	71.43	30.86
Germany	0.50	2.55	17.34
Guadalupe	40.83	322.37	—
Ireland	3.78	5.15	44.84
Malta	23.58	41.74	63.90
Nigeria	0.11	0.34	3.04
USA	0.90	11.79	30.74

Source: Author's adaptation of WTO data

Tourism's contribution to GNP

A country's economic performance can be measured by analysing its gross national product (GNP), i.e. the total value of all goods and services produced plus its net revenues from abroad. Studying the contribution that tourism makes to a country's GNP gives an indication of the importance of tourism relative to other industry sectors. A country that depends heavily on revenue from tourism will have a high relative figure for contribution to GNP, and vice versa. Analysis of GNP figures over a period of time will demonstrate trends in tourism's economic significance, demonstrating its growth rate compared with other sectors of the economy. Table 5.1 gives examples of tourism's contribution to the GNP of selected countries, plus details of exports.

The data included in Table 5.1 clearly demonstrate the variations in the economic importance of tourism in different countries. Tourism plays a relatively small part in countries whose economies are principally based on manufacturing; in Germany, for example, receipts from tourism make up only 0.50 per cent of GNP, 2.55 per cent of merchandise exports and 17.34 per cent of total commercial services exports. In stark contrast to this, tourism receipts for Malta contribute nearly one-quarter of total GNP, more than 40 per cent of merchandise exports and nearly two-thirds of commercial services exports, demonstrating the economic significance of tourism to the Mediterranean island. The statistics in Table 5.1 also indicate the differences in reliance on tourism in Africa's developing nations, with figures of 6.51 per cent and 0.11 per cent for tourism's contribution to GNP in the Gambia and Nigeria respectively. The data also shows that, although the USA is the world's number one country in terms of receipts from tourism, the industry contributes less than 1 per cent to the country's total GNP.

For those countries whose economies rely heavily on receipts from tourism there is always the danger of an over-dependence on the industry, making governments and commercial operators vulnerable to reductions in demand caused by internal and external factors, such as changes in consumer tastes and fashions, political upheavals, natural disasters, economic recession and fluctuations in exchange rates. Public agencies must be alert to this potential problem and seek to diversify their economies, thereby reducing the risk factors associated with an over-dependence on a single industry.

Factors affecting tourism's contribution to GNP

Bull (1991) identifies five major factors which determine tourism's role in GNP (note that Bull refers to Gross Domestic Product (GDP) rather than GNP, although there is little difference in their use as a measure of national income). The factors he identifies are:

- *The stock of resources.* Natural resources, built facilities, human and financial resources are all essential prerequisites of successful tourism development.

- *The state of technical knowledge.* In general, economic returns from tourism will tend to be highest in those countries with high levels of technical expertise.

- *Social and political stability.* Since tourism is consumed at the point of production, real or perceived problems in the destination area will have an adverse affect on visitor numbers and hence receipts from tourism.

- *Attitudes and habits.* The view taken by host communities towards tourists and individual tourists' propensity to travel will directly influence the development of tourism.

- *Investment.* Government and commercial investment in capital projects and 'soft' items such as promotion, training and business support will all affect the patterns and rates of growth of tourism development.

As these factors demonstrate, both the demand-side and supply-side of the tourism system have a bearing on the extent to which tourism activity contributes to a country's GNP. In this respect, tourism is no different from any other industry sector.

Tourism and the balance of payments

In simple terms, the balance of payments is a statement of the international flows of currency and capital items to and from a particular country. The items that appear on a country's balance of payments are classified as either 'visible' or 'invisible'; visibles are tangible goods such as cars, electrical products and raw materials, whereas invisible items include banking, insurance, shipping and tourism. Tourism has a major impact on the balance of payments position in many countries, particularly the developing nations of the world and those that have a heavy economic reliance on tourism. The 'tourism balance' of a particular country will consist of all receipts from its overseas visitors less payments made by its own residents on travel abroad. This means that countries which have a significantly higher proportion of incoming as opposed to outbound tourists will have a healthy surplus on the tourism account part of its balance of payments. Conversely, a country that has greater payments made by its residents on travel abroad than revenue received from incoming tourists will show a deficit on its tourism account. The examples of Spain and Germany given in Figure 5.1 demonstrate this position well. The figure shows that Spain had a positive and growing balance of payments tourism account between 1990 and 1994, whereas Germany's tourism balance was in deficit over the same time period, with more money spent by German people on travel abroad than was entering the country from overseas tourism. The actual figures for Spain show that its tourism balance in 1994 was +14 644 million ECU whereas Germany has a figure of –26 003 million ECU (Eurostat, 1996).

Figure 5.1: Tourism's contribution to the balance of payments in Spain and Germany, 1990–94

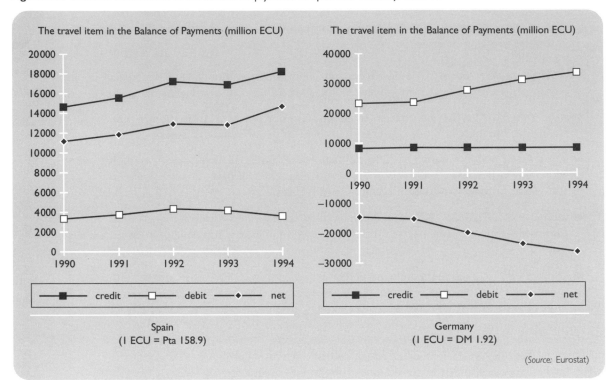

Spain
(1 ECU = Pta 158.9)

Germany
(1 ECU = DM 1.92)

(*Source:* Eurostat)

The multiplier concept

The money spent by tourists in a destination area has both direct and indirect economic benefits. Clearly, enterprises offering facilities for tourists, such as hotels, attractions and transport operators, benefit directly from tourist spending, but there are also many indirect beneficiaries, for example shops, petrol stations, banks and a variety of other businesses that provide goods and services for tourists. Since some of the money spent by tourists in an area is recirculated and re-spent in the local economy, thereby generating extra income, the actual economic benefit to the area is greater than the original amount spent by the tourists. The extent to which the original spending is recirculated in the local economy to boost overall income is known as the multiplier concept or income multiplier and can be explained with the help of the following example. A couple pay £200 for a weekend break in a seaside hotel in Brighton; a proportion of the £200 received by the hotelier will be paid to staff as wages and to local suppliers of goods and services, thereby remaining in the local economy. The staff will spend some of their wages in local shops and for local services, while the hotel's suppliers will themselves have wages to pay and will use the services of local firms. All of this local spending creates extra income which is recirculated and retained in the local economy. A proportion of the original £200 spent by the couple is likely to be lost to the local area, for example in payments to national contract catering suppliers or furniture companies located further afield; this loss of revenue to the local area is known as a 'leakage' from the local economy.

Researchers have shown that the precise value of an income multiplier will vary from one destination to another and also between different sectors of the tourism industry. A farm guesthouse, for example, may well have a higher income multiplier than a large city centre hotel that is part of a multinational chain. This is because the guesthouse is more likely to buy its food and other services locally, thereby retaining a greater proportion of its revenue in the local economy. The hotel, in contrast, will use a range of suppliers outside its immediate locality as part of national distribution agreements. The dividends paid to the hotel's shareholders are also a leakage to the local economy, since many will live away from the city. At the international level, particularly in developing countries, governments that are keen to develop tourism industries that are sustainable in the long term must adopt policies to ensure that as much tourist expenditure as possible is paid in wages and salaries to local people, and for locally produced goods and services.

The multiplier concept can also be used to calculate the potential increases in a range of economic factors related to tourist activity, such as employment, government revenues, imports and sales output.

Tourism and economic development

There is increasing interest in the role that tourism can play in economic development at national, regional and local levels. This is evident in urban and rural areas of both developed and developing nations. Tourism may be included as part of a multi-faceted development proposal, perhaps an urban regeneration scheme or as part of a strategy to stem outward migration from rural areas. Tourism is sometimes used as a vehicle to present a favourable image of an area that is undergoing structural economic change.

The development of tourism gives rise to a wide variety of economic benefits and costs, many of which are attributable to variations in the economic structures of destination areas and their geographical locations. The most obvious distinction is that between developed and developing countries. Developing countries usually have low levels of income, uneven wealth distribution, high levels of unemployment and underemployment, low levels of industrial development, a heavy dependence on primary industries and high levels of foreign ownership of manufacturing and service industries.

One of the principal appeals of tourism as a vehicle for economic development lies in the rapid and continued growth in international tourist arrivals. It is likely that increased affluence in western societies will stimulate still greater demand for international, long-haul tourism at the expense of domestic travel. The developing nations of the world are likely to benefit the most from this process.

Employment in tourism

Tourism's ability to create jobs is one of the prime motives for governments and other public agencies to encourage and stimulate the growth of the industry. When compared with creating employment in the manufacturing sector, service sector jobs in tourism are seen as a relatively cheap and easy way of making employment opportunities available, since the associated capital start-up costs are generally considerably lower. What is not always fully appreciated, however, is the level of commitment and investment necessary to recruit and train staff whose performance is crucial to the presentation of a positive and professional image of the industry. The horizontal nature of the international tourism industry, spanning a wide range of interrelated industry sectors, makes the collection and analysis of comparable data on employment in tourism difficult. Different regions of the world use different data collection methodologies and some tourism sectors do not fall within the standard industrial classification (SIC). Also, many tourism businesses are run by the self-employed and may not appear in readily available employment statistics. On the positive side, however, such a diversity does means that jobs in tourism are created in many economic sectors in all parts of the world. Direct employment in tourism occurs in hotels and other types of accommodation, transport operations, travel agencies, tourist attractions, government departments and tour operators, to name but a few. Tourism also has the ability to stimulate the creation of employment opportunities in sectors not directly associated with the industry, as the following examples indicate (World Travel and Tourism Council, 1996):

- *Traditional travel service jobs*: include employment in airlines, hotels, restaurants, attractions, car rental companies, tour operators and travel agents.

- *Government travel service jobs*: include employment in tourism promotion and information offices, national park or monument guides, air traffic controllers, highway safety and maintenance staff, and lifeguards on tourist destination beaches. They also include customs and immigration officials at land borders and airports.

- *Travel and tourism capital investment jobs*: on the public side, including design and construction of highways, parks and airports; on the private side, including employment in the conception and construction of aircraft, hotels/resorts, vacation homes, travel company office buildings, cruise ships, and some retail shops and restaurants.

- *Travel product jobs*: provide goods and services to travellers and travel companies, and run the gamut from film developers, to accountants, to dry cleaners, to butchers, to shoemakers, to sign makers.

At the international level, the forecast growth in tourism to beyond the start of the new millennium will create additional direct and indirect jobs in the industry. The World Travel and Tourism Council (WTTC) estimates that by 2006, tourism will generate employment for more than 385 million workers, representing 11.1 per cent of the total global workforce (see Figure 5.2).

Not surprisingly, it is the countries in the Asia/Pacific region that are forecast to experience the fastest rates of growth in future tourism employment, as the data in Table 5.2 indicate. This table clearly demonstrates the dominance that the different areas of the Asia region will have in terms of growth in world tourism employment. Indeed, WTTC estimates that the Asia/Pacific region will account for more than 80 per cent of new travel and tourism-related job creation up to 2006 (World Travel and Tourism Council, 1996).

Tourism employment issues

We have seen that tourism is a major force in global job creation. There are, however, a number of issues that concern the nature of tourism employment, many of which are linked to the problem of seasonality in the industry. The fact that tourism can often only provide seasonal work rather than continuous employment means that it sometimes attracts staff who are less than committed to their task; they see a job in tourism as a convenient 'stop gap' measure rather than a serious career opportunity. There is little incentive to put the time and effort into acquiring the necessary skills and qualifications, which results in a workforce that is generally lacking in basic service industry skills. Coupled with low pay and poor working conditions in certain sectors of the industry, jobs in tourism are often considered to be of low quality and offering little status.

Governments and commercial operators must work together to break this vicious circle and improve the status of jobs in tourism. Public agencies must develop manpower planning strategies that will chart the demand and supply of tourism-related employment and provide incentives for private tourism operators to release staff for training in

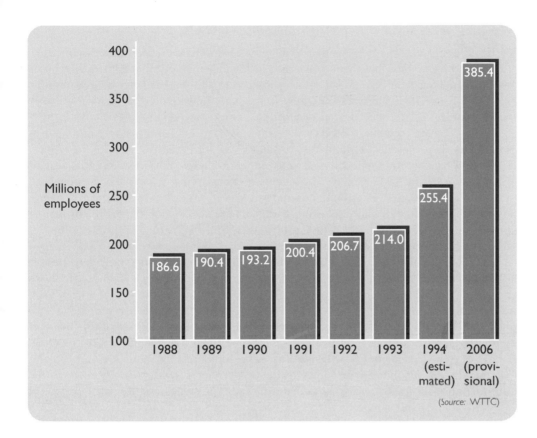

1988	1989	1990	1991	1992	1993	1994 (esti-mated)	2006 (provi-sional)
186.6	190.4	193.2	200.4	206.7	214.0	255.4	385.4

(Source: WTTC)

Region	Extra jobs created (millions)	Percentage growth
North-east Asia	74.62	69.5
South-east Asia	20.33	84.6
South Asia	16.24	45.6
North America	4.95	27.3
Eastern Europe	4.16	26.0
Sub-Saharan Africa	2.93	22.3
European Union	2.60	13.1
Middle East	1.13	31.5
Latin America	1.11	15.1
Other Western Europe	0.63	22.6
Oceania	0.48	23.1
Caribbean	0.46	19.4
North Africa	0.38	11.7

Source: WTTC

Table 5.2:
Regional growth
in employment
in travel and
tourism,
1996–2006

operational and management skills. In countries that have a high dependence on tourism
for their economic well-being, strategies must be developed to reduce the over-reliance
on employment in tourism in order to minimise the economic and social problems that
may arise if the tourism industry enters a recession.

Negative economic impacts of tourism

We have highlighted the benefits that tourism can bring to the economies of countries, regions and local areas, but the industry also has its negative economic impacts, such as the loss of labour from traditional, primary industries to the seemingly more glamorous jobs in tourism. This pattern was apparent in the early development of tourism in many Mediterranean island and mainland destinations, where workers quit their jobs in agriculture and fishing to work in hotels and restaurants, causing labour supply problems in the primary industries. These problems are still to be found today in many of the world's developing nations. Another economic problem associated with tourism revolves around price rises in destination areas. Local residents in some tourist resorts may be penalised by having to pay higher prices for goods and services at peak periods of tourism demand. Increases in land prices can also make it difficult for local people, particularly young couples, to afford to buy property in a tourist area. This is a particular problem in areas with a high proportion of second homes, which tend to inflate local house prices. Host communities can also be disadvantaged when local shops and service providers are lost in favour of retail outlets geared specifically to the needs of tourists, such as gift shops and cafés. This is particularly problematical in rural areas, where the loss of a local facility can often mean having to make a long journey to reach the nearest alternative supplier. Local people may be further disadvantaged by having to contribute to the cost of tourist facilities and services that they will never use, for example tourist information services and promotional activities. The development of infrastructure and facilities for tourism can also divert resources away from other capital projects, such as the construction of hospitals and schools. Where tourism is substituted for another type of economic activity this is referred to as the 'displacement effect'.

Notwithstanding these negative economic impacts of tourism, the industry has the potential to deliver significant economic benefits, as the following case study of the economic impacts of tourism in Australia clearly demonstrates.

Case Study: Economic impacts of tourism in Australia

Introduction

Australia relies heavily on the tourism industry as part of a planned programme of economic development. It has experienced considerable growth in international visitor arrivals in the 1990s, rising from 2.2 million in 1990 to 3.7 million in 1995 (see Tables 5.3 and 5.4), the results of the global economic recovery, explosive growth in travel from the Asian 'tiger' economies, growing interest in the environment and aggressive marketing by the Australian Tourist Commission. Below, we investigate details of tourism's economic impact in Australia and the future demand and expenditure trends.

Gross domestic product (GDP)

The tourism industry contributed an estimated 6.6 per cent to Australian GDP expenditure in 1993–94, of which around 75 per cent (4.8 per cent of GDP) was attributable to domestic tourism.

Domestic tourism expenditure

Expenditure derived from domestic tourism was Aus$32.5 billion in 1993–94, of which Aus$19.0 billion was attributed to overnight tourism and Aus$13.5 billion to spending on day trips. An additional

Year	Visitor arrivals
1988	2 249 300
1989	2 080 300
1990	2 214 900
1991	2 370 400
1992	2 603 300
1993	2 996 300
1994	3 361 700
1995	3 725 800

Source: Australian Bureau of Statistics

Table 5.3: International visitor arrivals to Australia, 1988–95

Origin	Arrivals	
Japan	782 700	
Other North-east Asia	496 100	
Hong Kong		131 700
Korea		168 000
Taiwan		152 000
South-east Asia	566 000	
Indonesia		135 000
Malaysia		108 200
Singapore		202 400
Thailand		81 300
New Zealand	538 400	
UK and Ireland	365 300	
Other Europe	386 700	
USA	304 900	
Rest of world	285 700	
Total	3 725 800	

Source: Australian Bureau of Statistics

Table 5.4: Origin of overseas visitor arrivals to Australia, 1995

Aus$3.8 billion was spent domestically by outbound tourists, for example on travel agency services, travel to and from the international airport and international air fares paid to Australian carriers.

Export earnings

In 1995–96 international tourism to Australia generated export earnings of Aus$14.1 billion, up 16.0 per cent on 1994–95. This accounted for 12.8 per cent of Australia's total export earnings (12.6 per cent in 1994–95) and 63.1 per cent of services exports (61.2 per cent in 1994–95).

Employment

In 1993–94 tourism directly accounted for employment of approximately 535 600 people, 6.9 per cent of the total workforce. It is estimated that by 2003 tourism will be employing 685 000 people.

Economic impacts of tourism in Australia continued

Inbound nights and expenditure

In 1995 overseas visitors to Australia stayed a total of 79.9 million nights (up 7.9 per cent on 1994), averaging 23 nights (24 nights in 1994). Spending by adult visitors (aged 15 and over) averaged Aus$1936 in Australia (excluding pre-paid package tour expenditure).

Domestic tourism

In 1995, Australian residents took 59.7 million trips of at least one night's duration within their own country and spent 251.8 million nights away from home.

Long range forecasts

Table 5.5 gives forecasts of tourism's future growth and economic significance in Australia, as supplied by the Tourism Forecasting Council.

Table 5.5: Australian tourism's long-range forecasts

	Projection	Year of projection	Average annual growth
International visitors	8.8 million	2005	8.9 per cent from 1995
International visitor nights	154 million	2005	6.8 per cent from 1995
Tourism export earnings	Aus$31 billion	2005	8.8 per cent from 1995
Domestic trips	53.5 million	1998–99	1.9 per cent from 1992–93
Domestic visitor nights	238 million	1999–2000	2.0 per cent from 1993–94

Source: Australian Tourism Forecasting Council

(*Information courtesy of the Australian Department of Industry, Science and Tourism*)

Discussion points and essay questions

1. What factors, internal and external to Australia, are likely to affect the successful achievement of the forecasts for export earnings from tourism?
2. What economic factors will influence the performance of commercial enterprises working in the Australian tourism industry?
3. Which sectors of the Australian tourism industry are likely to experience the greatest growth in employment in the future?
4. Domestic tourism is forecast to have a relatively small growth rate up to the end of the century. What measures could the Australian government implement to boost this rate of growth?

Socio-cultural impacts of tourism

The impact that tourism has on the social and cultural lives of communities is one of the most important issues debated by tourism researchers, academics and other commentators today. There is a general consensus that while tourism's well-documented negative environmental effects can be significantly reduced with appropriate planning and management, the socio-cultural consequences of tourist activity have the potential to be far more damaging in the long term, sometimes taking generations to eradicate. This is the case particularly in the developing nations of the world, many of whose strong cultural identities and traditions are coming to light through tourist travel for the first time in their history. Sadly, the same concern for such serious consequences is seldom voiced in a concrete fashion by tourism industry operators, although many do now include mention of tourism's negative social and cultural effects in their policies and mission statements. As with all economic sectors, the growth of tourism will have both positive and negative socio-cultural impacts, although it is the detrimental effects that have attracted the most attention. While it is important to appreciate that many of the social and cultural problems associated with the growth in tourism are likely to have happened anyway in the course of time, the pace of tourism growth often accelerates their development and acts as a powerful, sometimes unstoppable, force for change.

Tourism's negative socio-cultural impacts

If poorly planned, developed or managed, tourism can have a number of damaging impacts at local, national, regional and international level. Some of the most important are as follows:

- *Overcrowding.* An influx of tourists at the height of the season forces local residents to endure the inconvenience of disruption to their normal daily routines. This can lead to resentment and hostility between visitors and host communities, and is a particular problem in small rural communities that often lack the infrastructure and services of sufficient scale to meet tourists' demands; some of the fishing ports and villages of Cornwall and Devon in the UK are good cases in point.

- *Distortion of local customs.* Tourists are sometimes presented with a commercialised and stylised presentation of a destination's cultural identity, for example its music and dance, which may lack authenticity.

- *Loss of native languages.* Large numbers of tourists visiting foreign resorts over a long period of time can have an effect on the indigenous language. In a mass market resort such as Benidorm on Spain's Costa Blanca, it is much more likely that you will hear English or German spoken in the hotels, bars and restaurants, rather than Spanish.

- *'Demonstration effect'.* This is the term given to the outcome of the mixing of peoples from widely different cultures in tourist settings and is most evident in developing countries. The hosts seek to emulate the values and aspire to the material possessions of their more wealthy visitors; this can lead to an irreversible change in social and political values on the part of the host community, sometimes with unsettling consequences.

- *Loss of traditional industries.* Traditional industries, such as fishing, forestry, mining and agriculture, can be lost when workers are tempted by jobs in tourism. Indigenous craft industries may be lost if a tourist area substitutes local goods for imported, mass-produced tourist goods.

- *Fragmentation of communities.* Tourist areas that prove popular with visitors may develop large communities of second-home owners and expatriates, whose ability to pay higher prices for housing and land tends to force local people to move away from the area and may change political and cultural activities permanently.

- *Alterations to religious codes.*   Tourism businesses in resort areas may ignore religious codes and customs in their desire to provide tourists with what they want, for example shops opening on the Sabbath and cancellation of religious festivals.
- *Rise in social problems.*   Tourism can be the catalyst for a variety of social problems and anti-social behaviour. The tourists themselves may behave badly, while the temptation of tourism can lead local people into increased criminal activity, including fraud, prostitution, sex tourism, drug abuse and vandalism. Tourism accelerates and exacerbates many of these social ills.

Planners and operators responsible for tourism development need to be aware of the potential social and cultural damage that the industry can have on destination areas and develop strategies to minimise the problems. Later in this chapter we consider how this can be achieved.

Positive socio-cultural impacts of tourism

Given that many of the prime motivations for tourist travel are concerned with social and cultural experiences, for example meeting new people and exploring cultural sites, the industry can be said to have positive effects on travellers in this regard. Host communities too can benefit from the socio-cultural impacts of tourism in a number of ways. They can benefit from the mixing of people with different lifestyles and from diverse cultural and linguistic backgrounds. This is achieved most effectively through the types of tourism that are designed to bring visitors into direct contact with their hosts and to experience their way of life, for example types of agrotourism enterprises, youth exchange visits, village tourism and home swap programmes. Tourism can also contribute to improvements in the quality of life for the local residents of tourist resorts by offering them an enhanced programme of cultural and social events, designed primarily to satisfy the tourists' requirements but also available to the host communities, for example live shows, theatre performances and discothèques. Local people may also benefit from sports and leisure facilities funded out of tourist revenue. Another positive socio-cultural aspect of tourism is the contribution that it can make to the conservation of an area's cultural heritage by, for example, helping to maintain cultural traditions and preserving heritage sites. Finally, by helping to maintain a clean and attractive environment, tourism can instil a sense of civic pride in local residents, who may use the fact that tourism is important to their area as a springboard for further environmental and socio-cultural activities.

Environmental impacts of tourism

Tourism and the environment, whether natural or man-made, are inextricably linked. Indeed, without an attractive environment, tourism will not flourish and remain sustainable in the long term. In this section we use the term 'environment' to mean the physical setting within which tourist activity takes place; for example the coastal resorts, tracts of countryside, historic cities, mountain ranges, lakeland settings, picturesque villages, museums and galleries that provide the stimulus for so much tourist travel. The tourist experience does, however, embrace a mixture of physical, economic, cultural and social factors, and impinges on both the places where tourism takes place and the people who live there. The previous sections of this chapter have highlighted tourism's economic, social and cultural impacts.

The dramatic growth of international tourism since the 1950s has brought with it considerable environmental impacts, mostly detrimental; the ribbon development of high-rise hotels in some Mediterranean and American resorts, litter in the foothills of the Himalayas and cars in traffic jams on the approach roads to the English Lake District are vivid images that highlight the problems caused by the explosion of mass tourism throughout the world. But it is important to maintain a sense of perspective when considering tourism's harmful environmental impacts. 'Honeypot' areas that attract large volumes of tourists will continue to exist in the world's popular destinations and resort areas, and will need careful planning and management to sustain the physical environment, cultural identity and the integrity of the visitor experience. Much tourist activity, however, is dispersed throughout countries and regions, causing few problems to natural and cultural environments. France is a good case in point; although it is the world's number one destination in terms of international visitor arrivals, it does not immediately spring to mind as one of the countries of the world that has particular environmental problems associated with tourism. France's diverse history, culture, geography and gastronomy have served to spread the economic benefits of tourism throughout its regions, thereby minimising the industry's negative environmental impacts. On a related issue, it could be argued that the development of package holidays, although responsible for the mass movement of large numbers of tourists, has actually minimised tourism's harmful environmental effects, by concentrating tourism in relatively small resort areas or tourist 'enclaves'. The obverse of this argument is that small numbers of tourists travelling in remoter regions may well be contributing more to the destruction of environments and cultures than the mass tourists on package holidays.

Tourism's environmental problems

The negative effects of tourism exist at the macro and micro level. At the macro or global level, the fact that much tourism is consumed at the point of production means that it will inevitably have some negative impacts on resorts and destination areas. There is ample evidence to demonstrate that unplanned and inappropriate tourism development, often by land speculators with little interest in or knowledge of the tourism industry, has left its mark on many of the world's most popular tourist resorts and destinations. Today, there is a greater acceptance by governments and developers of the need to build and manage tourism infrastructure and superstructure that is in harmony with its environment. This may be for truly altruistic reasons, but more often than not is based on sound financial judgements, such as the need to make a return on investment in the long term. A new hotel development, for example, that does not blend sensitively with its natural environment may be unappealing to tourists, who may choose alternative accommodation that respects environmental principles, especially given the increasing concern for the environment shown by many tourists throughout the world.

Although the tourism industry is beginning to improve its environmental performance in terms of the visual impact of developments, there are still areas where improvements can be made. Some of tourism's harmful environmental impacts include:

- *Water supply.* Destination areas are often located in parts of the world where water is in short supply and the extra demand from tourists can jeopardise local supplies, thereby disadvantaging local communities. One particular aspect of the growth of tourism, namely the development of golf courses, uses quantities of water that are hard to justify, particularly in areas of poor supply.
- *Physical erosion.* This takes the form of the wearing away of natural features, such as river banks, mountain passes, soil and vegetation by tourists and their vehicles, plus the destruction of archaeological sites and historic monuments.

- *Water pollution.* Pollution of lakes, rivers, canals and coastal waters results from poorly managed sewage treatment and waste disposal processes, and the use of motor-driven pleasure craft.
- *Loss of wildlife habitats.* Ecological destruction and despoliation of the ecology of flora and fauna may occur through overuse by tourists and their vehicles. 'Fragile' habitats, for example coastal dunes, wild meadows, deserts and mountain areas, are particularly at risk from the pressures of tourism.
- *Waste disposal.* Litter in the landscape is both an eyesore and a potential health risk, while improper disposal of waste by tourism operators can lead to long-term environmental problems.
- *Air pollution.* Congestion in historic cities, excessive use of private transport for tourism and pollution associated with air travel are all problems that governments and the tourism industry must address.
- *Noise pollution.* This can result from the overcrowding of facilities and different modes of tourist transport.

At the micro level, tourism's negative environmental effects are concerned with the use of natural resources by tourism companies and facilities in the course of their normal daily operations. As well as helping the environment, it makes good business sense to use resources sparingly and to minimise waste by recycling and other processes. The installation of CFC-free appliances, unleaded fuel in vehicles, recycled paper products and energy-efficient lighting, heating, water and waste management systems, all contribute to a reduction in tourism's detrimental environmental impacts.

Positive environmental impacts

As well as contributing to harmful effects on the environment, tourism can also act as a catalyst for environmental improvements. The revenue earned from tourism can help destination areas to conserve natural and built resources, such as national parks and ancient monuments, which often provide the initial motivation for travel by tourists. Tourism revenue can also be used to improve the general environment of a destination area, thereby making places even more attractive to tourists, for example amenity planting in public parks and gardens, upgraded 'street furniture' (such as lighting, pedestrianisation, public seating and litter bins), improved signage, clearance of derelict land, and renovations to buildings. Such environmental improvements are also beneficial to local communities and can help to create a positive image for a destination, thereby making it more attractive to inward investment of all kinds. On an international scale, tourism to remote areas, such as the rain forests of South America and Papua New Guinea, and hitherto undiscovered Pacific islands, can help expose detrimental environmental activities, for example unplanned tree felling, destruction of coral reefs and damage to wildlife species. Pressure groups, such as Tourism Concern (see case study later in this chapter) and Friends of the Earth, campaign for sensitive tourism development that is respectful of local environments and customs.

Solving the problems of tourism's harmful impacts

There is widespread agreement in the tourism industry and among other interested commentators that the best way of solving tourism's negative environmental and socio-cultural impacts is to for the public and private sectors to work in partnership to develop integrated policies and practices that are sustainable in the long term. These two key concepts of partnership and sustainability are the platforms on which the future planning, development and management of tourism must be based. Chapter 6 on planning and development in tourism considers each in greater detail, but it is important to stress the 'principles for sustainable tourism' at this point since they underpin much of the action and many of the initiatives taking place at the operational level of the tourism industry. These principles, as agreed by the Tourism and the Environment Task Force (English Tourist Board, 1991), are as follows:

- The environment has an intrinsic value which outweighs its value as a tourism asset. Its enjoyment by future generations and its long term survival must not be prejudiced by short term considerations.
- Tourism should be recognised as a positive activity with the potential to benefit the community and the place as well as the visitor.
- The relationship between tourism and the environment must be managed so that the environment is sustainable in the long term. Tourism must not be allowed to damage the resource, prejudice its future enjoyment or bring unacceptable impacts.
- Tourism activities and developments should respect the scale, nature and character of the place in which they are sited.
- In any location, harmony must be sought between the needs of the visitor, the place and the host community.
- In a dynamic world some change is inevitable and change can often be beneficial. Adaptation to change, however, should not be at the expense of any of these principles.
- The tourism industry, local authorities and environmental agencies all have a duty to respect the above principles and work together to achieve their practical realisation.

The remainder of this chapter is concerned with the practical approaches that can be implemented to help reduce tourism's detrimental environmental and socio-cultural impacts, starting with the importance of involving host communities in tourism development.

Community involvement in the tourism decision-making process

There is growing interest in the belief that early and continued involvement of local communities in decisions concerning tourism development in their locality can help to alleviate many of the industry's negative impacts. This notion is founded on the symbiotic relationship that exists between visitors, local communities and destination areas, as shown in Figure 5.3.

This figure illustrates the interdependence of the visitor, the host community and the place in tourism. These three elements interact with each other and create the negative and positive economic, socio-cultural and environmental impacts discussed earlier in this chapter. Host communities vary in their ability and willingness to absorb and benefit from tourist activity. One difficulty is that whereas the costs of tourism are often plain to see, the benefits may be hidden, although just as real. It is also the case that tourism's costs and benefits are distributed unevenly and that those who bear the brunt of the costs, whether economic, social or environmental, may not always be those who receive the benefits. A further issue concerning community involvement in tourism decision-making is determining who should present the community's views and represent their interests.

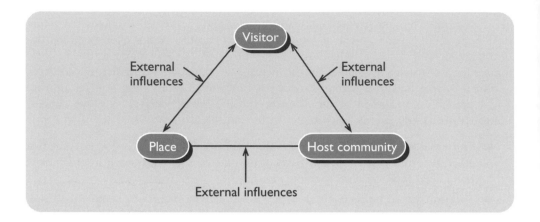

It is inevitable that some people will feel let down if their particular concerns are not addressed. Nevertheless, there are practical measures that can be taken to involve host communities more in their local tourism systems, for example the establishment of local tourism forums where ideas can be exchanged and issues aired, concessionary admission schemes for local people to tourist attractions and facilities, and public awareness programmes highlighting the benefits of tourism to communities.

Carrying capacity

Many of tourism's adverse socio-cultural and environmental problems stem from over-crowding and the over-use of facilities; in simple terms, too many tourists in an area will spoil their own enjoyment, inconvenience local people and cause damage to the environment. Controlling the number of tourists in an area, therefore, seems an obvious way of reducing their harmful effects. It can be argued that every tourist area or facility has a carrying capacity, i.e. a threshold number of visitors above which the resource and the quality of the visitor experience deteriorate. Carrying capacity is sometimes categorised into:

- *Physical capacity*: the spatial, finite capacity of a tourist resort or facility, such as the land available, number of bed spaces and car parking spaces.
- *Perceptual capacity*: relates to the threshold level that determines the quality of the visitor experience or host community's acceptance of tourists.
- *Biological capacity*: the threshold above which damage or disturbance to flora and fauna becomes unacceptable.

The precise carrying capacity of an area or facility, however, is not always easy to establish, since people have different tolerance thresholds; what is an overcrowded resort to one person may be an enjoyable place to another. Capacity can also vary according to the time of year; a fragile habitat, such as the beaches on Turkey's southern coastline that are the breeding grounds of loggerhead turtles, can tolerate heavy use by tourists at most times of the year, but will have a low biological capacity when the turtles are actually laying their eggs in the sand. Imposing limits on tourist use through the establishment of maximum thresholds may also cause resentment, both with tourists who may be denied access to facilities and with commercial tourism operators who may object to what they see as intervention in the market.

In addition to simply applying a quota system to the number of tourists using a resort or facility, there are a number of management techniques that can be used to control visitor numbers, such as differential pricing, guided tours, moving walkways and 'rides', advance booking systems and timed ticketing systems.

Visitor management

Whether or not the number of tourists to an area constitutes sufficient of a problem to threaten its carrying capacity, all visitors to resorts, attractions and destinations need to be managed in some way. This may be no more than arranging the safe transfer between an arrival/departure airport and the tourists' resort accommodation. In areas of high tourism demand, however, visitor management becomes a tool that can be used to min-imise the industry's adverse environmental, cultural and social impacts. In addition to the types of techniques discussed in the previous section on carrying capacity, planners and managers can influence tourists' movement patterns and behaviour with the help of sign-posting, information leaflets and broadcasts, visitor centres, zoning of areas, temporary restrictions on entry, waymarked routes, audio-visual displays, promotion of public trans-port services and a range of other measures.

A good example of developing and implementing principles for visitor management is found in the work of the North Pennines Tourism Partnership in the UK. In seeking to achieve its objective of increasing the range of active and informal countryside activ-ities in this remote area of northern England, the Partnership has adopted the following set of principles:

1. Encourage activities which draw upon and respect the particular character and attributes of the North Pennines Area of Outstanding Natural Beauty.

2. Encourage quiet, non-motorised activities which do not adversely affect the eco-logy of the area, local communities, the enjoyment of other countryside users, or the interests of land managers.

3. In order to minimise damage to the countryside, it will be necessary for some activities to be dispersed to spread the load, while others may need to be focused on adequately robust areas and/or at particular times of the year.

4. Activities which simply use the area as a venue and do not depend upon its par-ticular characteristics for full enjoyment of the activity, should not be encouraged.

5. Ensure that visitors are aware of the opportunities for recreation in the North Pennines and have the confidence, ability and understanding to enjoy it in a con-siderate way.

6. Ensure that visitors are aware of and respect the ecological importance of the area.

7. Encourage providers and participants in countryside recreation to recognise the human factors which have shaped and are still shaping the area, and highlight the link between conservation and existing management of the countryside, and its enjoyment by the public.

8. Where possible, provision for informal recreation should be linked to public trans-port and this information highlighted in any promotional literature.

9. Activities should be promoted only where the land and wildlife affected are robust enough to withstand damage and disturbance, and where adequate provision has been made for management and maintenance.

10. Promotion of activities should stress the special nature of the area and the need to respect and conserve the countryside.

In line with the above general principles, the Partnership has developed a number of strategies in order to further 'green tourism' in the area, namely:

- To promote as visitor activities walking, cycling, riding and cross-country skiing.
- To promote visitor interests such as photography, painting, crafts, birdwatching and practical conservation.
- To encourage the development of low-impact themed holidays involving these activities and interests.
- To encourage accommodation providers to hire out or lend bicycles, binoculars, waterproofs, etc.
- To encourage accommodation providers to take an interest in their local footpath network and the overall environment so as to be able to inform and encourage visitors.
- To guide organisers of events to act in accordance with these principles.
- To develop 'green charters' or codes of practice for adoption by outdoor activity centres, riding establishments and all other individuals or organisations who promote the use of the area for any interests.
- To encourage activity centres and establishments to include practical conservation work in their programmes and develop links with countryside management projects.
- To incorporate the above in its Business and Training Initiative.

Traffic management

As the ownership of private cars has increased sharply since the end of the Second World War, so the use of cars and other vehicles for excursions and longer tourist trips has grown dramatically, resulting in problems of erosion, air pollution, loss of land to car parks and congestion in many popular tourist destinations. The problem is particularly acute in historic cities, coastal resorts and national parks, where private cars and coaches often spoil the very ambience that attracted the tourists in the first place. Among the techniques used to manage tourist traffic are the following:

- *Signposting*: to attract drivers away from sensitive or over-used areas in order to spread tourism's impacts.
- *Public transport initiatives*: to encourage car owners to leave their vehicles at home or in car parks away from the tourist areas they are visiting, as a way of reducing congestion and providing a safer and cleaner environment.
- *Road closures*: whether permanent or seasonal, road closures can help alleviate particularly acute congestion problems, for example in towns and villages that have narrow streets or where historic buildings are suffering from the wear and tear of traffic.
- *Park and ride schemes*: when car-borne visitors leave their vehicles outside a popular tourist resort or historic city and travel by train, coach, bicycle, boat or some other form of transport.
- *Road pricing*: used in towns and cities to reduce the use of cars through charging tolls.

Whichever practical steps are taken to reduce the harmful impacts of tourist traffic, it is important to introduce measures that are part of an integrated plan in order to have maximum effect.

Education through information and marketing

The techniques and tools that a tourist area uses to inform and 'educate' its visitors can have a significant influence on its popularity and the movement patterns and behaviour of its visitors. Before tourists arrive in an area, the messages and images conveyed in brochures and other publicity materials can influence destination choice. Indeed, some resort areas are deliberately omitted from promotional materials altogether as a way of discouraging visitor arrivals, the technique known as 'demarketing'. Tourist destinations can use marketing techniques to encourage visitors out of peak season in order to ease congestion and other adverse impacts. They may also seek to influence the mix of visitors to the area, for example by encouraging users of public transport rather than car drivers, independent tourists rather than groups, or visitors who stay overnight rather than day visitors. Once in a destination area, tourists can be helped and influenced by the important work of tourist information centres (TICs), tour guides, representatives and local people.

One of the most recent initiatives in this field is 'Green Globe', a worldwide environmental management and awareness programme for the travel and tourism industry (see case study later in this chapter). As part of its programme of work to advance the cause of environmentally friendly and culturally sensitive tourism, Green Globe produces a leaflet for travellers, with a list of practical tips on holiday preparation and planning, which includes the following points of advice:

- Look at the environmental content of brochures and ask companies about their environmental policy.
- Take time to think about your holiday plans.
- Take time to learn in advance about the place you intend to visit.
- Consider what you really need to take with you.
- Only take environmentally friendly detergents and shampoos.
- Choose natural oils.
- Take a camera to record any wildlife you see.
- Take a few small gifts from your home country.

While on holiday, the Green Globe 'tips for travellers' leaflet suggests that visitors should:

- Look at personal travel options – choose public transport, cycling and walking, where appropriate.
- Ask your hosts where they go in their off-duty hours to enjoy their leisure.
- In rural areas, try to use small, locally owned accommodation.
- If beaches are dirty, let your travel representative know.
- Try out local food dishes and specialities.
- Buy locally made crafts.
- Ask your holiday representative about local environmental issues.
- Try to get to and from the airport by public transport.
- If travelling by car, ensure your vehicle is well maintained and energy efficient.

Through a sensitive approach to the promotion of tourist areas, public sector bodies can inform prospective visitors and, at the same time, make a contribution to a reduction of tourism's detrimental impacts. Non-governmental agencies can also seek to influence the patterns of tourism development, as the following case study on Tourism Concern demonstrates.

Case Study: Tourism Concern

What is Tourism Concern?

Tourism Concern is a membership organisation established in 1989 to bring together British people with an active concern for tourism's impact on community and environment, both in the UK and worldwide. The organisation is working for change in tourism and insists that tourism takes account of the rights and interests of those living in the world's tourist areas. Tourism Concern aims to look past the cosmetic 'green issues', such as recycling and energy conservation, to the way that tourism affects the people living in destination areas, their communities and their environments. It seeks to raise awareness of tourism's impacts, informs and influences decision-makers at all levels, and provides a comprehensive information base. Through its membership network, global contacts and resource collection, Tourism Concern is a respected centre for advice and information on tourism's impacts on environment and culture.

What does Tourism Concern stand for?

Tourism Concern advocates:

● Tourism that is just, yielding benefits that are fairly distributed.

● Tourism that is participatory, recognising the rights of residents to be involved in its development and management.

● Tourism that is sustainable, putting the long-term social and environmental health of holiday areas before short-term gain.

How is Tourism Concern organised?

Tourism Concern is made up of a voluntary membership body, led by an elected council, operating to a written constitution. It is supported by membership subscriptions, donations, grants and involvement in joint projects. There are links to a global network of like-minded organisations sharing information and occasional joint action. Tourism Concern has a full-time co-ordinator, supported by part-time staff and volunteers. Its base is in London.

What is Tourism Concern doing?

● *Campaigning*: to see that tourism is recognised by governments and development agencies as a key issue; to raise issues of injustice, like the harassment of those who speak out against developments in certain countries.

● *Networking*: to bring together different sectors to work on local and global projects such as the Himalayan Tourist Code, now distributed by the tourism industry, and Guidelines for Sustainable Tourism Development.

● *Informing*: the public, mounting exhibitions and providing literature to heighten awareness of tourism issues; providing speakers and information for the press, broadcasts and conferences.

● *Developing*: a resource base of information on the issues.

● *Educating*: by contributing to teaching resources on tourism's impact and exploring new ways to integrate tourism issues into education.

(*Information courtesy of Tourism Concern*)

Discussion points and essay questions

1. How can Tourism Concern influence the development of tourist resorts and facilities that conform to the principles of sustainable development?

2. What factors will affect Tourism Concern's success in meeting its aims?

3. Do campaigning organisations like Tourism concern have a role to play in regulating the tourism industry?

4. What measures can Tourism Concern implement to persuade governments of the need for planned tourism development?

Environmental impact assessments (EIAs)

The rise in the awareness of, and concern for, the environment has meant that tourism organisations are becoming more involved in measuring the effects they have on their environment, whether on their doorstep or many thousands of miles away. This is often as a direct result of a national or local government regulation linked to the planning and development process. It is now very common for the developers of large tourism projects to be asked to carry out an appraisal of the costs and benefits of the development from an environmental point of view. The most common technique for carrying out such an evaluation is the environmental impact assessment (EIA), which can be applied to a wide range of planned tourism developments. The EIA is a structured process which aims to:

- Identify the costs and benefits of a particular development
- Establish who will lose and who will gain if the development goes ahead
- Examine alternative courses of action and their likely impacts
- Consider ways of reducing impacts if the project is given the green light

For tourism enterprises already in existence, the technique of environmental auditing is gaining in popularity. Some pioneering work by the Inter-Continental Hotel Group, which has resulted in a manual of procedures giving consideration to the environmental consequences of all its business activities, has led to many large hotel companies, airlines and tour operators examining their activities and processes from an environmental standpoint. Some organisations have used their concern for the environment as a marketing tool, hoping to capitalise on the growing market for tourism products and services that are truly respectful of the world in which we live.

Industry initiatives

Operators in the mainstream international tourism industry are slowing waking up to the fact that they need to give consideration to the potentially damaging effects that tourism can have on the environment and host communities. Pressure from a travelling public that is more environmentally and culturally aware is forcing airlines, tour operators, destination planners and accommodation providers to implement the principles of sustainable tourism and introduce measures to limit adverse impacts. It is no longer uncommon to find statements of environmental policy in the holiday brochures of the mass market tour operators, giving advice to holidaymakers on how to protect local environments and respect host communities, their cultures and traditions.

Many major travel and tourism companies, including Thomson Holidays, British Airways and Inter-Continental Hotels, have developed environmental policies and train staff in their implementation. The British Airways 'Tourism for Tomorrow Awards' recognise environmentally responsible tourism developments on a worldwide basis. Recent global winners have included Whale Watch Kaikoura, New Zealand and the Sea to Sea Cycle Route across the north of England. A recent initiative that spans industry sectors and world regions is Green Globe, an environmental management programme geared specifically to the needs of the international tourism industry.

Case Study: Green Globe

Introduction

Green Globe is a worldwide environmental management and public awareness programme for the travel and tourism industry. Its prime objective is to provide a low-cost, practical means for all travel and tourism companies to undertake improvements in environmental practice. Green Globe was developed by the World Travel and Tourism Council (WTTC), a global coalition of industry Chief Executive Officers, with the involvement of the Earth Council and its Chairman Dr Maurice Strong, former Secretary General of the 1992 Rio Earth Summit. The concept has the broad support of the United Nations Environment Programme (UNEP).

Green Globe goals

Green Globe's stated aims are:

- To increase systematically environmental responsiveness throughout the travel and tourism industry, its suppliers and its customers.
- To encourage the widest possible global participation from companies of all sizes and sectors.
- To promote and emphasise the synergy between good environmental practice and good business.
- To identify and demonstrate, through the Green Globe logo, the commitment of travel and tourism companies to environmental improvement.
- To highlight leading examples of best practice and outstanding progress through Achievement Awards.

Membership of Green Globe

Since the programme's launch in 1994, Green Globe's membership has grown steadily to a total of 350 members in 74 countries in March 1996. Membership is open to travel and tourism organisations of any size, type and location that are committed, at Chief Executive Officer level or equivalent, to improvements in environmental practice. Members must also agree to abide by the WTTC environment guidelines (or an industry equivalent), to participate in annual surveys and to accept the Green Globe conditions of membership. Many of the world's leading travel and tourism businesses have joined the programme, along with small and medium-sized companies in all five continents. Some, such as Holiday Inn Worldwide and Inter-Continental Hotels and Resorts, have not only joined Green Globe at corporate level, but have brought many of their individual hotels into the programme. Currently, members include companies with household names, such as British Airways, American Express, Thomas Cook Group, Boeing, Hertz and Avis, plus a variety of smaller private, public and voluntary sector organisations, for example Simply Travel, Sunvil Holidays, Stroud District ▷

Council (UK), Borneo Adventure, Tourism Vancouver, the Youth Hostels Association (England and Wales), and Durham Convention and Visitor Bureau (UK).

How does Green Globe work?

Green Globe helps its member organisations to develop environmental programmes suited to specific requirements and which bring numerous business benefits. Green Globe members have access to:

- *Advice* – in tailoring company practices to changing environmental needs
- *Tools* – to help evaluation and to improve performance
- *Information* – on good environmental practice and cost-saving techniques
- *Recognition* – of an organisation's environmental commitment

In addition, members can call upon the services of experienced environmental advisers supplied by Green Flag International (GFI), whose international network and team of tourism experts can advise on all aspects of environmental practice in the industry. Green Globe also publishes training, education and information materials, including a series of self-help guides that focus on practical operational issues, such as energy saving, recycling, waste management and air quality, as well as corporate policy matters, including environmental mission statements and assistance in establishing environment committees. The WTTC's Environment Research Centre is an international information source for the tourism industry. The centre collects, analyses and updates data from all Green Globe members and develops programme support material. Green Globe assists in public awareness of the importance of the international tourism industry and the work of its members through a range of PR events and initiatives, such as its Achievement Awards, corporate logo and media relations activities.

Members' achievements

The success of Green Globe depends on its ability to demonstrate that it has a role in the development of a more sustainable tourism industry. Crucial to this success is the work undertaken by its members in their goal of enhanced environmental performance. The 1995/96 Green Globe Annual Review features the projects of a variety of the programme's members, including the initiatives of Canadian Pacific Hotels, which include recycling guests' newspapers, using biological pest control in hotel gardens and redistributing part-used bars of soap to charitable organisations. Also included in the Annual Review is the East Japan Railway Company, which has set environmental targets to be achieved by 2001 in a number of areas, including the reduction in energy consumption per passenger kilometre by 10 per cent, in CO_2 emissions by 10 per cent, and in NO_x emissions by 40 per cent per unit from its thermal power plant. It is clear from studying the Annual Review that Green Globe members across all world regions and in all sectors of the industry are delivering environmental benefits.

(*Information courtesy of Green Globe*)

Discussion points and essay questions

1. What are the advantages and disadvantages associated with the fact that Green Globe is a trade programme and not a governmental initiative?
2. What factors will influence the degree of success that Green Globe has in persuading industry partners to join?
3. Is it realistic to assume that Green Globe's goals will be achieved without government regulation of the tourism industry?
4. What are the benefits to an individual organisation of joining Green Globe?

Chapter summary

In this chapter, we have investigated the often contentious issue of the impacts of tourism on economies, cultures and local communities. The significant positive economic effects of tourism, including contributions to gross national product, balance of payments benefits, employment creation and economic development, have been analysed in detail. Invariably, however, it is tourism's negative impacts that are often of greater concern to those outside the industry, and many within it, and the chapter has sought to examine the negative economic, environmental and socio-cultural effects of tourism from the global to the local level. It has identified practical measures that can be applied to reduce tourism's harmful impacts, based on the application of the principles for sustainable tourism and, in particular, greater community involvement in the tourism decision-making process.

Discussion questions

1. Critically analyse the relative merits of industry initiatives and government legislation as mechanisms for reducing tourism's negative impacts.

2. What practical steps could a local community take to become more involved in tourism decision making?

3. Why should a mass market tourism company bother to become involved in initiatives to reduce the harmful effects of international tourism?

4. Examine the use of the price mechanism as a way of contributing to the environmental improvement of tourist areas.

References and further reading

● British Tourist Authority/English Tourist Board (1996) *Tourism Intelligence Quarterly*, Vol. 17, No. 4, BTA/ETB, London
● Bull, A (1991) *The Economics of Travel and Tourism*, Pitman, Melbourne
● Burns, P and Holden, A (1995) *Tourism: A New Perspective*, Prentice Hall, Hemel Hempstead, UK
● English Tourist Board (1991) *Tourism and the Environment: Maintaining the Balance*, ETB, London
● Eurostat (1996) *Tourism in the European Union: Key Figures 1994–1995*, Eurostat, Brussels/Luxembourg
● Krippendorf, J (1989) *The Holiday Makers*, Butterworth-Heinemann, Oxford, UK
● Murphy, P (1985) *Tourism: A Community Approach*, Routledge, London
● World Travel and Tourism Council (1996) *Progress and Priorities 1996*, WTTC, London

Chapter Six

Planning and Development in Tourism

Chapter Overview

This chapter investigates the concepts of planning and development in tourism, building on the analysis of tourism's negative and positive impacts in Chapter 5. We consider the reasons why tourism needs an effective planning system and the different contexts within which planning takes place, from the international to the local level. The stages in the tourism planning process are explained in detail and we consider key aspects of policy formulation in tourism, the starting point for most countries' tourism development. We investigate the twin themes of sustainability and partnerships in relation to tourism planning and development, with the help of case studies and industry examples. The chapter concludes with an analysis of tourism in the developing countries of the world.

Key Topics

- The rationale for tourism planning
- The context of tourism planning
- Stages in the tourism planning process
- Tourism policy formulation
- Planning for sustainable tourism development
- Partnerships in tourism planning and development
- Tourism in developing countries

Introduction

There is a widely held belief among the world's travellers that tourism 'just happens', as if by magic! Tourists give little thought as to how their travel arrangements have been organised or how destinations strive to cope with a regular influx of visitors. The expectation of a stress-free holiday experience away from the hustle and bustle of everyday life provides little inclination for such seemingly mundane thoughts! Regrettably, this same indifference to tourism's short- and long-term development has been all too apparent in certain sectors of the international tourism community. Tourism has been seen as a convenient 'cash cow' by governments and commercial operators alike, providing valuable foreign currency or a regular income over a relatively short lead time. Public bodies and the private sector have been guilty of 'short-termism', giving little thought to the longer-term negative environmental and socio-cultural impacts of tourism that we investigated in Chapter 5. Happily this situation is now beginning to change as the economic and political significance of international tourism grows apace. Today, a structured and sensitive approach to tourism planning and development is considered to be an essential prerequisite of a sustainable tourist industry. Governments and other public agencies invest considerable time and effort in setting the policies and priorities within which the commercial side of the tourism industry can operate and host communities can be shielded from the worst excesses of the industry while reaping its considerable benefits. The most successful private sector operators also spend time on developing their business objectives and planning their strategies for future growth.

Planning and development in tourism

The purpose of all tourism planning activity is to guide future actions in order to meet predetermined objectives in a way that reduces potential conflicts and maximises benefits. As such, planning is an essential prerequisite of tourism development and also lays the foundations for effective management (see Figure 6.1).

The relationship between planning, development and management in the tourism context shown in Figure 6.1 can best be explained with the help of the following example. The government of a former Eastern Bloc country has decided that tourism should form an integral part of its future development strategy, as it moves from an economy based on manufacturing to one where service industries will become more dominant. With the help of internal and external agencies, it engages in a tourism planning exercise to determine its policies and priorities for development. Once finalised, the resulting tourism plan becomes the basis for all future tourism development in the country, whether undertaken by commercial enterprises or public bodies. The tourist facilities and destinations that emerge as part of the overall plan will need to be managed in a way that meets tourists' demands and expectations, while making the best use of resources. Thus, the three concepts of planning, development and management work in concert to achieve the country's objective of maximising the economic benefits of tourism and minimising its harmful impacts.

Figure 6.1:
The relationship between tourism planning, development and management

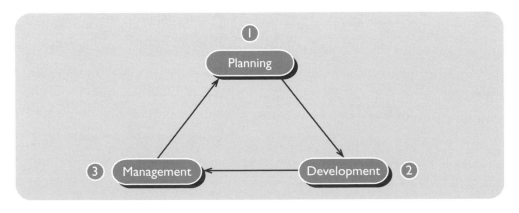

The rationale for tourism planning

As we saw in Chapter 5 on the impacts of tourism, the consequences of unplanned tourism development are clearly seen in many of the world's most popular destinations and resorts. Although there are examples of areas that have flourished in the past without a planned approach to tourism development, today's competitive tourist industry demands an integrated approach to planning and development if destinations are to be sustainable in the long term. There are many different reasons for engaging in tourism planning, which can be summarised under the following categories:

- Economic
- Commercial
- Environmental
- Organisational
- Socio-cultural

Chapter 5 emphasised the importance of tourism's economic benefits. Effective planning can help to maximise the industry's economic returns through, for example, manpower planning and targeted development assistance for tourism projects. The environmental rationale for tourism planning is concerned with conserving the physical nature and integrity of tourism destinations and facilities, whether natural or man-made. Planning can help to minimise negative effects on tourist environments and is crucial to the ability of an area to maintain its tourism appeal. Sensitive approaches to planning can also help to alleviate the socio-cultural impacts of tourism and to foster a positive interaction between tourists and host communities, respecting each other's traditions, cultures and values. The commercial rationale for tourism planning involves a number of interrelated themes that work together to help tourist destinations remain competitive and develop viable tourism industries, for example planning appropriate marketing strategies and activities, presenting a favourable image of a destination, developing facilities that continue to meet market requirements and making the most effective use of available physical, human and financial resources. Tourism planning also contributes to the effectiveness of tourism organisations by, for example, encouraging co-operation between tourism operators, identifying public/private sector partnership opportunities, maximising grant-aid from external sources, offering training events and generally developing a co-ordinated approach to tourism development.

The context of tourism planning

Planning for tourism occurs within a range of contexts and at a variety of levels. It is also carried out by many different types of commercial and non-commercial tourist organisations, large and small. The interrelationship between the different levels of tourism planning is shown in Figure 6.2.

Figure 6.2 depicts an ideal scenario where each level in the tourism planning process has an identified position in a hierarchical structure. Thus, in an ideal world, the planning of an individual tourist facility would only take place within the context of local, regional, national and international planning considerations. Although highly desirable, this is not always achievable, given the scarcity of resources and the many conflicting demands on public and private sector enterprises.

Tourism planning at the international level is not particularly well developed, but bodies such as the World Tourism Organisation (WTO) and World Travel and Tourism Council (WTTC) undertake programmes that seek to influence the way tourism develops on a global scale. The case study of the WTO in Chapter 2 demonstrates its wide-ranging programme of activities, such as technical co-operation for development, practical work in

Figure 6.2:
Interrelationships
in tourism
planning

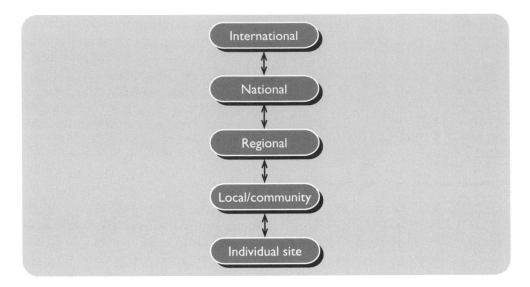

the field of sustainable tourism development and the collection of data on international tourism, all of which inform the debate on the future of tourism planning and its practical application. The WTO has prepared tourism planning studies for many countries and regions of the world, and is the major publicly funded agency representing the international tourism industry. The WTTC (see case study in Chapter 2) is a coalition of tourism industry representatives from all sectors of international tourism, including airlines, hotel companies and car rental firms. It aims to alert governments and the public in general to the full economic potential of travel and tourism. In terms of planning and development, the WTTC supports the concept of a global tourism industry that is sustainable in the long term, through its association with Green Globe (see case study in Chapter 5). In terms of individual commercial sectors of the tourism industry, there is a limited amount of planning at international level, co-ordinated by bodies such as the International Air Transport Association (IATA) and the International Civil Aviation Organisation (ICAO). Regional organisations operating at a global level include PATA (the Pacific Asia Travel Association), ASEAN (the Association of South East Asian Nations) and the CTO (the Caribbean Tourism Organisation). Multinational corporations, which by definition operate across international frontiers, must plan internationally as well as at a national level in order to remain competitive.

Tourism planning is generally most developed at the national level, where countries or states seek to maximise tourism's economic benefits through the development and implementation of a structured tourism planning process. The most visible part of a country's tourism planning machinery is its national tourism organisation, or NTO, which as we saw in Chapter 2 has a wide range of responsibilities and undertakes a variety of activities. Its principal role, often in conjunction with other government departments and industry representatives, is the establishment of a national tourism policy, which lays down the parameters and priorities for future tourism development. In addition to policy formulation, which we investigate in more detail later in this chapter, tourism planning at the national level addresses a range of interrelated factors, including:

● Manpower planning
● The development and implementation of tourism marketing strategies
● Sustainable development

- Seasonality in tourism
- Transport and other infrastructure developments
- Accommodation provision and quality standards
- Tourism education and training strategies

Tourism development will also be influenced by national planning policies that, although not specific to tourism, nonetheless impact on the industry to a greater or lesser extent. These would include, for example, transport policies, priorities in training and education, environmental protection, land use planning, regional planning and agricultural policy.

Approaches to tourism planning at the regional level differ markedly between countries. Those that have strong regional identities and administrative frameworks, for example France and Spain, place a heavy reliance on regional tourism planning to complement national plans. At the other extreme, some countries choose not develop regional tourism planning strategies, relying on national guidelines to stimulate and control development. Between these two extremes lie many countries that have vestigial regional planning frameworks which, as in the case of UK tourism, rely heavily on a combination of local authority and tourism trade sponsorship for their success.

Currently, planning at the local or community level is undergoing something of a renaissance in world tourism, the result of heightened interest in approaches to sustainable tourism development and the need to respect the rights of host communities in tourism areas. To what extent the problems associated with tourism development at local level can be addressed remains to be seen, but there are many ways that local people can be involved in the tourism decision-making process, as was discussed in greater detail in Chapter 5. There is a growing awareness among planners that early involvement of local communities in tourism developments can bring dividends, both for the local people themselves and for the visiting tourists who receive an enhanced experience in their destination area. Much of the pioneering work undertaken as part of the English Tourist Board's Tourism Development Action Programme (TDAP) initiative has been based on the importance of community involvement in tourism planning and development.

Planning at the individual tourist site or facility level is very specific and is governed by the relevant planning guidelines and regulations existing in the locality. Increased concern for the environment and sustainable development principles, however, may influence the final location of a tourist facility, its design and appearance, the landscaping of the site and the energy efficiency of the buildings.

Corporate planning

From our consideration so far of tourism planning, it would be easy to be misled into thinking that planning is only undertaken by public sector tourism organisations, but this is far from the case. In the same way that governments formulate policies and plans for tourism development in their countries, commercial tourism enterprises of all sizes need to plan for the future in order to grow their businesses and continue to maximise the use of their resources. Larger tourism companies develop mission statements to inform all those with an interest in the organisation why they are in business and what they are hoping to achieve. Working within this mission, many companies develop strategic plans to be implemented in the short to medium term. Strategic planning is a flexible, continuous, developmental and action-orientated activity that seeks to answer the following questions:

1. What do we want to achieve?
2. Where are we now?
3. Where do we want to be in the future?

Figure 6.3: The
strategic planning
process for
commercial
tourism
enterprises

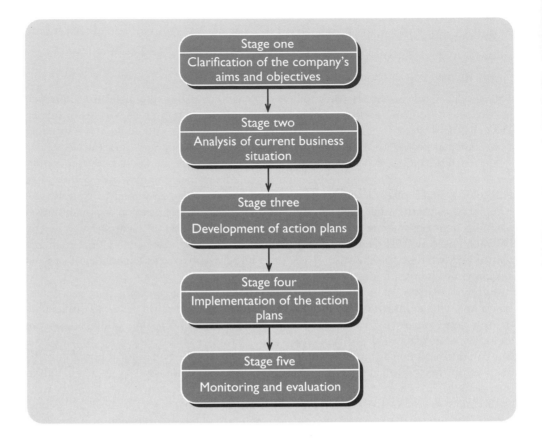

Figure 6.3: The strategic planning process for commercial tourism enterprises

4. What do we have to do to get there?

5. How will we know when we have arrived?

In attempting to answer these questions, the company will undertake a strategic planning process that will follow the five stages shown in Figure 6.3.

The figure indicates that the clarification of the company's aims and objectives is the first stage in the strategic planning process. Without an agreed vision of what it is trying to achieve, a company may lack direction and a clear sense of purpose. As an example, the primary aim of the Thomas Cook Group, one of the most successful companies in the international tourism industry, is '. . . *to be the best and most profitable travel-driven service businesses in the world*' (Thomas Cook Group, 1994).

Although profit maximisation is a basic objective of private sector tourism companies, it is by no means the only aim to which they aspire. Many people start tourism businesses for lifestyle reasons, perhaps enabling them to live in a country with a pleasant climate or make a business out of a hobby or pastime. Objectives for individual enterprises will be very diverse and will reflect the philosophy of the owners or managers, the size of the organisation and its stage of development. Every company's objectives, which must be realistic, achievable and set within a defined time frame, will be influenced by all those who have an interest in the business. Known as stakeholders, these may include shareholders, directors, employees, trade unions, suppliers or finance companies. Stage two of the process is an analysis of the company's current business situation, investigating both internal and external factors and influences on its performance. This is often accomplished with the help of a SWOT (strengths, weaknesses, opportunities, threats) analysis or a PEST analysis, which considers the political, economic, social and technological factors likely to affect the company's future activities. Having carried out its situation analysis the company is ready to develop action plans to meet its stated aims and objectives. These will include detailed aspects of planning and management, such as budgets, marketing activities and the deployment of human resources. Stages four and five of the strategic planning process will involve the company putting their plans into action and measuring actual against planned performance, making any necessary adjustments or alterations to the plans in the light of their implementation.

Business planning

Whereas a company's strategic planning considers its broad objectives and future policies over the medium term, typically a three- to five-year timescale, organisations need short-term operational plans as a way of meeting specific targets or developing particular projects. A business plan, reviewed on an annual basis and including an annual budget, is the most appropriate tool for this task. Such a plan will give managers a focus for their work and the freedom to organise, co-ordinate, motivate and control their financial, physical and human resources to achieve optimum efficiency and effectiveness.

Business plans have a variety of applications in the international tourism industry. For example, they are used by organisations when they are:

- Considering diversification into a new market sector
- Developing new products
- Seeking extra finance from external sources
- Establishing a new enterprise
- Expanding an existing operation
- Changing working practices

Typical examples of when business plans are prepared would include a hotel that is planning to add a leisure facility to its existing building, a museum that is considering an expansion of its retail operation or an airline that is investigating the feasibility of adding another aircraft to its fleet. The dynamic nature of international tourism means that business planning is common in all sectors of the industry, irrespective of a company's scale of operations. Increased competition dictates that tourism businesses must constantly evaluate the products and services they offer to their customers and revisit their corporate objectives.

The structure of a business plan will be influenced by the purpose for which it is being prepared. Two common reasons for developing a business plan are to examine the feasibility of expansion or to help management make the best use of its existing resources. Those that concentrate on the feasibility of expansion will include sections on:

- The proposed product or facility expansion
- The market in which the organisation operates
- Details of the management team that will be implementing the plan
- Legal aspects of the plan
- Financial considerations including projections and funding requirements

Business plans whose primary purpose is to help management make the best use of resources often concentrate more on internal systems and procedures, aiming to reduce costs while maintaining an efficient operating environment. Whatever the purpose of the business plan, financial indicators and forecasts, such as cash-flow projections, anticipated profit and loss figures, and balance sheets, will be of prime importance throughout.

Figure 6.4:
Stages in the
tourism planning
process (after
Inskeep, 1991)

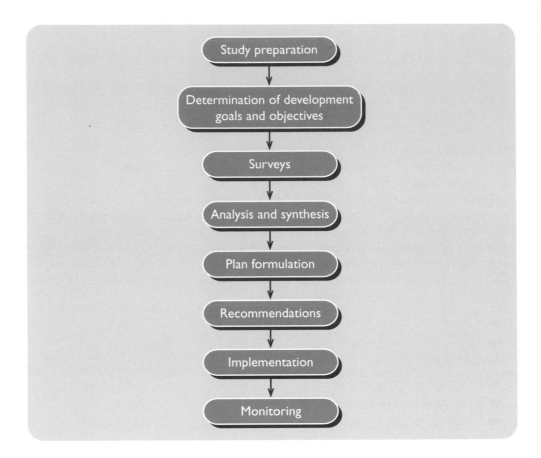

Stages in the tourism planning process

Inskeep (1991) suggests that there are eight basic stages in the tourism planning process, applicable to any national or regional planning situation, as shown in Figure 6.4. The first stage is careful preparation of the study so that it achieves its main aim of providing appropriate development guidance. This stage involves agreement on the project terms of reference, selection of the team members, appointment of a steering group to oversee the project, and organising the study activities. The determination of development goals and objectives is an early stage in the planning process. Time spent defining and refining the project's objectives early on will pay dividends at later stages in the process. The precise objectives of the tourism development must balance the economic, environmental and socio-cultural impacts that the development will generate, and should stress priorities where there is potential conflict. Although the goals and objectives are agreed at this early stage, the development process must be sufficiently flexible as to allow further focusing and alterations as the project proceeds. The survey stage of the planning process is generally very wide-ranging and involves collecting data, both qualitative and quantitative, on the characteristics of the development area and the current demand/supply situation in terms of tourist activity. Working from the general to the specific, this stage of the process will entail the analysis of global tourism patterns and trends, any existing data on current tourism arrivals, an inventory of all the elements of the existing and planned tourist infrastructure and facilities, plus coverage of the economic, environmental, social and cultural aspects of the plan. Stage four of the process involves the structured analysis and synthesis of the data collected at stage three to arrive at a number of important outcomes, including:

- *A market analysis.* This will detail the expected level and type of demand, and should include target numbers of tourists.
- *The required supply of tourism facilities.* From the market analysis it will be possible to plan the number and types of accommodation, transportation and attractions, plus manpower levels.
- *Infrastructure requirements.* Improvements to existing infrastructure and the development of new infrastructure can be determined from the data collected at stage three.
- *Environmental, social and cultural effects.* This will involve establishing carrying capacities and proposing mechanisms to limit detrimental impacts while at the same time maximising tourism's beneficial effects.

An important part of this stage is the identification of major opportunities and/or constraints for developing tourism. This provides a focus for formulating recommendations and identifies how to maximise the opportunities and overcome the constraints. Stage five of the planning process is the formulation of the tourism plan, incorporating the tourism policy. This stage is best approached by preparing and evaluating alternative development scenarios, since there is seldom one ideal set of principles, but rather optimal choices that balance costs and benefits. The alternatives are evaluated according to a range of factors, including how they meet the development objectives, maximising economic returns, reinforcing positive tourism impacts and minimising the detrimental environmental and socio-cultural effects of tourism development. The next stage of the planning process is the formulation of the institutional recommendations, drawn up with due regard to the views of the project steering committee. The final two stages of the process, implementation and monitoring, address how the plan will be actioned and the detection of any problems that arise, so that appropriate remedial action can be taken.

Having completed all the stages of the tourism planning process, and following the general sequence of events described above, the final tourism plan should include all of the following major elements (after Inskeep, 1991):

- Tourism development objectives
- General background analysis
- Infrastructure analysis and recommendations
- Tourist attractions and activities, and their performance
- Tourist facilities and services, and their improvements
- Recommended extent and forms of tourism
- Market analysis and projections
- Recommended tourism development policy and structure plan
- Economic analysis and recommendations
- Environmental considerations and recommendations
- Socio-cultural considerations and recommendations
- Institutional considerations and recommendations
- Marketing and promotion recommendations
- Plan implementation and monitoring

Tourism policy formulation

The formulation and agreement of policies for tourism is an essential prerequisite of successful tourism development and management. A tourism policy establishes a framework within which informed decisions on development can be made, as the following list of Japan's tourism policies (from JNTO) demonstrates:

1. Promoting international exchange through tourism
   - International exchange and co-operation
   - Developing attractive tourist resorts
   - Encouraging longer, safer travel
   - Hosting conventions

2. Promoting international tourism in local regions
   - Tourism Action Program in the Nineties (TAP 90s)
   - 'New sites of discovery'
   - International culture villages
   - International convention facilities
   - International exchange centres

3. Improvement of tourist facilities
   - Accommodation in Japan
   - Government assistance to hotels
   - Tourist and recreation facilities
   - Development of resort areas
   - Registered international tourist restaurants
   - Subsidies for promoting the tourist industry

4. Travel agency business
   - Regulations on travel agency business
   - Consumer protection on tourism

5. Transport
   - Rail transport
   - Road transport
   - Air transport
   - Marine transport

6. International tourism co-operation and international exchange
   - Technical co-operation
   - Co-operation with international organisations
   - Bilateral tourism exchange program

7. Protection of tourism resources
   - Protection of natural resources
   - Protection of the cultural heritage

The lead role in policy formulation must rest with governments and their executive agencies, since policies, once implemented, affect entire countries and their communities. All governments produce statements of intent across their full range of activities, for example in defence, the economy, foreign affairs, education, housing, social services and health provision. Policies on tourism are not universally developed by all the world's nations, especially those developing nations and emerging Eastern Bloc states yet to embrace tourism development. Those countries that have developed tourism find that the revenue earned from tourism can help to achieve other economic, technological and social policy objectives. In the west African countries of Sierra Leone and the Gambia, for example, export earnings from tourism are used to develop education and health services, and to improve the countries' infrastructure, such as their road and telecommunications networks.

Tourism policies will differ from one country to another, but there are a number of basic requirements that an effective policy will seek to address. These include:

● *Objectives of tourism development.* The key feature of the tourism policy will be why the country has decided to develop tourism, expressed as realistic and measurable objectives. In the vast majority of cases the prime objective will be economic, for example foreign currency earnings, employment creation and economic development. Supporting objectives may be social, cultural or environmental, for example the mixing of people from different cultural backgrounds or the preservation of wildlife habitats. In reality, the objectives included in the tourism policy are likely to cover a variety of economic, environmental and socio-cultural reasons for progressing tourism development.

● *Rate of growth of tourism.* This is an important issue since the faster the growth rate the harder it is likely to be to control any potential and actual detrimental impacts of the tourism development. A cautious growth rate will allow the host nation and communities to adjust to the influx of tourists, while at the same time allowing sufficient time for infrastructure and superstructure development, and training of workers.

● *Types of tourist development.* The policy should indicate the extent to which either domestic or international tourism, or both, are to be developed. Each type of tourism has its own requirements in terms of tourist facilities and amenities. The policy can include reference to the type of tourists that the country is seeking to attract; nowadays, it is common for tourism policies to include reference to the encouragement of 'high quality' tourism, loosely translated as high spending tourists! Nonetheless, such a statement illustrates to developers the type of tourism that is likely to be encouraged and, perhaps of greater importance, the types of development that are likely to be frowned upon.

● *Private and public sector responsibilities.* The division of roles and responsibilities between the private and public sector in tourism should be clearly stated in the policy. Traditionally, the public sector has been responsible for infrastructure provision and tourism promotion, although private/public sector partnerships are becoming increasingly common.

It is frequently the case that the specific elements of a tourism policy are set within a framework of sustainable development, encouraging a type of tourism that is respectful of environments, cultures and communities in the short and long term, as the following case study on tourism policy formulation in Wales demonstrates.

Case Study: Policy formulation in Wales – Tourism 2000

Introduction

In 1994, the Wales Tourist Board published its Tourism 2000 strategy document to guide the way in which Welsh tourism is developed and marketed leading up to the year 2000. It aims to ensure that a proper balance is maintained between different policy objectives, enabling the industry to continue to benefit Wales. It has been developed in consultation with the Wales Tourist Board's public and private sector partners, and seeks to ensure that the industry's joint endeavours remain complementary and cost effective.

Objectives and principles

The Tourism 2000 strategy has as its starting point the following mission statement:

The Wales Tourist Board seeks to develop and market tourism in ways which will yield the optimum economic and social benefit to the people of Wales. Implicit in this objective is the need:

- *to offer high standards of product quality and of service;*
- *to sustain and promote the culture of Wales and the Welsh language;*
- *to safeguard and enhance the natural and the built environment.*

In order to achieve these aims, the Board works in partnership with statutory agencies, local authorities, the private sector and other bodies.

The Board's mission statement is based upon the principle of sustainable development. The strategic challenge facing tourism is summarised in the document as follows:

- *Tourism already makes an important economic contribution to Wales. Developed appropriately, it can play a bigger role in the future, alongside other industries;*
- *to flourish in the future, tourism in Wales needs to offer products of high quality and of good value, in order to meet the needs of discerning consumers within a highly competitive market place;*
- *tourism development must respect the environment (in all its facets) and must proceed with the support of the community;*
- *therefore, the Tourism 2000 strategy must be asset-led, market-related and aimed at achieving sustainable development.*

Policy statements

There are a total of 142 policy statements included in the Tourism 2000 strategy document, arranged on a sectoral and thematic basis. Their purpose is to guide the actions of the Board and to offer policy advice to its partners. For ease of analysis, the policy statements can be grouped under the following five categories:

1. Environment, culture and community (policies 1–33)
The Tourism 2000 strategy recognises the need for the industry to forge a special relationship with the environment and the community. The principles for environmental and community sustainability provide a basic framework for the Board's policies, but codes of conduct are not enough; they need to be supported by practical initiatives. Organisations in Wales are used to working together ▷

on environmental and community projects. The strategy urges all concerned with the tourism industry to remain pioneers.

2. Places to stay (policies 34–66)

The Tourism 2000 strategy asserts that accommodation services are the keystone of tourism. The strategy seeks to foster a viable accommodation sector, offering a good choice of places to stay which are in tune with market needs, offer good quality and bring benefit to host communities. A balance will be sought between safeguarding existing enterprises which can adapt and remain competitive, and encouraging new enterprises geared to capturing new markets.

The strategy suggests that the self-catering sector will be favoured by demographic trends and that it is important to Wales. The Board's policies are aimed at ensuring that this sector thrives and remains cost-competitive. The serviced sector has been more heavily hit by recession, but is well placed to deliver products consistent with the overall strategy. Policy emphasis is placed on improving the performance of existing serviced accommodation stock, and encouraging new development where there is potential.

3. Things to do (policies 67–95)

The strategy appreciates the important role that attractions play in helping to complete a holiday or day visit and the fact that, apart from being a rewarding experience in their own right, they often provide the reason for making the trip. Tourism 2000 recognises the need to offer a good range of things for visitors to do, which should reflect and respect the diversity and quality of Welsh assets. They also need to cater for changing market needs, to be of good quality and to be durable.

The strategy recognises that there is a need to develop some new high quality attractions. In Cardiff and Swansea, for example, there is scope to create a critical mass of attractions and cultural facilities to raise the international profile of Wales. The Board will not, however, encourage new attractions whose effect would simply be to displace efficient existing ones.

The strategy attaches importance to the arts and to special events. It also appreciates that Wales is well placed to cater for activity holidays, although these need to be developed sensitively for environmental reasons.

4. Infrastructure services (policies 96–119)

Tourism 2000 recognises that accessibility from the principal visitor markets is crucial to determining the number of visitors coming to Wales. Once in Wales, visitors need good information to help them make the most of their stay. They also need other basic facilities, whose quality will influence perceptions of Wales.

The strategy welcomes the introduction of management measures to reduce the impact of road traffic on the community and the environment. It considers that maintaining the rail network is important, especially with regard to rural Wales, the South Wales valleys and the Irish sea ports.

5. Customer care, management and training (policies 120–142)

The Tourism 2000 strategy maintains that quality has become the watchword for the 1990s. It goes on to say that in tourism, competing on quality means not only producing the right product, but also delivering good service – promptly, courteously and with enthusiasm. The strategy gives the Board the opportunity to re-affirm its commitment to good standards and to refine its quality assurance schemes. The Board's policies stress the importance of good standards of customer care. The strategy recognises that effective training is essential and that the industry must be more aware of visitors with special needs.

Implementing the strategy

In themselves, the objectives and policy statements contained in Tourism 2000 do not define strategic priorities for tourism. To provide a degree of objectivity to the exercise, the strategy includes a number of targets to be achieved by the year 2000, relating to the annual growth in domestic tourism trips and revenue, overseas visitor numbers and their spending, and employment in the tourism industry in Wales.

The strategy sets out a vision for the future, of a Welsh tourism industry that is competitive in terms of both quality of facilities and standards of customer care, and the diversity of the holiday experience that is on offer. In short, as the Tourism 2000 document states, the Wales Tourist Board sees a tourism industry that is sustainable in the longer term in both environmental and economic terms, and is integrated within the community.

(*Information courtesy of the Wales Tourist Board*)

Discussion points and essay questions

1. What factors, internal and external to Wales, are likely to affect the successful achievement of the strategy's targets?

2. Why does the Tourism 2000 strategy place such an emphasis on sustainability?

3. The strategy talks of tourism being a highly competitive industry; which are Wales's main competitors on the domestic and international tourism scene?

4. What factors will influence the degree of commitment and enthusiasm with which the different sectors of the tourism industry in Wales will respond to the policy statements and work in partnership with the Wales Tourist Board to achieve its future vision?

Planning for sustainable tourism development

We saw in Chapter 5 on the impacts of tourism that, if the international tourism industry is to flourish, then future development must be founded on the principles for sustainable tourism. Sustainable tourism is an emerging concept that has grown out of increased concern about the negative environmental and socio-cultural impacts of unplanned tourism development. An extension of 'green tourism', which focuses on environmental concerns, sustainable tourism is part of a much wider global debate on sustainable development, highlighted by the *Brundtland Report* in 1987 and the Earth Summit in Rio in 1992. The sustainable approach to tourism development implies that the natural and cultural resources of tourism are conserved for continuous use in the future, while still bringing benefits to the present society. This builds on the definition included in the *Brundtland Report* (United Nations, 1987), which states that sustainable development is:

> '. . . development that meets the needs of the present without compromising the ability of future generations to meet their own needs'.

Planning for sustainable development is acutely important in tourism, since so much tourism development depends on attractions related to the natural and cultural environments of destination areas. Without a commitment to sustaining the very resources that attract tourists in the first place, the industry cannot prosper.

It is important to stress that the concept of sustainable tourism goes far beyond minimising environmental impacts. Central to the concept is the need to protect and respect the integrity of communities and cultures, and to involve local communities in tourism planning and development issues. Chapter 5 examined in detail some of the practical steps that can be taken to help achieve these aims.

Partnerships in tourism planning and development

There is general consensus across the whole of the international tourism industry that partnership arrangements are the most effective way of achieving success in planning and development. Partnerships and collaborative ventures can help to unite the multiplicity of interests throughout all sectors of the diverse tourism industry. The UK Department of National Heritage (now the Department for Culture, Media and Sport), in its 1997 tourism strategy document *Success through Partnership* (Department of National Heritage, 1997), states that its mission in relation to UK tourism is:

'To develop tourism as a high-quality, profitable and sustainable activity, through a partnership of industry, government and the tourist boards, so as to realise the growth potential of the industry and the associated social and cultural benefits for the nation'.

This illustrates a common partnership arrangement in tourism, where the private sector works in conjunction with the public sector on a wide range of issues, such as tourism policy formulation, infrastructure provision, the development of tourist facilities and amenities, marketing and promotion, and training. There are many examples of such partnership arrangements at all levels of the industry, for example:

- The publicly funded World Tourism Organisation working with its private sector affiliate members drawn from all sectors of the international tourism industry.
- National tourism organisations (NTOs) working collaboratively with tourism industry operators to develop attractions and facilities.
- Regional tourist boards providing a range of services for their commercial members, including hoteliers, attractions operators and coach companies.
- Local authorities co-ordinating the development of privately funded tourist facilities in their areas.

Partnership arrangements are also found *within* the private sector and the public sector of tourism. It is common for commercial operators to work together for mutual interest, for example hotels and tourist attractions creating joint products, tour operators contracting with accommodation providers and coach operators, and farm tourism enterprises undertaking joint purchasing and promotional schemes. Different levels of the public sector also work in partnership to pool resources for maximum effect; a local authority tourism department, for example, may work with its regional tourist board to develop new holiday packages.

Whatever the precise collaborative working arrangements, effective partnerships offer a number of advantages, including:

- Maximising the economic benefits of tourism
- Helping to minimise tourism's negative environmental and socio-cultural impacts
- Maximising the use of resources
- Spreading the risks of tourism development

Collaborative arrangements between tourism industry partners in the same geographical area are particularly effective, as the following case study of York demonstrates.

Case Study: Partnerships in tourism development – York

Introduction

The City of York is one of the leading tourism destinations in Britain, offering UK and overseas visitors a wide variety of museums and other attractions, the historic architecture of the city itself, plus a wide range of shopping and accommodation facilities. Tourism is vitally important to the economy of York, as shown by research from Touche Ross consultants carried out in 1994, which indicated that some 4 million visitors each year are attracted to the city, spending more than £250 million and supporting over 10 000 jobs. Of the 4 million visitors, 600 000 were overnight stay visitors who accounted for more than 1.5 million visitor nights in the city's accommodation. A significant proportion of the tourism revenue is accounted for by visitors' shopping spend, contributing substantially to the continued prosperity of city centre shops in the face of out-of-town retail competition. Other important data from the Touche Ross research showed that, of the 4 million visitors to York in 1993:

● 199 000 stayed in the main hotels

● 379 000 stayed in other accommodation

● 1 125 000 were on day visits primarily for leisure purposes

● 2 250 000 were on day visits primarily for shopping purposes

● Average length of stay of overnight visitors was 2.7 nights

● Of all visitors to York, 67 per cent were day visitors and 33 per cent staying visitors

Although the research highlighted the positive aspects of the York 'product' and the significant economic benefits of tourism to the city, there was also a note of caution, with the comment that *'there is no room for complacency'*. There was evidence that some of the attractions in York were experiencing reductions in their visitor numbers (see Table 6.1). Moreover, York faces increasing competition as a regional tourist and shopping destination from places such as Leeds, with the new Royal Armouries attraction, Halifax, with its Eureka! Museum for Children, and Bradford, the home of the National Museum of Photography, Film and Television.

Table 6.1:
Visitor numbers to selected attractions in York, 1993–94

Attraction	Number of visitors
York Minster	2 000 000 (estimated)
Jorvik Viking Centre	676 935
Castle Museum	428 587
National Railway Museum	399 120
Cliffords Tower	136 289
York City Art Gallery	126 304
Yorkshire Museum	120 000
Archaeological Resource Centre	53 852
Treasurer's House	50 744

Source: York City Council

SWOT analysis

As part of their research, the consultants analysed a number of factors that affect the competitiveness of York as a tourist destination. These were set out as a SWOT analysis, as follows:

1. Strengths
   - Strong national and international identity
   - Superb built heritage

2. Weaknesses
   - Poor market intelligence
   - Difficulty in identifying growth markets
   - Lack of re-investment by leading attractions
   - Limited exploitation of synergies between attractions

3. Opportunities
   - Development of the Castle Museum
   - Potential for further developing inbound markets

4. Threats
   - Lack of monitoring methods to assess performance and make adjustments
   - Environmental damage/capacity constraints
   - Shopping tourism may 'suffocate' leisure tourism
   - Fading appeal of Jorvik

The consultants' implications arising from the SWOT analysis for York fell into three distinct areas, as follows:

1. There is little need for broad-based destination marketing of York since there is already a strong positive image of the city.
2. There is need for comprehensive and continuous market research, given the increasingly competitive and fast-moving market for tourist destinations.
3. York will need to develop a flagship tourist attraction in order to maintain its position as a popular leisure destination.

A tourism strategy for York

At the beginning of 1995, representatives of the tourism industry in York met as the York Tourism Forum to discuss the report of the research by Touche Ross. A small strategy group was established and asked to translate the consultants' findings into a strategy and action plan for the city, which would be recommended to the whole of the tourism industry in York. The strategy group included representatives from the following organisations:

- York City Council
- Yorkshire and Humberside Tourist Board
- York Visitor and Conference Bureau
- York and North Yorkshire Chamber of Commerce
- North Yorkshire Training and Enterprise Council
- York Attractions Group
- York Archaeological Trust
- GMB trade union

Partnerships in tourism development – York continued

The strategy group reported back to the Forum in July 1995 and the 'First Stop York' tourism initiative was born. The strategic goals of the initiative were to create, through partnership between the public and private sectors, a tourism industry in York where:

1. Economic and employment benefits are maximised.

2. The city is recognised as a high quality tourism destination that is continually being enhanced, in terms of both product and customer service.

3. A wide range of quality jobs is available, with training and career opportunities.

4. The potentially negative environmental and social impacts of the tourism industry are managed so that both the quality of life for residents and the enjoyment of York by visitors are enhanced.

5. Local citizens can appreciate the benefits of tourism in York and therefore give it their support.

6. Those engaged in the industry in York possess the means to understand and respond to national and international trends in their business.

Based on the outcomes of the Touche Ross research, the strategy group identified a number of core principles and objectives of the 'First Stop York' initiative, including:

● *Intelligence gathering*: the monitoring of local, regional, national and international trends as an aid to informed planning and management.

● *Product development*: including the continuation of a clear image for the city, encouraging re-investment in attractions and facilities, and improving evening facilities in the city.

● *Product marketing and packaging*: to adopt a highly targeted and co-ordinated approach to marketing the city, particularly the short break opportunities, and adopt a single, clear, high quality brand for the York product. To market York as a year-round destination.

● *Bookability and management*: including the introduction of booking systems that will facilitate easy access to the York product for potential visitors, improving facilities for the arrival of visitors to the city and ensuring equal access to all sections of the community.

● *Centre of excellence*: to improve job quality, training and career prospects for those working in the tourism industry and to develop a high quality and consistent approach to providing services to the visitor.

● *Citizens' support*: increasing understanding of the tourism industry among local people and developing a greater understanding of residents' concerns about the development of tourism in the city.

● *Partnership*: to develop a co-ordinated, partnership framework for the management, implementation and monitoring of all activities resulting from the strategic plan for tourism in York.

Action points

Building on the initiative's strategic goals, core principles and objectives, members of the strategy group have devised a series of specific action points, published as an action plan, with detailed timing, leadership and cost implications. The action points concerned with the objective of improving product marketing and packaging, for example, include the establishment of the 'First Stop York' brand, with its associated logo, artwork and displays and a commitment by all partners to corporate, trade-related marketing activities, to include trade fairs, liaison with tour operators and trade advertising. Further product marketing action points include a year-round campaign led by the York Visitor and Conference Bureau aimed at UK and overseas visitors, an enhanced rail campaign ▷

with Regional Railways, targeting of incoming visitors through the exploitation of Yorkshire and Humberside Tourist Board's links with the British Tourist Authority (BTA), linkages with Eurotunnel and Eurostar, liaison with air operators and development of the incentive travel market.

(*Information courtesy of York City Council*)

Discussion points and essay questions

1. Why is it important for tourist destinations such as York to have accurate intelligence gathering capabilities?

2. What impacts can tourism development have on local people in destinations such as York and why is it important to involve local residents in future tourism development plans?

3. What particular roles do private sector operators, and the different public sector organisations involved with tourism in York, play in the implementation of the strategy?

4. How has a partnership approach to tourism development helped York and its tourist industry?

Tourism in developing countries

As aircraft technology develops, and tourists' ability and desire to explore new long-haul destinations increases, many of the developing nations of the world are emerging as important tourist areas. Increased standards of living in developing countries are also enabling their residents to travel abroad more frequently. Although international tourism remains the preserve of developed western societies, with more than 90 per cent of all international tourist arrivals centred on the three 'hubs' of Europe, the Americas and the Asia/Pacific region (World Tourism Organisation, 1996), developing countries are showing significant growth in tourism when compared with industrialised countries and the emerging nations of central and eastern Europe, as Table 6.2 indicates.

These data show that, while industrialised countries absorbed more than half of the world's tourist arrivals in 1995, they experienced a loss of five percentage points in world market share since the beginning of the 1990s. In contrast, developing nations recorded the fastest growth rate of international arrivals in 1995 and a gain of more than 2 per cent in their market share during the first half of the 1990s. Data on receipts from international tourism indicate a similar pattern; the developing countries' share of international tourism receipts grew from 26.6 per cent in 1990 to 30.5 per cent in 1995, at the expense

Table 6.2: International tourist arrivals in selected country groupings

Country groupings	Tourist arrivals (thousands)			Annual % change		Market share (% of world total)	
	1990	1994	1995	95/94	95/90	1990	1995
World total	459 233	546 269	567 033	3.80	4.31	100.00	100.00
Industrialised countries	284 268	314 676	321 385	2.13	2.48	61.90	56.68
Developing countries	128 242	157 280	170 050	8.12	5.81	27.93	29.99
Central/East Europe	46 723	74 313	75 598	1.73	10.10	10.17	13.33

Source: WTO

of the industrialised nations whose share fell from 71.6 per cent to 65.1 per cent over the same time period (World Tourism Organisation, 1996).

Increasingly, the governments of developing nations, particularly those that have few exploitable natural resources, are coming to realise that tourism offers many economic and political benefits, including:

- Injections of foreign currency
- Employment opportunities
- Infrastructure improvements
- Diversity of economic activity
- Credibility on the world stage

The growth of tourism in developing countries, however, is not without its problems. Multinational hotel groups, airlines and tour operators have been quick to exploit tourism's potential in the developing nations by working with governments on tourism projects. Some have been criticised, however, for making little contribution to the local economies in developing countries, for failing to employ sufficient local people and for offering low contract rates for accommodation. In addition to these problems, the growth of tourism has led to concern about the long-term social and cultural impacts that tourism might have in developing countries. The bringing together of people from widely different social backgrounds can lead to a loss of cultural identity and a loss of authenticity on the part of the host communities, for example local people are encouraged to perform ethnic and religious rituals that conform to the tourists' image of an area, but which may bear little relation to the reality of their situation. The affluence of the incoming visitors can also affect young people in the developing countries, who may be tempted to forego their education in favour of providing services for the tourists. In the worst cases, drug abuse, crime and prostitution may flourish as a result of tourism development.

It is for these reasons that the governments in developing nations, and non-governmental organisations such as Tourism Concern and Friends of the Earth, are working towards tourism development that is sustainable in the long term, by giving attention to prior planning and responsible management.

One country that is working to develop a sustainable tourism industry is Botswana in southern Africa, the subject of the following case study.

Case Study: Tourism development in Botswana

Introduction

Botswana lies in the heart of southern Africa, bordered by South Africa, Namibia, Zimbabwe and Zambia. The tableland of the Kalahari Desert covers the bulk of southern Botswana and nearly one-fifth of the country is designated as National Park. The majority of the population lives in the south-east around the capital Gabarone, Serowe and Kanya along the border with South Africa.

Tourism infrastructure

Sir Seretse is Botswana's principal international airport, located 10 miles to the north of Gabarone. The airport was opened in the mid-1980s and gave the country direct access to the international community, with British Airways and Air France operating regular flights. There is another airport ▷

in the north of the country at Kasane, close to the border with Zambia, and a number of smaller airports for internal travel. Work is in progress to upgrade the internal rail system, and the road system boasts over 1200 miles of surfaced highway.

Tourism statistics

Data from the Botswana Department of Tourism show that tourist arrivals more than doubled between 1980 and 1990 (see Table 6.3). The most significant growth in numbers coincided with the opening of Sir Seretse International Airport in the mid-1980s. Table 6.3 also demonstrates that there has been a shift in the proportions of domestic and international tourists over the same time period; domestic tourists accounted for 57 per cent and overseas visitors 43 per cent of all arrivals in 1980, but the figures for 1990 were 40 per cent and 60 per cent respectively. Arrivals from the UK and Ireland jumped from 5824 in 1980 to nearly 36 000 in 1990. Preliminary statistics for 1995 show that the number of international arrivals to Botswana grew by 6.4 per cent on the 1994 figures (World Tourism Organisation, 1996).

Table 6.4 shows the expenditure of visitors to Botswana between 1981 and 1990. Not surprisingly, expenditure rose sharply from 1985 onwards as a result of the opening of Sir Seretse International Airport. Total expenditure in 1990 amounted to 182 million Pula (approximately £43 million).

Botswana's tourism product

The Botswana government's selling proposition is 'high cost, low volume', i.e. a small number of high-spending tourists. In line with this proposition, the Department of Tourism has increased the entry and camping fees to National Parks in order to discourage mass tourism. They pursue a policy of sustainable tourism, leaving the country's ecosystem in a balanced state. There are wildlife management areas, which are zoned for sustainable wildlife utilisation, protecting one of the country's major tourist assets.

Although there is no grading system, all hotels generally maintain a reasonable standard, particularly those in the main centres in the east of the country. Hotels and motels with the most modern facilities are to be found around Gabarone. There is a wide range of safari lodges and camps, some very basic and some with every luxury, attracting the high-spending tourists from Europe, North America and the Far East.

Tourism promotion

The Department of Tourism produces a variety of brochures and posters, in English, French and German. Videos are also available in these languages. Staff from the Department attend major travel trade fairs, such as ITB Berlin and the World Travel Market in London, so as to forge links with tour operators and airlines, thereby further developing their products and promotional outlets. Meetings are also arranged with major tour wholesalers to persuade them to include Botswana in their sales manuals and tour programmes.

(*Information courtesy of Botswana Director of Tourism*)

Discussion points and essay questions

1. What is the rationale for Botswana adopting a 'high cost, low volume' approach to tourism development?
2. Who funds infrastructure improvements in developing countries such as Botswana?

Tourism development in Botswana continued

Table 6.3: Total arrivals in Botswana by country of residence, 1980–90

Country of residence	1980	1981	1982	1983	1984	1985	1986	1987	1988	1989	1990
Botswana	351 134	330 860	398 173	448 240	434 035	436 779	468 340	449 224	513 313	622 196	561 596
Total excluding Botswana	263 581	226 940	297 678	302 329	338 750	326 950	381 205	432 323	384 335	691 041	844 295
Africa	247 761	213 960	274 475	282 808	297 424	290 602	333 167	382 908	333 783	612 457	759 197
South Africa and Namibia	202 833	149 980	193 570	189 152	226 972	216 263	239 179	247 449	254 241	309 747	363 840
Zimbabwe	30 984	48 960	57 225	75 614	52 071	60 694	55 067	96 933	44 869	249 283	338 264
Zambia	7 269	9 740	16 580	8 637	8 082	3 912	21 402	18 480	15 242	25 241	26 454
Swaziland	1 785	1 360	1 320	2 317	1 146	1 480	2 861	2 618	2 714	2 614	3 997
Lesotho	2 202	1 500	2 200	2 101	2 620	2 531	3 090	4 003	4 771	5 601	5 026
Rest of Africa	2 688	2 420	3 580	4 987	6 533	5 722	11 568	13 425	11 946	19 971	21 616
Asia and the Pacific	1 294	1 180	2 241	1 853	3 804	4 022	4 018	5 303	5 204	7 303	8 771
Asia	704	720	1 301	1 229	2 482	2 693	2 820	3 454	2 976	3 722	4 328
Australia and New Zealand	590	460	940	624	1 322	1 329	1 198	1 849	2 228	3 581	4 443
Europe	11 341	8 940	16 541	13 156	31 708	26 388	37 473	36 918	37 737	60 075	65 473
UK and Ireland	5 824	3 900	8 689	6 160	17 982	13 045	19 074	17 896	18 712	25 735	35 973
Rest of Europe	5 517	5 040	7 852	6 996	13 726	13 343	18 399	19 022	19 025	34 340	29 500
America	3 185	2 860	4 421	4 512	5 814	5 938	6 547	7 194	7 611	11 206	10 854
USA	2 587	2 200	3 681	3 937	4 827	5 248	5 724	5 961	6 162	9 374	8 533
Rest of America	598	660	740	575	987	690	823	1 233	1 449	1 832	2 321
Total	614 715	557 800	695 851	750 569	772 785	763 729	849 545	881 547	897 648	1 313 237	1 405 891

Source: Botswana Director of Tourism

Table 6.4: Expenditure by visitors to Botswana, 1981–90

	Number of visitors	Number of visitors who declared expenditure	Declared expenditure (Pula)*	Average expenditure (Pula)	Average length of stay (days)	Average daily expenditure per visitor (Pula)	Total expenditure ('000 Pula)
1981	271 060	179 610	12 686 660	70.63	5.4	13.08	19 146
1982	300 413	181 362	19 041 928	104.99	4.8	21.87	31 542
1983	350 453	211 504	24 541 482	116.03	5.9	19.67	40 664
1984	325 204	201 997	28 226 271	139.74	5.9	23.68	45 443
1985	333 871	203 698	27 341 308	134.22	4.9	27.39	44 814
1986	368 499	228 900	47 533 084	207.66	4.3	48.29	76 522
1987	406 008	264 974	49 701 271	187.57	4.9	38.28	76 155
1988	340 436	211 389	38 275 779	181.07	4.9	36.95	61 642
1989	582 871	398 517	73 780 097	185.14	4.5	41.05	107 911
1990	759 867	513 949	126 544 749	246.22	4.8	50.87	182 037

* £1 sterling ≃ 4.20 Pula

Source: Botswana Director of Tourism; based on declarations made by departing visitors

3. What internal and external factors are likely to affect Botswana's tourism development in the next 10 years?

4. How can the government of Botswana ensure that its tourism development is sustainable in the longer term?

Chapter summary

In this chapter we have explored the twin concepts of planning and development in international tourism, and their relationship to resource management. We have seen that the three concepts of planning, development and management need to work in harmony if a country or region is to maximise tourism's economic benefits and minimise its detrimental effects. The often ignored concept of planning for tourism at the corporate level has been tackled, with an introduction to strategic planning in the industry. The chapter has investigated the different contexts and levels within which tourism occurs, plus the stages in the tourism planning process. We have seen that tourism policy formulation is an essential prerequisite of successful tourism development, since it establishes the framework within which informed decisions on future developments can be made. We have analysed the concept of sustainability in the tourism planning process and the role of partnerships in tourism planning and development. There is little doubt that the twin themes of sustainability and partnerships will be of great significance to the future development of international tourism. The chapter concluded with an analysis of the principal issues concerning tourism in developing countries, which are increasingly turning to tourism as a way of harnessing economic, political and social development.

Discussion questions

1. With the aid of national and international examples, consider the relationship between planning, development and management in the context of tourism.

2. Why is tourism planning not particularly well developed at the international level?

3. What is the significance of tourism planning at the corporate level?

4. Critically assess the role of partnership arrangements in tourism planning and development.

References and further reading

● British Tourist Authority/English Tourist Board (1996) *Tourism Intelligence Quarterly*, Vol. 17, No. 4, BTA/ETB, London
● Burns, P and Holden, A (1995) *Tourism: A New Perspective*, Prentice Hall, Hemel Hempstead, UK
● Department of National Heritage (1997) *Success through Partnership: A Strategy for Tourism*, DNH, London
● Gunn, C (1994) *Tourism Planning*, Taylor & Francis, New York
● Hall, C M (1994) *Tourism and Politics*, Wiley, Chichester, UK
● Holloway, J C (1994) *The Business of Tourism*, 4th edition, Longman, Harlow, UK
● Inskeep, E (1991) *Tourism Planning: An Integrated and Sustainable Development Approach*, Van Nostrand Reinhold, New York
● Pearce, D (1989) *Tourist Development*, Longman, Harlow, UK
● Thomas Cook Group (1994) *Annual Report and Accounts*, Thomas Cook, London
● United Nations (1987) *World Commission on Environment and Development, Our Common Future (the Brundtland Report)*, Oxford University Press
● World Tourism Organisation (1994) *National and Regional Tourism Planning: Methodologies and Case Studies*, Routledge, London
● World Tourism Organisation (1996) *International Tourism Overview 1995*, WTO, Madrid
● World Travel and Tourism Council (1995) *Agenda 21 for the Travel and Tourism Industry*, WTTC, London

Chapter Seven

Tourism Marketing

Chapter Overview

This chapter considers the role and significance of marketing within the global tourism industry, drawing on case studies and up to date industry examples. We investigate key aspects of the concept and application of marketing, such as marketing objectives, segmentation, market orientation and customer service, before analysing marketing research in tourism. The application of the marketing mix to the tourism industry is considered in detail, highlighting the importance of a balanced approach to implementing marketing plans. We also investigate the important topic of destination marketing, where problems of multi-ownership and multiple product offerings pose many challenges to the tourism marketer. The chapter concludes with an explanation and appraisal of the application of the strategic marketing planning process to the tourism industry.

Key Topics

- Understanding the concept of marketing in the context of international tourism
- Marketing research in tourism
- Application of the marketing mix to the tourism industry
- Market segmentation in tourism
- Destination marketing
- Strategic marketing planning in tourism

Introduction

All those managing tourism organisations in the public and private sectors are well aware of the importance of marketing to the success of their enterprises. A company developing a new hotel complex, for example, may have top-class facilities for guests and the latest computerised management information systems, but if it fails to market the hotel effectively, the venture will not reach its full business potential and may even fail through insufficient sales revenue. Applying traditional marketing concepts and techniques to the tourism industry, however, can be problematical. This is due in no small part to the fact that tourism is a very diverse and fragmented industry, as we saw in Chapter 2; indeed many would argue that applying the term 'industry' to tourism is a misnomer in itself, given that it is made up of a wide range of interrelated sectors, each of which could justifiably be classed as an industry in its own right, such as airlines, hotels and tourist attractions. This fragmentation makes co-ordinated marketing activities more difficult to plan and implement successfully. The predominance of small business enterprises in the international tourism industry also influences the application of marketing concepts and mechanisms. Many of the operators of tourism businesses lack the necessary finance and management skills to be able to make informed marketing decisions, often with little or no relevant marketing research to consult. In addition, the 'tourism product' has certain unique characteristics not found in other service sector industries, meaning that the transfer of traditional marketing approaches to tourism is not always possible without refinement and adjustment. Nonetheless, marketing does command a significant share of both public and private tourism resources, as the competition for domestic and international visitors intensifies. National Tourist Organisations (NTOs) and commercial operators invest heavily in all aspects of tourism marketing, from research through strategic marketing planning to promotion. The remainder of this chapter looks in detail at these and other topics.

Understanding the concept of marketing

Although the importance of marketing is widely accepted throughout the international tourism industry, there are many misconceptions about the marketing concept in general and its application to the tourism industry in particular. One of the most common is the belief that marketing is the same as advertising; although advertising often features prominently in the marketing plans and promotional campaigns of tourism companies, it is just one part of a much wider process that encompasses marketing research, product development and public relations activities, to name but a few. It is understandable why confusion sometimes occurs given the very visible and high-profile nature of tourism advertising. Another myth surrounding marketing is that it is the same as selling. Again, selling is a vital part of the marketing process in international tourism, but it is just that, a part of the much wider process. A further misconception about marketing is that it only takes place in private sector enterprises. It is true that the historical development of the concept of marketing was most apparent in the commercial world. Today, however, the majority of public sector tourism organisations are actively involved in marketing their products, services and destinations, since they too have 'customers'. A final myth surrounding marketing is that it is a 'one-off' activity. This could not be further from the truth; marketing must be viewed as a continuous process over the medium to long term, allowing an organisation to develop a profitable relationship with its customers. Over time, customers' needs and requirements change, and the successful tourism enterprise will be the one that recognises this fact and develops its products and services accordingly.

The cyclical nature of the marketing process in tourism is shown diagrammatically in Figure 7.1. As the figure shows, the identification of customer needs is the starting point for all effective marketing activities. Knowing where customers come from, their demographic profiles, whether they are satisfied with facilities, how much they are willing to pay, and so on, provides an invaluable research base on which to make informed marketing decisions. Stage two of the marketing process, namely developing products and

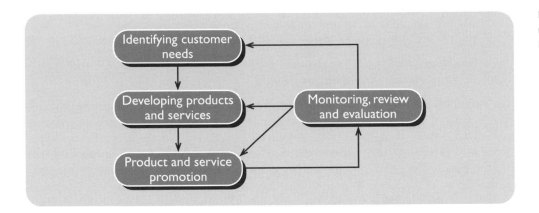

Figure 7.1: The marketing process in tourism

services, is far less risky when the characteristics and profiles of customers are known. This enables tourism providers to offer products that have the right features and benefits, are offered for sale at the right price and are made available via the most appropriate distribution channels. Having developed the correct products and services, stage three of the process is concerned with promoting them effectively. As we shall see later in this chapter when we investigate the marketing mix, there are many ways of promoting tourism products and services, including advertising, direct marketing and public relations activity. The final stage of the marketing process indicates that all marketing takes place in a constantly changing business environment. As such, organisations must regularly monitor, review and evaluate their marketing strategies and plans to ensure that they remain relevant and effective.

It is important to stress the dynamic nature of the marketing concept. Kotler (1994) suggests that the marketing discipline is undergoing fresh reappraisal in the light of the vast global, technological, economic and social challenges facing today's companies. Former assumptions, concepts, skills, tools and systems for marketing are being redeveloped for making sound business decisions. These are general statements aimed at all industry sectors, but if we couple them with the dynamic nature of international tourism, it is clear that today's marketers in tourism are faced with managing regular, significant changes in their internal and external business environments.

Marketing defined

Although many managers and operators working in the tourism industry consider that marketing is the single most important management function in their organisation, most would be hard pressed to come up with a meaningful definition of the concept when asked. This is not a criticism of the people working in tourism, but more an illustration of the complexity of the subject, particularly when applied to the very diverse sectors within the global tourism industry. Marketing is concerned with identifying customer needs, developing products and services to meet these needs, and delivering the products and services to the customer at the right time, in the right place and at the right price. Philip Kotler, perhaps the world's most respected authority on the subject of marketing, defines marketing as:

> '. . . a social and managerial process by which individuals and groups obtain what they need and want through creating, offering and exchanging products of value with others'. (Kotler, 1994)

This definition emphasises that notion of exchange within marketing, i.e. that there must be a stated or implied demand and an ability to supply for a market to exist.

The UK Chartered Institute of Marketing (CIM) defines marketing as:

'. . . the management process responsible for identifying, anticipating and satisfying customer requirements profitably'.

This definition has a number of important elements that will help us understand better what we mean by marketing. Firstly, the fact that marketing is a management process means that it ranks alongside human resources, operations, finance and other management functions in terms of the operations of an organisation. The precise importance given to marketing will depend in part on the attitude of management, but more importantly on the nature of the business and the markets in which it operates. The case study on the work of the Australian Tourist Commission (ATC) towards the end of this chapter, for example, indicates that marketing is given a very high priority in helping the ATC achieve its ultimate objective of maximising the numbers of overseas tourists visiting Australia. The second important point about the CIM definition of marketing is that of identifying and anticipating customer requirements, which are crucial for any tourism organisation, large or small. A variety of marketing research activities can be used to discover what customers like and dislike about products and services, with appropriate action being taken as and when required. Thirdly, satisfying customer needs is all about developing products and services that the customer will want to buy and the various techniques that can be used to promote their sale, including direct selling, advertising and public relations. The fourth important point is that the company engaged in the marketing activity must be profitable in its endeavours. This applies equally to private and public sector organisations, even though profit maximisation may not be the prime objective of the latter.

Marketing objectives

We shall see later in this chapter that the identification of marketing objectives is an important early phase of strategic marketing planning for tourism enterprises. Marketing objectives are usually developed in harmony with an organisation's overall goals and objectives. British Airways, for example, has the ultimate goal of becoming:

'. . . the best and most successful company in the airline industry'. (British Airways, 1993)

In order to help achieve this goal, the company has developed a range of specific marketing objectives, for example to secure a leading share of the air travel business worldwide with a significant presence in all major geographical markets, to excel in anticipating and quickly responding to customer needs and competitor activity, and to provide overall superior service and good value for money in every market segment in which it competes. The successful achievement of these marketing objectives will contribute significantly to helping BA fulfil its ultimate goal.

The wide variety of organisations operating in the international tourism arena all set themselves specific marketing objectives so as to provide a framework within which their marketing resources can be used to best effect and their performance measured. These objectives will be a reflection of many internal and external factors that affect the organisation, including its organisational ethos, the business environment in which it is operating, its management style and, perhaps most importantly, whether it operates in the public or private sector of the industry. Private sector tourism operators seek to maximise profits by providing products and services geared to the needs of their customers. Public sector tourism organisations have wider social, environmental, political and economic objectives, such as the provision of facilities for local communities, urban regeneration, political credibility on the world stage or habitat protection. Marketing objectives developed to achieve these wider aims will necessarily differ from those seen in the commercial sector. Although profit maximisation is not the primary objective of public sector tourism organisations, those that are funded from national, regional or local government sources or are agencies of central government, are expected to offer value for money and account for their wise use of public resources. As such, public bodies increasingly adopt a more commercial approach to their activities and the distinction between marketing in private and public sector tourism is becoming less apparent.

Market orientation

Figure 7.1 indicates that the identification of customer needs is a vital first step in the tourism marketing process. Organisations that place customer requirements at the heart of their marketing activities are said to be adopting a market orientation, whereas those that focus on products and services while ignoring customer needs are considered to be product orientated. All tourism organisations must strive to adopt a market orientated philosophy if they are to be successful in retaining and increasing their market share. A tourism enterprise that concentrates too heavily on developing products and services without researching customer attitudes and preferences, is unlikely to reach its full business potential. A true market orientation in the tourism industry involves facilities being open when it is convenient for the customers, not the operators, meals being served in hotels at times suitable to the guests, and transport companies running services at times that are convenient for travellers, to name but a few. Adopting a market or customer orientation is often part of a wider shift in the philosophy of an organisation, which may include a more 'open' management style, improved customer care systems and a more responsive sales environment.

Social marketing

While it is quite justified from a purely commercial viewpoint to place the needs of the market at the forefront of an organisation's marketing activities, tourism companies need to be aware of the consequences of their actions, on the environment, their customers, members of staff and society in general. In Chapter 5 we explored the rise of sustainable tourism and the work of organisations such as Green Globe and Tourism Concern in their endeavours to promote a brand of tourism that is both environmentally sound and culturally responsible. In any marketing work that they undertake, individual tourism operators too must ensure that their actions do not harm the very environments and cultures that their customers have often travelled so far to enjoy. Tour companies, transport operators and destination areas are increasingly alerting prospective travellers to the potential harm that their presence can have, particularly in the remoter and more inaccessible regions of the world. Many include advice and information in their brochures and other publicity materials, while others train their staff on the ground in responsible environmental and cultural practices.

Strategic versus tactical marketing

Strategic marketing is marketing activity that is planned well in advance and has clear medium-term and long-term objectives, for example a US tour operator that aims to capture

50 per cent of the ex-US market to South Africa within three years of its launch and to become the number one US company offering packages to South Africa within 5–7 years. Tactical marketing is an altogether more short-term operational activity, often in response to unforeseen or unplanned problems or opportunities. The need for extra public relations activity after a holiday accident, discounting to counteract competitors' price reductions and the promotion of a new range of holiday products to meet a short-term increase in demand, are all examples of tactical marketing in tourism. In an increasingly competitive global marketplace, it is often necessary for tourism companies to implement a variety of tactical marketing approaches simply to retain their market share. Later in this chapter, we explore strategic marketing planning in tourism and the part that it plays in the growth of tourism enterprises.

Market segmentation

The process by which the total market for a product or service is sub-divided into identifiable groups with similar needs, wants and characteristics, is known as market segmentation. It is one of the most important principles in the marketing of products and services, not least in the tourism industry. The main benefit of segmentation is that it allows an organisation to target particular individuals or groups, making them the focus of its concentrated marketing activities. Market segmentation is, therefore, a tool that the marketer can use to satisfy the requirements of his or her particular customers, while at the same time minimising wastage of resources and improving organisational effectiveness.

The major market segmentation variables available to marketers are as follows:

1. Socio-economic
   - Social class
   - Occupation
   - Income level
   - Home ownership

2. Geographic
   - Country
   - Region
   - Population size
   - Population density

3. Psychographic
   - Lifestyle characteristics
   - Motivations
   - Attitudes
   - Interests

4. Demographic
   - Age
   - Education
   - Gender
   - Family composition
   - Ethnic group

5. Behavioural
   - Benefits
   - Usage rate
   - Frequency
   - User status

The precise variables that an individual tourism organisation uses will depend on a number of factors, such as the products it is selling, the characteristics of its customers and its marketing objectives. As the list indicates, there are five main types of segmentation variables, each with its own sub-classes. Historically, marketers in the UK have used the classification developed by JICNARS (Joint Industry Committee for National Readership

Social grade	Social class	Typical occupations
A	Upper Middle	Higher managerial, administrative and professional (e.g. judges, surgeons)
B	Middle	Intermediate managerial and administrative (e.g. lawyers, teachers, doctors)
C1	Lower Middle	Supervisory, clerical, junior management (e.g. bank clerks, estate agents)
C2	Skilled Working	Skilled manual workers (e.g. joiners, welders)
D	Working	Semi- and unskilled manual workers (e.g. drivers, postmen, porters)
E	Those at lowest level of subsistence	Pensioners, widows, casual workers, students, unemployed people

Surveys) for segmentation on the basis of socio-economic factors. This classification groups people according to their 'social class', based on the occupation of the head of the household (see Table 7.1).

The underlying principle of the JICNARS classification is that the people in each category will have generally similar values, display similar patterns of purchasing behaviour and have similar levels of disposable income. Clearly, there are a number of anomalies with such a classification system, for example:

● It is unrealistic to assume that all people in one category will have broadly similar characteristics. The managing director of a major international airline, for example, may follow the same hobbies as, say, a semi-skilled manual worker in category D.

● If the sales director of a major tour operator is made redundant he or she will immediately move from category A to category E.

● Skilled manual workers may well have higher disposable incomes than people in category A, depending on how they choose to spend their money.

Problems with the implementation of the rather 'rigid' socio-economic classification have led marketers to look towards using market segmentation techniques based on lifestyle criteria, to provide a more realistic base on which to make their marketing decisions. Psychographic variables such as motivations, attitudes and interests often give a clearer understanding of an individual's purchasing behaviour.

Whichever variables are used by a tourism organisation when segmenting a market, it is clear that the process relies heavily on accurate data concerning existing and potential customers, obtained through a variety of marketing research methods.

The customer service function in tourism marketing

Any analysis of the marketing of tourism products and services cannot overlook the importance of customer service to the success of organisations. In the international tourism industry, the creation and distribution of tourism products and services involves a significant amount of interaction between suppliers and their customers. This is due, in part, to the fact that many tourism products are consumed at the point of production, for example a businesswoman on a working trip to Brussels will experience the various components of the tourism process as they happen. Also, staff in tourism enterprises are often an integral part of the product being sold; the success of an excursion as part of an overseas package holiday, for example, will depend in no small part on the professionalism and attitude of the staff hosting the trip. Both these factors highlight the important role that the employees working in tourism have to play in ensuring success for their organisations.

There are many reasons why tourism enterprises need to continually invest in staff training to provide the highest possible standards of customer care. Companies operating in certain highly competitive sectors of the tourism industry, for example travel agencies, tour operators and airlines, have concluded that they can no longer compete on price alone. Margins have been driven so low as to make the future viability of some organisations uncertain. As an alternative strategy, some companies have sought to differentiate themselves by offering superior standards of customer service, and promoting this as their USP (unique selling proposition). Also, customer expectations are changing rapidly, making it especially important for organisations to seek to offer enhanced levels of customer service. Factors such as increased educational opportunities, more travel to foreign countries, the growth of the service sector at the expense of manufacturing industry, greater mobility and the rise of 'consumerism', have all contributed to the rise of a new breed of customers in tourism, who are demanding improvements in both product quality and standards of customer service.

At the organisational level, investment in improving standards of customer service can have definite internal benefits. Companies that have successfully introduced enhanced customer care programmes have experienced fewer complaints from customers and staff, lower staff turnover, improved security, reduced staff absenteeism, improved departmental co-operation and staff who are happier in their work.

Marketing research in tourism

Successful marketing in public and private sector tourism organisations is founded on an effective marketing research base. All organisations need to have detailed information on their existing customers, as well as data with which to plan for the future, a concept known as forecasting. As we saw in Figure 7.1, identifying customer needs is an essential first stage in the marketing process in tourism, from which products and services geared to customer needs can be developed and their success monitored. Without the structured, objective and focused approach to the collection of data that a well-designed marketing research study can offer, decisions taken by marketing managers in tourism are unlikely to be wholly effective.

Market research is the collection and analysis of data about customers and its use for management purposes. To the marketing professional, the term 'marketing research' is a wider, all-embracing concept that includes price research, product research, promotion research and research into consumer behaviour. The complexity of today's global tourism industry means that successful operators cannot rely solely on market research data, but must invest in a variety of marketing research techniques in order to remain competitive. Marketing research data, from whatever source, are essential to all tourism organisations and provide a sound base on which effective marketing decisions can be made. All tourism organisations need feedback from their existing customers on the products they buy, and many will want to know why people are not using their facilities but prefer what a competitor is providing. It is the job of marketing research to provide such information in as objective a form as possible. This need for unbiased data is why many larger tourism organisations commission outside specialists to carry out the research on their behalf. However, not all marketing research activity is necessarily a costly or elaborate affair. The proprietor of a small hotel, for example, will constantly receive informal feedback from guests on their opinion of the hotel's facilities or standards of service, making the necessary adjustments to systems and practices to improve matters. What he or she doesn't always know, of course, are the opinions of the people who say nothing; this is where a marketing research technique such as a self-completed questionnaire survey or customer comment form may provide more reliable and honest information.

Marketing research may be required at any stage of the tourism marketing process, perhaps linked to a feasibility study to investigate the expansion of an existing tourist attraction or to consider alterations to the pricing levels on a cruise liner. Most managers would agree that marketing research plays a vital role in helping their organisations remain buoyant in the increasingly competitive international tourism industry. More specifically, marketing research can:

- Identify new market opportunities or sales outlets
- Help pinpoint specific business problems, for example why has there been a steady drop in demand for a particular product or at a particular facility?
- Identify problems and suggest solutions, such as what proportion of a destination area's budget should be spent on improving infrastructure and how much on marketing and promotional activities?
- Allow a tourist organisation to plan for the future with confidence
- Monitor the reaction of customers to products, services and facilities
- Project an image of an organisation that cares about its customers and respects their views and comments
- Reduce costs by highlighting ineffective practices and systems
- Monitor trends in the tourism industry and its constituent sectors

A marketing research exercise can be carried out by staff already employed in an organisation or, as was suggested earlier in this chapter, it may be undertaken by outside specialist consultants. The 'in house' option has the advantage of being cheaper and under the direct control of the organisation and its management, but this could itself introduce bias and a degree of subjectivity that may render the results meaningless. Larger tourism organisations are likely to employ their own marketing research professionals who will be responsible for commissioning research, analysing data and reporting back to other departments and senior managers. Most tourism enterprises will not be able to afford the luxury of having their own specialist marketing research staff and will look to external agencies to meet their research needs. Such services can be provided by advertising agencies, market research agencies, universities and colleges.

Sources of marketing research data

There are many different types of marketing research data from a variety of sources available to those managing and planning tourism enterprises. Some information, although not specific to the tourism industry, is nonetheless useful for marketing purposes, for example data on trends in employment and changes in population structures. More specific tourism-related data, such as company financial figures, global tourism trends and visitor profiles at attractions, provide organisations with an invaluable information base on which to plan their future marketing activities. Marketing research information is available from two principal sources: material that is already available through a variety of published sources is known as secondary data, whereas primary data refers to new information that is collected for the first time and is often specific to an individual company, for

Figure 7.2: Various marketing research sources in tourism

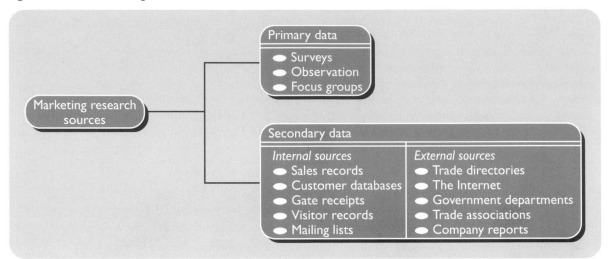

example a survey of visitors to a tourism destination. Figure 7.2 gives examples of the types of information available from both sources.

Figure 7.2 indicates that secondary marketing research data are available from internal and external sources. Much of the information that an organisation needs for marketing purposes may already be available from its own internal sources, such as sales returns, customer databases and mailing lists. It is surprising that tourism organisations often fail to make the best use of their internal records for marketing purposes, sometimes because of problems with accessing large amounts of data. The precise choice of secondary sources will depend on the objectives of a particular marketing research exercise.

Primary research data

Although there is an increasing amount of relevant and up-to-date secondary data available on tourism at international, national and local levels, it is likely that an organisation, at some stage in its development, will need to collect information that is either specific to its own operations or not already available in a published form. The collection and subsequent analysis of this information is known as primary research.

An organisation wanting to collect primary data has three main options available to it, namely:

- Surveys
- Observation
- Focus groups

Surveys Conducting a survey is the most common method of collecting primary data in the tourism industry. It involves the collection of data from a proportion of a total 'population', which researchers refer to as the sample. In this context, 'population' means the total number of people who could be interviewed. For example, the owner of a visitor attraction may decide to interview a 5 per cent sample of all visitors to the attraction on a particular day during the season. If the total number of visitors is 10 000 (the population), 500 interviews (the sample) will need to be undertaken. Sampling is carried out because it is usually impractical to interview the whole 'population'. It is a very precise statistical technique that we investigate further below.

There are three main types of survey that can be used to collect primary data:

- Face-to-face interview survey
- Self-completed questionnaire survey
- Telephone survey

A face-to-face interview survey involves an interviewer asking questions of a member of the general public, known as the respondent, and recording his or her answers and comments on a questionnaire. This type of survey is very common in all sectors of the tourism industry, from destination resorts to transport providers. Face-to-face interviews can be carried out in a number of different locations, for example in a tourist area, at a respondent's home or place of work, in the street or *en route* to a holiday area, perhaps at a frontier post or a toll booth. The face-to-face interview is a good way of obtaining both quantitative and qualitative data. Quantitative refers to factual information such as the age of respondents, where they live, how far they have travelled to a destination, how much they have spent on holiday and the type of transport they have used. Qualitative data refer to the respondents' opinion or attitude to a particular facility, product or service, and provide managers with direct feedback on the views of their customers. Typical questions that would produce qualitative data are as follows:

- How would you rate the standard of service you received at the holiday centre?
- How could the facilities be improved for disabled people?
- If the company were to introduce a loyalty bonus scheme for travel, would you use it?
- Which feature of the visitor attraction did you like the most?
- What is your opinion of the food in the restaurant?
- What was your general impression of the resort complex?

Face-to-face interviews have a number of advantages when compared with other survey methods. One advantage is that the interviewer is able to answer any difficulties that the respondent may have with particular questions. The interviewer can also use prompts to encourage the respondent to elaborate on his or her answers, thereby gaining further valuable information. A further advantage is that visual aids, such as charts and photographs, can be used by the interviewer when asking questions. The main disadvantage of the face-to-face interview technique concerns cost. Recruiting and training interviewers can be expensive and the associated administrative load can be high. Face-to-face interviews are also more time-consuming than techniques such as telephone interviews. They are, nonetheless, used very widely in the tourism industry as a means of providing valuable information for organisations to improve their products and services.

Unlike face-to-face interviews, self-completed questionnaire surveys do not involve the use of interviewers, thereby making them a less expensive option for many tourism businesses. They are also a more flexible technique, but they do have some disadvantages. Response rates are typically lower than for comparable face-to-face surveys; this can sometimes be improved by sending a reminder to the respondent. Also, if a respondent does not fully understand a question, there is no interviewer to ask for clarification. Self-completed questionnaire surveys are used extensively in tourism, as a relatively low-cost method for obtaining both qualitative and quantitative data on customers and usage. Many tour operators carry out a postal survey of returning holidaymakers, asking them to complete a questionnaire related to their holiday experience (see Figure 7.3). The information contained in these questionnaires gives valuable feedback from clients and

Figure 7.3: An extract from a self-completed questionnaire (courtesy of Thomson Holidays)

Thomson
Skytours   PORTLAND DIRECT

CUSTOMER SATISFACTION SURVEY

Enjoyed your holiday? We hope you have, because we work very hard to ensure that our customers have a really good time. But we need your help to make things even better. Your opinions are very important to us, and by completing this questionnaire you will help improve the standard and quality of future holidays.

All questionnaires are returned to RSL, an independent market research company. The answers to the questions are analysed, and the results are reported regularly. If you would prefer not to receive any information from a member of the Thomson group of companies or, through our agent, from other selected companies, please tick this box ☐. Thank you.

Please ✔ appropriate box, or write in answer as requested

YOUR HOLIDAY DETAILS...

▶ **Which holiday company are you with?**

Thomson ☐   Skytours ☐
Other ☐   Portland ☐
Write in ....

▶ **Board arrangements:**

Full board ☐   Flexible dining ☐ (combining B/B & H/B)
Half board ☐   Self catering ☐
Bed/breakfast ☐   Room only ☐
   All inclusive ☐ (all meals, drinks etc. included)

▶ **The name of your resort(s) or the name of your tour/safari/cruise**

....
....

▶ **The name of your Hotel(s)/Villa/Apartments (name all accommodation stayed in)**

....
....

▶ **Number of nights abroad:**

6 or less ☐   8-13 ☐   15-20 ☐
7 ☐   14 ☐   21 or more ☐

▶ **If accommodation not included in your holiday price, was this a:**

Airfare/ flight only ☐   Flydrive ☐ (flight & rental car only)

▶ **If accommodation not specified until you arrived in resort, was this a:**

Late availability/ Square Deal ☐   Club Freestyle ☐
   Price Breaker ☐

▶ **How did you book this holiday?**

Direct with holiday company ☐
With a travel agent ☐

▶ **With which travel agent did you book this holiday?**

A.T. Mays ☐   Co-op Travelcare ☐
Thomas Cook ☐   Callers Pegasus ☐
Lunn Poly ☐   Dawson & Sanderson ☐
Going Places ☐   Midlands Co-op ☐
Other ☐ ➔ Write in ....

▶ **Was this a Young at Heart or Home & Away holiday?**   Yes ☐   No ☐

▶ **How long before departure was the holiday booked?**

Less than 1 week ☐   5-6 months ☐
1-4 weeks ☐   7-8 months ☐
1-2 months ☐   9-10 months ☐
3-4 months ☐   Longer ago ☐

▶ **Not counting this one, how many holidays abroad have you been on in the past three years:**

	None	One	Two	Three or more
With Thomson/ Skytours/Horizon	☐	☐	☐	☐
With Portland	☐	☐	☐	☐
With other package holiday companies	☐	☐	☐	☐
Independently arranged (non-package)	☐	☐	☐	☐
To this resort/island	☐	☐	☐	☐
To this accommodation	☐	☐	☐	☐
Self-catering	☐	☐	☐	☐

Figure 7.3: (cont'd)

OUT & ABOUT...

▶ **Did you yourself:**   Yes   No

▷ Go to the Welcome Get-Together ....

▷ Go on any Thomson company excursions ....

▷ Rent a car for/during your holiday ....

▶ **Please rate:**   Excellent   Good   Fair   Poor

▷ Arrangements for collecting car.............................

▷ Car hire overall ....

▶ **Booked with:**   Hertz   Dollar   Other company

▶ **Was the car:**   Pre-booked in the UK   Booked in resort via our Representative   Booked independently in resort

ANY PROBLEMS?...

▶ **Did you experience any problems during your holiday?**   Yes   No

▶ **Regarding these problems, how many times did you contact:**

     None   One   Two   Three   If more, please write number of times in boxes ➡

▷ A Thomson company Representative ..   Representative

▷ A member of the cabin crew ......   Cabin crew

▶ **How soon after first contact was your problem resolved or otherwise concluded?**

Immediately   Within 1 day   Within 2-3 days

Within 4-7 days   After 8 days or more   Never

▶ **How satisfied were you with the action taken?**

Completely   Mostly   Partly   Not at all

HOLIDAY EXPERIENCE...

▶ **How did this holiday compare with the impression you gained from the brochure?**

Better   The same   Worse   Did not use brochure

▶ **How likely are you to choose the same Thomson company for your next package holiday?** (ie. Thomson, Skytours or Portland)

Definitely   Probably   Possibly   Not likely

▶ **With which company did you take your last package holiday abroad?**

Thomson, Horizon or Skytours   Portland   Airtours   Cosmos   Unijet

Sunworld   Aspro   Inspirations   Kuoni   Sunset

Virgin   First Choice   Other ➡ Write in ....

▶ **Where did you go for your last package holiday?**

Mainland Spain   Portugal/Madeira   Greece (inc. islands)   Morocco/Tunisia/Egypt   Canary Islands

Majorca   Ibiza   Minorca   Cyprus   Malta

Florida   Caribbean   Other (Europe)   Write in ....   Other (Rest of World) Write in ....

▶ **Not counting this one, which of the following types of holiday abroad have you taken in the past three years?** (not necessarily with Thomson companies, all holidays both package and independent)

Cities/short breaks   Winter sun holiday   Winter sports

Specialist holiday for over 55s   Longhaul   Lakes & mountains

Summer sun holiday   Flights only   Cruise

is often the starting point for changes to products or services. It is common to find self-completed questionnaires at attractions and in accommodation facilities, for customers to complete and either return by post, or leave behind before they depart. Some tourism organisations provide an incentive, such as a free gift or discounted product, in order to increase the number of completed questionnaires.

Telephone surveys are gaining in popularity in the tourism industry, as a way of getting a fast response to an event, facility or service. They are used widely in the USA, but are largely restricted in the UK to trade activities, such as following up enquiries from buyers who have attended exhibitions, such as the 'World Travel Market' held every year in London. Companies specialising in selling timeshare also use telephone surveys to target likely customers. Conducting a survey by telephone can certainly give a speedy response and, if trained operators are used, many interviews are possible in a given time period. Disadvantages include the fact that it is not possible to use visual stimulus materials and the likelihood that people will feel that they have had their privacy invaded and will refuse to co-operate with the interviewer.

Questionnaire design   It is important for tourism organisations to remember that designing a questionnaire is a task best left to professionals. Many managers think that questionnaire design is a relatively easy part of the marketing research process, but often end up with a great deal of information that is of little use for marketing purposes. Specialists in the design of questionnaires suggest following the sequence shown in Figure 7.4 to ensure an effective finished product.

As the figure indicates, the questionnaire design sequence begins with listing the expected 'outcomes' of the survey, i.e. what it is hoped the survey will achieve. These are then used as the basis for the formulation of a set of questions, the answers to which will

Figure 7.4: Stages in effective questionnaire design

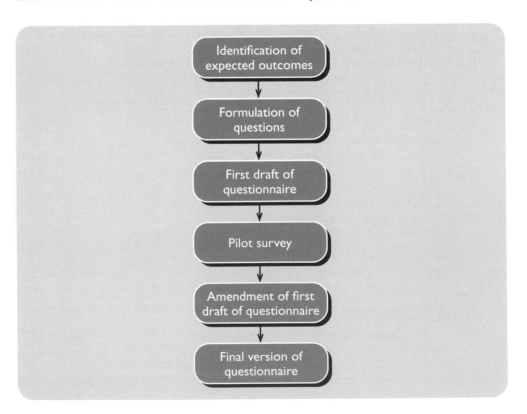

help achieve these outcomes. A draft questionnaire is produced next and used in a pilot survey; this is a 'dry run' of the main survey with a small number of respondents to check understanding and suitability of the questions. The draft questionnaire is then amended in the light of the pilot survey to produce a final version for use in the survey.

Sampling   In the majority of marketing research studies, it is not feasible to survey all the people who use a tourism facility or buy a tourism product. Instead, the organisation must rely on the responses of a proportion of the total 'population', known as the sample. If the selection of the sampling unit (the target population to be surveyed), sample size (how many are to be interviewed) and sampling procedure (the method by which the respondents are selected) are based on proven statistical methods, the responses of the people interviewed should mirror those of the total 'population' within known limits of accuracy. The sampling method chosen must reduce bias to a minimum. For example, if a major European hotel group wanted to collect data on customer perception at its 325 establishments spread evenly across Europe, but carried out 80 per cent of the surveys in France, the results would clearly be biased and not representative of the group as a whole.

The sampling procedure may be either random or quota. For a random survey, individuals are pre-selected from a sampling frame, such as the electoral roll or a database. The interviewer is asked to carry out interviews of selected respondents chosen at random. Many UK government surveys are carried out in this way. When using the quota sampling method, the interviewer is given instructions as to the number of respondents he or she must interview in certain categories, for example defined by age, sex or social class.

The sample size will determine the level of accuracy of the data. Generally speaking, the larger the sample size the better, but the increase in accuracy becomes less significant as the sample size is increased. Provided that proven statistical methods have been used to select the sample, a survey consisting of approximately 2000 interviews will give an accurate reflection of the public's view of general matters to a 95 per cent confidence level (in other words, 19 out of 20 surveys will fall within a stated 'margin of error'). In reality, it would be rare for a market research agency to carry out a survey with a sample size of less than 100, even if only broad impressions were needed.

Observation   Observation is a very useful, and often neglected, form of primary data collection in tourism. In its simplest form, observation is a management practice that involves an organisation employing a person to study the behaviour of others as a way of improving its products and services. It is particularly suitable for visitor attractions such as theme parks, craft galleries and museums. It does not always involve people actually watching what others do and recording the details systematically. Nowadays, there are sophisticated techniques such as closed circuit television (CCTV) and time-lapse photography that can be used to produce valuable information on the flow of people and traffic at tourist facilities. Electronic tally counters are used in attractions, leisure centres and tourist information centres to monitor usage. On occasions, staff may be asked to 'mingle' with visitors or customers and to eavesdrop on their conversations without revealing their identity. People are often far more honest about their true feelings when talking in private than they would be when asked questions as part of a visitor survey.

Observation has an important role to play in researching competitors' products. There are very few products, services and facilities in the tourism industry that are truly unique, most having been based on an idea seen elsewhere. It is not uncommon for hoteliers, travel agents and airlines, for example, to use the facilities of competitors in order to pick up new tips and improve their own products. Tourism companies sometimes employ 'mystery shoppers' to visit competitor facilities (and sometimes even their own facilities!) anonymously to check on standards of service and the range of products on offer.

Focus groups   A focus group is a marketing research technique used to collect in-depth information on customers' purchasing habits, for example to explore the reasons why they choose one travel product or company in preference to another. This kind of in-depth information is not easy to obtain from questionnaire surveys or observation, but focus group sessions give respondents the time to reflect and consider in detail why they make the decisions they do. A focus group, or panel interview as it is sometimes called, usually consists of up to 10 consumers under the guidance of a trained interviewer, who will use a number of techniques to explore the innermost thoughts and values of the members of the group. The sessions are generally video-recorded for future analysis and will often cause companies to make changes to their product range or promotional activities. Given the intensive nature of the focus group, it is an expensive method of gaining primary research material and tends, therefore, to be used mainly by larger tourism organisations, primarily in the private sector of the industry.

Secondary research data

Many marketing research studies involve the collection of a mixture of primary and secondary sources of information. Secondary data is information that is already available, usually in written form, but increasingly now made available via computers and other electronic sources, for example the Internet and CD-ROM databases. Marketing research that makes use of secondary data sources is sometimes referred to as 'desk research'. The main advantage offered by secondary research when compared with primary data collection methods is that it can save both time and money. There is a great deal of secondary research data available to organisations working in all sectors of the tourism industry. The most easily accessible comes from its own internal sources, while external data are available from a range of commercial and public sector sources.

Internal sources of secondary data   Much of the information that an organisation needs for marketing purposes may already be held within its various departments and management systems. An examination of existing files, databases and records should be a first priority before external research sources are consulted, in order to save time and money. The following internal information sources, held by any organisation that is operating professionally in the tourism industry, may reveal useful data for marketing research purposes:

- Sales receipts
- Financial returns
- Customer records
- Survey findings
- Mailing lists

The advent of computerised management information systems makes this kind of information so much more accessible and useful for marketing research studies. Indeed, systems can now be programmed to generate frequent reports specifically geared towards the needs of the marketing personnel in an organisation.

External sources of secondary data   As the worldwide tourism industry continues to grow, an increasing amount of specific secondary research data on tourism is being generated to service this expansion. The World Tourism Organisation (WTO) and World Travel and Tourism Council (WTTC) supply statistical data on an international scale, while organisations such as the Organisation for Economic Co-operation and Development (OECD) and the Pacific Asia Travel Association (PATA) provide regional, international data. Statistics on tourism at a national level are made available by government departments or government-sponsored agencies (see the case study below on the work of the Bureau of Tourism Research in Australia). In the UK, tourism enterprises have access to a wide range of information on tourism provided by government and commercial sources, including:

- Annual reports of the national tourist boards and the British Tourist Authority (BTA)
- Annual reports of the regional tourist boards/tourism companies
- The International Passenger Survey (IPS)
- The United Kingdom Tourism Survey (UKTS)
- The British National Travel Survey (BNTS)
- *Business Monitor MQ6 – Overseas Travel and Tourism*, published by the Stationery Office
- Annual reports of commercial tourism organisations, for example British Airways, Thomas Cook, Thomson Travel Group and Airtours
- Trade associations including ABTA, AITO and IATA
- Eurostat
- Professional bodies such as the Tourism Society

In destination areas, information on the economic importance of tourism will be collected by regional bodies, local authorities and trade associations. The following case study on the Australian Bureau of Tourism Research investigates the activities of a data collection agency operating at national, international and sectoral levels.

Case Study: Australian Bureau of Tourism Research

Introduction

The Bureau of Tourism Research (BTR) is a non-statutory agency of the Australian government, administered through the Commonwealth Department of Industry, Science and Tourism. Commonwealth, State and Territory governments directly provide the majority of BTR's budget, but it also derives revenue from publication and data sales, and from consultancy services provided to a range of clients. The BTR has professional independence in the conduct of its work programme.

Mission

BTR's mission is to provide independent, accurate, timely and strategically relevant statistics and analyses to the tourism industry, government and the community at large, in order to enhance the contribution of tourism to the well-being of the Australian community.

Objectives

BTR's mission is achieved through five key objectives:

1. To provide a national focus for the collection, analysis and dissemination of tourism and related data
2. To provide relevant, timely and high quality tourism statistics

Australian Bureau of Tourism Research continued

3. To analyse and distribute tourism data in such a way as to encourage its widespread and effective use in tourism industry development

4. To undertake or co-ordinate research on priority issues in the tourism field

5. To promote an understanding and awareness of the role of tourism research in the development of Australian tourism

Research products

The Bureau conducts two major national travel surveys, the *International Visitor Survey* (IVS) and the *Domestic Tourism Monitor* (DTM). The principal features of these two surveys, including frequency, description and key data items, are shown in Table 7.2.

Data from the IVS and the DTM are made available in a wide variety of formats, including:

- Quarterly publications
- Annual publications
- Detailed tables
- Special tabulations
- Compact disc

Table 7.2: Key features of the International Visitor Survey and Domestic Tourism Monitor

Survey/publication title, frequency and description	Key data items
International Visitor Survey (IVS)	*Characteristics of visitors*: Country of residence, nationality, age/sex, occupation, reasons for visit
Ongoing: quarterly and annual	*International itinerary*: Stopovers, time away from home, previous visits to Australia
Survey of the characteristics, behaviour and expenditure of international visitors to Australia	*Australian itinerary*: Length of stay, city of arrival/departure, transport used, region of stay, accommodation used, places and attractions visited, sports, entertainment and cultural activities
	Travel arrangements: Inclusive package tour, travel party, prepaid arrangements, type of booking agent, information sources
	Expenditure: Average expenditure per visitor and per item
	Reactions: Satisfaction/dissatisfaction
Domestic Tourism Monitor (DTM)	*Characteristics of travellers/non-travellers (people)*: Age/sex, occupation/income/life cycle, origin
Ongoing: quarterly and financial year	*Travel behaviour*: Origin and destination, purpose and duration of trip, transport and accommodation used, month returned from trip
Survey of level of domestic travel, and characteristics/behaviour of domestic tourists	*Market shares*: Share of trips generated by State/Territory received
Basis of reporting: trips/visits/nights	

Source: BTR

The BTR also conducts the *Domestic Tourism Expenditure Survey* (DTES), which focuses on overnight trips, day trips and the Australian component of overseas trips.

The Bureau uses other secondary sources of tourism statistics supplied by other agencies, including:

- *Tourism Forecasts*: provided by the Tourism Forecasting Council
- *Overseas Arrivals and Departures*: from the Australian Bureau of Statistics
- *Survey of Tourist Accommodation*: conducted by the Australian Bureau of Statistics
- *Service Industries Surveys*: supplied by the Australian Bureau of Statistics
- *International Scheduled Air Transport*: from the Commonwealth Department of Transport and Regional Development
- *Air Transport Statistics – Domestic Airlines*: from the Commonwealth Department of Transport and Regional Development
- *Yearbook of Tourism Statistics*: from the World Tourism Organisation

Other BTR products include reports on tourism and the economy, regional tourism reports, occasional papers and conference papers.

(*Information courtesy of the Bureau of Tourism Research, Canberra*)

Discussion points and essay questions

1. Who are the principal users of the data collected by the Bureau of Tourism Research?

2. Do you consider that the collection on statistics on Australian tourism is best handled by one central body, rather than through State and Territory governments?

3. How might the Australian government justify its funding of the Bureau?

4. How does the Bureau help the development of Australian tourism products

The marketing research process in tourism

Although the nature of any marketing research carried out will vary between different tourism organisations, influenced by such matters as the size of the organisation, the sector in which it operates, its turnover and the importance it attaches to the process, there are a number of clearly defined stages that any marketing research process needs to go through, as shown in Figure 7.5.

As the figure shows, the first stage in the marketing research process in tourism is the identification of the objectives of the research. This could be as simple as discovering the average age of visitors to a theme park or as complex as an international airline investigating the feasibility of introducing a new fares and pricing strategy across all its networks. Objectives that are clearly defined, realistic and measurable will not only provide a focus for the research activity, but also enable those who have commissioned the research to evaluate whether or not it has met its intended aims. Clarity at this important first stage in the marketing research process is far more likely to provide information later on that is useful for decision-making purposes by an organisation's marketing staff.

Stage two of the process calls for developing the most efficient and effective strategy for gathering the information needed to satisfy the objectives identified at stage one. This will involve decisions about the most appropriate research methods to be used (the methodology), whether any, or all, of the information needed to meet the research

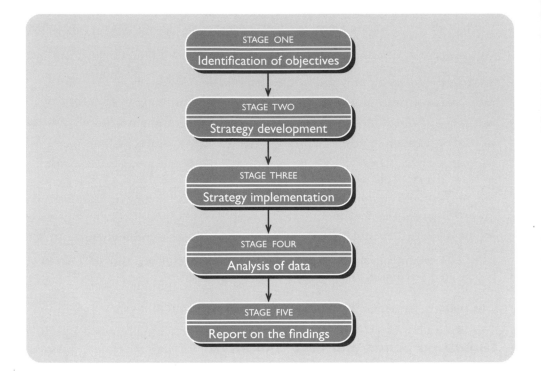

objectives is already available from other sources and what timescale is envisaged for the project. The strategy will also seek to answer questions concerning costs, appropriate research instruments, who will carry out the research, whether any primary research will be needed and which secondary sources and agencies may be able to help with the work.

The third stage of the marketing research process is the implementation of the agreed strategy, i.e. the collection of the data. This is often the most expensive stage in the operation, particularly if the chosen methodology involves the recruitment and training of a large number of interviewers. The least expensive type of research study tends to be one that involves the collection of information from secondary sources alone, sometimes referred to as a desk study or desk research. An example of a marketing research study that involves both primary and secondary data collection would be a travel agency chain that is researching the feasibility of opening further branches in locations throughout the UK. Typical primary research for this may include a small-scale interview survey of shoppers in the cities concerned and a telephone survey of a sample of businesses within a 25-mile radius of each location. Secondary data consulted are likely to include economic and demographic information produced by local government agencies and reference to national and local travel trade directories.

Once the collection of the data is completed, stage four of the process can begin. This is the analysis of the information, which may be carried out manually or with the aid of a computer program. Depending on the complexity of the study, a range of statistical techniques is available to help with this part of the process.

The final stage of the marketing research process is reporting on the findings of the study. In the majority of cases, a written report will be produced for distribution to those who have commissioned the study, perhaps preceded by a draft to solicit comments and make necessary amendments. It is helpful if the main elements of the study and its recommendations are included at the beginning of the final written report as an executive summary. This allows the reader to gain an understanding of the main issues without having to study the whole report in detail. Nowadays, it is becoming increasingly common to supplement the written report with a formal presentation by its authors, at which those who commissioned the study can question them in greater depth about their findings and recommendations. Such an event will generally take place after the distribution of the final report, so as to allow time for those who commissioned the work to study it in detail.

Applying the marketing mix to the tourism industry

The marketing mix is one of the most important concepts in the marketing of tourism products and services. It is commonly referred to as the 4 Ps, namely product, place, price and promotion, although some researchers have extended the concept to 7 Ps by including people, process and physical components (see Booms and Bitner, 1981). Tourism organisations in both the private and public sectors of the industry are constantly striving to achieve the optimum balance between the four variables of the marketing mix in order to meet their marketing objectives. Like many aspects of marketing in tourism, the precise nature of the marketing mix implemented by a particular organisation will vary over time. Successful tourism organisations respond to internal and external influences by constantly monitoring and adjusting the elements of their marketing mix. A newly opened facility, for example, will need greater emphasis on promotion in its early stages of development in order to attract customers. As the facility becomes established, promotional budgets can be reduced and more emphasis can be placed on product development and enhancement. It should also be stressed that, although the elements of the marketing mix may be studied in isolation, in reality there is a great deal of overlap and integration between the four components. The marketing mix is shown in diagrammatic form in Figure 7.6 and its constituent parts are discussed in more detail in the following sections of this chapter.

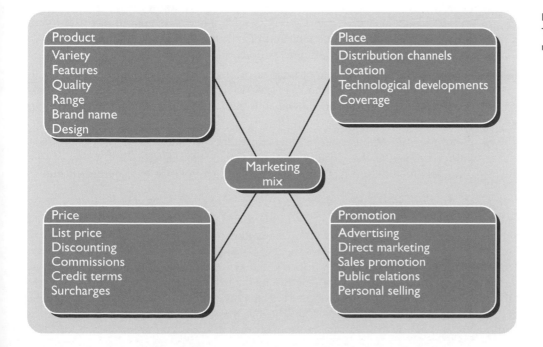

Figure 7.6:
The marketing mix in tourism

Product
Variety
Features
Quality
Range
Brand name
Design

Place
Distribution channels
Location
Technological developments
Coverage

Marketing mix

Price
List price
Discounting
Commissions
Credit terms
Surcharges

Promotion
Advertising
Direct marketing
Sales promotion
Public relations
Personal selling

Product

The product is at the core of all marketing activity, since it represents the main benefit received by the customer. To use the term 'product', however, when considering a service industry such as tourism can be a little misleading. The tourism industry does not produce tangible goods such as television sets or cars, but rather a range of experiences and services geared to the needs of particular market segments. Indeed, tourism is often thought of as an industry that succeeds by 'selling dreams'. The tourism product is, thus, an amalgam of several products and services, the individual components of which are usually supplied by different organisations, both private and public sector. The sale of overseas package holidays, for example, will involve the combined efforts of a variety of suppliers, including airlines, tour operators, accommodation providers, travel agencies, destination management organisations, car hire companies and coach operators. On a wider scale, the destinations visited by tourists can be considered to be products in their own right, since it may well be the appeal of the destination that prompted the desire to travel in the first place.

Characteristics of tourism products

Tourism products exhibit a range of specific characteristics, the most important of which are:

- *Intangibility.* Unlike manufactured goods, it is not possible to touch a tourism product such as a package holiday or short break. Operators rely heavily on brochures and other promotional items to sell their tourism products.
- *Inseparability.* The majority of tourism products are consumed at the point of production; a family on an overseas package holiday, for example, will experience the flights, transfers, accommodation and excursions as they happen. This highlights the crucial role played by the staff who attend to the tourists; they too are an important and integral part of the product being sold to the customers.
- *Perishability.* An airline seat or hotel bed not sold today cannot be stockpiled and resold at a later date, thereby representing a lost sales opportunity to the company concerned. Price reductions and discounting can be introduced as a way of stimulating sales within given time periods.
- *Ownership.* The purchasers of tourism products do not generally buy the title to the goods. The family on the overseas package holiday, for example, will take home their experiences and dreams, not the hotel room or aircraft that were part of their holiday!
- *Heterogeneity.* Maintaining product consistency is difficult with tourism products. Influences such as the weather, attitude of staff, time of year and quality of food can alter the same product purchased at different times or by different customers.

The product life cycle concept

All tourism products undergo changes during their lifespan. External and internal influences on organisations, together with changes in consumer demand, affect the development of a given product from the moment it is made available to the general public to the time it is ultimately withdrawn from the market. Although it is difficult to predict the precise dynamics of a particular tourism product, it is possible to chart a number of stages that products go through in the course of their evolution, as depicted in the product life cycle concept or PLC (see Figure 7.7). The five stages in the product life cycle are as follows:

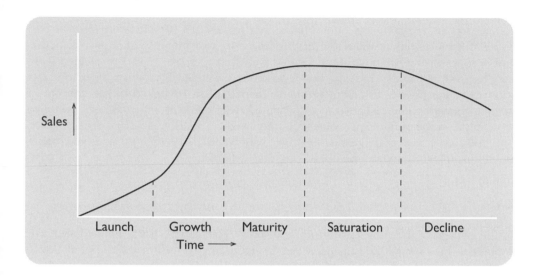

Figure 7.7: The product life cycle (PLC) concept

1. *Launch.* Sales will slowly increase once a product is launched on to the market.
2. *Growth.* Demand accelerates during the growth phase once the product's existence becomes more widely known.
3. *Maturity.* Growth in sales slows down at this point, perhaps as a result of competitors' products. At this stage, the company will need to decide whether to stimulate further sales through increased promotional work, remodel the product or allow demand for the product to continue to fall.
4. *Saturation.* Sales have reached a plateau at this stage.
5. *Decline.* Demand for the product falls steadily.

Although the product life cycle concept was originally developed within the manufacturing sector as a way of helping predict sales activity and product adoption by customers, it can also be applied to service sector industries including tourism. Its retrospective view and rather simplistic approach to product evolution, however, have led to criticism that its usefulness as a forecasting tool in tourism is rather limited. Indeed, making marketing decisions on the basis of such an imprecise concept could even be considered foolhardy, since a drop in demand for a product may be merely a temporary phenomenon. Also, predicting the exact timing of changes between one stage in the cycle and another is particularly difficult. Nonetheless, the product life cycle concept can help the marketer to plan and execute different marketing tactics and strategies to correspond with the various stages of the cycle and, as such, it has a role to play in the strategic marketing planning process for tourism products.

Butler (1980) suggests that the product life cycle concept can be applied successfully to the development of tourist destinations, a point that is covered in greater depth in the section of this chapter looking at destination marketing.

Branding tourism products

Branding is commonplace in the marketing of fast-moving consumer goods (FMCGs), such as cosmetics, food and household cleaning products, and is a technique that is increasingly common in the marketing of tourism products. As the tourism industry matures and its range of products becomes ever greater, assigning a brand name to a product, for example a Disney resort, Hilton hotel or Hertz rented car, helps distinguish it from its competitors and, by so doing, offers customers a buying cue. A tourism organisation also hopes that its customers will show brand loyalty, by continuing to choose its products and services over and above those offered by its competitors. A variety of incentives, ranging from discounts to loyalty bonus schemes, is offered by tourism operators as a way of retaining their customers' business. Branding can be linked to the concept of market segmentation (see earlier in this chapter), with different brands being developed to meet the needs of different segments of the market. Thomson Holidays, the UK-based tour operator, is a very good example of this, with brand names such as 'lakes and mountains', 'small and friendly', 'young at heart' and 'à la carte'.

Place

In the context of the tourism industry, the 'place' component of the marketing mix is concerned not only with destinations and the location of tourist facilities, but also with how they are made available to the customer, including the channels of distribution and how these are being influenced by developments in new technology.

Location of tourist facilities

Location is clearly an important factor for many types of tourism enterprises, particularly those that survive on a high volume of 'passing trade'. A hotel that is situated in a remote countryside location away from major centres of population may struggle to attract custom and will need to devote a greater proportion of its resources to marketing than, for example, a hotel located in the centre of a popular tourist city. The developers of major tourist attractions will choose locations that are close to major centres of population in order to attract visitors from as wide a catchment area as possible. A good example of this is Chessington World of Adventures, a theme park located 12 miles south of London, which has a catchment of 18 million people living within a 2-hour drive of the attraction. It has free parking for cars and coaches, and is served by frequent bus, coach and train services. The managers of successful natural, historic and cultural attractions, where the location is 'fixed', make their facilities as accessible as possible through carefully planned visitor and traffic management schemes, including public transport programmes. Travel agencies that are part of large multiple chains are usually found in the most accessible, and most expensive, high street locations. Independent agents, who may not be able to justify the high rent and rates of town centre locations, will nonetheless want to be in a position that is not too far away from a town's main shopping areas.

The examples in the preceding paragraph clearly indicate that location is closely linked to accessibility. It is important for all tourism organisations to make their facilities and services accessible to all sections of the community, including those with special needs. It makes good business sense to spend time assessing a facility from the visitors' point of view, so as to minimise their inconvenience and provide an enjoyable experience for all.

By their very nature, the location of destinations is 'fixed'; physical factors, such as climate, topography and geology, give an area its visible, natural characteristics, which are often the stimulus for a tourism trip. The skill for the marketer is to ensure that the benefits of the destination's associated tourism products, such as accommodation, attractions, entertainment and transportation, are developed from the tourists' perspective and are made known to prospective travellers through the appropriate promotional channels. A destination may have an international reputation, but if its products and services fail to meet customers' needs, the area will not flourish and its reputation may be tarnished.

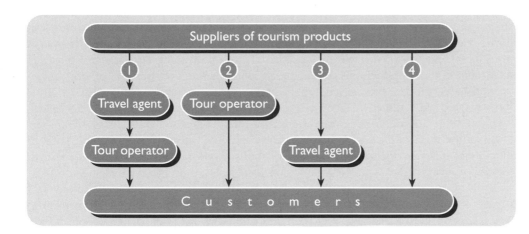

Figure 7.8:
Channels of distribution in the tourism industry

Channels of distribution in tourism marketing

The suppliers of tourism products, for example hoteliers and transport operators, sometimes make their services available direct to the customer, but more often than not use the services of an intermediary, such as a travel agent or tour operator, as indicated in Figure 7.8. As the figure shows, there are four main channels for the distribution of tourism products. Route 1 on the diagram is the channel most commonly associated with the sale of mass market package holidays; tour operators take on the role of wholesalers by assembling the components of the package and offering them for sale through travel agents. Some tour operators by-pass the agent and offer their products direct to the customer (route 2). Portland Holidays, part of the Thomson Travel Group, is one such 'direct sell' operator, all of which profess to being able to offer the public cheaper holidays since they pay no commission to travel agents. Occasionally, a travel agency will market its own tours to its clients (route 3), offering a level of personal service and attention to detail not always found in packaged products. Finally, some suppliers of tourism products sell directly to the public. This is common in domestic tourism, where the tourists have a good knowledge of the products on offer and easy, direct access to the suppliers, for example hotels, coach companies, self-catering accommodation providers, caravan parks, camping grounds and holiday centres.

Developments in information technology systems are increasingly influencing the distribution channels in international tourism. Within the travel industry, computer reservation systems (CRS) and global distribution systems (GDS) have revolutionised the sales of airline and other travel products since they were first developed in the USA in the late 1960s. Systems such as Sabre, Worldspan and Galileo offer travel professionals a wealth of information and the ability to make and confirm reservations instantly. In the consumer marketplace, developments in CD-ROM technology and the Internet offer prospective travellers an alternative way of researching their travel plans and making their own holiday bookings, without ever consulting a travel agent or tour operator. Such developments are destined to revolutionise many aspects of people's daily lives, not least how they make their travel purchases.

Price

In the highly competitive environment of international tourism, price determination is crucial to the success of all organisations in the industry. Daily fluctuations in the price of holidays and other travel products are a fact of life in the majority of the enterprise economies of the world, reflecting changes in demand for products and services. Tourism operators have to react to the pricing tactics of their competitors and alterations in global exchange rates, while at the same time monitoring their own internal costs, in order to increase or even retain their market share. Of all the components of the marketing mix in tourism, decisions on pricing are perhaps the most difficult to make, given the perishability of the products on offer and the constant fluctuations in demand. Tour operators are often forced to finalise the prices of their holidays many months before the holidays go on sale, in order to publish their brochures at the earliest possible opportunity, in the hope of stealing a march on the competition in the race for sales. Another difficulty is that the price of the majority of tourism products fluctuates in response to seasonal demand. Prices for ex-UK family package holidays to the Mediterranean coastal resorts in Spain, for example, reach a peak in the UK school holiday periods of July and August, when demand is at its highest. The proprietor of a country house hotel in the Cotswolds, on the other hand, will offer reductions in the price of off-season, winter breaks as a way of filling spare accommodation capacity.

We have seen that demand plays a crucial part in the process of price formulation in tourism, but there are many other internal and external factors that will influence an organisation's pricing decisions, for example its overall objectives and organisational goals. Commercial operators will price at a level that maximises their returns, whereas a public sector organisation will be influenced by its social or community aims when setting pricing levels, perhaps offering concessionary rates to disadvantaged groups. An understanding of competitor behaviour is also important when setting pricing levels. Most tourism enterprises operate in markets where there are many competing suppliers, all striving to gain a competitive advantage. Price movements by one company can often trigger a 'domino effect' of discounting by its competitors. When considering pricing levels, a tourism organisation will also need accurate information on the costs of providing its products, as a first stage in determining pricing strategies. Organisations also need to take account of general economic and demographic trends when establishing their prices; for example, when an economy is in recession and consumer spending on non-essential items is suppressed, prices may need to be reduced in order to attract extra custom.

Pricing policies in tourism

Having considered the factors that can have an influence on a tourism organisation's pricing decisions, we now need to investigate the options open to the organisation when determining its pricing policies. It should be remembered that any policy decisions on price will change over time, in response to a combination of the types of internal and external factors discussed in the preceding paragraph.

Tourism enterprises can take one of two broad-based approaches when fixing their prices, the first based solely on the costs of providing the product, the second taking into account the level of demand associated with the product. The most common example of the former is the technique known as cost-plus pricing, or accountants' pricing, where the final price of a product is calculated by adding a profit margin to its associated variable and fixed costs. Although it is important for any organisation to know the true costs of developing its products, this rather simplistic approach to price determination fails to take into account the fluctuations in demand for products and services. It is more usual for tourism operators to implement pricing policies based on the demand for their products or services. Examples of this demand-orientated approach include:

- Competitive pricing
- Penetration pricing
- Discrimination pricing
- Price skimming

Competitive pricing, sometimes referred to as 'the going rate', assumes that organisations will match the price of their competitors when selling broadly similar products and services. This is considered a dangerous long-term strategy since profit margins are driven down, sometimes to the point where it may be uneconomic for a tourism company to continue trading. Discrimination pricing involves charging different prices to different segments of the market for the same product or service. For example, people who travel alone and require single occupancy in their accommodation are sometimes charged a premium for this service. Tourist attractions usually offer a range of prices, such as child rates, concessionary prices for senior citizens and discounted group rates. Penetration pricing, also known as a 'loss leader' strategy, is used by tourism operators wanting to break into a new market where there are already a number of existing product providers. Prices will be set sufficiently low in order to persuade customers to switch their allegiance. Price skimming is when a high price is charged initially for a new product or service that is made available for the first time. Early pricing on the Eurostar cross-Channel rail service between England and France is a good example of price skimming.

Promotion

Promotion is the most visible of the four components that together make up the marketing mix in tourism. Tourism organisations use a variety of promotional techniques to communicate information and 'messages' to their existing and potential customers, with the aim of persuading them to buy their products. As well as encouraging sales, promotion can also help achieve a number of associated aims, such as projecting a favourable image of a company, developing long-term relationships with customers, reminding customers of the availability of products, and informing customers of the benefits of one product over another. As well as communicating directly with their customers, it is important to remember that tourism enterprises also use a variety of promotional techniques to communicate with a range of 'trade' contacts, for example:

1. Consumer
   - Television advertising
   - Direct mail
   - Holiday shows
   - Newspaper editorial
   - Point-of-sale materials

2. Trade
   - Trade exhibitions
   - Staff discounts on products
   - Sales bonuses
   - Advertising in travel trade journals
   - Product training

Tourism organisations use a mixture of 'above the line' and 'below the line' techniques when devising their promotional strategies. Advertising is the most popular 'above the line' technique, while 'below the line' activities include direct marketing, sales promotion, brochure distribution and public relations work. Being a service industry, personal selling also has an important role to play in the promotion of tourism products and services.

Advertising

Advertising is the use of paid media by an organisation to inform existing and potential customers and persuade them to buy its products. Advertising plays such a pivotal role in the promotion of tourism products and services that it would be easy to conclude that

Table 7.3: Advantages and disadvantages of selected advertising media

Media type	Advantages	Disadvantages
Newspapers and magazines	● Relatively inexpensive ● Segmentation possible ● Flexibility ● Use of colour possible	● Can be poor production quality ● 'Static' medium ● Smaller advertisements may have little impact
Television	● Access to a large audience ● High degree of creativity ● Sound, vision and colour ● Repetition easy	● Expensive medium ● High production costs ● Difficult to target market segments
Radio	● Immediacy ● Relatively inexpensive ● Segmentation possible ● Repetition easy ● Low production costs	● 'Background' medium ● Limited audience numbers ● Can be poor production quality ● Lack of visual impact
Cinema	● 'Big screen' impact ● Segmentation possible ● Access to young audience ● Local and regional coverage	● High production costs ● Limited market
Transport and outdoor advertising	● Low 'cost per site' ● Flexibility	● Localised coverage ● High production costs
Electronic media (e.g. Internet, Teletext, fax shots)	● Novelty value ● Speed ● Segmentation possible ● Use of graphics and images	● Expensive initial investment ● Limited market currently

it is the *only* promotional tool used by tourism organisations. This, however, is far from the case, with many smaller tourism operators relying heavily on 'below the line' techniques to stimulate sales. Nonetheless, there are very few tourism organisations that do not use advertising to some extent in their promotional mix. The two main types of advertising used in tourism are:

● *Consumer advertising.* This is where a tourism organisation advertises directly to its customers, for example an airline placing an advertisement in a national daily newspaper or a travel agent advertising a promotional event in its local newspaper.

● *Trade advertising.* This is where tourism organisations advertise their products and services to other tourism businesses, for example a tour operator or a car hire company placing an advertisement in a travel trade newspaper that is read by travel agents.

It is common for most tourism companies to use a mixture of trade and consumer advertising in their promotional mix.

The channels through which organisations advertise their products are known as media (a single channel is a medium). Popular media used by tourism enterprises include newspapers and magazines, television, radio, cinema, transport, outdoor and electronic advertising. The respective advantages and disadvantages of each of these are shown in Table 7.3.

The choice of media for an advertising campaign will depend on such factors as the target audience, the message being conveyed, the product or service on offer and the promotional budget. Advertising agencies specialise in devising, implementing and monitoring campaigns and advising clients on media selection.

The role of brochures

The production and distribution of brochures is an important part of the promotional mix of the great majority of tourism organisations, whether operating in the private or public sector of the industry. Brochures are used to inform potential purchasers of the features and benefits of tourism products, with the hope of converting enquiries into sales. The intangible nature of tourism products gives brochures a special significance in the industry. Bookings are often made on the strength of the words and images depicted in holiday brochures, making their design and content of particular significance in tourism. In addition, operators have to ensure that all the material included in their brochures conforms to UK and European Union legislation, including the Package Travel Directive. Price competition in many sectors of the tourism industry, notably mass market tour operating, has led companies to produce further editions of original brochures in the same season, in order to publish new pricing information and special offers.

Direct marketing

Direct marketing is the term used to describe the various techniques an organisation can use to communicate directly with its customers, without using the services of an intermediary, as a way of conveying information and generating sales. It is particularly suitable for smaller companies with limited promotional budgets, since, if planned and executed effectively, direct marketing has the potential to be more cost-effective than any other promotional tool, the result of the precise targeting that the technique allows. Existing customers can be contacted to introduce them to new products and special offers, while new customers can be identified and encouraged to purchase products and services through direct channels.

Direct mail is the best-known method of direct marketing and is used extensively in all sectors of international tourism, for example a visitor attraction mailing a brochure to all households within a 10-mile radius, a hotel automatically sending a Christmas card to all past guests on its database or a travel agency sending a quarterly newsletter to all its current clients. Achieving success in any direct mail campaign necessitates a methodical approach to planning and implementation, following a number of clearly identified stages (see Figure 7.9).

Figure 7.9 indicates that a successful direct mail campaign begins with specifying what the campaign hopes to achieve, by formulating the campaign objectives. These could be, for example, the promotion of a new product or service, changing the image of an organisation or selling spare capacity in a holiday programme. Once the objectives are established, the budgets and timescale for the campaign must be agreed, and the mailing list confirmed. The list could be a database of existing customers or may be a targeted list purchased with a particular objective in mind, such as a mailing by an outdoor activity centre to all the members of a local ramblers' association, using its membership list. Having finalised the contents of the direct mail package, which generally consists of a personalised letter, promotional item and reply device (for example a freepost address or a reply-paid return envelope), the mailing can take place. If response rates are low, it may be necessary to run a follow-up mailing to act as a reminder to customers. Once the direct mail campaign has finished, it is important to evaluate the results so as to identify what was successful and what needs changing for future campaigns.

Figure 7.9:
Stages in the
execution of a
direct mail
campaign

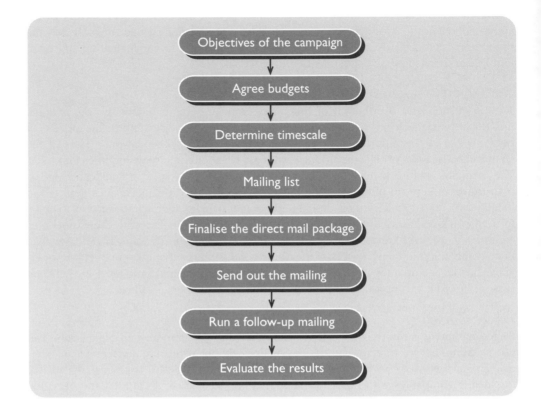

Other types of direct marketing used in the tourism industry include telemarketing, direct response advertising and door-to-door leaflet distribution. Telemarketing is used extensively in business-to-business activities, where one company provides services and facilities for another. For example, the sales staff of a tour operator may telephone all the people who enquired about its holiday programmes at a recent travel trade promotion. Direct response advertising is any type of advertising that asks a member of the public or trade to respond in some way. This could be by completing a coupon, calling a telephone number, visiting a facility or sending a fax. This allows the organisation to build up a mailing list at the same time as servicing the enquiry. Door-to-door leaflet distribution is particularly suitable for reaching a local or regional market. In the tourism industry, it is popular with hotels, restaurants, visitor attractions and leisure facilities. A certain amount of market segmentation is possible, with particular postcode areas being targeted in terms of, for example, family composition, social class or age.

Sales promotion

Tourism organisations use a wide variety of sales promotion techniques to sell their products and services. Some target customers directly, for example posters in travel agencies, public holiday exhibitions, discount vouchers, loyalty schemes, free gifts and discounts, while others are aimed at staff working in tourism to encourage extra sales activity and reward high achievers; these include bonus payments, discounted holidays and other travel products, gift vouchers and hospitality at trade launches. It is common practice for tour operators and airlines to offer financial and other incentives to travel agency staff to encourage them to sell their products.

The essential feature of all sales promotion techniques in tourism is that they are temporary, short-term inducements. They may be undertaken as a direct response to competitor activity or be part of a wider promotional campaign, integrated with, for example, advertising or direct marketing.

Public relations

Public relations, or PR as it is more commonly known, is used extensively in the tourism industry, as a way of communicating with potential customers and presenting a favourable public image. In the tourism arena, one of the most successful exponents of PR is Richard Branson, chairman of the Virgin Group, which includes Virgin Atlantic Airways, Virgin Hotels and Virgin Holidays. He makes effective use of the media by planning unusual events and staging publicity 'stunts', for example his attempt in 1997 at the circumnavigation of the earth in a hot air balloon.

Public relations is defined by the UK Institute of Public Relations (IPR) as:

'. . . the planned and sustained effort to establish and maintain goodwill and mutual understanding between an organisation and its publics'.

It is an all-embracing term, covering relations with the media, customer relations, trade relations, image projection and staff attitude. The last word of the IPR definition is deliberately used in the plural, since a tourism enterprise must develop and maintain goodwill with a wide variety of individuals and external organisations, including suppliers, trade unions, local government officers, regulatory bodies, the press, voluntary groups, neighbours, distributors and financial institutions. If used carefully, PR is a very cost-effective way of helping tourism organisations survive and grow. Specifically, PR can:

● Help publicise products and services
● Communicate a favourable image when an organisation is experiencing difficulties
● Influence specific target groups
● Generate interest in an organisation
● Build a favourable image of an organisation
● Attract the best staff to an organisation

PR is perhaps most commonly associated with press and media relations. Successful tourism organisations build lasting relationships with appropriate media contacts, in the hope of gaining valuable 'free publicity'. This may be personal contact with reporters on local, regional or national newspapers, feature editors on relevant trade and consumer magazines, or television and radio stations. The most common tool for keeping media contacts up to date with news is the press release, which can be sent to newspapers, magazines and TV/radio stations. Familiarisation ('fam') trips are frequently used in tourism to give journalists first-hand experience of a product or facility to help with and influence their writing.

Personal selling

Personal selling is an essential part of the marketing process in international tourism. It not only provides enterprises with the financial resources necessary for survival and growth, but also plays an important role in supporting an organisation's customer service function. The highly personalised nature of the delivery of many tourism products and services means that the bulk of staff working in the industry are likely to be involved in some form of sales activity during the course of their work. Personal selling involves persuasive communication between a seller and a buyer, which is designed to encourage the customer to purchase the products or services on offer. The prime objective of personal selling is, therefore, to make a sale. It is, however, a much more wide-ranging activity and should be seen by those managing and working in tourism as a continuous process that can help build customer loyalty, develop long-term relationships between companies and their customers, and provide lasting benefits in enhanced standards of customer service.

Destination marketing

Destinations are the focal point of much domestic and international tourist activity. We saw in Chapter 2 that a single destination can be thought of as the 'umbrella' under which the many interrelated sectors of the tourism industry operate. Tourists visit destinations for a variety of cultural, social, recreational, educational, religious and business reasons, often attracted by a mixture of imaginative promotional activities using skilfully developed images of the area. Successful marketing of a destination, however, involves much more than just promotional work and image projection. Destination marketing must also concern itself with effective marketing research that leads to the correct deployment of all aspects of the tourism marketing mix, i.e. product, place, price and promotion, within the framework of a high quality customer service strategy and a costed strategic marketing plan. This illustrates the complex nature of the marketing of tourism destinations, which is further complicated by a number of factors concerning destinations themselves, including the fact that they exist at varying geographical scales, encompass multiple products, exhibit a multi-ownership pattern and serve the needs of a variety of markets. These factors were considered in greater detail in Chapter 2 on the structure and organisation of the international tourism industry.

The destination life cycle

We saw earlier in this chapter that all tourism products undergo a similar pattern of growth, development and ultimate decline, a concept known as the product life cycle (see Figure 7.7). It can be argued that since destinations are merely an amalgam of tourist products and facilities, they too will undergo a similar growth pattern, from low initial visitor numbers to mass tourism. In his tourist area life cycle (TALC) concept, Butler (1980) suggests that tourist destinations first go through an exploration stage when small numbers of visitors are attracted by the unspoilt nature of an area. This is followed by an involvement stage, during which local initiatives begin to provide facilities for the visitors. During the third development stage, large numbers of tourists visit the destination and control passes out of local hands. The fourth stage, consolidation, sees the rate of increase of visitor numbers declining followed by a period of stagnation, at which peak visitor numbers have been reached. There then follows a period of decline, during which the authorities may decide to rejuvenate the destination, by further investment in facilities or the exploitation of new markets, or may allow it to 'wither on the vine'. As with the application of the product life cycle concept to tourism, the TALC concept has its limitations. It has its uses as a conceptual framework for the retrospective analysis of destination development, but as a strategic planning or marketing tool its use is limited.

One destination that has enjoyed significant growth in visitor numbers is Australia, the subject of the following case study which investigates how the country is marketed overseas.

Case Study: Destination marketing – Australia

Introduction

By any country's standards, Australia has experienced dramatic growth in international tourist arrivals since the mid-1980s, to become one of the fastest-growing destinations in the world. In 1994/95, overseas visitor arrivals reached a new record level of 3.5 million, an 11.6 per cent rise on the 1993/94 figures. Direct visitor expenditure is estimated to have risen by 18.3 per cent to Aus$6.7 billion in 1994/95 over 1993/94, while foreign exchange earnings from inbound tourism climbed 16 per cent to a new high of Aus$12.3 billion (Australian Tourist Commission, 1995). The global economic recovery, explosive growth in travel from the Asian 'tiger' economies, growing interest in the environment, and aggressive marketing by the Australian Tourist Commission, have all contributed to this unprecedented pattern of growth in tourism to Australia.

The Australian Tourist Commission

The Australian Tourist Commission (ATC) is a statutory authority established under the Australian Tourist Commission Act 1987, with the principal task of marketing Australia internationally as a tourist destination. Its stated mission is to '. . . . *market Australia internationally to become the chosen destination for overseas visitors – for the economic and social benefit of all Australians*' (Australian Tourist Commission, 1995). Under the 1987 Act, the ATC's main objectives are to:

1. Increase the number of visitors to Australia from overseas

2. Maximise the benefits to Australia from overseas visitors

3. Ensure Australia is protected from adverse environmental and social impacts of international tourism.

The Commission is governed by a 10-member board, which reports to the Australian Federal Minister for Tourism. The ATC markets Australia to consumers and the travel industry in more than 30 countries around the world from its head office in Sydney and overseas offices in Los Angeles, New York, Hong Kong, Singapore, London, Frankfurt, Tokyo, Osaka and Auckland.

Working with the private sector and State and Territory tourism authorities, the ATC's promotional activities include consumer advertising on television and in print, an extensive programme of media visits and public relations, and co-ordination of the Australian tourism industry's participation in travel missions and trade shows around the world. The Commission also assists in product development, information distribution and retailer education programmes, with the aim of increasing the amount and variety of Australian product available overseas. Its work is divided into head office functions and activities in its various world markets, as the next two sections of this case study explain.

Marketing in the regions

Japan is Australia's largest single tourism market, with visitor arrivals climbing 7.5 per cent between 1994 and 1995 to a record high of nearly 750 000 (Australian Tourist Commission, 1995). The full picture of the origin of overseas visitors to the country is shown in Figure 7.10, which indicates that Asia is Australia's largest tourism source region with 28.3 per cent of all international arrivals in 1994/95, followed by Europe with 21.1 per cent.

Not surprisingly, the majority of the ATC's promotional budget is targeted at its three prime markets of Japan, Asia and Europe, as shown in Table 7.4. These three regions alone accounted for some 77 per cent of all ATC and industry sponsored spending on promotional activities in 1994/95. ▷

Destination marketing – Australia continued

Figure 7.10:
Origin of overseas visitors to Australia by region, 1994/95

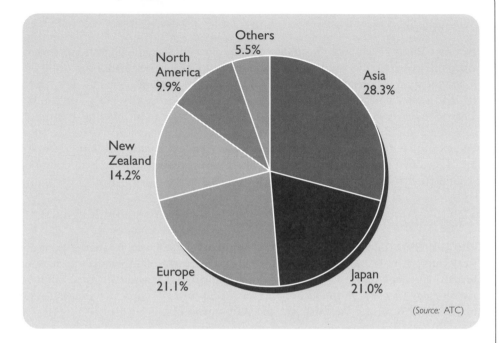

(Source: ATC)

Table 7.4:
Promotional expenditure in Australia's key overseas markets, 1994/95

Region	ATC expenditure (Aus$)		Industry sponsorship (Aus$)	
	Consumer marketing	*Trade marketing*	*Consumer marketing*	*Trade marketing*
Japan	12.9m	1.4m	4.2m	0.5m
Europe	11.2m	2.5m	6.3m	2.3m
Asia	12.3m	1.7m	3.0m	1.3m
The Americas	7.7m	1.8m	4.3m	1.4m
New Zealand	1.2m	0.3m	1.0m	0.08m

Source: ATC Annual Review, 1995

Marketing objectives, strategies and tactics differ for each of Australia's prime source regions for overseas tourists, although the principal aim is to increase the visitor arrivals and expenditure from them all. The marketing objectives for the Americas region, for example, are to:

● Increase visitor arrivals and maintain high levels of desire to visit Australia

● Develop a stronger and more persuasive brand image for Australia

● Enhance Partnership Australia programmes (see below) to increase product and information distribution

● Establish Australia as a viable holiday destination for stays of less than 14 days

● Further develop the conventions, incentive and special interest travel segments.

Objectives for Japan in particular, and Asia in general, include further enhancement of Australia's tourism products and greater travel agency staff training to increase their knowledge of Australia as a holiday destination. Promotional work in Europe seeks to build a strong, positive image of Australia as a desirable holiday destination and increase the range of holiday products available to potential travellers.

The marketing strategies implemented in Australia's major overseas markets include a mixture of consumer and travel trade activities. Consumer marketing activities include television and press advertising, public relations work centred on hosting journalists and overseas television programmes, and the production of a variety of destination sales brochures and guides. Travel trade marketing activities include attendances at major exhibitions around the world, including the World Travel Market in London and ITB Berlin, and a wide range of joint marketing schemes with industry partners.

In addition to its promotional work in its established source regions of the world, the ATC spent a total of Aus$590 000 in 1994/95 on targeted promotional activities in a number of emerging markets, including South Africa, the Middle East and Oceania (excluding New Zealand). The Commission believes that continued political stability and positive economic growth will result in higher levels of disposable income within these emerging markets, leading to continued increases in visitor arrivals to Australia.

Head office marketing activities

From its head office in Sydney, the ATC works with State and Territory tourism authorities and industry partners through an initiative known as Partnership Australia, to improve Australia's international competitiveness, reduce duplication of effort and deliver new products to consumers. This national co-operative marketing venture was launched in January 1994 and, to date, has included campaigns in the USA aimed at special interest travellers, golfers from Malaysia, honeymooners from the UK and France, and rural tourists from Asia. Co-operation on joint tactical advertising campaigns has expanded the range of competitively priced holiday choices available and generated strong interest. Partnership Australia telephone helpline services have been set up in Europe, North America, Asia, Japan and New Zealand to provide information, answer trade and consumer enquiries, and service requests for literature.

Working with travel industry partners, the ATC invested nearly Aus$1 million in 1994/95 in product development, helping to exploit new markets in, for example, cruise shipping, backpacker, rural and cultural tourism. To attract the growing special interest travel market, the ATC promoted a variety of attractions aimed at enriching the image of Australia as a holiday destination.

The aims of the trade marketing services department of the ATC are to provide effective co-operative marketing opportunities for the Australian tourism industry, co-ordinate Australian participation in trade shows in Australia and overseas, and improve the flow of information to the industry. The Commission places a high priority on working with Australian tourism operators to help them market their products internationally, through participation in co-operative programmes such as trade events and joint advertising schemes.

Marketing research plays a major role in developing the ATC's marketing strategies and identifying market segments offering the highest potential for travel to Australia and the highest yield. In 1994/95, an extensive research programme was carried out to help develop the advertising strategy and creative execution for new global campaigns to be implemented in 1995/96.

(*Information courtesy of the Australian Tourist Commission*)

Destination marketing – Australia continued

Discussion points and essay questions

1. Analyse the part that the Australian Tourist Commission has played in the dramatic growth in overseas visitor arrivals to Australia since the mid-1980s.

2. How has the Partnership Australia initiative helped the country's tourism operators?

3. How are the ATC's activities likely to change in the next 15 years in response to increased competition in international tourism?

4. Do you envisage a shift in the balance between trade and consumer marketing activities in the future marketing of Australia as an international tourism destination?

Strategic marketing planning

So far in this chapter we have investigated the various factors that a tourism organisation must consider when deciding on its marketing activities, including formulating marketing objectives, undertaking marketing research, determining the balance in its marketing mix and agreeing communication channels. To be truly effective, the organisation must approach each of these items in a systematic fashion, by implementing the process known as strategic marketing planning. By so doing, it will not only increase the chances of its activities being successful, but also make best use of its resources, help forecast future trends, allow measurement of its marketing performance and provide a focus for action. In short, strategic marketing planning helps an organisation secure its future profitability by developing its market share. Figure 7.11 indicates the principal stages in the strategic marketing planning process in tourism.

Figure 7.11:
The strategic marketing planning process in tourism

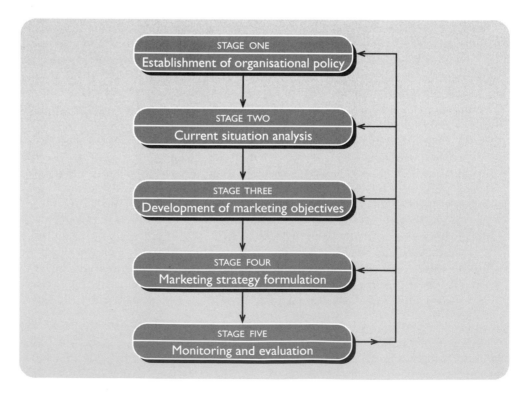

STAGE ONE
Establishment of organisational policy

STAGE TWO
Current situation analysis

STAGE THREE
Development of marketing objectives

STAGE FOUR
Marketing strategy formulation

STAGE FIVE
Monitoring and evaluation

Figure 7.11 demonstrates that the starting point of the strategic marketing planning process in tourism is the establishment of an overall organisational policy, followed by an analysis of its current business situation, both internal and external to the organisation. This leads on to the development of specific marketing objectives. Stage four is the formulation of the marketing strategy, i.e. the process by which the objectives identified at stage three will be achieved. The final stage in the process involves monitoring and evaluation, so that all preceding stages can be adjusted and adapted in response to changing circumstances.

The strategic marketing planning process is sometimes presented as a series of questions, which equate to the five stages shown in Figure 7.11 as follows:

● Stage one – what do we want to achieve?

● Stage two – where are we now?

● Stage three – where do we want to be?

● Stage four – how do we get there?

● Stage five – how do we know when we've arrived?

Each of the five stages of the process shown in Figure 7.11 will now be considered in greater depth.

Organisational policy

Before a tourism organisation can begin to think about specific marketing plans and priorities, it must be clear what it is trying to achieve, by defining its corporate goals. These goals are sometimes expressed as a mission statement or, in the case of public sector bodies, an organisational policy. Such statements are intended to convey to all those with an interest in the organisation, whether members of staff, customers, shareholders or the public in general, the type of business it is in and where it sees itself going in the future. Aspects of the organisation's philosophy and/or values may also be included in such statements. By way of example, the mission of the Wales Tourist Board is as follows:

'The Board seeks to develop and market tourism in ways which will yield optimum economic and social benefit to the people of Wales. Implicit within this objective is the need:

● *to sustain and promote the culture of Wales and the Welsh language,*

● *to safeguard the natural and built environment.*

In order to achieve its aims, the Board works in partnership with statutory agencies, local authorities, the private sector and other bodies'. (Wales Tourist Board, 1993)

Clearly, a public sector body such as the Wales Tourist Board has wider social, community, cultural and environmental aims than private sector tourism enterprises, which have profit maximisation as their first priority.

Current situation analysis

This stage in the strategic marketing planning process in tourism seeks to answer the question 'where are we now?'. Progression to the next stages of the process must be based on an objective assessment of a tourism organisation's internal and external operating environment and current business situation. Sometimes referred to as a marketing audit, this is most commonly achieved with the help of the following analytical techniques:

- PEST analysis
- SWOT analysis
- Product portfolio analysis

The benefits of each will now be discussed in greater detail.

PEST analysis

A PEST analysis is a structured process that allows an organisation to investigate the major external factors (**p**olitical, **e**conomic, **s**ocial and **t**echnological) that may impact on its current and future operations. The PEST (or STEP) analysis will be specific to an individual tourism organisation, but is likely to focus on the following factors of interest in the context of international tourism:

- *Political*: for example national/regional government influence, GATS (general agreements on trade in services), European Union policies, local government priorities, legislation, regulation/deregulation and regional development.
- *Economic*: such as taxation, business sponsorship, exchange rates, disposable incomes, inflation, unemployment levels and recession.
- *Social*: including demographic trends, changes in lifestyle, education, community issues, environmental awareness, holiday entitlements, working practices and retirement issues.
- *Technological*: for example transport developments, global communications, sales and reservation systems, management information systems, personal computer use and virtual reality.

SWOT analysis

Whereas a PEST analysis focuses on external factors that may influence an organisation's operations, a SWOT (**s**trengths, **w**eaknesses, **o**pportunities and **t**hreats) analysis seeks to assess its current business situation by investigating aspects of both its external and internal environment, by considering, among other things, its management style, human resources, facilities, suppliers, customers, competitors and products. An example of a SWOT analysis for a hypothetical tourist attraction is as follows:

1. Strengths
   - National reputation
   - Large regional catchment
   - High levels of customer satisfaction
   - Good staff morale
2. Weaknesses
   - Underdeveloped staff training policy
   - Declining visitor numbers
   - Outdated car parking facilities
   - Poor public transport links
3. Opportunities
   - Proximity to high-speed rail link to the Channel Tunnel
   - Inward investment by Japanese firms
   - Economy coming out of recession
4. Threats
   - New attraction being developed nearby
   - Proposed extension to government health and safety legislation
   - Likely increase in bank base rate

The discipline of producing a SWOT analysis should lead an organisation to build on its strengths, take action to reduce weaknesses, exploit opportunities and counter any real or perceived threats to its operation.

Product portfolio analysis

As well as investigating its internal and external business environments, a tourism enterprise is likely to critically assess its range of products as part of the current situation analysis stage of the strategic marketing planning process. It will seek to answer such questions as 'do the products on offer still meet customer needs?' and 'are there sufficient brands within the product range to cater for our target markets?'. The rationale of undertaking an analysis of a portfolio of products is to continually assess relative growth rates and resource demands. A well-known model for assisting the process of portfolio analysis is the Boston Consulting Group (BCG) matrix, which charts the rate of market growth against a product's relative market share (see Figure 7.12).

As Figure 7.12 indicates, products with high growth rates and a high share of the market are the 'stars' of the portfolio. 'Cash cows', with a low market growth rate but a high market share, tend to be market leaders in mature markets and are excellent generators of cash. A product with a high rate of market growth but a low relative market share is known as a 'question mark' and will need extra resources to help move it into the 'stars' sector. Finally, the 'dogs' have both low rates of market growth and low market shares, a sure recipe for removing the product from the portfolio altogether. Tourism organisations can chart their own products on the BCG matrix and use the process to make informed decisions on future products and services.

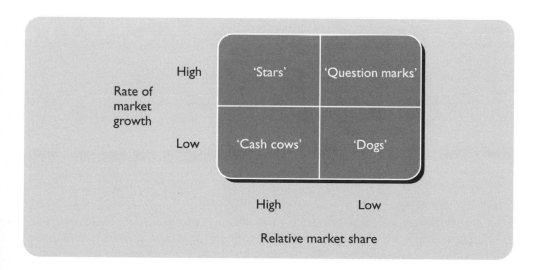

Figure 7.12:
The Boston Consulting Group matrix

Marketing objectives

Having determined its organisational policy and completed its situation analysis, the tourism organisation can now begin to answer the question 'where do we want to be?' by setting specific marketing objectives, the third stage of the strategic marketing planning process. A useful tool to help with this task is the product–market matrix developed by Ansoff (1988). Ansoff's matrix suggests that an organisation has four possible courses of action open to it when setting its marketing objectives, namely:

- *Market penetration*: attempting to sell more of a current product in an existing market, for example an airline introducing an enhanced customer service programme on its transatlantic routes to entice customers from its competitors.
- *Market development*: trying to sell a current product in a new market. British Airways' development of strategic alliances with Qantas and American Airlines is a good example of market development through selling in different geographical areas.
- *Product development*: involves developing new products for an existing market. The introduction of corporate hospitality at tourist attractions is an example of product development in the tourism industry.
- *Diversification*: attempting to launch a new product in a new market. This is a particularly high-risk scenario, given that there are so many unknown factors. Euro-sites, part of the UK-based Airtours tour operating company, successfully diversified into the self-drive continental camping market in the early 1980s.

Over and above any considerations of product and market changes suggested by the application of Ansoff's matrix, a tourism organisation may need to implement specific marketing objectives, such as increasing the scale of its operations, restricting its product range or changing the emphasis of its promotional activity. Whatever is decided must reflect the organisation's overall objectives and the findings of the current situation analysis.

Marketing strategy

In determining its marketing strategy or strategies, a tourist organisation is trying to answer the question 'how do we get to where we want to be?'. The success of the marketing planning process is determined to a great extent by an organisation achieving the correct balance in its marketing mix, i.e. product, place, price and promotion, so as to achieve its stated marketing objectives. A tourism enterprise can choose one of a number of options when implementing its marketing strategy, for example:

- *Undifferentiated marketing.* This is when a single marketing mix is offered to the total market for a product or service. This is unlikely to succeed in tourism since buyers have markedly different characteristics.
- *Differentiated marketing.* This approach tailors specific marketing strategies to clearly identified market segments; a tour operator, for example, will develop different products for different age groups.
- *Concentrated marketing.* This involves choosing to compete in only one sector of the market and developing the most effective marketing mix to achieve success in sales. Eurocamp, the self-drive camping specialist company, is a good example of a tourism enterprise that concentrates on one sector of the market.

Whatever strategy or strategies are finally developed, and associated marketing plans produced, it is important that clear financial and operational targets are set for completion of the work and a time deadline agreed at the outset.

Monitoring and evaluation

The final stage of the strategic marketing planning process in tourism seeks to answer the question 'how do we know when we've arrived?', through careful monitoring and evaluation of the plan. Sadly, this aspect of the process is often neglected, with management and staff thinking that their work is done once the marketing strategy is implemented. Without consistent monitoring of the process, in order to make any necessary adjustments, and objective evaluation of each stage, the plan may not reach its full potential. Managers must have access to reliable and regular information on sales and marketing activity in order to achieve the desired results.

Chapter summary

This chapter has investigated the significance of marketing in international tourism, drawing on case studies and industry examples of best practice. We have investigated the marketing concept and its application to tourism, in particular the fluid and cyclical nature of the tourism marketing process. The importance of marketing research in tourism has been highlighted, with analysis of the principal sources of primary and secondary research data. We have examined market segmentation in tourism and the application of the four main elements of the marketing mix – product, price, place and promotion. The need for a balanced approach to the formulation of the marketing mix and subsequent marketing plans was stressed. The chapter has also considered the importance of destination marketing, where multi-ownership and operation pose challenges to the tourism marketer. The chapter concluded with an appreciation of the importance of a logical, objective approach to tourism marketing, through the application of the strategic marketing planning process, with its five clearly defined stages.

Discussion questions

1. Is marketing in tourism any different from marketing in other service sectors of the economy?

2. Why is it important to undertake marketing research as part of a tourism organisation's overall marketing activities?

3. Is market segmentation a necessary part of a successful marketing strategy?

4. How can private and public sector organisations ensure the co-ordinated marketing of tourist destinations?

5. Critically analyse the strategic marketing planning process of a tourism enterprise with which you are familiar.

References and further reading

● Ansoff, H (1988) *The New Corporate Strategy*, John Wiley & Sons, New York
● Australian Tourist Commission (1995) *Australian Tourist Commission Annual Review 1995*, ATC, Sydney
● Booms, B and Bitner, M (1981) 'Marketing strategies and organisation structures for service firms', in Donnelly, J and George, W (eds), *Marketing of Services*, American Marketing Association, Chicago

- British Airways (1993) *Annual Report and Accounts 1992–93*, BA, London
- Butler, R (1980) 'The concept of a tourist area life cycle of evolution', *Canadian Geographer*, Vol. 24, Pergamon Press, Oxford, UK
- Holloway, C and Robinson, C (1995) *Marketing for Tourism*, 3rd edition, Longman, Harlow, UK
- Kotler, P (1994) *Marketing Management*, 8th edition, Prentice-Hall International
- Middleton, V (1994) *Marketing in Travel and Tourism*, 2nd edition, Butterworth-Heinemann, Oxford, UK
- Wales Tourist Board (1993) *The Wales Tourist Board 1988–1993*, WTB, Cardiff

Chapter Eight

The Future of Tourism – Issues for the Millennium

Chapter Overview

This chapter aims to crystallise many of the issues and topics discussed in the preceding chapters of this book, by concentrating on the future of tourism at what to many commentators is a critical time in its history. It looks at future demand for tourism, in terms of both tourist numbers and the factors that will influence demand. Supply-side issues concerning the main sectors of the tourism industry are considered, along with the concept of sustainable tourism and its position in the future of the industry. Finally, the chapter considers the future role of governments and other public agencies in international tourism.

Key Topics

- The scale of future demand for international tourism
- Key factors influencing future tourism development
- Future sectoral developments in tourism
- The role of sustainability in the future of tourism
- Future governmental influence in tourism

Introduction

No book on international tourism can ignore the issues facing the industry in the future and the influences on its development. This book began by suggesting that tourism finds itself at something of a crossroads in its development; on the one hand it is heralded as 'the world's biggest industry', with impressive and growing economic credentials, while at the same time its recognition on the world stage as a truly significant economic and political activity has yet to fully materialise. An increasing number of countries are scaling down their public investment in tourism development and marketing, and the European Union seems reluctant to recognise the economic potential of the industry. The future could be either one where tourism truly comes of age in the global arena, or one in which the industry, through unco-ordinated approaches and a sometimes mixed message, fails to realise its considerable potential. The remainder of this chapter explores these issues.

Future demand for international tourism

Analyses from the World Tourism Organisation (WTO), World Travel and Tourism Council (WTTC), national governments and major industry operators all conclude that the growth in domestic and international tourism of the last half-century will continue up to and well beyond the year 2000. Tourism is destined to play an increasingly important economic and political role on the world stage. WTO forecasts that the growth in international tourist arrivals to 2005 will be approximately 4 per cent per annum, giving a total figure of some 650 million international arrivals by 2000. WTTC's research estimates that this growth in demand for tourism will generate a total output of US$7.1 trillion and create 130 million new jobs in the international travel and tourism industry by 2006 (World Travel and Tourism Council, 1996).

Although overall demand for tourism at a global level is set to continue in the foreseeable future, there will clearly be winners and losers in terms of international tourist arrivals in different world regions. Chapter 3 highlighted the fact that Europe is already losing its share of the international tourism market, principally to countries in the Far East and the Pacific Rim, but will this trend continue in the future and how does Europe's position compare with other parts of the world? Figure 8.1 provides the answers to these questions.

The data from the World Tourism Organisation shown in Figure 8.1 indicate that the east Asia/Pacific region will continue to grow at the fastest annual rate between 1990 and 2000, closely followed by its near neighbour south Asia. Africa, the Americas and the Middle East are all forecast to have annual growth rates above the world average of 3.8 per cent for the ten-year period. Only Europe, with a predicted growth rate of 2.7

Figure 8.1:
International tourism regional growth rates, 1990–2000

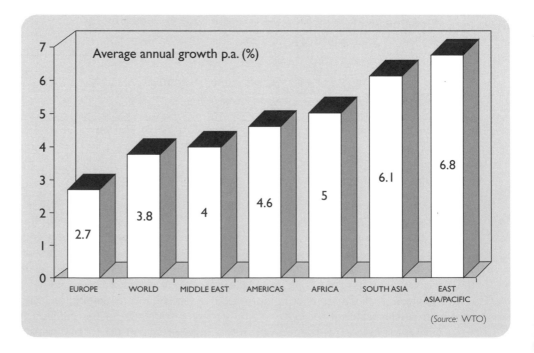

(Source: WTO)

per cent per annum, falls below the world average, finding itself at the bottom of the league in terms of the growth of international tourist arrivals.

It is clear that countries in the Asia/Pacific Rim region are in an excellent position to benefit from the predicted growth in international tourism; but why exactly is the region forecast to have the highest rate of growth of any part of the world? The most important factors that contribute to this scenario are:

- Rapid economic growth projected in many Asia/Pacific countries
- Intensification of intra-Asia/Pacific trade
- Continuing air transport liberalisation
- Opening of new airports (for example Macau, Hong Kong, Osaka, Kuala Lumpur and Bangkok)
- Low tourist numbers at present in several countries with high travel potential, including China and Vietnam
- Assumption of increased tourist movements between China and Chinese Taipei
- Increases in disposable incomes and propensity to travel

Although these factors are specific to the Asia/Pacific region, they are reflected in the influences on the demand for tourism at the international level, as discussed in the following section of this chapter.

Factors affecting future tourism demand

The growth of international tourism will be influenced by a wide variety of social, economic, political, environmental, cultural and technological factors, the most important of which are considered in the remainder of this section.

Demographic trends   The ageing of the population in western, industrialised nations (the major tourism generating countries) will have important effects on the nature of demand for tourism products and services in the future. Changes in household composition, such as increased numbers of one-parent families and couples choosing not to have children or to delay having children until later in life, will also influence tourism demand.

Technological developments   Continuing developments in transportation will reduce travel times and make the remoter regions of the world more accessible to tourists. Sensitive planning will be needed to minimise the possible detrimental effects on these destination areas. Airport expansion will continue, particularly in the Asia/Pacific Rim region. Technology will also influence the way that tourism products are promoted and sold, for example the viewing of virtual reality simulations of resort facilities prior to making a booking and sales via networked computer systems such as the Internet.

Emerging economies   The World Bank forecasts that the developing nations of the world, including the former Soviet states, will achieve economic growth rates of around 5 per cent per annum, compared with only 2.7 per cent in the richer, industrial countries (British Tourist Authority/English Tourist Board, 1996). If these forecasts prove to be correct, within a generation China will overtake the USA as the world's biggest economy and as many as nine of the top 15 world economies will be from today's third world nations. According to the World Bank figures, the top ten economies are likely to be China, USA, Japan, India, Indonesia, Germany, South Korea, Thailand, France and

Taiwan. Given that past patterns of international tourism growth have closely followed global economic prosperity, we are likely to see a very different pattern of demand for tourism at the international level in the future, with the emergence of a distinct east–west movement of tourists from the 'tiger economies' of the Far East.

Political stability   World regions that have a high proportion of countries with stable political regimes are likely to gain in terms of tourism, at the expense of politically unstable nations.

Changing work patterns   Developments such as home working, the growth of short-term contracts and multi-tasking (one person carrying out a number of different job roles) will have significant effects on the nature of tourism demand, with a continuation of the trend away from long (4+ nights) holidays to short breaks, and leisure pursuits being followed at non-traditional times, for example the growth of the 24-hour city concept.

Increased environmental awareness   The rise of the 'green' movement of the 1970s and 1980s will continue in the future, with increased demand for tourism products and services that espouse the principles of sustainable development.

Globalisation of the industry   Moves by major players in the international tourism industry to increase their influence and domination of global markets may reduce consumer choice. On the other hand, greater deregulation of industry sectors, coupled with the emergence of a more discerning travelling public, is likely to result in greater choice for consumers.

The 'new tourist'

In terms of the future demand for international tourism, it is currently fashionable to talk of the rise of the 'new tourist', an individual who will shun the homogenised, mass market tourism products and destinations in favour of a more adventurous, active and individualised approach to holiday-taking. The 'new tourist' will be well educated, discerning, demanding, environmentally aware and prepared to pay a premium for high quality products and services. In many respects, such tourists already exist in western society, albeit in relatively small numbers. As international tourism expands, the number of 'new tourists' will undoubtedly grow, but their numbers will always be overshadowed by the bulk of tourists who will continue to buy packaged holiday products, visit popular destinations and make their holiday choices primarily on the basis of price.

Future sectoral developments

So far in this chapter we have considered the future *demand* for tourism. The many sectors of the international tourism industry, the supply side, will also undergo significant changes in response to market fluctuations and changes in consumer habits. The following sections investigate the major influences on accommodation, air travel, tourist attractions and travel intermediaries.

The accommodation sector

As world tourist arrivals continue to grow up to and beyond 2000, the accommodation sector of the global tourism industry will continue to expand, especially in the growth regions of the world, including east Asia and the Pacific, south Asia and Africa. There will be many factors that influence the nature of tourist accommodation, for example:

- *Greater concern for product quality.* Operating in a highly competitive environment, providers will need to supply high quality accommodation for an increasingly demanding and discerning travelling public.
- *Customer service.* Increased investment in staff training by hotels and other accommodation providers will help improve profitability.
- *Value for money.* All guests, whether on business or leisure travel, will expect good value for money, regardless of the price paid for the accommodation.
- *Changes in demographics and family structures.* Factors such as the ageing of the population and more single-parent households will affect product development and marketing strategies.
- *Changing work patterns.* More women in the workforce, greater home working and the move towards more contract and part-time employment will influence the demand for tourist accommodation.
- *Health and fitness.* Accommodation providers can capitalise on the trend towards healthy lifestyles by providing suitable facilities for guests, such as fitness suites and leisure facilities.
- *New technology.* Changes in technology will affect patterns of booking and could be used by accommodation providers to control many of the mundane operations associated with the sector, thereby freeing staff to concentrate on delivering enhanced levels of customer service.

Successful providers of hotels and other types of accommodation will continue to offer products that are targeted at particular market segments. The trend towards branding accommodation products, so cleverly exploited by the Accor Group in its European hotels, will be further refined in order to match these market segments with readily identifiable accommodation types.

Future developments in air travel

The world's dominant airlines will continue to develop global networks through takeovers or strategic alliances with partner airlines. The focus of much activity in this field will be on routes serving countries in Asia, which according to IATA's international air traffic forecasts will be the world's fastest growing region at 8.7 per cent per annum between 1996 and 2000 (International Air Transport Association, 1996). Annual growth rates of international passenger numbers for other world regions over the same time period are:

- South Pacific   7.3 per cent
- Latin America   6.9 per cent
- Europe   6.6 per cent
- North America   6.4 per cent
- Africa   5.9 per cent
- Middle East   5.0 per cent

Forecasts for *total* air traffic – international and domestic – give a fairer indication of the future growth patterns of the airline sector. Total passenger traffic is expected to grow at an average annual rate of 6.3 per cent between 1995 and 2000, giving a forecast passenger total in 2000 of 1748 million, a growth of 460 million (36 per cent) on the 1995 figure of 1288 million.

The attractions sector

The attractions sector will always play a crucial role in the international tourism industry. Given that it is a highly competitive and dynamic industry sector, there are many issues that the operators of attractions, and those responsible for their planning and development, will need to consider in the future; of particular concern are:

- *Visitor management.* By their very nature, attractions are a 'magnet' for people and their vehicles to what is often a small, closely defined area. This can lead to congestion, physical erosion, pollution and a general despoilation of the visitor experience. Planners and managers in cities, country areas and coastal resorts will need to implement policies that minimise the negative environmental and social impacts of tourist attractions.

- *Authenticity.* Attractions and events are sometimes criticised for conveying images that fail to appreciate and value the true cultural identity of destination areas, resulting in a loss of authenticity. This can be reduced by sensitive management of attractions and the early involvement of local communities in their development.

- *Advances in technology.* Tourists who are exposed to new technologies in their work and everyday lives are looking to attractions to provide a similarly stimulating environment while they are at leisure. Developments such as virtual reality, CD-ROM technology and the Internet will increasingly become part of the attractions sector.

- *Nature of the visitor experience.* As well as appreciating technological improvements in tourist attractions, today's increasingly discerning tourists will be looking for the highest quality in both product presentation and customer service.

The future for travel intermediaries

The fortune of travel agents and tour operators in the future will be dependent on the state of the international tourism industry. There is little doubt that tourism is set to grow steadily in terms of international visitor arrivals. Travel to and within the east Asia, south Asia and African regions is forecast to grow at the fastest rate, so travel intermediaries operating in these areas have ample opportunity for growth. With most regions of the world emerging from the economic recession of the early 1990s, the prospects for travel agents and tour operators are favourable. Nevertheless, the fiercely competitive nature of these sectors of the tourism industry will mean that the profit margins of agents and operators will continue to be squeezed. Successful travel intermediaries will need to respond to a variety of factors that are likely to shape the demand for their services in the future, for example:

- *Continued growth in the long-haul market.* Helped by new aircraft technology and the consequent availability of charter flights, destinations such as the USA,

Australia, the Caribbean and the Pacific Rim will continue to be popular with both package and independent tourists.

- *Growth in independent travel.* The trend away from inclusive tours towards more independent travel is likely to continue. In order to retain market share, tour operators will need to offer more flexibility in the design of their holidays, while some travel agents will seize the opportunity and offer a more customised service to their clients.

- *Growth in short holidays and breaks.* Both domestic and outbound operators will continue to provide short breaks to meet growing demand. Developments in transportation, such as the Channel Tunnel, improvements in rail services and the deregulation of European air fares will stimulate increases in this sector.

- *Demand for activity and health-related holidays.* Growing interest in health and fitness will offer an opportunity for travel organisers to develop greater variety in their activity programmes.

- *Continuation of the trend towards late bookings.* Changes in lifestyle and work patterns will mean a shorter lead time for travel purchases.

- *Greater concern for quality.* Concern over indifferent standards of package holidays have dogged the tourist industry in recent years, making it crucial for tour operators to put quality at the top of their agenda when planning new products.

- *Heightened concern for the environment.* Customers will expect their travel intermediaries to operate in a manner that is respectful of the long-term well-being of the environment when choosing the elements of their packages.

Sustainable tourism – the way ahead?

One possible solution to the environmental and socio-cultural problems associated with tourism is to adopt and engender sustainable development principles. We saw in Chapter 5 that sustainable tourism is an emerging concept that has grown out of increased concern about the negative environmental and socio-cultural impacts of unplanned tourism development. An extension of 'green tourism', which focuses on environmental concerns, sustainable tourism is part of a much wider global debate on sustainable development, highlighted by the *Brundtland Report* in 1987 and the Earth Summit in Rio in 1992. The sustainable approach to tourism development implies that the natural and cultural resources of tourism are conserved for continuous use in the future, while still bringing benefits to the present society. Although gaining favour with academics and researchers, there remains the problem of converting principles of sustainability into practical measures to protect environments and cultures. It is likely that the range and variety of tourism products based on the principles of sustainability will increase in the future, but the incorporation of such principles into mass market products will remain a distant hope.

Agenda 21 and the tourism industry

Agenda 21 is a comprehensive programme of action adopted by 182 governments in June 1992 at the United Nations Conference on Environment and Development (UNCED), better known as the 'Earth Summit'. It provides a blueprint for securing the sustainable future of the planet, from now into the twenty-first century. Agenda 21 is the first ument of its kind to achieve widespread international agreement, reflecting a global

document of its kind to achieve widespread international agreement, reflecting a global consensus and political commitment at the highest level. Although not legally binding, Agenda 21 has moral and practical force. One of its greatest strengths lies in the fact that it was not produced by experts for governmental consent, but rather was negotiated, word by word, by representatives of the governments that will be responsible for its implementation. In short, Agenda 21 represents a commitment to an important strategic thrust, which now requires specific initiatives from all levels of society and from business communities.

Tourism's contribution to the Agenda 21 debate has been summarised and advanced by the World Travel and Tourism Council (WTTC, 1995). The WTTC has translated Agenda 21 into a programme of action for the tourism industry, highlighting priority action points for both the public sector and commercial operators. For government departments, national tourism organisations, companies and representative trade organisations, the WTTC sees the overriding aim in relation to Agenda 21 as establishing systems and procedures to incorporate sustainable development considerations at the core of the decision-making process and to identify actions necessary to bring sustainable development into being. The WTTC sees Agenda 21 as being at the heart of the debate about the future development of tourism, which if it is to survive and prosper in the long term, must take action now.

Future government involvement in tourism

Throughout the chapters of this book, the fact that tourism is essentially a private sector industry has been clearly highlighted. There has, nonetheless, been acknowledgement of the important regulatory and co-ordinating role played by public agencies in tourism at international, national, regional and local levels. As world nations move away from centralised states to modern, free-market economies, it is likely that the trend of less public involvement, and investment, in tourism development and marketing is likely to continue and even accelerate. Governments and public agencies will see their role in international tourism as facilitators for the private sector rather than as providers of services and facilities in their own right. The strategic role of governments in tourism will remain important and may well grow, in such matters as manpower planning, training, enterprise development, development control, infrastructure improvements and economic development.

Chapter summary

This chapter has indicated that international tourism will continue to expand in the short term and that the supply side of the industry will be faced with many challenges in meeting the needs of an increasingly discerning travelling public. All sectors of the industry will need to adapt to changed circumstances. The influence of the principles of sustainable tourism will continue, albeit in terms of a 'niche' market. That there is potential for international tourism to achieve a global economic significance is not in doubt. What is in question, however, is whether this disparate industry has the necessary co-ordination and influence, not to mention responsive management structures and a well-trained workforce, to realise its economic and political potential to the full.

Discussion questions

1. What are the main demographic factors that will influence the future nature of international tourism?

2. What are the key economic issues facing small and medium-sized tourism enterprises as they strive to grow their businesses in the future?

3. Is there a good argument for reductions in the public funding of tourism?

4. What influence do you think the principles for sustainable development will have on the future of international tourism?

5. What part will technology play in helping to shape the tourism industry of tomorrow?

References and further reading

- British Tourist Authority/English Tourist Board (1996) *Tourism Intelligence Quarterly*, Vol. 17, No. 4, BTA/ETB, London
- International Air Transport Association (1996) *Annual Report 1996*, IATA, Geneva
- World Travel and Tourism Council (1995) *Agenda 21 for the Travel and Tourism Industry*, WTTC, London
- World Travel and Tourism Council (1996) *Progress and Priorities 1996*, WTTC, London

Glossary of terms

- **'Above the line'.** Refers to marketing and promotional activity for which a commission is normally paid by the chosen media to an advertising agency, for example advertising by a tourism organisation on television, at the cinema, in newspapers and magazines, or on commercial radio.

- **ABTA.** Stands for the Association of British Travel Agents, the trade body that represents over 90 per cent of all travel agents and tour operators in the UK. The Association is a self-regulatory body run by its membership, via a network of councils and committees, with members appointed by member travel agents and tour operators.

- **Agenda 21.** A set of principles for future sustainable development agreed at the Earth Summit in Rio in 1992. Agenda 21 has since been interpreted and expanded at national, regional and local level in many of the world's countries. Many communities in the UK have developed their own action plans, referred to as Local Agenda 21.

- **Allocentric.** One of a number of types of tourist behaviour developed by Plog in 1977 as part of a research study for airline companies. Allocentrics are people who enjoy travel and cultural exploration, are in above-average income groups, independent in mind and body, and adventurous.

- **'Below the line'.** Refers to marketing activity for which commission is not normally paid to an advertising agency, but the work is carried out on a fee basis instead; for example, an agency may charge a fee of £2000 to carry out a small direct mail campaign for a travel company. As well as direct mail, other below-the-line activities include public relations, sales promotions and merchandising.

- **Branding.** The practice of giving a product or service a distinctive name or logo, in the hope that it will become easily identifiable from its competitors and take on a certain identity. Common brand names used in the tourism industry include Holiday Inn, Hertz and Lunn Poly. Organisations hope that customers will show brand loyalty, by buying their particular products above all others.

- **Break-even load factor.** A measure of the number of seats that need to be sold on an airline flight, as a proportion of total seats available, before all operating, marketing and administrative costs are covered. It is only when the break-even load figure has been reached that the airline will begin to make a profit on the flight.

- **Business tourism.** The category of the tourism industry concerned with travel for business purposes, rather than travel for leisure purposes. Business tourism includes travel for meetings, exhibitions, trade fairs, conferences, conventions and incentive travel.

- **Cabotage.** Refers to airline and shipping routes within a country's national territory, for example flights between London and Glasgow, and even between London and Gibraltar. Such routes are not subject to international agreements on fares, making residents of the country eligible for reduced-rate tariffs, sometimes called cabotage fares.

- **Carrying capacity.** The maximum number of people that a resort, site or other area can sustain, before there is a reduction in the quality of the visitor experience or adverse effects on either the physical environment or the host community.

- **Catchment area.** The geographical limit from within which a tourism facility draws its customers. The size of the catchment area will depend on a number of factors, such as the availability and quality of transport links, the uniqueness of the facility and the population density of the area.

- **Chartered air services.** When aircraft are commissioned for a set period of time, flying to a particular destination and able to offer reduced fares by setting high load factors. Most package holidays that include air travel will use charter flights (known as inclusive tours by charter).

- **Commission.** A payment made to an agent for selling the products and services of a principal; for example, a travel agent is paid a commission for selling a tour operator's package holidays. The commission is usually an agreed percentage of the selling price, which may be increased for higher sales levels.

- **Day visitor.** A term which describes a tourist who makes a visit which does not involve an overnight stay away from his or her normal place of residence.

- **Demarketing.** The technique of withdrawing marketing activity from a product or service so as to dissuade customers and thereby reduce demand. In tourism, it can be applied to a destination that has become too popular and is giving rise to complaints of overcrowding and damage to the environment.

- **Demographic factors.** Concern the characteristics of the population of a country or region, for example age structure, proportion of males and females, social class, level of income and employment status.

- **Demonstration effect.** Seen most often in developing countries, when members of the host communities begin to imitate the patterns of behaviour of their (often) wealthier Western visitors. Some residents are curious about and may yearn for the consumer goods belonging to the tourists, such as cameras, personal stereos and radios.

- **Deregulation.** The withdrawal of local or central government control over industries to encourage greater competition between companies, for example the airline industry in the USA and the coach industry in the UK.

- **Determinants.** The economic, social, political and technological factors that influence a person's demand for travel and leisure products, irrespective of any motivations he or she may have.

- **Direct marketing.** The term used to describe the various techniques that an organisation can use to sell its products and services on a personalised basis direct to the consumer, without the need for an intermediary. These include direct mail, telemarketing, door-to-door distribution and direct response advertising.

● **Direct sell.** When a tourism organisation sells its products and services direct to the consumer, rather than through an intermediary, sometimes called a 'middle man'. In the package holiday industry, direct sell operators, such as Portland Holidays and Eclipse Direct (formerly Tjaereborg, Sunfare and Martin Rooks), suggest that they can sell holidays more cheaply since they do not have to pay commission to travel agents.

● **Displacement effect.** When tourism development has the effect of taking employment and other economic resources away from other industries, for example the development of tourism in some Mediterranean countries has taken jobs away from primary sector industries, such as fishing and agriculture.

● **Domestic tourism.** The type of tourism where people take holidays, short breaks and business trips in their own country.

● **Economic impacts.** Refer to the positive and negative effects of tourism on national and local communities, for example wealth generation, employment creation, urban regeneration and contributions to gross national product (GNP).

● **Ecotourism.** Defined by the Ecotourism Society as 'purposeful travel to natural areas to understand the cultural and natural history of the environment, taking care not to alter the integrity of the ecosystem, whilst producing economic opportunities that make the conservation of natural resources financially beneficial to local citizens'.

● **ECU.** Stands for European Currency Unit, an artificial currency made up of the trade-weighted averages of the currencies of the member states of the European Union.

● **'Empty nesters'.** A term used by tourism marketers to denote couples whose children have moved away from the household, thereby increasing their available disposable income.

● **Entrepreneur.** An individual who is prepared to take a risk and accept a challenge or undertake a venture that has no guarantee of success. Richard Branson, chairman of the Virgin Group, is often cited as a good example of an entrepreneur working in the tourism industry.

● **Environmental impacts.** Refer to positive and negative impacts of tourism, for example initiatives such as the Britain in Bloom competition and the Seaside Award, helping to improve local environments for both locals and visitors. Problems associated with the environmental impacts of tourism include litter, pollution, physical erosion and loss of habitats.

● **European Blue Flag Campaign.** A scheme that provides a comparison between standards of cleanliness and management at European resort beaches. Launched in 1987, the European Year of the Environment, a Blue Flag is awarded to resort beaches which have achieved the guideline standard of the EU Bathing Water Directive.

● **Eurostat.** The official body that collects, analyses and publishes statistical data on matters concerning the European Commission and member states of the European Union (EU). Officially known as the Statistical Office of the European Communities, Eurostat publishes two main sets of documents – general publications and statistical documents.

● **Excursionists.** Another term used to denote day visitors.

● **External business environment.** A term used to denote certain factors that may have an effect on an organisation, its operation and profitability. Sometimes referred to as the macro environment, they are often factors over which the organisation will have little control, such as the state of the national economy, the level of unemployment, changes in the social structure, government legislation and technological advances.

● **Familiarisation visit.** An educational trip which gives travel agents, tour operators and other members of the travel trade, the opportunity of trying tourism facilities and services at first hand, so that they are in the best position to advise clients on their holiday choices.

- **Globalisation**. The process whereby large companies and markets become increasingly multinational, through company takeovers, strategic alliances, vertical and horizontal integration, allowing businesses to switch operations around the world with ease.

- **Green tourism.** A general term used to describe a type of tourist activity which aims to be respectful of the environment in which it takes place and the communities that live there. Variously described as alternative tourism, appropriate tourism, intelligent tourism, 'soft' tourism, responsible tourism and ecotourism, 'green' tourism is characterised as small-scale activities which make use of local produce and labour and aim to produce a holiday experience that is an alternative to mass tourism.

- **'Honeypot'.** The term used to describe the convergence of visitors in popular tourist destinations.

- **Horizontal integration.** The process whereby companies at the same level in the distribution chain merge to gain competitive advantage, for example a large hotel chain taking over a small independent hotel or the takeover of Dan Air by British Airways.

- **Host community.** A term used in the debate on sustainable tourism to denote a place where people go for holidays and the people who live there. There is a growing acceptance that the wishes of host communities in relation to tourist development need to be given a higher priority, to allow minimum disruption to their lives, while at the same time providing economic benefits.

- **IATA.** Stands for International Air Transport Association, a voluntary international trade body representing the interests of more than 80 per cent of the world's major airlines. IATA's principal aim is to promote safe, regular and economic air travel.

- **Impacts of tourism.** These are generally characterised as economic, environmental, socio-cultural and political. Tourism impacts may be either positive or negative.

- **Inbound (incoming) tourism.** A form of international tourism which deals with people entering another country from their own country of origin or another country which is not their home.

- **Incentive travel.** A type of business tourism concerned with offering holidays and leisure products as incentives for staff.

- **Inclusive tour (IT).** Another term used for package holiday.

- **Inclusive tour by charter (ITC).** The term used for a package holiday where the travel component is made up of a charter flight, as opposed to a scheduled flight. The vast majority of mass market package holidays use this arrangement.

- **Inclusive tour by excursion (ITX).** A package holiday where the travel component consists of a scheduled flight, rather than a charter flight. In the UK this arrangement is less common and more expensive than an inclusive tour by charter.

- **Infrastructure.** Refers to facilities such as airports, communications, roads, railways, water supply and sewerage services, i.e. all those services that need to be in place before tourism development of any kind can go ahead. A country's infrastructure is generally financed and built by the public sector, or is part of a public/private partnership arrangement, with private sector operators developing the tourism superstructure.

- **Integration.** Refers to tourism organisations merging their operations for commercial advantage. The most common types in tourism are horizontal and vertical integration.

- **Internal business environment.** A term used to denote those influences and factors that are close to a tourism organisation and over which it has some degree of control. Sometimes called the micro environment, these include customers, staff, facilities and suppliers.

- **Internal tourism.** Refers to domestic and inbound tourism.

- **International tourism.** Refers to inbound and outbound tourism.

- **Invisibles.** These are services whose value is shown on a country's balance of payments, i.e. those items that cannot be seen or touched, for example banking, financial services, shipping and tourism.

- **Leakage.** The loss of revenue from a local or national economy as a result of, for example, fluctuations in exchange rates, payments to shareholders, taxation and purchases of goods and services from external distributors.

- **Leisure tourism.** The category of tourism concerned with travel for leisure purposes, rather than travel for business purposes. Leisure tourism includes taking holidays at home and abroad, visiting friends and relatives (VFR) and travel for a variety of reasons, such as for health and fitness, sport, education, culture, religious and spiritual.

- **Macro environment.** Another term used to denote the external business environment.

- **Market orientation.** A philosophy concerned with researching the needs of the market and providing tourism products and services that customers will want to buy. It is more concerned with giving customers complete satisfaction than purely concentrating on the details of the products and services that are supplied.

- **Market research.** The process of gathering information on existing and potential customers and its use for management purposes.

- **Market segmentation.** The technique of sub-dividing the total market for a tourism product or service into different groups, each with similar characteristics. Market segmentation enables an organisation to target a particular group, whose members become the focus of all its marketing efforts.

- **Market share.** The proportion of a total market that is held by an organisation, in relation to its main competitors. In tourism, market share is usually measured either by volume, for example the number of holidays sold to a particular destination, or by value, for example the revenue generated by sales to a particular country.

- **Marketing.** The process concerned with identifying customers' needs and supplying products and services in the right place, at the right time and at the right price. It is defined by the Chartered Institute of Marketing as 'the management process for identifying and satisfying customer needs profitably'.

- **Marketing consortium.** A grouping of independent tourism businesses or other organisations working together for a common purpose or benefit.

- **Marketing mix.** Commonly referred to as the 4 Ps, the marketing mix refers to product, price, place and promotion, and the emphasis placed on each component in seeking to achieve marketing objectives.

- **Marketing objectives.** The specific aims or goals that an organisation has in mind when planning and implementing its marketing activity.

- **Marketing research.** The term used to describe the process of gathering and analysing data which affects a wide range of factors that influence the marketing process of an organisation. Unlike market research, which is concerned specifically with customers and their attitudes to products and services, marketing research is a more all-embracing activity, involving, for example, product research, promotion research and price research.

- **Marketing strategy.** Refers to the overall means by which an organisation hopes to meet its marketing objectives.

- **Mass tourism.** The term used to describe the movement of people in large numbers for leisure tourism purposes, a characteristic of the latter half of the twentieth century in Western, developed countries.

- **Merchandising.** A range of methods adopted by travel and tourism retailers to stimulate customers to purchase at the point-of-sale (POS). This may include brochure racks, posters, hanging cards, displays and signs.

- **Micro environment.** Another term used to denote the internal business environment.

- **Mid-centric.** One of a number of types of tourist behaviour developed by Plog in 1977 as part of a research study for airline companies. Midcentrics make up the bulk of tourists to a particular destination, i.e. the mass market. They tend to move in after resorts have been discovered by the more adventurous allocentrics.

- **Mission statement.** A brief explanation of an organisation's fundamental purpose. Its aim is to convey to all those with an interest in the organisation, be they staff, share-holders or the public in general, what business it is in, where it sees itself going and how it will relate to its environment and other organisations.

- **Motivators.** These are factors within the psychological make-up of an individual that help influence his or her patterns of tourist behaviour.

- **Multinational corporation.** A company that operates across international frontiers, with its headquarters in one country and operating interests in a number of others.

- **Multiplier effect.** An economic concept which, when applied to tourism, shows that the money spent by visitors to an area is re-spent in the local economy and is actually worth more than its face value.

- **National tourism.** Refers to domestic and outbound tourism.

- **'Niche' marketing.** The process of targeting small, readily identifiable sections of a tourism market, each with clearly defined characteristics, rather than trying to cover it all.

- **Outbound tourism.** The form of international tourism which concerns people travelling away from their main country of residence for leisure or business purposes.

- **Package Travel Directive.** A European Union Directive that seeks to give people buy-ing package holidays greater protection in law and access to compensation when things go wrong.

- **Passenger load.** The number of people travelling on a particular journey.

- **PEST analysis.** A technique used by an organisation to investigate the business envir-onment in which it operates, with a view to helping determine its future strategies. PEST stands for political, economic, social and technological, which are the main factors that influence organisations.

- **Primary data.** Refers to data that is collected for the first time, usually as part of a mar-ket research study.

- **Principal.** The name given to a company that a travel agent does business with and whose products and services it sells.

- **Private sector tourism.** The sector of the tourism industry that is concerned principally with commercial activities and maximising profits. The majority of tourism organisations are private sector enterprises, for example hotels, airlines, travel agencies, tour operators, car hire firms, tourist attractions and transport operators.

- **Product development.** The techniques and processes that an organisation will undertake to make its product portfolio as appealing as possible to existing and potential customers.

- **Product orientation.** A business philosophy and management style that focuses on the details of products and services supplied rather than the needs of customers.

- **Product portfolio.** The mix of products or services offered by a tourism organisation to its customers.

- **Promotional mix.** The different promotional techniques that a tourism organisation will use to raise awareness of its products and services, and stimulate sales. These could include advertising, direct marketing, sales promotion and public relations activities.

- **Psychocentric.** One of a number of types of tourist behaviour developed by Plog in 1977 as part of a research study for airline companies. Psychocentrics tend to be mainstream in their behaviour, rather unadventurous when it comes to travelling, prefer familiar surroundings and have below-average income levels.

- **Public sector tourism.** The sector of the tourism industry concerned with providing a service to a local community or society in general, rather than having profit maximisation as a prime objective.

- **'Pump priming'.** The process of providing initial capital for a tourism enterprise, usually from public funds, in order to stimulate its growth and development.

- **Qualitative data.** Refers to information, often gathered as part of a market research process, that is concerned with an organisation's standing in the marketplace, rather than an exact measurement of its performance. An example of qualitative data would be tourists' opinions of an attraction.

- **Quantitative data.** Factual information that can be measured, often gathered as part of a market research process, for example the number of visitors to a theme park, the stock of accommodation in a holiday resort or the country of origin of visitors to Britain.

- **Racking policy.** Refers to the tour operators' brochures that a travel agent will have on display in the agency.

- **Scheduled air services.** Flights that operate to a published timetable on specific routes. Unlike charter flights, scheduled services are committed to operate even if the load factor is very low.

- **Seasonality.** Refers to variations in the demand for tourism products and services at different times of the year.

- **Seat-only sales.** The name given to purchases of flight tickets without any accommodation or other services provided.

- **Secondary data.** Information available from existing sources, usually in written form, but increasingly now available from electronic media such as CD-ROMs and the Internet.

- **Section 4 grants.** Funds that were made available to tourism businesses under the 1969 Development of Tourism Act to encourage new tourism projects. Although initially available in England, Scotland and Wales, the English Tourist Board no longer has powers to distribute 'section 4' grants.

- **Self-catering accommodation.** Regarded as any type of accommodation where guests take care of themselves and where, unlike serviced accommodation, there are no, or very few, services provided for them during their stay.

- **Serviced accommodation.** Refers to hotels, guesthouses and any other type of accommodation where guests are offered a range of different services during their stay, such as food, portering, valet services and possibly entertainment.

- **Shoulder periods.** Times of the year either side of tourism's peak season.

- **Socio-cultural impacts.** Positive and negative effects of tourism on societies and communities, and their cultural traditions.

- **Standard Industrial Classification (SIC).** A system that places jobs in various employment categories in order to analyse movements in particular occupations and provide indicators of trends in employment generally.

- **Strategic alliance.** When two or more enterprises work collaboratively for mutual benefit or self-interest.

- **Strategic marketing.** The medium- to long-term process of determining how best a tourism organisation can achieve its marketing objectives.

- **Superstructure.** Any construction that takes place above ground and which uses a pre-existing infrastructure. In the case of tourism, superstructure projects would include hotels, attractions and transportation.

- **Sustainable tourism.** A concept that seeks to address the long-term environmental and socio-cultural issues surrounding uncontrolled tourist development worldwide. An extension of 'green' tourism, it is part of a much wider global debate on sustainable development, highlighted by the Brundtland Report in 1987 and the Earth Summit in Rio in 1992.

- **SWOT analysis.** One of the most common techniques that an organisation can undertake to try and establish where it stands in the marketplace and what it needs to do to maintain or improve its competitive position. SWOT stands for strengths, weaknesses, opportunities and threats.

- **Tactical marketing.** Short-term marketing activity carried out in response to unforeseen or unplanned occurrences in the marketplace.

- **Target audience.** The individuals that a tourism organisation seeks to attract and influence via its marketing activity.

- **Target marketing.** The practice of selecting particular groups or individuals (known as the target market), and using the different components of the marketing mix to encourage them to buy or use products or services.

- **Tourism balance.** The difference between the value of a country's earnings from inbound tourism and the expenditure by its residents on overseas tourism.

- **Tourist enclave.** A clearly defined enclosed area within which tourists are isolated from the residents of a destination (the host community), sometimes for security and safety reasons.

- **Tourist generating country.** Refers to the country of origin of a traveller, as opposed to the tourist receiving country, which is his or her destination country.

- **Tourist receiving country.** The destination country that travellers arrive at, as opposed to the tourist generating country, which is the origin of their journey.

- **Travel propensity.** The proportion of a population who are actively involved in travel, whether for business or leisure purposes. Travel propensity is higher in Western, developed countries than in the developing nations of the world.

- **Travel trade.** The term used to describe all the commercial sectors within the tourism industry, including travel agents, tour operators, coach operators, car hire firms, airlines, ferry companies and providers of specialist support services.

- **Unique selling proposition (USP).** Denotes the particular benefit that one product or service is said by its promoters to have over another product or service, i.e. the reason why customers will choose that item instead of all other competitors.

- **Vertical integration.** The process whereby companies at different levels of the distribution chain are linked in some way in order to gain competitive advantage.

- **VFR.** Stands for visiting friends and relatives, an important revenue source for most nations involved in tourist activity.

- **Viewdata.** A computer-based interactive system used by travel agents to display information on VDUs and to access the computerised reservation systems of principals, mainly airlines and tour operators, via a telephone line.

- **Virtual reality.** A technology that allows a user to enter and interact with images generated by a computer.

- **Visibles.** Manufactured items and goods whose value is shown on a country's balance of payments.

- **World Tourism Organisation.** The established inter-governmental agency for tourism policies worldwide, representing public sector tourism bodies from the majority of countries in the world.

Selected Bibliography

- Ashworth, G and Goodall, B (1990) *Marketing Tourism Places*, Routledge, London
- Bull, A (1991) *The Economics of Travel and Tourism*, Pitman, Melbourne
- Burkart, A and Medlik, S (1981) *Tourism: Past, Present and Future*, Heinemann, London
- Burns, P and Holden, A (1995) *Tourism: A New Perspective*, Prentice Hall, Hemel Hempstead, UK
- Burton, R (1995) *Travel Geography*, Pitman, London
- Cooper, C *et al.* (1993) *Tourism: Principles and Practice*, Pitman, London
- Davidson, R (1992) *Tourism in Europe*, Pitman, London
- English Tourist Board (1991) *Tourism and the Environment: Maintaining the Balance*, ETB, London
- Gamble, W (1989) *Tourism and Development in Africa*, John Murray, London
- Gunn, C (1994) *Tourism Planning*, Taylor & Francis, New York
- Hall, C M (1994) *Tourism and Politics*, Wiley, Chichester, UK
- Hall, D (ed.) (1991) *Tourism and Economic Development in Eastern Europe and the Soviet Union*, John Wiley & Sons
- Holloway, C (1994) *The Business of Tourism*, 4th edition, Longman, Harlow, UK
- Holloway, C and Robinson, C (1995) *Marketing for Tourism*, 3rd edition, Longman, Harlow, UK
- Inskeep, E (1991) *Tourism Planning: An Integrated and Sustainable Development Approach*, Van Nostrand Reinhold, New York
- Kotler, P (1994) *Marketing Management*, 8th edition, Prentice-Hall International
- Krippendorf, J (1989) *The Holiday Makers*, Butterworth-Heinemann, Oxford, UK
- Lea, J (1988) *Tourism and Development in the Third World*, Routledge, London
- Lickorish, L (1991) *Developing Tourism Destinations*, Longman, Harlow, UK
- Mathieson, A and Wall, G (1982) *Tourism: Economic, Physical and Social Impacts*, Longman, Harlow, UK
- Middleton, V (1994) *Marketing in Travel and Tourism*, 2nd edition, Butterworth-Heinemann, Oxford, UK

● Mill, R and Morrison, A (1992) *The Tourism System*, Prentice-Hall International

● Murphy, P (1985) *Tourism: A Community Approach*, Routledge, London

● Pearce, D (1989) *Tourist Development*, Longman, Harlow, UK

● Pearce, D (1995) *Tourism Today: A Geographical Analysis*, Longman, Harlow, UK

● Pompl, W and Lavery, P (1993) *Tourism in Europe: Structures and Developments*, CAB International, Wallingford, UK

● Poon, A (1993) *Tourism, Technology and Competitive Strategies*, CAB International, Wallingford, UK

● Ryan, C (1991) *Recreational Tourism: A Social Science Perspective*, Routledge, London

● Smith, V (1989) *Hosts and Guests: The Anthropology of Tourism*, 2nd edition, University of Pennsylvania Press, Philadelphia

● Urry, J (1990) *The Tourist Gaze*, Sage, London

● Van Harssel, J (1994) *Tourism: An Exploration*, 3rd edition, Prentice-Hall International

● Williams, A and Shaw, G (1991) *Tourism and Economic Development – Western European Experiences*, Belhaven Press, London

● Witt, S, Brooke, M and Buckley, P (1995) *The Management of International Tourism*, Routledge, London

● World Tourism Organisation (1994) *National and Regional Tourism Planning: Methodologies and Case Studies*, Routledge, London

Index

Accessibility, 210
Accommodation and catering, 27
    Australia, 29
    branding, 73
    classification of accommodation, 27
    commercial, 28
    employment in UK, 110
    future developments, 232–3
    future supply, 29
    grading schemes, 113
    in Europe, 71
    market segmentation in Europe, 73
    non-commercial, 28
    self-catering accommodation, 28
    serviced accommodation, 28
    UK, 110, 114
Accor, 73
Advertising, 213
    consumer, 214
    media, 214
    trade, 214
Agenda 21, 235–6
Air travel, 30
    chartered, 31
    deregulation, 30, 71, 110
    domestic services, 31
    European airlines, 68
    future developments, 233
    growth in passenger numbers, 31
    liberalisation, 90
    scheduled services, 31
    seat-only sales, 31
    types of, 30
    UK, 107, 109
Allocentrics, 20
Alton Towers, 115

Amadeus, 43
Ansoff's matrix, 225
Areas of Outstanding Natural Beauty (AONBs), 118, 119
Asia-Pacific region, 15, 231
Association of British Travel Agents (ABTA), 121
    bonding, 123
    membership, 122
Association of Independent Tour Operators (AITO), 125
    aims, 125
    bonding, 125
    Campaign for Real Travel Agents, 126
Attractions (see tourist attractions)
Australia
    destination marketing in, 219–21
    economic impacts of tourism, 146
    export earnings, 147
    international visitor arrivals, 147
    origin of overseas visitor arrivals, 147, 220
Australian Bureau of Tourism Research, 203–5
Australian Tourist Commission, 219

Balance of payments, 65, 141, 142
Bank Holiday Act 1871, 5
Best Western, 114
Billy Butlin, 6
Biological capacity, 154
Blackpool Pleasure Beach, 74, 115
Bonding, 123, 125
Boston Consulting Group matrix, 225
Botswana, 182–5
Branding, 73, 209

Britannia Airways, 40
British Airways, 30, 102, 190
British Incoming Tour Operators' Association (BITOA), 127
British Tourist Authority (BTA), 96, 103, 129
    funding, 104
    objectives, 103
    structure and operation of, 104
Brochures, 39, 215
Brundtland Report, 176, 235
Business planning, 169
Business tourism, 10, 12
Business travel, 37
Butler, 218

Campaign for Real Travel Agents, 126
Camping and caravanning, 113
Car travel, 96, 107
Carrying capacity, 154
Center Parcs, 112
Channel Tunnel, 32, 70, 107, 110
Chartered Institute of Marketing, 190
Chernobyl, 64
Clarkson, 6
Coach travel, 107, 108
    deregulation, 33
Commercial providers, 24
Commission, 37
Community involvement in tourism, 153–4, 167
Competitive pricing, 212
Computerised reservation systems (CRS), 43, 211
Consumer protection, 90
Consumer society, 6, 194
Corporate planning, 167

Crown Classification Scheme, 113
Cruising, 32
Cultural tourism, 86
Cunard, 5
Customer service, 175, 193
Cyprus Tourism Organisation, 75
    marketing, 77
    structure of, 76

Demand for tourism, 10, 11, 14
    determinants of, 18
    influences on, 18, 231
    future, 230
    motivators, 19
    patterns of international
        demand, 14–15
    regional demand, 15, 16
    seasonality, 17
Demographic trends, 231
Demonstration effect, 149
Department for Culture, Media and
    Sport, 34, 129
Deregulation of travel, 30, 33, 70
Destination marketing, 218
    Australia, 219
Destinations, 25
    composition, 25
    image, 20
    life cycle, 218
    marketing, 218
    UK, 106
    world's top destinations, 16–17
Determinants of tourism demand,
    18
Developing countries, 181
    Botswana, 182
Development of Tourism Act 1969,
    96, 131
Differential pricing, 18
Direct mail, 215–16
Direct marketing, 215
    campaign, 216
Direct-sell operators, 38
Discrimination pricing, 212
Disneyland Paris, 74
Distribution channels, 211
Domestic tourism, 7, 11, 64
    operators, 127
Dr Richard Russell, 5

Earth Summit, 176
Eastern Bloc, 61–2
Economic development, 143
Economic impacts of tourism,
    139
    balance of payments, 141–2
    contribution to GNP, 140
    employment, 139, 143
    in Australia, 146–8
    leakages, 142

multiplier concept, 142
    negative, 146
Economic significance of tourism,
    7, 139
    in Europe, 81
Education, 20
Employment in tourism, 143–5
    Australia, 147
    direct, 144
    in the UK, 100
    indirect, 100
    issues, 144
    regional growth in, 145
    world tourism, 145
English Tourist Board, 129, 131
    funding, 3, 132
    objectives, 131–2
Environmental impact assessments,
    159
Environmental impacts of tourism,
    150
    environmental problems, 151
    erosion, 151
    in Europe, 87
    industry initiatives, 159
    pollution, 152
    positive, 152
    solutions, 152–3
    environmental impact
        assessments, 159
Europe
    changing face of, 59
    economic developments in, 59
    image, 59
    'new Europe', 60
    politics of, 59
    share of international tourist
        arrivals, 63
    structural funds, 90
European Commission, 66, 83
European Parliament, 83
European tourism, 57
    accommodation, 71–3
    action plan to assist tourism, 85
    airlines, 68
    arrivals, 63
    Directorate General (DG XXIII),
        83
    domestic and incoming tourism,
        64
    Eastern Bloc influences on, 61
    economic significance of, 57–8,
        81, 84
    future issues concerning, 91
    hotels, 72
    liberalisation of travel, 70
    markets for incoming tourism, 65
    package travel regulations, 90
    philoxenia programme, 88–9
    public sector involvement in, 74

receipts, 63
    regional variations in, 66
    role of the European Union in,
        81
    structure of the industry, 66–7
    tourism balance of payments, 65
    tourist flows, 62–3
    trans-European transport
        networks, 68–9
    transportation, 67
    world share of international
        arrivals and receipts, 58, 63
European Tourism Action Group,
    80
European Travel Commission, 78
    funding of, 79–80
    members, 78
    structure of, 79
European Union
    action plan to assist tourism, 85
    indirect effects on tourism, 90
    legislation, 84
    Maastricht Treaty, 82, 84
    member states, 60, 82
    philoxenia programme, 88, 89
    role in tourism, 81, 83
    single market, 90
    structure of, 82
    Treaty of Rome, 82
    tourism measures in, 84
European Year of Tourism, 85
Eurostar, 32, 68
Events, 34
Excursionists, 10

Farm tourism, 112
Fast-moving consumer goods
    (FMCGs), 209
'Fifth freedom' rights, 71
Florida, 26
Fly-cruise, 32
Focus groups, 202
Freddie Laker, 6

Galileo, 43
Gambia, 173
Gender, 20
General Agreement on Trade in
    Services (GATS), 54
Germany, 141, 142
Global distribution channels
    (GDS), 211
Globalisation, 42, 232
Government role in tourism, 236
'Grand Tour', 4
Great Exhibition in London, 5
Greeks, 3
Green Globe, 157, 160
    goals, 160
    membership, 160

'Green tourism', 176
Gross national product (GNP)
    tourism's contribution to, 140
    factors affecting, 141
Gulf War, 15

Heritage, 116
Historical developments in tourism,
    3, 7
Holiday camps, 6
Holiday centres, 112
'Honey pot' areas, 151
Horizontal integration, 128
Hospitality sector, 27
Host community, 154
Hotels
    European, 72
    UK, 112
    world stock of, 28

Impacts of tourism, 10, 11, 138,
    164, 165, 171, 176
    economic, 139–48
    environmental, 150–2
    socio-cultural, 148–50
Inbound tourism, 11
Inclusive tour by charter (ITC),
    31
Incoming tour operators, 127
Independent travel, 235
Industrial Revolution, 4, 95
Infrastructure, 25, 30, 44, 45, 106,
    171, 175
Intasun, 124
Integration, 42
    in UK travel, 127–8
Inter-Continental Hotel Group,
    159
Internal tourism, 11
International agencies, 24, 50
International Air Transport
    Association (IATA), 31, 37,
    71
International tourism, 7, 11, 14
    developing countries, 181
    employment in, 145
    future demand, 230
    growth in arrivals and receipts,
        15
    organisation, 23
    regional demand, 15, 16
    role of public sector in, 44
    structure, 24–5
Internet, 202
Investment in tourism, 141

Japan
    public sector tourism
        organisation in, 44
    tourism policies in, 172

Japan National Tourist
    Organisation, 46
    activities of, 48
    budgets and revenue sources of,
        49–50
    structure of, 47
Jet aircraft, 6, 96
JICNARS, 192

Kotler, 189

Landmark Trust, 111
'Leakage', 143
Legislation, 46
Leisure tourism, 12
Life cycle
    destination, 218
    product, 209
    stage in, 20
Local authorities and tourism, 129,
    134
Location, 210
Long haul travel, 6
Lunn Poly, 40

Management
    relationship to planning and
        development, 164
Manpower planning, 166
Market orientation, 191
Market research, 194
Market segmentation, 73, 192
    in European accommodation,
        73
    lifestyle, 193
    variables, 192
Marketing (see also tourism
    marketing)
    concentrated, 226
    Cyprus, 77
    definition, 189
    destination, 218
    differentiated, 226
    direct, 215
    joint, 114
    mix, 207
    objectives, 190, 225
    promotion, 213
    research, 194
    social, 191
    strategic, 191, 222
    strategy, 226
    tactical, 191
    undifferentiated, 226
Marketing mix, 207
    place, 210
    price, 211
    product, 208
    promotion, 213

Marketing research, 194
    benefits of, 195
    Australian Bureau of Tourism
        Research, 203–5
    focus group, 202
    observation, 201
    primary data, 196
    process in tourism, 205–7
    qualitative data, 197
    quantitative data, 197
    questionnaires, 197–200
    sampling, 201
    secondary data, 202
    self-completed questionnaires,
        197, 198–9
    sources of data, 195, 196
    surveys, 196
Maslow's hierarchy of needs, 19
Mass tourism, 3
Mid-centrics, 20
Mission statements, 167
Monopolies and Mergers
    Commission, 128
Motivators, 18
Multinational corporations, 25, 43
Multiplier concept, 142

National Express, 107–8
National Parks, 117–19
National tourism, 11
National tourism organisation
    (NTO)
    functions of, 45
National tourist boards, 131
National Trust, 103, 112
Non-commercial providers, 24
North Pennines Tourism
    Partnership, 155
Northern Ireland Tourist Board,
    129, 131
Not-for-profit sector, 24

Observation, 201
Oil Producing and Exporting
    Countries (OPEC), 15
Olympic Games, 3
Organisational policy, 223
Outbound tourism, 11

Package tours, 6
    taken by UK residents, 97
Partnerships, 91, 165, 173, 177
    in York, 178
Passenger shipping, 32
Penetration pricing, 212
Peninsular and Oriental Steam
    Navigation Company (P&O), 5
Perceptual capacity, 154
Personal mobility, 20
Personal selling, 217

PEST analysis, 224
Physical capacity, 154
Place, 210
Planning (see tourism planning)
Plog, 20
Politics of tourism, 8, 232
Price, 211
    pricing policies, 212
    skimming, 212
Private sector tourism, 13–14
Product, 208
    life cycle, 209
    mix, 18
    portfolio analysis, 225
Promotion, 213
    consumer, 213
    techniques, 18
    trade, 213
Psychocentrics, 20
Public relations, 217
Public sector tourism, 44
    bodies, 24
    functions of agencies in, 45
    in Europe, 74
    in the UK, 128–9
Purpose of travel, 12

Qualitative data, 197
Quantitative data, 197
Questionnaires, 197–200
    design, 200–1
    self-completed, 197, 198–9

Race, 20
Rail transportation, 31, 69
Railways, 5
Reformation, 3
Regional tourist boards, 132–4
Regulation, 46, 77
Road transport, 33
Romans, 3–4
Rural tourism, 87
Russian Federation, 61

Sabre, 43
Sales promotion, 216
Sampling
    quota, 201
    random, 201
Scottish Tourist Board, 129
Sea transport, 107
Seaside resorts, 5
Seasonality, 17–18, 144
Seat-only sales, 31
Self-catering accommodation, 28,
    112
Serviced accommodation, 28, 111
Short breaks, 114
Sierra Leone, 173
Signposting, 156

Single market, 90
Situation analysis, 223
Social marketing, 191
Social mobility, 7
Social tourism, 87
Socio-cultural impacts of tourism,
    148, 177
    negative, 149
    positive, 150
Socio-economic classification, 193
Spa resorts, 4
Spain, 26–7, 142
Sport and recreation centres, 117
Stakeholders, 101, 168
Standard industrial classification
    (SIC), 143
Steam power, 5
Strategic marketing, 191
    planning, 222
Strategic planning, 167–8
Superstructure, 26
Surveys, 196
Sustainable development, 53, 81,
    130, 176
    Agenda 21, 235
    Brundtland Report, 176
Sustainable tourism, 176, 235
    principles of, 153
SWOT analysis, 178–9, 224

Tactical marketing, 191
Technology, 114, 231
TGV (train de grande vitesse), 31
Theme parks, 35, 116
    in Europe, 73, 74
Thomas Cook, 5
    Group, 168
Thomson Tour Operations, 41–2,
    198–9
    future of, 42
Thomson Travel Group, 40, 128
    future of, 42
Timeshare, 113
Tour operators, 38
    direct-sell, 38
    domestic, 38
    future for, 234
    incoming, 38
    issues, 39
    key activities of, 39
    market research, 39
    mass market, 38
    position of, 38
    specialist, 38
    top five in the UK, 124
    types in the UK, 123–7
Tourism
    and economic development, 143
    classification according to
        purpose of travel, 12

community involvement in,
    153
definitions, 9
economic significance, 2, 7, 98
employment in, 143
future of, 229
government involvement in, 129,
    236
historical development, 3
image perception, 8, 182
in developing countries, 181
in the Industrial Revolution, 4
in the twentieth century, 6
in the UK (see UK tourism)
influence of steam power, 5
percentage of world exports, 2
politics of, 8, 232
public sector, 44, 128, 134
supply, 10, 11
training, 46, 87, 114, 130, 135
types of, 11
Tourism balance, 141
Tourism Concern, 158
Tourism demand (see demand for
    tourism)
Tourism development, 8, 164
    Botswana, 182–5
    objectives of, 173
    pace of, 8
    rate of growth, 173
    types, 173
Tourism Development Action
    Programme (TDAP), 167
'Tourism for Tomorrow Awards',
    160
Tourism industry
    characteristics, 13
    core components, 24
    structure, 24
Tourism impacts (see impacts of
    tourism)
Tourism marketing, 187
    advertising, 213
    concept, 188
    direct, 215
    distribution channels in, 211
    in Cyprus, 77
    marketing mix, 207
    objectives, 190
    process, 189
    promotion, 213
    research process, 205–6
    segmentation variables, 192
    targeted, 18
Tourism plan, 171
Tourism planning, 164
    business planning, 169
    carrying capacity, 154
    community involvement in,
        153–4, 167

context of, 165
corporate planning, 167
regional level, 167
interrelationships in, 166
national level, 166
rationale for, 165
tourism plan, 171
stages in the process, 170–1
strategic planning, 168
sustainable tourism, 176
UK government, 129
Tourism policy, 45, 172
in Wales, 174
organisational, 223
Tourism products, 208
branding, 209
characteristics of, 208
product life cycle, 208–9
Tourism Society, 9
Tourist area life cycle concept
(TALC), 218
Tourist attractions, 33
commercial, 33
cultural, 117
European, 73
funding, 119
future developments, 234
heritage, 34
issues, 35, 119
leisure shopping, 35
man-made, 34, 116
museums, 34
natural, 34, 117
non-commercial, 33
sports facilities, 35
technology and, 119
theme parks, 35, 73
top UK, 115
types of, 34
UK, 114–15, 119
visitor experience, 119
York, 178

Tourist boards
in the UK, 131–4
regional tourist boards, 132
Tourist information centres (TICs),
132, 157
Tourist information services, 45
Trade associations, 24, 50
Traffic management, 156
Transportation, 7, 8, 29, 31, 67
trans-European networks, 68, 69
UK, 106, 109
Travel agents
functions, 120–1
future for, 234
products, 37
role of, 36–8
UK, 120–1
Travel intermediaries, 35–6
future for, 234–5
issues concerning, 39
Travel principles, 37

UK tourism, 94
accommodation, 110, 114
airports, 109
attractions, 114, 119
classification of, 101, 105
commercial operators, 101
core elements of, 105
Crown Classification Scheme,
113
destinations, 106
Development of Tourism Act
1969, 96
employment in, 100
future of, 135–6
government involvement in,
129–31
gross domestic product (GDP),
98
historical development of, 95–6
hotels, 112

local authorities and, 134–5
overseas visitors, 98–100
public sector, 128, 129
significance of, 97
stakeholders in, 101
structure of, 100, 105
tourist boards, 131–4
training, 130, 135
transportation issues, 106, 109
United Nations Statistical
Commission, 9

Venice-Simplon Orient Express, 32
Vertical integration, 43, 124, 128
Visiting friends and relatives (VFR),
12, 27
Visitor management, 155–6, 157
Voluntary sector, 24

Wales Tourist Board, 129, 174,
223
World Tourism Organisation
(WTO), 2, 51
future of, 53
mission, 51
structure of, 52
World Travel and Tourism Council
(WTTC), 2, 53
organisation of, 54
Millennium Vision, 54
World Travel and Tourism
Environment Research Centre
(WTTERC), 53
World Travel Market, 200
World War One, 6
Worldspan, 43

York, 178–81
attractions, 178
Youth Hostels Association (YHA),
110
Youth tourism, 87